Second Edition

FUNDAMENTALS OF ORGANIZATIONAL COMMUNICATION

Knowledge, Sensitivity, Skills, Values

Developed under the advisory editorship of
Thomas W. Bohn, Dean, School of Communications,
Ithaca College

Second Edition

FUNDAMENTALS OF ORGANIZATIONAL COMMUNICATION

Knowledge, Sensitivity, Skills, Values

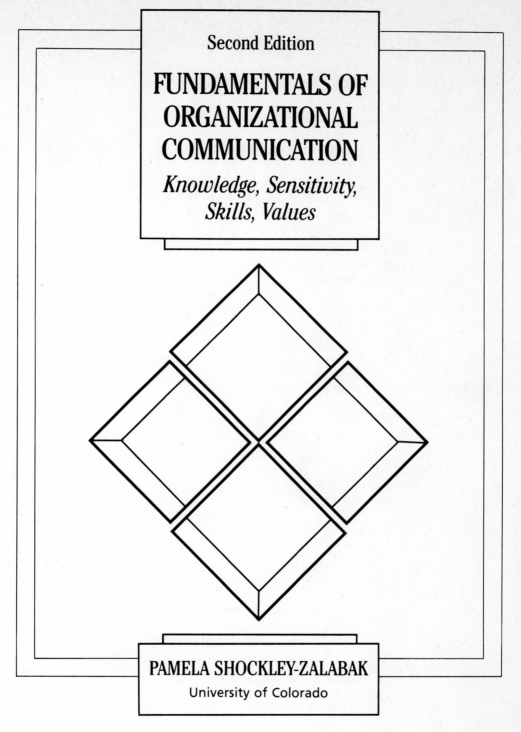

PAMELA SHOCKLEY-ZALABAK

University of Colorado

Longman
New York & London

**Fundamentals of Organizational
Communication, 2E**

Copyright © 1991 by Longman Publishing Group
All rights reserved.
No part of this publication may be reproduced,
stored in a retrieval system, or transmitted
in any form or by any means, electronic, mechanical,
photocopying, recording, or otherwise,
without the prior permission of the publisher.

Longman, 95 Church Street, White Plains, N.Y. 10601

Associated companies:
Longman Group Ltd., London
Longman Cheshire Pty., Melbourne
Longman Paul Pty., Auckland
Copp Clark Pitman, Toronto

Executive editor: Gordon T. R. Anderson
Production editor: Helen B. Ambrosio
Text design: Betty Sokol
Cover design: David Levy
Production supervisor: Anne Armeny

Library of Congress Cataloging in Publication Data
Shockley-Zalabak, Pamela.
    Fundamentals of organizational communication : knowledge,
sensitivity, skills, values / Pamela Shockley-Zalabak.—2nd ed.
        p.   cm.
    Includes bibliographical references.
    ISBN 0-8013-0622-1
    1. Communication in organizations.   I. Title.
HD30.3.S55   1990
658.4′5—dc20   90-34906
                                                       CIP

2 3 4 5 6 7 8 9 10-HA-9594939291

~CONTENTS~

APPENDIX

~ P R E F A C E ~

Effective communication in organizations is widely considered to be necessary both for the attainment of organizational goals and for individual productivity and satisfaction. How can we respond to this emphasis on organizational communication? Is it possible to prepare for jobs in the corporations of the 1990s and 2000s, and if so, how? What communication competencies are the corporate world seeking? Even more basic, how do we begin to define what organizational communication competency is?

This text explores the development of key communication competencies for the 1990s and beyond. It is organized for an interaction of theory, practice, and analysis through an emphasis on *knowledge, sensitivity, skills,* and *values*.

Among the issues of central importance are: What constitutes communication competency? Why in this text do we broadly develop communication competencies rather than merely survey key disciplinary concepts? And what happens to key disciplinary concepts in this process?

The question of what constitutes communication competency has been a major topic in recent research. The framework I prefer is comprehensive, with four basic components—process understanding, interpersonal sensitivity, communication skills, and ethical responsibility. When applied to organizational communication, competency develops from increased understanding of the communication process; ability to sense accurately the meanings and feelings of oneself and others in the organization; improved skills in speaking, conflict management, and decision making; and finally, a well-defined sense of organizational as well as interpersonal ethics.

Why a competency-based approach? The answer is simple: Organizing material by competency components is academically relevant and important to contemporary organizations. Studies of corporate America have described intense informal communication as the key to excellence in the 1990s and beyond. Further, a recent major employer's survey found that accurately processing information within organizations, though necessary, was not sufficient for excellence; the surveyed employers want individuals who take personal responsibility for building relationships that contribute to quality communication. The *sensitivity* and *values* components in our competency framework specifically address this need.

THE COMPETENCY FRAMEWORK

Knowledge

Knowledge is developed through presentation of theoretical concepts important to the study of organizational communication. To this end, we will examine various frameworks for understanding organizational communication, communication implications of major organizational theories, and communication processes in organizations.

Sensitivity

To develop the sensitivity component, we will study and analyze various roles and relationships within organizations. Individual sensitivity can be developed by analyzing the impact of personal behaviors in organizational settings. We will examine such situations as individuals in organizations, dyadic relationships (specifically supervisor-subordinate relationships), group processes, conflict, and leadership and management communication.

Skills

The skills component is designed to help students develop both initiating and consuming communication skills. We will identify key organizational communication skills (e.g., decision making, problem solving, fact-finding, and presentations) and provide analysis and practice opportunities appropriate for each. Also, analysis opportunities provided in case studies, in-baskets (decision-making exercises based on a series of written messages), and simulations will contribute to skill development.

Values

The values component is key to the integration of knowledge, sensitivity, and skills. To understand the realities of organizational life, we must first examine how individual and organizational values or ethics can shape organizational communication behavior. We will have an opportunity to develop values and ethics through case studies that present ethical dilemmas and value issues in organizational settings. We will adopt different value positions and ethical perspectives to analyze cases, recommend courses of action, and predict outcomes.

Each chapter of this text attempts to contribute to competency development through the constant interaction of theory, practice, and analysis. Chapters are preceded by a statement of objectives and a short case study illustrating the concepts to be studied. Key terms and concepts are identified in margins, and chapters end with a concept summary and a workshop posing questions and issues in each of the competency areas—knowledge, sensitivity, skills, and values. The appendix provides additional practice and analysis opportunities.

Part One of this book is designed to develop *knowledge* through an understanding of what contributes to comprehensive communication competency and how we can understand this phenomenon called organizational communication. The chapters in Part One emphasize major organizational theories and their communication implications.

Part Two is designed to develop the *sensitivity* component of communication competency. Chapters in Part Two describe individuals in organizations and their intrapersonal, interpersonal, and small-group experiences. A particular emphasis will be the study of conflict and leadership. Research indicates that conflict and leadership may well be the focal processes for effective communication in organizations. Texts in organizational communication frequently treat these topics mechanically, without emphasizing underlying subtleties such as organizational climate or the complex interactions of individual predispositions, strategies, and tactics. We will support our understanding of individual preferences in these crucial areas of organizational behavior by using self-assessment instruments.

Competency in the *skill* component is developed in Part Three, where chapters identify key applications and career options for organizational communication skills and make specific suggestions for skill development.

The interaction of personal, organizational, and professional ethics and values is the subject of Part Four. The *values* component of communication competency is presented with particular emphasis on how organizational values contribute to organizational culture and effectiveness.

Finally, the appendix contributes to the comprehensive development of all four competency components through an interaction of theory, practice, and analysis. Materials in the appendix are to be used as supplements to the other chapters to foster an application of learning through practical and realistic examples.

I wrote this book for four primary reasons: my research interests in organizational communication; my experiences with students who appreciate the importance of the study of organizational communication; my twenty-plus years of business experience in both the private and public sectors; and my fundamental belief that organizations and the discipline of organizational communication must undergo significant change as we approach the twenty-first century. These experiences and beliefs, when taken together, have been invaluable to me in relating theory to practice and in projecting competency needs for the future.

I am grateful for the help and support of many individuals in the development of this manuscript. My colleagues in the Communication Department at the University of Colorado at Colorado Springs and throughout the country have provided support, ideas, feedback, and contributions important to this book. Special thanks go to the individuals who reviewed the first edition and whose insights guided this effort.

In preparation of this text, I appreciate the encouragement offered by Tren Anderson, executive editor at Longman, and the assistance of Sherwyn Morreale, my research associate and Helen Ambrosio, associate managing editor at Longman. I also want to thank the many special students at the University of Colorado at Colorado Springs who reviewed and critiqued most of the exercises, in-baskets, and cases contained in the text.

On a personal note, I wrote this book with the guidance, love, and support of my family. My father and mother, Jim and Leatha Shockley, have influenced more than they will ever know a special pursuit of learning. To my husband, Charles, whose love, support, work, and encouragement have been continuous, I shall always be grateful.

This book was written for students who want to change and improve organizations, who are willing to take risks in striving for excellence, and who love and appreciate human communication. Therefore, to students (past, present, and future) and to my family (most particularly Charles and Mom and Dad), I dedicate this book.

Second Edition

FUNDAMENTALS OF ORGANIZATIONAL COMMUNICATION

Knowledge, Sensitivity, Skills, Values

PART ~I~

Organizational Communication: Theories/Assumptions/Processes

In Part One we will discuss the changing communication requirements brought about by an information age. We will describe the need for communication competency in an information society, defining competency as a combination of our personal *knowledge, sensitivity, skills,* and *values.* We will explore the process nature of human communication and describe how communication can be understood in organizational settings. We will identify two major frameworks for understanding organizational communication—the functional and meaning-centered approaches—and use these approaches to analyze communication implications from leading organizational theories.

Part One is designed to develop *knowledge* competencies in order to understand the process of communication and how that process can be observed in organizations. *Sensitivity* competencies will be developed through self-analysis and through exploring a variety of assumptions about human behavior in organizations. *Skills* will be developed and practiced through self-assessment and case studies. *Values* development will be encouraged by emphasizing the importance of communication for organizational excellence.

1

Part Two will change our focus from the organization as a whole to individuals and how they relate to organizations. We will also identify individual competencies needed for organizational excellence. In Part Three we will develop competencies for decision making and problem solving and will identify professional applications of organizational communication. Part Four will illustrate the importance of individual and organizational values and ethics for organizational communication. Finally, the Appendix contains case studies, guest essays, and a self-assessment instrument designed to develop communication competency by applying theory to practice and analysis opportunities.

CHAPTER

~ O N E ~

Organizational Communication: A Competency-Based Approach

Developing competencies through . . .

KNOWLEDGE

Describing communication in the information society
Defining and describing communication competency

SENSITIVITY

Understanding communication as a key to organizational excellence
Developing awareness of our personal communication competencies

SKILLS

Assessing personal development needs
Practicing analysis capabilities

VALUES

Understanding communication competency as a personal and organizational need
Clarifying a contemporary "good communicator theme"

THE INFORMATION SOCIETY

We live, work, and play in the communications era. Sophisticated communications technologies have changed the way we do everything. As students you are being challenged to sort through more sources of available information than students at any other period in human history. Millions of routine jobs have disappeared, and new and more stimulating jobs requiring communications expertise are being created. In every aspect of our lives we are influenced by information generated and distributed by the people and machines of the communications era.

As an individual you are likely to spend most of your working life employed in an "information" job. You are more likely to create, process, or distribute information than you are to be directly involved in the production of goods. There is a greater need for salespeople, teachers, computer programmers, lawyers, financial analysts, secretaries, managers, bankers, consultants, engineers, doctors, architects, and social workers, and a decreased need for manufacturing assembly workers, miners, toolmakers, machinists, builders, and welders. With more than half of America's work force and gross national product already in knowledge industries, most agree with scholar Daniel Bell (1976) that we are in the postindustrial **information society.**

Information society—environment in which more jobs create, process, or distribute information than directly produce goods. The environment is characterized by mass production of information, which requires the constant learning of new activities and processes.

One of the most important characteristics of the "information" era is the rapid change associated with mass production of information, change requiring all of us to be constantly involved in the learning of new activities and processes. Most of us have already experienced rapid change brought about by new technologies. For example, although checks can still be written by hand, many of us pay our bills with plastic cards and use computer terminals to deposit or withdraw money from our bank accounts. We can still go to the movies or we can bring the movies to our homes through videocassettes or discs. We can write letters and memos to send through "regular" mail or we can use sophisticated electronic mail systems to send and receive rapidly all types of correspondence. Most students reading this book are in traditional classrooms with "live" instructors. But for some students now, and more in the future, "live" means that the instructor is telecast from a remote site to a classroom equipped with audio and video interconnects. And for all of us, whether we began in grade school or at a much later age, becoming "computer literate" is a requirement of our times.

We have so much information that for both individuals and organizations the challenge is how to deal with our information alternatives. John Naisbitt, in his best-selling book *Megatrends* (1982), contends that "we now mass-produce information the way we used to mass-produce cars." This daily increase in information (based on innovations in communications and computer technology) brings with it rapid change in activities, processes, and products. The Massachussetts Institute of Technology Commission on Industrial Productivity in a *Scientific American* report (Berger et al., 1989) underscores fast-paced change when it characterizes successful U.S. organizations by their ability to make simultaneous improvements in quality, cost, and speed of bringing new products to market while operating with less hierarchy (managers) and incorporating frequent technological innovations.

Workers in the communications era of microelectronics, computers, and telecommunications have an abundance of information for decision making and a growing concern for information overload. We can routinely communicate across both geography and organizational levels. It is not unusual, for example, for employees of an organization in Boston to interact with their counterparts in Los Angeles, whom they have never met, while both groups are preparing a portion of a single report or recommendation. And for a growing number of individuals this report can be generated without ever leaving their homes as they "telecommute" from automated home work stations to offices around the globe.

As William Work (1982), retired executive secretary of the Speech Communication Association, has so aptly suggested, the communications era places increasing demands on our individual communication abilities. These demands are best met with the perspective that becoming and staying competent is an ongoing process requiring lifelong learning.

COMMUNICATION—THE KEY
TO ORGANIZATIONAL EXCELLENCE

In this information society the key to **organizational excellence** is effective communication. Communication systems within organizations—both human and technological—are responsible for creatively solving increasingly complex problems. People using the machines of the communications era must coordinate large volumes of information for the performance of new and dynamic tasks. There is widespread recognition, however, that excellence in organizational problem solving is more than the efficient management of large volumes of facts. Organizational excellence stems from the dedicated commitment of people—people who are motivated to work together and who share similar values and visions about the results of their efforts.

Viewing communications as the key to organizational excellence is not new. As early as 1938, Chester Barnard, in his now-famous work *The Functions of the Executive,* described as a primary responsibility of executives the development and maintenance of a system of communication. Research spanning the last fifty years has linked organizational communication to managerial effectiveness, the integration of work units across organizational levels, characteristics of effective supervision, job and communication satisfaction, and overall organizational effectiveness. In fact, numerous scholars have gone so far as to suggest that organizations are essentially complex communication processes that create and change events. For both

Organizational excellence—ability of people to utilize technology for the creative solving of increasingly complex problems.

the industrial society of the past and the information society of today and tomorrow, there is broad agreement that organizational communication plays a significant part in contributing to or detracting from organizational excellence.

With this emphasis on the fast-paced information society and the importance of human communication, questions arise concerning what skills and abilities organizations need from their future employees. How should individuals prepare themselves for the information responsibilities and opportunities that almost inevitably will be a part of the future? What does it take to contribute to organizational communication excellence?

Put simply, organizations of today and tomorrow need competent communicators at all organizational levels. With more complex decisions, rapid change, more information, and less certainty about what the decisions should be, excellence in the information society depends on the abilities, commitment, and creativity of all organizational members. As a result, students, communication teachers and researchers, and active organizational members must work together to understand what contributes to organizational communication competency and how best to develop personal potential.

EXCELLENCE IN COMMUNICATION— COMMUNICATION COMPETENCY

Quintilian's ideal of the "good man speaking well" is not as far removed from contemporary concepts of organizational communication competency as history might suggest. In fact, when Vincent DiSalvo (1980) surveyed twenty-five recent studies describing the need for communication skills in organizations, he discovered a contemporary "good" communicator theme. Today's organizations need people who can listen, write, persuade others, demonstrate interpersonal skills, gather information, and exhibit small-group problem-solving expertise. The MIT commission (Berger et al., 1989) lends further support to these findings when it concludes that the effective use of modern technology requires involved and responsible people to develop capabilities for planning, judgment, collaboration, and analysis of complex systems. In other words, organizations in our information society need flexible and creative people who have diverse and well-developed communication abilities. But how do we determine if we are competent organizational communicators? Who decides? On what do we base our conclusions?

Communication competency—comprises knowledge, sensitivity, skills, and values. Competence arises from interaction of theory, practice, and analysis.

Researchers differ in how they define **communication competency.** Some believe a person is competent if he or she knows what is appropriate in a specific situation, whether that behavior actually occurs or not. A student, for example, who realizes that class participation is required for a high grade may choose not to participate, yet the student can be considered competent because of the knowledge or awareness of the appropriate behavior. Other researchers extend the competency concept beyond knowledge of appropriate behaviors to include actual language performance and the achievement of interpersonal goals. The student, from this latter perspective, must not only recognize appropriate participation behaviors but also participate in order to demonstrate communication competency.

Stephen Littlejohn and David Jabusch (1982) have proposed a particularly useful definition of communication competency for the organizational setting. They suggest that communication competency is "the ability and willingness of an individual to participate responsibly in a transaction in such a way as to maximize the outcomes of shared meanings." This definition requires not only knowledge of appropriate behaviors but also motivation to engage in communication that results in mutual understanding. In other words, communication competency involves our personal willingness and ability to communicate so that our meanings are understood and we understand the meanings of others. Regardless of differences in perspectives, organizational communication competency relates to message encoding and decoding abilities—the process of communication initiation and consumption.

When we begin to think about our personal communication competency, we quickly realize that we form impressions of our own competency while making evaluations about the competency of others. We try to decide what is appropriate for us as well as for others, and we determine whether that behavior is effective in a particular circumstance. In other words, my impression of my own competency and the competency of others is related to my evaluation of whether we exhibited the "right" behaviors and achieved "desirable" results in a particular situation. But determining what is "right" and "desirable" is not always easy. Think for a moment about your personal experiences. Have you ever been in a situation where others thought you did a good job although you were disappointed in yourself? Who was right? Were you competent or incompetent? Can both be correct?

Earlier we said organizational excellence depends on the communication competencies of all organizational members. Specifically, we described the need for creative problem solving among diverse groups of people who often share little common information. With this emphasis on communication and technology, the real question becomes what individuals should do to prepare themselves to meet the communication needs in their futures. In other words, how do we develop and evaluate our communication competencies?

Our answer begins by returning to the Littlejohn and Jabusch approach to communication competency. Littlejohn and Jabusch (1982) contend that competency arises out of four basic components—process understanding, interpersonal sensitivity, communication skills, and ethical responsibility. Process understanding refers to the cognitive ability to understand the dynamics of the communication event. Interpersonal sensitivity is the ability to perceive feelings and meanings. Communication skill is the ability to develop and interpret message strategies in specific situations. The ethical component of competency is the attitudinal set that governs concern for the well-being of all participants in taking responsibility for communication outcomes. Finally, Littlejohn and Jabusch believe that competence comes from the interaction of three primary elements—theory, practice, and analysis. When applied to the organizational setting, the Littlejohn and Jabusch approach can be modified and expanded to include the competency components this book seeks to develop: *knowledge, sensitivity, skills,* and *values.*

ORGANIZATIONAL COMMUNICATION—A COMPETENCY-BASED APPROACH

This book is designed to help you develop communication competencies for effective organizational communication. The goal of the book is to provide theory, practice, and analysis opportunities that contribute to knowledge, sensitivity, skills, and values important for organizational excellence.

Knowledge competency— ability to understand the organizational communication environment.

Knowledge—the ability to understand the organizational communication environment. **Knowledge competency** will be developed through the exploration of the interactive, process nature of human communication. We will examine what organizational communication is and the major theoretical approaches for its study. We will explore the roles of individuals in organizations and examine communication implications of major organizational theories. Finally, vital organizational subjects such as conflict, leadership, and problem solving will be discussed.

Sensitivity competency— ability to sense accurately organizational meanings and feelings.

Sensitivity—the ability to sense accurately organizational meanings and feelings. **Sensitivity competency** will be developed through the examination of our personal "theories-in-use" about communication and organizations. Individual preferences for leadership and conflict will be assessed, as well as the impact of personal differences and similarities within organizational settings. Emphasis will be placed on how we develop "shared meanings" with others.

Skills—ability to analyze accurately organizational situations and to initiate and consume organizational messages effectively.

Skills—the ability to analyze accurately organizational situations and to initiate and consume organizational messages effectively. **Skills competency** will be developed through analysis and practice opportunities. Specifically, analytical skills will be developed by applying *knowledge* and *sensitivity* to case studies and individual experiences. Problem-solving and conflict-management skills also will be presented and practiced.

Values—importance of taking personal responsibility for effective communication, thereby contributing to organizational excellence.

Values—the importance of taking personal responsibility for effective communication, thereby contributing to organizational excellence. **Values competency** will be developed through discussion of personal responsibility for participation in organizational communication. Ethical dilemmas relating to organizational communication and the importance of values to organizational culture will be examined. Finally, case studies will be used to illustrate ethical and value issues common in organizations.

SELF-ASSESSMENT OF PERSONAL DEVELOPMENT NEEDS

The material in the next eleven chapters is designed to help you develop important competencies for organizational communication. But before you begin to study that material, please complete Table 1.1 on pages 11–13. The following chapters will be more meaningful if you approach theory, practice, and analysis opportunities with a personal assessment of your current strengths and weaknesses.

TABLE 1.1
Self-Assessment of Personal Development Needs

The following organizational communication competencies are presented for your self-evaluation. For each area you are asked to determine whether your present competencies are highly developed, moderately developed, somewhat limited, or needing development.

As I begin this course I would describe my KNOWLEDGE in . . .	Highly Developed	Moderately Developed	Somewhat Limited	Needing Development
1. defining and understanding organizational communication as . . .			✓	
2. understanding major theories of how organizations work as . . .			✓	
3. determining how an individual experiences organizational life as . . .			✓	
4. describing what organizational conflict is and how it relates to productive organizations as . . .				✓
5. identifying characteristics of leadership and management communication as . . .		✓		
6. understanding decision making and problem solving as . . .			✓	
7. locating career opportunities in organizational communication as . . .				✓
8. distinguishing between values and ethics in organizational communication as . . .		✓		

Continued on next page

TABLE 1.1—*continued*

As I begin this course I would describe my SENSITIVITY to . . .	*Highly Developed*	*Moderately Developed*	*Somewhat Limited*	*Needing Development*
9. my personal responsibilities for organizational communication as . . .			✓	
10. how "shared realities" are generated through organizational communication as . . .				✓
11. why and how people work together as . . .		✓		
12. what motivates me and what is likely to motivate others as . . .			✓	
13. the importance of interpersonal relationships with supervisors, peers, and subordinates as . . .		✓		
14. personal preferences for a variety of approaches to conflict as . . .		✓		
15. personal preferences for leadership and management communication as . . .		✓		
16. organizational influences for decision making and problem solving as . . .				✓
17. past achievements, values, and skills that can guide career choices as . . .				✓
18. how values and ethics contribute to organizational effectiveness as . . .		✓		
As I begin this course I would describe my SKILLS in . . .				
19. analyzing a variety of organizational problems as . . .			✓	
20. developing effective organizational messages as . . .			✓	
21. engaging in active listening as . . .			✓	
22. contributing to supportive organizational environments as . . .		✓		

	1	2	3	4	5
23. participating in productive conflict management as . . .				✓	
24. leadership communication as . . .				✓	
25. leading and participating in effective group meetings as . . .				✓	
26. fact finding and evaluation as . . .					✓
27. gathering information for decision making and problem solving as . . .			✓		
28. analyzing data for decision making and problem solving as . . .			✓		
29. developing and making public presentations as . . .					✓
As I begin this course I would describe my VALUES for . . .					
30. accepting personal responsibility for communication as . . .			✓		
31. relating individual communication behavior to organizational effectiveness as . . .		✓			
32. using conflict for productive outcomes as . . .				✓	
33. determining how leaders and managers should behave as . . .			✓		
34. influencing my career choices as . . .			✓		
35. understanding organizational values, ethics, and dilemmas as . . .			✓		

After you have completed your self-evaluation, compile a complete list of items for which you rated your competencies as highly developed. Next compile lists for those competency items rated moderately developed, somewhat limited, and needing development. Use these lists to help establish personal objectives for the study of this text. All of the competencies evaluated in your self-assessment will be presented in the following chapters with theory, practice, and analysis opportunities.

SUMMARY

The information society is a reality of our lives that places increasing importance on our individual communication competencies. Organizations of today and tomorrow must depend on people and the machines of the communications era to solve problems creatively and to adapt to rapid change. In this fast-paced environment, organizational excellence is directly related to effective communication from all members of the organization. To prepare for the communication responsibilities and opportunities of the future, individuals need to develop broad-based communication competency. Communication competency is best understood as a complex interaction of knowledge, sensitivity, skills, and values. The goal of this book is to develop these competencies through an interaction of theory, practice, and analysis.

WORKSHOP

1. Review a copy of the Sunday edition of your city's largest newspaper. Identify all of the stories that relate to an "information age" and the technologies of the communications era. Bring copies of selected articles to class for group discussion.
2. In small groups, identify the "information industries" in your community. Compare lists among your groups.
3. Either individually or as an entire class, identify as many jobs as you can that are essentially "information" jobs.
4. Interview a professional in your community. Ask this person to describe what it takes to be a competent communicator in his or her particular job. Compare your findings with other class members.
5. Small groups should use The Case against Hiring Karen Groves, which follows, to determine how communication behaviors influenced Hockaday's management team to vote against hiring Karen Groves. (See pages 14–15.)
6. Make a list of all the communications technologies you currently use. Survey your home, school, work, business, social, and leisure environments for communications technologies. Make a list of the technologies with which you expect to become more familiar.

The Case against Hiring Karen Groves

John Murphy, the head of personnel for Hockaday Corporation, was excited about the application of Karen Groves to become Hockaday's new training director. Karen's educational background in organizational communication and business, her work in the training department of a major competitor of Hockaday's, and her excellent letters of recommendation made her an appealing candidate. John's initial interview with Karen had gone well and he was anxious for her to meet Hockaday's management staff, who approved John's hiring decisions for major company positions.

John was surprised and dismayed when Hockaday's president reported to John that the staff did not favor hiring Karen. According to the president, Karen surprised the group when she said _____ and _____. They did not believe she would be good for Hockaday's because of her _____.

In groups of four to six members each, fill in the blanks to account for what might have happened to create the case against hiring Karen. Describe how the communication abilities of all involved may have contributed to the negative decision. Following individual group discussions, each group should present to the class as a whole their members' description of the situation and how they believe communication affected the outcome.

SUMMARY OF COMPETENCY COMPONENTS:

KNOWLEDGE, SENSITIVITY, SKILLS, VALUES

KNOWLEDGE

Communication demands increase in an information society.

Communication competency is described as a combination of knowledge, sensitivity, skills, and values.

SENSITIVITY

Communication is identified as key to organizational excellence.

Personal competencies are considered important for organizational life.

SKILLS

Assessment skills are developed through self-evaluation and practice-and-analysis activities.

VALUES

Communication competency is considered important for an information society.

REFERENCES AND SUGGESTED READINGS

Barnard, C. 1938. *The functions of the executive.* Cambridge, MA: Harvard University Press.

Bell, D. 1967a. Notes on the post industrial society (I). *The Public Interest* 6: 24–35.

Bell, D. 1967b. Notes on the post industrial society (II). *The Public Interest* 7: 102–18.

Bell, D. 1976. Welcome to the post industrial society. *Physics Today* 29(2): 46–49.

Bell, D. 1979. Communications technology—for better or for worse. *Harvard Business Review*, 57(3): 20–42.

Bell, D. 1980. Techne and themis. In *The winding passage*. 1–65. Cambridge, MA: Abt. Books.

Berger, S., M. Dertouzos, R. Lester, R. Solow, and L. Thurow. 1989. Toward a new industrial America. *Scientific American* 260(6): 39–47.

Bostrom, R. N. 1984. *Competence in communication: A multi-disciplinary approach.* Beverly Hills, CA: Sage.

Boyatzsis, R. 1982. *The competent manager: A model for effective performance.* New York: Wiley.

Bronowski, J. 1958. The creative process. *Scientific American* 199(3): 59–64.

Clampitt, P., and C. Downs. 1983. Communication and productivity. Paper presented at the Speech Communication Association Convention, November, Washington, DC.

DiSalvo, V. S. 1980. A summary of current research identifying communication skills in various organizational contexts. *Communication Education* 29: 283–90.

Farace, R., P. Monge, and H. Russell. 1977. *Communicating and organizing.* Reading, MA: Addison-Wesley.

Goldhaber, G., M. Yates, D. Porter, and R. Lesniak. 1978. Organizational communication: 1978 state of the art. *Human Communication Research* 5(1): 76–96.

Goodall, H. L., Jr. 1982. Organizational communication competence: The development of an industrial simulation to teach adaptive skills. *Communication Quarterly* 30(4): 282–95.

Hacker, K., C. Carmichael, and K. Hirsch. 1986. Organizational culture and the design of computer-mediated communications systems: Issues for organizational communication research. Paper presented at the Speech Communication Association Convention, November, Chicago.

Jablin, F., R. Cude, K. Wayson, A. House, J. Lee, and N. Roth. 1989. Communication competence in organizations: Conceptualization and comparison across multiple levels of analysis. Paper presented to the Organizational Communication Division of the International Communication Association, May, San Francisco.

Jabusch, D. M., S. W. Littlejohn, and G. K. Levison. 1981. *Elements of speech communication: Achieving competency.* Boston: Houghton Mifflin.

Johnson, J. R. 1983. A developmental-biological perspective of human communication competency. *The Western Journal of Speech Communication* 47(3): 193–204.

Kennedy, G. 1969. *Quintilian.* New York: Twayne.

Kotter, J. 1982. What effective general managers really do. *Harvard Business Review* 60(6): 156–67.

Likert, R. 1967. *The human organization.* New York: McGraw-Hill.

Littlejohn, S. W., and D. M. Jabusch. 1982. Communication competence: Model and application. *Journal of Applied Communication Research* 10(1): 29–37.

McCroskey, J. C. 1982. Communication competence and performance: A research and pedagogical perspective. *Communication Education* 31: 1–7.

McCroskey, J., and L. McCroskey. 1986. Communication competence and willingness to communicate. Paper presented at the Speech Communication Association Convention, November, Chicago.

Monge, P. R. 1982. Communicator competence in the workplace: Model testing and scale development. In *Communication Yearbook 5*, ed. M. Burgoon, 505–27. New Brunswick, NJ: Transaction Books.

Naisbitt, J. 1982. *Megatrends*. New York: Warner Books.

O'Connell, S. 1988. Human communication in the high tech office. In *Handbook of organizational communication*, eds. G. Goldhaber and G. Barnett, 473–82. Norwood, NJ: Ablex Publishing.

Pavitt, C., and L. Haight. 1986. Implicit theories of communicative competence: Situational and competence level differences in judgments of prototype and target. *Communication Monographs* 53(3): 221–35.

Peters, T. J., and R. H. Waterman, Jr. 1982. *In search of excellence*. New York: Harper & Row.

Redding, W. 1972. *Communication within the organization: An interpretive review of theory and research*. New York: Industrial Communication Council.

Roberts, K., C. O'Reilly, C. Bretton, and L. Porter. 1974. Organizational theory and organizational communication: A communication failure? *Human Relations* 27(5): 501–24.

Rogers, E. 1988. Information technologies: How organizations are changing. In *Handbook of organizational communication*, eds. G. Goldhaber and G. Barnett, 437–52. Norwood, NJ: Ablex Publishing.

Rubin, R. B. 1985. The validity of the communication competency assessment instrument. *Communication Monographs* 52(2): 173–85.

Rubin, R. B., and J. D. Feezel. 1986. Elements of teacher communication competence. *Communication Education* 35(3): 254–68.

Rubin, R. B., and S. A. Henzl. 1984. Cognitive complexity, communication competence, and verbal ability. *Communication Quarterly* 32(4): 263–70.

Schall, M. 1983. A communication-rules approach to organizational culture. *Administrative Science Quarterly* 28(4): 557–81.

Smith, A. F., and S. A. Hellweg. 1985. Work and supervisor satisfaction as a function of subordinate perceptions of communication competence of self and supervisor. Paper presented to the Organizational Communication Division of the International Communication Association, May, Honolulu.

Snavely, W. B. 1985. The impact of perceptions of the superior on subordinate job stress. Paper presented to the Organizational Communication Division of the International Communication Association, May, Honolulu.

Snavely, W. B., and E. V. Walters. 1983. Differences in communication competence among administrator social styles. *Journal of Applied Communication Research* 11(2): 120–35.

Spitzberg, B. H. 1983. Communication competence as knowledge, skill, and impression. *Communication Education* 32(3): 323–29.

Spitzberg, B. H., and W. R. Cupach. 1984. *Interpersonal communication competence*. Beverly Hills, CA: Sage.

Staley, C. C., and P. S. Shockley-Zalabak. 1985. Identifying communication competencies for the undergraduate organizational communication series. *Communication Education* 34(2): 156–61.

Stoddard, T. D. 1980. Business communication as a competency based general education course. *Journal of Business Communication* 17(5): 51–60.

Swenson, D. H. 1980. Relative importance of business communication skills for the next ten years. *Journal of Business Communication* 17(2): 41–49.

Tubbs, S., and T. Hain. 1979. Managerial communication and its relationship to total organizational effectiveness. In *Communication and productivity*, P. Clampitt and C. Downs. Paper presented at the Speech Communication Association Convention, November 1983, Washington, DC.

Weick, K. 1976. Educational organizations as loosely coupled systems. *Administrative Science Quarterly* 21(1): 1–19.

Wheeless, V., and C. Berryman-Fink. 1985. Perceptions of women managers and their communicator competencies. *Communication Quarterly* 33(2): 137–47.

Wiemann, J. 1977. Explication and test of a model of communicative competence. *Human Communication Research* 3(3): 195–213.

Wiemann, J., and P. Backlund. 1980. Current theory and research in communicative competence. *Review of Educational Research* 50(1): 185–99.

Wiio, O., G. Goldhaber, and M. Yates. 1980. Organizational communication: Time for reflection? In *Communication yearbook 4*, ed. D. Nimmo, 83–98. New Brunswick, NJ: Transaction Books.

Work, W. 1982. Communication education for the twenty-first century. *Communication Quarterly* 30(4): 265–69.

Frameworks for Understanding Organizational Communication

Developing competencies through . . .

KNOWLEDGE

Defining and describing the human communication process
Identifying descriptions of organizations
Surveying definitions of organizational communication

SENSITIVITY

Understanding human communication as creating shared realities, shared meanings
Distinguishing among interpersonal, small-group, and organizational communication

SKILLS

Practicing analysis capabilities

VALUES

Understanding communication as fundamental to the process of organizing
Evaluating communication for ethics and effectiveness

The "What Business is This of Ours?" Case

John and Mary were the only two buyers in the purchasing department of Quality Engineering. Both had been with the company for several years and were experienced in handling purchases for the manufacturing, research, finance, and marketing areas of Quality. Mary typically handled purchases for the manufacturing and research areas, and John was the principal buyer for the rest of the organization. At times their individual work loads required that they cross departments and help each other. Their boss, Mike Anderson, the accountant for Quality, believed they were the best purchasing team with whom he had ever worked. He was proud of their efforts and willingness to cooperate with each other. He frequently commented to Quality management that John and Mary made money for the company by getting the best possible prices for goods and services.

Mike was surprised and concerned to overhear John and Mary in a heated discussion.

JOHN: I can't believe you are still using Anderson Printing as one of our suppliers. I told you last month that their last two orders for my groups were late and part of the printing had to be sent back because of errors. I told them then that I wouldn't accept any more of their bids on our jobs. It makes me look like a fool when I hear from them that you are still ordering their products for manufacturing and research. How can we enforce good quality from our suppliers if we don't present a united front?

MARY: Just a minute. Anderson Printing has been one of our good suppliers for over ten years. I know we have had some problems with them in the past year but I don't think we should drop them flat. They have pulled us out of a lot of jams when we needed printing in a big hurry. I never agreed to dropping them off our supplier list. You just told them they were gone and expected me to support your decision. You should have talked to me about it first. I don't care if you think you looked like a fool. We are in this together and need to make those types of decisions as a team.

JOHN: I'll admit we should have talked about it, but Anderson made me so mad on that last deal that I just told them they were through. I expected you to support me. We both want what is best for Quality. Our reputations are good because we always get the company the best products for the lowest price. I would have supported you.

MARY: Yes, I suspect you would have. But John, you can't lose your temper like that. We need to work together on these decisions.

You and I can usually work out a solution when we try hard enough. I don't want to drop any supplier on the spur of the moment, especially when we may have trouble replacing them. John, sometimes I think we have worked together so long that we take each other for granted. We are friends and I want it to remain that way, but that shouldn't stop us from doing business with each other as true professionals.

JOHN: Wait a minute. Are you saying that I don't act like a professional—

MARY: No, see what I mean? You get mad when I even suggest we might improve the way we do things.

JOHN: Well, I just think friends should support each other. I know I may not have handled the Anderson thing just right but as my friend I expected more support from you.

MARY: Oh, John, there you go again.

INTRODUCTION

Are John and Mary engaged in interpersonal or organizational communication, or both? Does the setting make the difference? Can we distinguish interpersonal and organizational communication? When we talk about developing our personal communication competencies, is it different for our personal and organizational lives? The answers to these questions lie in understanding what human communication is, how it works, and how organizations and human communication relate. In other words, frameworks for understanding organizational communication can be found in descriptions of human communication and organizations.

This chapter is designed to contribute to our knowledge by defining and describing the **human communication process** and identifying basic characteristics of organizations and organizational communication. *Sensitivity* competencies are developed through understanding human communication as the creation of shared realities and distinguishing among interpersonal, small-group, and organizational communication. *Skills* are practiced through application of *knowledge* and *sensitivity* competencies in exercises and case analysis. *Values* are developed through an understanding of the importance of communication in the process of organizing and an awareness that all communication is subject to evaluation for ethics and effectiveness.

Human communication process—construction of shared realities through social interaction.

BASICS OF HUMAN COMMUNICATION

Although the discussion between John and Mary is typical of human communication exchanges that occur daily in organizations, it also is typical of communication between two people regardless of the setting. In fact, the discussion between John and Mary illustrates some of the important basics necessary for understanding human communication.

Defining Communication

Analyzing the exchange between John and Mary will help us describe human communication. John and Mary are engaged in transferring information, they are eliciting responses from each other, and they are engaged in social interaction. Further, it is possible to say they are using symbols (words) to attempt to create shared meaning (mutual understanding) that will result in an effect on the two of them. Their disagreement about how to handle problems with Anderson Printing will influence not only what happens to Anderson as a supplier to Quality Engineering but their interpersonal relationship as well. Put another way, their exchange is an example of communication behaviors creating and shaping both relationships and events through a culturally dependent process of assigning meaning to symbols.

John wants Mary to share his "reality" that Anderson has made serious mistakes that disqualify it from providing goods and services to Quality. Furthermore, he expects Mary to accept another "reality"—that friends and co-workers should support each other's decisions even if decisions are made on the spur of the moment and in anger. Mary has a different set of "realities" she wants John to understand. While she agrees about recent problems with Anderson, part of her "reality" includes Anderson's past service to Quality and the possible difficulty of replacing its goods and services with another supplier. She also believes John should have included her in his decision. When John and Mary exchange their individual "realities," their communication is an attempt to construct "shared realities." Although they may not agree, their communication enables each to "share" the "realities" of the other.

The Communication Process

When John and Mary are constructing their shared realities, they are engaged in what we call the process of communication. Both John and Mary serve as *sources* and *receivers* of messages. Both engage in message *encoding* and *decoding* and in selecting verbal and nonverbal *channels* for message transmission. Both are influenced by their individual *competence* and their perception of the competence of the other. Each brings to the exchange a different set of *experiences* and each may view differently the context of their interaction. Thus, all of their messages are subject to distortion or *noise*. The *effect*, or what happens between John and Mary, is a result of the complex interaction of all these elements. Figure 2.1 illustrates a basic model of the human communication process in which John and Mary are engaged.

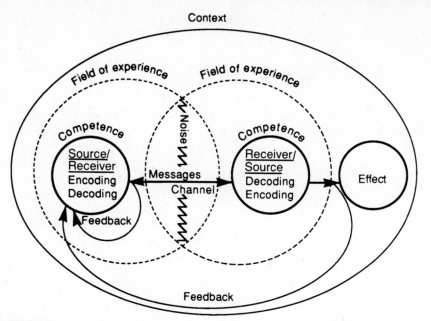

FIGURE 2.1
A model of essential components in communication.

ELEMENTS IN THE COMMUNICATION PROCESS

Source/Receiver

Each individual engaged in communication with others is both a message **source** and a message **receiver**. We talk (send messages) while closely monitoring the nonverbal reactions of others (receiving messages). We listen (receive messages) and determine how to respond (send messages). Often message-sending and -receiving activities occur so rapidly that they seem to be happening simultaneously.

Source/receiver—individuals send messages as sources and receive messages as receivers. The process is often so rapid as to appear simultaneous.

Encoding/Decoding

As a message source and receiver, each individual encodes and decodes messages. Message **encoding** is the process of formulating messages—choosing content and symbols to convey meaning. Message encoding is determining what we want to be understood (content) and how we believe it can best be presented (choosing symbols). Message **decoding** is the process of assigning meaning in the role of receiver to message symbols generated by the message source. Decoding is taking what we see and hear from others and deciding how it should be interpreted or understood. Both encoding and decoding are influenced by our communicative competence

Encoding/decoding—message encoding is the process of formulating messages, choosing content and symbols to convey meaning. Message decoding is the process of assigning meaning in the role of receiver to message symbols generated by the message source.

(knowledge, sensitivity, skills, and values), our past experiences, our perception of the competence of others, and the communication context.

Message

Message—symbolic attempt to transfer meaning; the signal that serves as a stimulus for a receiver.

The **message** is the symbolic attempt to transfer meaning; it is the signal that serves as a stimulus for a receiver. Sources send messages consisting of auditory, visual, olfactory, gustatory, or tactile stimuli in any combination of these five senses. Sources of messages intend meaning but messages in and of themselves do not carry meaning. Meanings, or interpretations of messages, are assigned when the receiver decodes the message. Messages serve as symbols for meaning and as such are subject to situational and cultural influences. In other words, to understand a message as a source intends requires an understanding of the source's symbol system (language and actions, and intent of language and actions) in a particular situation.

Channel

Channel—medium through which the message is transmitted.

The **channel** is the medium through which the message is transmitted. It is the link or links between source and receiver. Channels include the five senses and any technological means used for message transmission. Channels frequently are used in combination (verbal and nonverbal, oral and written, face-to-face, and telemediated) with certain channels generally more credible than others. When verbal and nonverbal messages appear to contradict, for example, researchers tell us that most people will find the nonverbal channel more credible than the verbal one. In other words, most of us believe it is more difficult to lie nonverbally than verbally. Channels can distort messages both technologically and in sensory reception. Indeed, the very selection of one channel over another may become a message in and of itself. Written channels, for example, are more often used than face-to-face channels for giving bad news. Receiving a memo from your boss—the bad-news channel—may be cause for alarm even before the actual message has been read.

Noise

Noise—distortion or interference that contributes to discrepancies between the meaning intended by the source of a message and the meaning assigned by the receiver.

Noise is the distortion or interference that contributes to discrepancies between the meaning intended by the source and the meaning assigned by the receiver. Noise can be anything—physical distractions, channel interference, communicative competence, communication context, or psychological predispositions. Noise is always present in one form or another, and the type or types of noise contribute to the meanings assigned to messages by receivers and to the encoding of new messages. Think for a moment about your reaction to receiving an important message from a person whose credibility you have reason to doubt. What meaning do you assign to the message based on your prior relationship with this individual? Assume next that you receive the same message from a trusted friend. Is your reaction different? What type of noise was generated by your past experiences with both individuals? How did that noise affect meaning?

Competence

Each individual brings knowledge, sensitivity, skills, and values to communication interactions. Our ability to understand appropriate behaviors, our willingness to engage in communication, and our ability to interact with others to generate shared realities all contribute to our impression of our own *competence*. Also, we continually evaluate and form impressions about the competence of those with whom we are communicating. Our impression of our own competence and the impression we have of the competence of others contribute to both encoding and decoding of messages. Ultimately competence contributes to communication effects and how we evaluate the effectiveness of our interactions.

Field of Experience

All parties in a communication interaction bring a specific set of experiences or background to bear on the interaction. What we do in a particular situation is related to how much we know about the situation from past experiences and whether we share any common past experiences. We may behave very differently in situations where we have considerable past experience than we would in situations that are new and unfamiliar. The **field of experience** is situation specific and may or may not relate to broader evaluations of self-competence. In other words, although we may feel less competent in situations in which we have little past experience, that impression does not automatically transfer to other circumstances in which we have more background.

Generally it is believed that the more common the field of experience among those communicating, the easier it is to share similar meanings or to construct shared realities. Have you ever tried, for example, to explain an American sporting event to a visitor from another country where the sport is not played and has never been televised? Did you even know where to begin? Chances are the lack of any prior experience on the part of your receiver (no common field of experience between you) required you to engage in considerable detail, making it difficult even to begin to describe

Field of experience—set of specific experiences or background all parties in communication bring to bear on the interaction.

the event. You can imagine that your approach would be entirely different if you were describing the same event to a longtime fan of the sport.

Communication Context

Communication context—
environment for the communication interaction.

The **communication context** is the environment for the communication interaction. Context includes not only the specific time and place of the interaction but also the roles, relationships, and status of communication participants. Most of us recognize that we communicate differently depending on how well we know people, what their formal position is in relation to us, and how visible our communication is to others. The way we express ourselves in the privacy of our own homes may differ from what we will say and do in our work environments. Openly disagreeing with a friend or co-worker is different from openly disagreeing with our boss. The way we express ourselves is related to whether we believe others to be more knowledgeable or competent or whether we believe we possess the best information in a specific setting. The way we express ourselves also reflects the expectations of the particular culture or environment in which we are communicating. We can say, therefore, that context is both culturally and physically influenced, and as with other elements in the communication process, perception of context can differ from one communication participant to another.

Effect

Effect—result, consequence, or outcome of communication exchanges.

The communication **effect** is the result, the consequence, or the outcome of the communication exchange. Effects can be observed to be directly related to communication interactions. When people have an argument and terminate relationships at the end of the argument, we witness what we would call an obvious effect. At other times, the effect is not immediately observable or is at best delayed in time and context. A student does not contribute to a group project; the project is completed and all group members receive the same grade. Nothing appears to happen until the next class project begins and members of the group ask the instructor to reassign the student to another team. Although less direct, this effect nevertheless should be understood as an outcome of previous communication exchanges.

In addition to being viewed in terms of results, the effect of an interaction is evaluated by communication participants for effectiveness and ethics. Did the outcomes result from the free, informed choices of all parties? Did one or more parties feel manipulated? Were all parties empathically supported? Were the best alternatives considered as a result of the interaction? It is in this evaluative area—ethics and effectiveness—that future interactions are influenced. Perceptions of whether past interactions were ethical and effective influence perceptions of the desirability of future communication.

THE CONSTRUCTION OF SHARED REALITIES

Human communication is the process of constructing **shared realities**—creating shared meanings. It is our attempt to have others understand our world as we do and our efforts to appreciate the world of those around us. The process is culturally and contextually influenced with success or failure in individual communication competencies—knowledge, sensitivity, skills, and values. As a process for the construction of shared realities, human communication is dynamic and ever-changing.

When this process occurs between two individuals with some type of ongoing relationship, we call the process *interpersonal communication*. When the process occurs among several individuals, we are describing *group communication*. When large numbers of people are involved (either personally or through technological channels), we call the process *public* or *mass media communication*. Finally, the human communication process in organizations is referred to as *organizational communication*, the subject of our text. Whether in interpersonal, group, public, mass media, or organizational contexts, the human communication process involves attempts to construct shared realities among people in order to generate shared meaning. Think back to the "What Business Is This of Ours?" case. What were the shared realities at Quality Engineering? Describe the fields of experience and the context of the interaction between John and Mary. What were the noise factors? Can you predict the effect of their interaction? Will they be able to work together in the future?

Shared realities—meanings resulting from the communication process; attempts to have others understand our world as we do and our efforts to appreciate the world of those around us.

CONCEPTS OF ORGANIZATIONS

We have been defining and describing the human communication process in a variety of possible contexts. Our particular interest is, of course, communication in organizations and how communication influences organizational processes and events. We will begin to explore the relationship between communication and organizations by first identifying what an organization is and what it does.

The term **organization** is applied to the results of the process of *organizing*. Organizing is an attempt to bring order out of chaos or establish organizations—entities where purposeful and ordered activity takes place. Organizing is accomplished through purposeful activities generated as a result of communication behaviors. In other words, the process we call organizing is accomplished through human communication as individuals seek to bring order out of chaos and establish entities for purposeful activities.

Amitai Etzioni (1964) has described organizations as social units or groupings of people deliberately constructed and reconstructed to strive for specific goals. As such, organizations are characterized by divisions of labor for goal achievement. These efforts also are directed by relatively

Organization—results of the process of organizing; dynamic systems in which individuals engage in collective efforts for goal accomplishment.

continuous patterns of authority and leadership. Interdependence exists both among organizational components and with the external environment. This complex interdependence requires coordination achieved through communication.

Consistent with the Etzioni view, Richard Farace, Peter Monge, and Hamish Russell (1977) have provided a description of organizations that reflects much of modern organization theory. They suggest that organizations can be best understood as

> two or more individuals who recognize that some of their goals can be more readily achieved through interdependent (cooperative) actions, even though disagreement (conflict) may be present; who take in materials, energy, and information from the environment in which they exist; who develop coordinative and control relationships to capitalize on their interdependence while operating on these inputs; and who return the modified inputs to the environment in an attempt to accomplish the goals that interdependence was meant to make possible.

This definition focuses on organizations as dynamic systems in which individuals engage in collective efforts for goal accomplishment. To remain dynamic, organizations must adapt to continually changing environments—both internally and externally. From this perspective of adaptation and change, organizations can be understood as active and dynamic mergers of human behaviors and technological operations. As such, organizations can be understood not only from their structure but also from how they continually create and change what they do and how they do it. This occurs through communication behaviors. Put another way, understanding what an organization is and how it works requires an understanding of the process of organizational communication.

DEFINITIONS OF ORGANIZATIONAL COMMUNICATION

Organizational communication—process through which organizations are created and in turn create and shape events. The process can be understood as a combination of process, people, messages, meaning, and purpose.

Organizational communication is both similar to and distinct from other types of communication. Organizational communication has sources and receivers who are engaged in encoding and decoding of messages. Messages are transmitted over channels distorted by noise. As with other forms of communication, organizational communication is related to the competencies of individuals, their fields of experience, the communicative context, and the effects or results of interactions. Yet organizational communication is more than the daily interactions of individuals within organizations. It is the process through which organizations create and shape events.

Organizational Communication as Process

As with other forms of communication, organizational communication is best understood as an ongoing process without distinct beginnings and endings. The process includes patterns of interactions that develop among organizational members and how these interactions shape organizations.

Because the process is ever-changing, it can be described as evolutionary and culturally dependent. In other words, the ongoing process of creating and transmitting organizational messages reflects the shared realities resulting from previous message exchanges and evolves to generate new realities that create and shape events.

Organizational communication is an evolutionary, culturally dependent process of sharing information and creating relationships in environments designed for manageable, cooperative, goal-oriented behavior. (Wilson, Goodall, and Waagen, 1986)

Organizational Communication as People

Individuals bring to organizations sets of characteristics that influence how information is processed. Organizational communication contributes to creating relationships and assists both individuals and organizations in achieving diverse purposes. Organizational communication occurs between and among people who share both work and interpersonal relationships.

Communication is an interactional process in which meaning is stimulated through the sending and receiving of verbal and nonverbal messages. An organization is a social grouping that establishes task and/or interpersonal patterns of relationships for the attainment of specific objectives. Thus, our working definition of organizational communication will be the study of the flow and impact of messages within a network of interactional relationships. (Tortoriello, Blatt, and DeWine, 1978)

Organizational Communication as Messages

Organizational communication is the creation and exchange of messages. It is the movement or transmission of verbal and nonverbal behaviors and the sharing of information throughout the organization. Communicators are linked together by channels, and messages are described with such terms as *frequency, amount,* and *type.* Concern is expressed for message fidelity, or the extent to which messages are similar or accurate at all links through the channels.

Organizational communication may be defined as the display and interpretation of messages among communication units who are part of a particular organization. An organization is comprised of communication units in hierarchical relations to each other and functioning in an environment. (Pace, 1983)

Organizational Communication as Meaning

Organizational communication creates and shapes organizational events. Role taking occurs as individuals engage in social interaction within the ever-changing organizational context. Organizational communication is the symbolic behavior of individuals and organizations that when interpreted, affects all organizational activities. It is the process through which organizational meanings are generated.

> *Meanings, then, do not reside in messages, channels, or perceptual filters. Rather, they evolve from interaction processes and the ways that individuals make sense of their talk. Process is not movement or transmission of messages. Instead, it refers to the ongoing, ever-changing sets of interlocked behaviors that create as well as change organizational events. (Putnam, 1983)*

Organizational Communication as Purpose

Organizational communication is organizing, decision making, planning, controlling, and coordinating. It is people, messages, and meaning. It is the process through which individuals and organizations attempt goal-oriented behavior in dealing with their environments.

> *Organizational communication is the process of creating and exchanging messages within a network of interdependent relationships to cope with environmental uncertainty. (Goldhaber, 1986)*

Can you now answer the question we asked at the beginning of the chapter about the differences between organizational and other types of communication? You should be able to. Whereas interpersonal and group communication occur in organizations, organizational communication is a more comprehensive process including, but not limited to, one-on-one and group exchanges. Competencies for organizational communication include interpersonal abilities, but organizational communication competencies also require effectiveness in complex and changing environments where diverse groups of people join in purposeful activity. The goal of this book is to help you identify and develop important competencies for organizational communication. The next several chapters will concentrate on knowledge, sensitivity, skills, and values important in interpersonal, group, and organization-wide contexts.

Let's return to our case study. Describe the interaction between John and Mary from an organizational communication perspective. Can you identify organizational factors influencing their exchange? Do John and Mary have a work relationship or are they communicating as friends? Can they be both? Is this an example of organizational goal-directed behavior? How might their exchange affect Quality Engineering?

It is difficult to be certain about our answers for this case. The chances are most of us feel the need for additional information about John and Mary and Quality Engineering. Yet the lack of complete information is very characteristic of many, if not most, of our organizational experiences.

In fact, it is probable that even with more information we can never be certain about all of the shared realities between John and Mary. Indeed, as we begin our study of organizational communication, a key to our personal development rests with our ability to analyze thoughtfully while recognizing the limits of our understanding.

SUMMARY

Human communication is the process through which we construct shared realities. Elements in the communication process include sources and receivers, message encoding and decoding, channels, noise, communicative competence, participant fields of experience, contexts, and effects. The process is evaluated for effectiveness and ethical behaviors, with these evaluations influencing future interactions. Organizations are the products of organizing activities and can be described as deliberately constructed social units designed to strive for specific goals. As such, organizations are dynamic mergers of human behaviors and technological operations. Organizational communication includes all of the elements in the human communication process. It is also the process through which organizations are created and in turn create and shape events. As such, organizational communication can be understood as a combination of process, people, messages, meaning, and purpose.

WORKSHOP

1. Identify all the organizations of which you are a member. Include the school you are currently attending. Describe shared realities for each organization. Discuss as a class the shared realities of your school.
2. Shared meanings or shared realities are what organizational communication is all about. My Meaning, Your Meaning, Our Meanings, an exercise to illustrate the importance of meanings and shared realities, is found below. Divide the class into groups of six members each and complete the exercise. Discuss what you have learned about meanings and shared realities. (See pages 33–34.)
3. The following case, "What Do You Mean I'm Not Getting a Raise?" illustrates organizational messages with multiple meanings. Study the case and attempt to understand how people receiving the same message can arrive at very different meanings. (See pages 34–35.)

My Meaning, Your Meaning, Our Meanings

Read each of the following five statements and write your response. You may agree, disagree, or take no position on the statement. Your response should accurately reflect the statement's meaning to you.

1. Oral skills are more important than written communication skills for most jobs. I (agree with, disagree with, don't know about) this statement. It means to me . . .

2. People who are the most intelligent make the best grades and are the most successful. I (agree with, disagree with, don't know about) this statement. It means to me . . .

3. The successful organizational member must be competitive and persuasive. I (agree with, disagree with, don't know about) this statement. It means to me . . .

4. The successful organizational member is more analytical than others and believes technical skills are more important than communication abilities. I (agree with, disagree with, don't know about) this statement. It means to me . . .

In groups of six, discuss your responses and compare similarities and differences. What influenced the similarities and differences in your answers? How do these influences contribute to the meanings we assign to messages?

Next, consider the following four professions: minister, salesperson, lawyer, television executive. As a group, attempt to determine how you think most people in these professions would react to the five statements. Again, what does this tell us about how meanings are influenced? How accurate can you be about your perceptions of the meanings others might assign?

Finally, as a group attempt to develop a response to each statement that all group members can support. (Total agreement is not necessary, only general support.) How do these group statements differ from your individual statements? Did your statements become a "shared reality" for your group? If so, why? If not, why not? (If time permits, compare your group's statements to other groups in your class. What are the similarities and differences? Are there any surprises?)

The "What Do You Mean I'm Not Getting a Raise?" Case

Jane Jackson, division manager of AMC, Inc., had spent the day in the cafeteria meeting with each of AMC's three manufacturing shifts. She had good news and had been eager to make the announcement that the company would not begin the layoffs rumored to occur at the end of the present round of contracts. Instead of layoffs, management had decided to freeze wages and evaluate in six months when cost-of-living and merit increases could resume. Jane had been careful with the announcement, reading exactly the press release from corporate headquarters.

Following her cafeteria meetings, Jane asked her section managers to meet with individual supervisors on each of the three shifts to determine how the news was being received. Jane had been concerned about the layoff rumors and expected a generally favorable response to the announcement. She was not prepared for her section managers' feedback. Several supervisors reported that although there was considerable relief that layoffs were not imminent, many workers did not understand that they would not receive their annual increases at performance appraisal time. Numerous workers believed management intended to consider layoffs again at the end of the six-month freeze period, and others thought the wage freeze meant no new people were being hired. Jane could not understand how all this confusion was possible. After all, everyone got exactly the same message.

What would you tell Jane about messages and meanings? What are the probable reasons for this confusion? What would you do if you were Jane and her section managers?

SUMMARY OF COMPETENCY COMPONENTS:

KNOWLEDGE, SENSITIVITY, SKILLS, VALUES

KNOWLEDGE

Communication is defined as the construction of shared realities.

Communication is viewed as process.

Elements in the communication process include sources, receivers, channels, noise, competence, experience, context, and effect.

Organizations are described as social units striving for specific goals.

Organizational communication is defined as the process through which organizations create and shape events.

SENSITIVITY

Communication is identified as symbolic behavior.

Communication is influenced by culture and context.

Communication meanings create and shape organizational events.

SKILLS

Analysis skills are developed through case study.

VALUES

Communication is considered the focal process for organizing.

Communication is evaluated for ethics and effectiveness.

REFERENCES AND SUGGESTED READINGS

Etzioni, A. 1964. *Modern Organizations*. Englewood Cliffs, NJ: Prentice-Hall.

Farace, R., P. Monge, and H. Russell. 1977. *Communicating and organizing*. Reading, MA: Addison-Wesley.

Goldhaber, G. 1986. *Organizational communication*. 4th ed. Dubuque, IA: Brown.

Krone, K., F. Jablin, and L. Putnam. 1987. Communication theory and organizational communication: Multiple perspectives. In *Handbook of organizational communication*, eds. F. Jablin, L. Putnam, K. Roberts, and L. Porter, 18–40. Newbury Park, CA: Sage.

Pace, R. W. 1983. *Organizational communication: Foundations for human resource development*. Englewood Cliffs, NJ: Prentice-Hall.

Putnam, L. 1983. The interpretive perspective: An alternative to functionalism. In *Communication and organizations: An interpretive approach*, eds. L. Putnam and M. Pacanowsky, 31–54. Beverly Hills, CA: Sage.

Tortoriello, T., S. Blatt, and S. DeWine. 1978. *Communication in the organization: An applied approach*. New York: McGraw-Hill.

Wilson, G., H. Goodall, and C. Waagen. 1986. *Organizational communication*. New York: Harper & Row.

CHAPTER

~T H R E E~

Theoretical Perspectives for Organizational Communication

Developing competencies through . . .

KNOWLEDGE

  Describing the Functional approach to organizational communication

  Describing the Meaning-Centered approach to organizational communication

  Distinguishing between the Functional and Meaning-Centered approaches

SENSITIVITY

  Understanding the importance of shared realities for organizational communication

  Identifying how organizational communication creates and shapes organizational events

SKILLS

  Developing analysis abilities using Functional and Meaning-Centered approaches

  Practicing analysis abilities

VALUES

  Viewing communication as the fundamental organizational process

  Relating organizational communication to organizational effectiveness

The Coronado Company's Quality Defects Case

Bill Drake, president of Coronado Manufacturing Company, could hardly believe the conclusions in the consultant's report. Product quality had always been a strength of Coronado Manufacturing, and now defective products were being blamed for declining sales in the company's small-appliance line. The report went on to say that the sales department for Coronado was not passing along customer complaints to anyone in manufacturing. Furthermore, Drake was confused by his own lack of personal knowledge about either customer dissatisfaction or problems in manufacturing. After all, he met weekly with the management team responsible for spotting these problems, and they all knew he felt the customer was number one.

Drake thought about the history of Coronado Manufacturing. Coronado had been founded some fifty years ago by Drake's father and uncle. Both men had worked most of their lives for a major manufacturer of small appliances well known for its quality products and customer concern. In founding Coronado both men had hired people who cared about quality and understood customers. In fact, stories were told about the founders personally emphasizing quality to newcomers on the manufacturing line and making "surprise" visits to customers to check on how "their" products were working. When Bill Drake's father retired, he had admonished Bill not to forget the basics that had made the business successful.

Bill Drake had assumed he was successfully carrying on Coronado's quality and customer traditions. Was the report accurate? Was his management team withholding information? How could he determine what to do?

Bill Drake is confronted with a management problem requiring immediate action. The decisions he makes, the action he takes, and what ultimately happens to Coronado Manufacturing provide examples of how organizational communication creates and shapes events.

INTRODUCTION

In Chapter 2 we defined organizational communication as the process through which organizations create and shape events. This chapter is designed to help us understand this process and to develop our competencies in determining how Bill Drake might approach his problem. The Functional and Meaning-Centered approaches will be presented as ways to understand the process of organizational communication and as frameworks to help analyze specific organizational situations and problems.

The Functional and Meaning-Centered approaches ask different questions about organizational communication. The *Functional approach* asks how and why communication works, whereas the *Meaning-Centered approach* asks what communication is. The Functional approach asks what purpose communication serves within organizations and how messages move. The Meaning-Centered approach asks if communication is the process through which organizing, decision making, influence, and culture occur. The Functional approach describes organizational reality in such terms as chains of command, positions, roles, and communications channels, whereas the Meaning-Centered approach defines as reality the symbolic significance of these terms. The Functional approach subordinates the importance of the individual to his or her organizational position and function, whereas in the Meaning-Centered approach the significance of the individual is the key focus.

After studying this chapter you will be able to answer several questions about Functional and Meaning-Centered approaches.

THE FUNCTIONAL APPROACH

1. What are the different types of organizational messages?
2. How do organizing, relationship, and change messages differ?
3. How can communication networks be described?
4. How do different communications channels affect messages?
5. What is communication load?
6. What is distortion in organizational communication?

THE MEANING-CENTERED APPROACH

1. How is "reality" generated through human interaction?
2. Why are communicating and organizing almost synonymous processes?
3. How does communication contribute to decision making?
4. How does influence work in organizations?
5. What are communication rules?
6. What is the difference between treating culture as something an organization has versus something an organization is?
7. What is meant by communication climate?

Think back to the Coronado Quality Defects case. Which of these questions should Bill Drake be asking? As you study the material in this chapter, try to determine how the Functional and Meaning-Centered perspectives can help Bill Drake solve his problem at Coronado Manufacturing.

This chapter contributes to *knowledge* competencies by describing and contrasting Functional and Meaning-Centered approaches to organizational communication. Individual *sensitivity* competencies are developed by examining the development of shared realities in organizations and individual communication behaviors that shape and change organizational events. *Skills* are developed and practiced by applying Functional and Meaning-Centered approaches to cases and exercises. Finally, *value* competencies are encouraged by describing communication as the fundamental organizational process and by relating organizational communication to organizational effectiveness.

THE FUNCTIONAL APPROACH

Functional approach—way of understanding organizational communication by describing what messages do and how they move through organizations.

The **Functional approach** helps us understand organizational communication by describing what messages do and how they move through organizations. This perspective describes communication as a complex organizational process that serves organizing, relationship, and change functions—what messages do. The way messages move through organizations is described by examining communication networks, channels, message directions, communication load, and distortion. The Functional approach suggests that communication transmits rules, regulations, and information throughout the organization. Communication establishes and defines human relationships, helps individuals identify with goals and opportunities, and is the process by which the organization generates and manages change. These functions occur during the repetitive patterns of communication interactions in which organizational members engage.

> THE FUNCTIONAL APPROACH
>
> Communication Functions
>
> Organizing
>
> Relationship
>
> Change
>
> Communication Structure
>
> Networks
>
> Channels
>
> Direction
>
> Load and Distortion

In Chapter 2 we described organizations as dynamic systems in which individuals engage in collective efforts to accomplish goals. We found that organizations can be understood not only in terms of their structure but also by the way they continually create and change what they do and how they do it. We claimed that, as such, organizations emerge and evolve through communication behaviors. The Functional approach describes organizations as dynamic communication systems with the various parts of the system operating together to create and shape organizational events.

Organizational Communication Systems: Component Parts

Before we can examine what messages do and how they move in organizations, we need to understand the concept of an **organizational communication system** on which the Functional approach is based. What are the main parts of the system? What parts work together to create and shape organizational events? How does communication contribute to keeping a system dynamic? What role does communication play in organizations that cease to exist?

In the Functional approach, information processing is seen as the primary function of organizational communication systems. It takes place in a number of related units that when taken together, are called *organizations* or *suprasystems*. The individual units, sometimes called *subsystems*, are related by some degree of structure and, when described as a whole, can be distinguished from other organizations in the environment by their boundary. The Coronado Manufacturing Company provides an example of an organizational communication system with its manufacturing and sales units, and Bill Drake as president represents a management unit. These units relate to each other to produce a product that customers in the external environment, outside the Coronado boundary, will buy. Coronado Manufacturing Company is the suprasystem with management, manufacturing, and sales subsystems. But the external environment is important to Coronado. Sales are slipping. Bill Drake needs external information (from the consultant and customers) to make decisions about internal operations, decisions that in turn will influence future sales.

> **Organizational communication system**—number of related units that operate together to create and shape organizational events. Information processing is the primary function of the units.

Communication Inputs

This relationship between external environment information and internal information processing is important for understanding organizational communication systems. Information in the external environment, commonly known as **communication inputs,** is any information that can potentially influence the decision making of the suprasystem (organization). It is crucial for an organization to have accurate and timely information inputs to adapt and change. Bill Drake realizes that the future of Coronado Manufacturing is related to the accuracy of the inputs about quality defects from his customers. Without this information his understanding of the sales problem is incomplete. Only with accurate information about quality problems can he make informed decisions.

> **Communication inputs**—information in the external environment that may influence the decision making of the organization.

Communication Throughput

When information enters the organization, the communication system begins a process known as **communication throughput,** or the transforming and changing of input information for internal organizational use. Bill Drake, in taking the consultant's report and evaluating what to do, is taking inputs and transforming them into organizational action. His decisions and

> **Communication throughput**—transforming and changing of input information for internal organizational use and the generation and transmission of internal information throughout the organization.

the decisions of people in sales and manufacturing can be described as throughput communication. In other words, the internal subsystems (management, sales, manufacturing) of Coronado are moving messages through the organization that will influence the production of products and ultimately customer satisfaction. The quality of throughput communication will determine whether or not the defects problem is solved. Even with accurate and timely inputs, the subsystems of Coronado require effective internal communication to increase sales. Bill Drake has reason to question the throughput communication of his organization when he realizes that despite weekly staff meetings, he was unaware of the quality problem.

Communication Output

Communication output—messages to the external environment from within the organization.

Messages to the external environment from within the organization are known as **communication output.** *Outputs* can be thought of as the results of the input and throughput process and are both intentional and unintentional. Coronado Manufacturing, through its sales force and advertising, generates intentional output communication. The defects in its products, however, have become unintentional output messages with important consequences. The low-quality message from the defective products is a potentially more powerful message than positive messages from advertising and sales campaigns.

Open versus Closed Systems

Open systems—organizations that continually take in new information, transform that information, and give information back to the environment.

Closed systems—organizations that lack input communication, making it difficult to make good decisions and stay current with the needs of the environment.

The response of the environment (in Coronado's case, the customers) to organizational communication is feedback that in turn becomes new inputs to the system. The way the organization responds to these new inputs with throughput efforts and new outputs determines whether we have an open or closed system. **Open systems** continually take in new information, transform that information, and give information back to the environment. By contrast, **closed systems** are characterized by a lack of input communication, making it difficult to make good decisions and stay current with the needs of the environment. Open systems use a variety of problem-solving approaches. There is no one best way to do things. We call this ability to use a variety of approaches *equifinality*, meaning there are many ways to reach system goals.

Bill Drake wants Coronado Manufacturing to operate as an open system. He is listening to customer complaints and trying to decide what to do. He can consider a new advertising campaign or new approaches from his sales staff. He knows, however, that he is unlikely to be successful until the defects problem is solved. In the long term, if Bill Drake pays no attention to sales or quality problems he increases the likelihood that Coronado Manufacturing will go out of business. However, as we can see from studying the Coronado case, Bill Drake has more than one way to approach his problems. He can work with both manufacturing and sales, he can work only with manufacturing, he can assign responsibility to others, he can retain much of the responsibility himself, and he has other options. There are a number of ways (equifinality) to solve Coronado's problems. Figure 3.1 illustrates the Coronado Manufacturing communication system.

Message Functions

When we talk about **message functions** within organizations we are talking about what communication does or how it contributes to the overall functioning of the organization. Numerous researchers have described message functions in attempts to understand how communication systems work. Daniel Katz and Robert Kahn (1966), for example, provide a message-function classification that includes production, maintenance, adaptation, and management communication. Howard Greenbaum (1976) talks about regulative, integrative, innovative, and informative-instructive networks. W. Charles Redding (1972) suggests that message flow can be classified by task, maintenance, and human concerns, and Leo Thayer (1968) identifies functions that inform, persuade, command, instruct, and integrate.

Message functions—what communication does or how it contributes to the overall functioning of the organization.

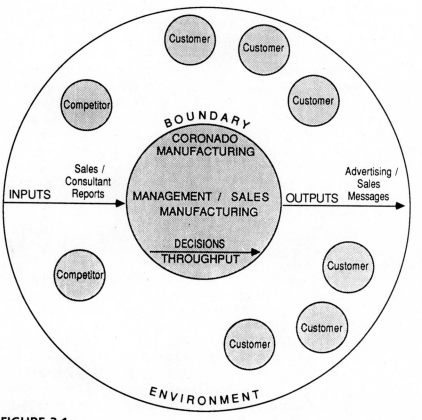

FIGURE 3.1
Coronado Manufacturing communication system.

In our attempt to understand organizational communication from the Functional approach, we will describe message functions in three broad categories: organizing functions, relationship functions, and change functions. Each function is seen as necessary for an open communication system, although the exact balance among message functions will vary by organizational type and circumstance.

Organizing Functions

People who work together talk more about doing tasks than any other subject. This is not a surprising finding. To engage in organized activity in pursuit of goals, people in organizations must develop and exchange messages about rules, regulations, policies, and tasks.

Organizing functions establish the rules and regulations of a particular environment. Policy manuals, employee handbooks, orientation training, newsletters, and a variety of other sources convey information about how the organization expects to work and what it requires of its members. These organizing messages define and clarify tasks, develop work instructions, and evaluate task accomplishment.

Organizing messages can be found in every aspect of our lives. The school you attend publishes standards for admissions and requirements for specific majors and degrees. Instructors establish requirements and define performance expectations. You converse with teachers and peers about assignments and responsibilities. All these messages and many more describe how your school is organized, how it is supposed to work, and how you fit into that process.

The adequacy and effectiveness of organizing messages can be evaluated by how well organizational members understand and perform tasks, how rules and regulations are understood and followed, and how adequately daily operations support organizational goals. In sum, the organizing function of communication guides, directs, and controls organizational activity.

Relationship Functions

The **relationship function** of organizational communication helps individuals define their roles and assess the compatibility of individual and organizational goals. *Relationship communication* contributes to individuals' identification with an organization or sense of "belonging" in their work environment. Frequently referred to as *integrative* or *maintenance messages*, relationship communication contributes to employee morale and maintains or integrates individuals with their work environments.

Communication establishes relationships between supervisors and subordinates and within peer groups. Relationship messages range from informal conversations to visible symbols of status such as large offices and reserved parking spaces. Job titles, awards, and promotions are other examples of relationship communication that determine how individuals identify or relate to the organization.

Organizing functions—messages that establish the rules and regulations of a particular environment.

Relationship functions—communication that helps individuals define their roles and assess the compatibility of individual and organizational goals.

Whereas organizing messages communicate how the organization operates, relationship messages establish the human interactions that make such operation possible. Chances are, for example, that your sense of belonging with your school or lack of it is closely related to your interpersonal interactions with teachers and other students. In fact, your ability to meet performance expectations successfully may be influenced by your relationship with your instructors and how comfortable you are in exchanging ideas with them. The same may be true of your relationship with other students. The quality of your work on a team project probably is influenced by how much you feel a part of—or integrated with—your group. The effectiveness of relationship messages is reflected in individual satisfaction with work relationships, productivity, employee turnover, overall support for organizational practices, and a variety of other less obvious ways.

Change Functions

Change functions help organizations adapt what they do and how they do it and are essential to an open system. Change messages occur in organizational problem solving, individual decision making, feedback from the environment, and numerous other choice-making situations. Change communication is the processing of new ideas and information as well as the altering of existing procedures and processes. It is essential for continual adaptation to the environment and for meeting the complex needs of individuals working together.

Change functions—messages that help organizations adapt what they do and how they do it; viewed as essential to an open system.

Experiences in decision-making groups help illustrate how change messages function. When working with a group of students to develop a class presentation, chances are you can recall messages speculating about the best approach and who should take what type of responsibility. Furthermore, you probably attempted to reduce the ambiguity of the assignment by determining what the instructor wanted and what would be appropriate for the time you had. Your group's ability to exchange innovative messages and adapt to the requirements of the assignment influenced your effectiveness and final grade. In the Coronado case, Bill Drake became aware of his quality problem through change messages—specifically, declining sales and a consultant's report. His attempt to correct the problem will require change messages with his sales and manufacturing staffs and new approaches to reverse the negative reactions of his customers.

The ultimate effectiveness of change communication is the survival of the organization. Without appropriate change, organizational systems stagnate and die. Change communication is necessary for innovation and adaptation and is the process through which the organization obtains new information, chooses among various alternatives, and weighs current practices against emerging needs. Timely and creative change communication is required for a dynamic and open system. The effectiveness of change messages can be determined by whether the organization gathers information from the best available sources and acts on that information with a timely, quality decision. Figure 3.2 illustrates organizing, relationship, and change functions.

Message Structure

Message structure—movement of organizing, relationship, and change messages throughout the organization and between the organization and its external environment.

The movement of organizing, relationship, and change messages throughout the organization and between the organization and its external environment is the **message structure** of organizational communication. The Functional approach to structure asks questions about the repetitive patterns of interactions among members of the organization (networks), the use of a variety of channels for communication, message directions, and the amount of messages and the types of distortions that can be expected to occur in organizational communication. In other words, the structure of organizational communication can be understood in terms of networks, channels, message directions, load, and distortion.

Communication Networks

Networks—formal and informal patterns of communication that link organizational members together.

Communication **networks** are the formal and informal patterns of communication that link organizational members together. Networks can be described by how formally or informally they are organized, by the links between people, and by the roles people perform as they link.

Communication networks develop as a result of both formal organization and informal social contact. Organizations divide work by function and task. Organization charts mapping out who reports to whom and in what

---

FIGURE 3.2
The Functional Approach

Organizing Messages

Rules and regulations
Organizational policies
Task definition
Task instruction
Task evaluation

Relationship Messages

Individual role definition
Individual/organizational goals
Status symbols
Integration among supervisor/
    subordinates, peers

Change Messages

Decision making
Market analysis
New idea processing
Environmental inputs
Employee suggestions
Problem solving

area of responsibility can be described as blueprints for the way decisions are to be made, the way conflicts are to be resolved, and which groups are responsible for "networking" to reach organizational goals. The formal organization (as illustrated by the organization chart just mentioned) prescribes who has the right to tell others what to do, who is to work together as a unit or team, and who has the final authority in disagreements. In other words, the formal act of organizing creates organizational communication networks or the formal communication system.

As individuals work together, interpersonal relationships develop that extend beyond the specific requirements of the work group. Informal networks emerge, with individuals exchanging diverse types of information related both to the organization and to their social relationships. The organizational "grapevine" is perhaps the most frequently discussed example of an informal network.

Supervisors and subordinates, task forces, committees, quality circles, and other types of decision-making bodies are examples of formal communication networks. Formal networks also are established with various forms of technology such as computers and video systems. Generally speaking, these telemediated networks are used to establish communication links that geographic separation would otherwise make difficult and costly. In our shift to an information society, these technological networks are of increasing importance and are projected to change the way we establish networks and broaden the scope of our network involvement.

Informal networks emerge as a result of formal networks and are formed by individuals who have interpersonal relationships, who exchange valuable information across reporting chains, and who disregard formal status and timing. Typically, informal networks exclude numerous individuals who are designated for network inclusion by the formal chain of command.

Formal and informal networks exist side by side; individuals maintain membership in both. Formal and informal networks contribute to organizational reality, and both networks change and shape organizational events. Message structure within organizations cannot be understood without evaluating how both formal and informal patterns of interaction take place.

Think about your own personal networks. What formal networks exist in the organizations of which you are a member? What types of networks exist in your school? How do you establish your informal networks? Which type of network is more meaningful to you? All of us are involved in both formal and informal networks. When we evaluate our personal experiences we can better understand how organizational networks function and how they contribute to the movement of organizing, relationship, and change messages (see Figure 3.3).

Richard Farace, Peter Monge, and Hamish Russell (1977) have identified three general properties of the links found in organizational networks: symmetry, strength, and reciprocity. They describe a *symmetrical link* as persons equally exchanging information during an interaction. In other

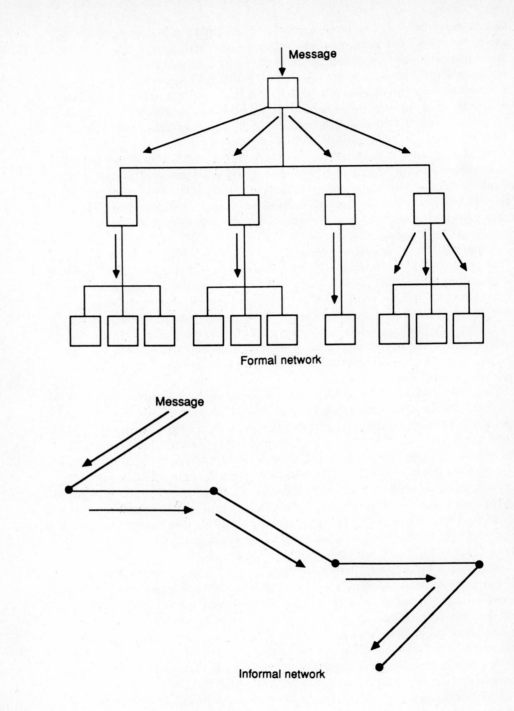

FIGURE 3.3
Illustrates message movement in formally organized and informal networks.

words, the network is symmetrical when both parties have approximately the same amount of give and take. Symmetrical links are common among peers when interacting about work problems or social interests.

The opposite of the symmetrical link is the *asymmetrical link*, where one individual gives more information than another. Common organizational examples of asymmetrical links are supervisors giving directions to subordinates or instructors lecturing to students. In most cases, more information is sent from supervisors to subordinates and from instructors to students than the other way around.

The network property of *strength* refers to the frequency and length of interactions among linked individuals. Strong links communicate more frequently than weak links and usually have longer periods of interaction. The strength of communication links predicts who is influential among organizational members. The stronger the communication link among people the greater the chances of linked individuals influencing each other's behavior.

The final property, *reciprocity*, describes the level of agreement among organizational members about their network links. In other words, do individuals agree or disagree about the type of link they have with each other? Disagreement about whether or not individuals are linked frequently can be understood in terms of the differing perceptions individuals bring to communication relationships. For example, a subordinate may perceive a symmetrical link to his or her supervisor, whereas the supervisor would describe the link as somewhat weak and certainly asymmetrical. Independent observation could help to understand the discrepancy; however, the perceptions of each individual would still influence their overall relationship.

Individuals perform diverse roles in networks. Common roles such as liaisons, bridges, gatekeepers, participants, nonparticipants, and isolates all function differently in communication networks. *Liaisons* link or connect groups with common information without being a member of either group. Bill Drake, as president of Coronado Manufacturing, can fulfill a liaison role for his sales and manufacturing units. He can describe his concern for the quality problem to both groups without being a member of either. An individual fulfilling a *bridge* communication role is a member of one group and transmits information from that group to another, actually forming a bridge between the two. If Coronado's manufacturing manager informs the sales group of changes to ensure increased product quality, the manufacturing manager will be acting as a network bridge between manufacturing and sales.

Gatekeepers are positioned in networks to control the flow of information through a communication chain. Gatekeepers routinely receive information and determine whether or not to transmit that information to the next link or links in the chain. Managers are gatekeepers in relation to their subordinates. Secretaries are gatekeepers as they filter messages and may even determine who can reach their bosses. Subordinates can keep problems from their managers in a gatekeeper role. Anyone in the network can function in this role.

We describe a network *isolate* as an individual with little or no communication links throughout the organization. Isolates often are apprehensive about communication and deliberately avoid interaction with others. However, few organizational members are complete isolates. Individuals or groups may be isolates from other groups. Competition between groups, for example, may weaken communication links and contribute to isolation, and individuals or groups may be isolated from certain communication functions while participating in others. An individual or group may be involved in the sending and receiving of organizing and relationship messages without being connected or linked (i.e., involved) in change messages or the innovative function.

Finally, there are the network participants and nonparticipants. *Participants* are individuals who participate in linked communication behaviors but who are not usually in liaison or bridge roles. They are typically seen as members of the group but not influential to other groups. *Nonparticipants* are formal members of groups but do not affiliate with others in the group to the extent that participants do. According to Gerald Wilson, H. Lloyd Goodall, and Christopher Waagen (1986), nonparticipants differ from isolates in that nonparticipants have demonstrated more communication and relationship abilities. Nonparticipants refrain from communication out of choice, not out of inability or fear.

Perceptions of various network roles differ. Although liaisons and nonliaisons are often similar in background, liaisons routinely enjoy higher organizational status than their nonliaison counterparts. Liaisons believe they have and are perceived by others to have more communication contacts and opportunities. Isolates, on the other hand, tend to withhold information and are less likely than others to facilitate communication flow. Isolates depend more than others on technology rather than interpersonal contact and in general have a lower self-concept and a higher need for security than their more communicatively linked counterparts. Figure 3.4 illustrates the communication links.

Communication Channels

Channels—means for the transmission of messages. Common means are face-to-face interaction, group meetings, memos, letters, electronic mail systems, computer-assisted data transmission, and teleconferencing.

Channels are the means for transmission of messages. Organizations typically have a wide variety of channels available for transmitting oral and written messages. Face-to-face interaction, group meetings, memos, letters, electronic mail systems, computer-assisted data transmission, and teleconferencing are among the channels commonly used in contemporary organizations. As we shift to an information society, emphasis is increasing on developing new and improved technical channels that speed information transfer and shorten decision-making response time. Indeed, it is fair to say the choice and availability of communication channels influences the way the organization can and does operate.

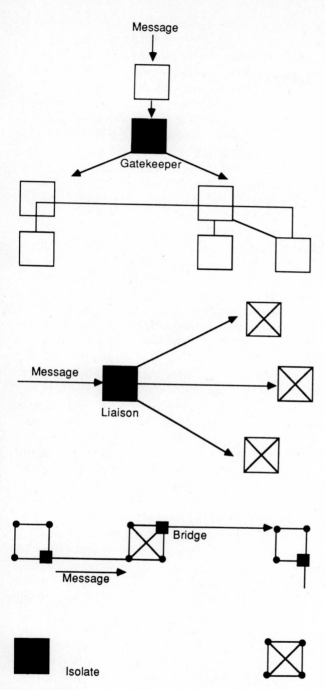

FIGURE 3.4
The black boxes illustrate gatekeeper, liaison, bridge, and isolate communication links.

Questions arise as to the effectiveness of various channels and what is communicated by channel selection. Although most of us take channel use for granted, selecting one channel over another can communicate subtle and important attitudes about both the message receiver and the message itself. For example, most of us like to communicate good news in face-to-face interaction. We enjoy the reactions of others and deliberately choose channels that permit close, "immediate" contact. If the news is not positive we may prefer another channel. Negative messages, more than good news, are likely to be transmitted in a less "immediate" channel such as letters or memos, the telephone, or a third-party announcement. In fact, research suggests that our attitude about the message and our willingness to have contact with the receiver significantly influence the channels we use for communication.

Attitudes about messages and receivers are not the only factors that influence channel selection. Power and status, work requirements, technical capability, and judgments about channel effectiveness all contribute to the mode or modes we use. High-status organizational members, for example, can determine what channels they personally want to use and what modes others must use in communicating with them. The president of the company can initiate face-to-face interaction with just about anyone in the organization. The chances are good, however, that not all organizational members can walk into the president's office for an unscheduled visit. In the Coronado case, Bill Drake can require the consultant to submit a report and recommendations in writing. Drake can require his sales and manufacturing people to meet with him and make detailed presentations of their ideas. It is unlikely that the consultant or the sales and manufacturing managers could make the same requirement of Bill Drake.

Judgments about channel effectiveness also guide organizational members in making communication choices. Face-to-face interaction has the strength of immediacy and the capacity to monitor nonverbal as well as verbal behavior. Face-to-face interaction also permits questions and immediate clarification of ambiguous messages. The face-to-face channel, however, does not provide support for complicated instructions requiring considerable technical detail. A financial report presented orally may be much less effective than if the same material had been summarized in writing. On the other hand, delivering an employee reprimand via the company's electronic mail system may be destructive and fail to gain the desired outcome.

Research on the effectiveness of channels supports what many organizational members know about the importance of the "immediate" mode of oral communication. Oral messages accompanied by supporting written messages have been described as the most effective method for transmitting information from management throughout the organization. Face-to-face oral methods without written accompaniment have been found to be effective for employee reprimands and in settling work disputes. Written channels are more effective when communication requires future employee action or is of a general nature. Directives, orders, important policy changes, and the need for immediate action are best communicated orally and accompanied by written support.

Judgments about channel effectiveness also are based on financial cost and individual skill levels. The cost of telemediated channels and the skills necessary to use computers and teleresources are important factors governing their selection as organizational channels. Access and availability of channels and the type of response needed also influence which channel or channels are effective in particular situations.

Bill Drake will be confronted with channel selection as he works on the defects problem. He will use internal channels, and once the problem is solved he must consider how to communicate to his customers. How would you advise Drake? Are particular channels more appropriate than others as he seeks to regain lost sales? Attempt to describe the criteria Drake should use for channel selection.

Message Direction

As messages move through channels, we begin to think about that movement in terms of **direction.** Researchers typically describe three primary message directions in organizations: downward, upward, and horizontal. *Downward* communication describes message movement from a person in a position of authority to a subordinate or subordinate group. It is characterized by those with higher authority developing messages to transmit to those lower in authority—authority being defined by the chain of command or the formal structure of the organization. We have downward communication, for example, when the board of regents for the university votes to raise tuition for the upcoming semester. The board formally informs the school's president, who in turn informs officials in admissions and records; finally, students, who will pay the new fees, are advised of the bad news.

Upward communication describes message movement that begins with lower organizational levels and is transmitted to higher levels of authority. As with downward communication, authority levels are defined by the formal organization. Subordinates are engaging in upward communication when they complain about working conditions to a supervisor, who in turn reports their concerns to higher management.

Horizontal communication moves laterally across the organization among individuals of approximately the same level and without distinct reporting relationships to each other. In others words, there is horizontal flow when various department heads come together to discuss common problems from their respective groups. This communication generally moves messages more quickly across the organization than if the messages were to follow the vertical chain of command.

Informal network flow cannot be described in terms of specific direction. The grapevine as an informal network may move both vertically and horizontally, all within the transmission of a single message. Messages may

Direction—description of the movement of messages in organizations based on authority or position levels of message senders and receivers; typically described as downward, upward, and horizontal communication.

move among people of different organizational authority levels without the message having anything to do with authority or reporting relationships. When the research engineer speculates about the feasibility of a new product with the head of the marketing department, different authority levels are represented. One is a manager and one is not. We do not, however, label that flow as up or down the chain of command because the exchange is about a subject not related to the position levels of the two individuals. Wayne Pace (1983) has described this interaction as cross-channel communication. Whether cross-channel or grapevine, informal network flow is not dependent on formal organizational structure and is more difficult to describe in terms of specific message directions.

Communication Load

Load—number of messages moving through the communication system; commonly referred to as load, overload, and underload.

The number of messages moving through the communication system is yet another variable important for describing the message structure of organizational communication. We commonly refer to the number of messages as communication **load,** or the volume, rate, and complexity of messages processed by an individual or the organization as a whole.

Load is a common term for most of us. In fact, it is a rare student who has not proclaimed him- or herself to be in information overload during midterms or final examinations. The concept of load, however, is not limited to the overload state. Load, for example, can be defined as the optimum or ideal volume, rate, and complexity of messages for a particular individual or the organization. Underload is present when the volume, rate, and complexity of messages to an individual or organization are lower than the capacity of the individual or system. Underload is frequently found when individuals engage in routine, repetitive tasks that have been thoroughly learned and no longer present challenges. This leads to boredom and the underutilization of human potential. Overload, on the other hand, occurs when the volume, rate, and complexity of messages exceed the system's capacity. It generates stress and strains the capacity of individuals to deal with information. In fact, one of the continuing concerns of the information society is that the ease with which we can use new technologies to process large volumes of messages is generating a permanent overload in many jobs—a situation that actually impairs rather than strengthens the decision-making process.

Message Distortion

Distortion—anything that contributes to alterations in meaning as messages move through the organization.

Closely related to the concept of load are the types of communication problems, or **distortions,** that occur as messages move throughout the organization. These distortions occur because of load, message direction, channel usage, and the very composition of the networks themselves. Put simply, distortions are anything that contribute to alterations in meaning as messages move through the organization. Distortions are noise in the organizational communication system.

Organizational communication is characterized by the serial transmission of messages. Messages pass first to individuals as receivers, who then become senders of information. Supervisors learn of changes in policies and have the responsibility to transmit those changes to a subordinate group. Messages are influenced by the numbers of people involved (the network), the channels for transmission (oral, written), and the direction of flow (vertical, horizontal, informal). Research consistently finds that original messages change or are distorted in the serial transmission process. Information is lost from or added to the message, interpretation of facts change, and new interpretations develop. Researchers Gordon Allport and Leo Postman (1947) have described systematic serial transmission distortions as *leveling*, dropping or minimizing part of the message; *assimilating*, altering the message to fit individual or group attitudes, beliefs, and expectations; and *sharpening*, making some parts of the message more important than originally intended.

These distortions in serial transmission are brought about in part by perceptual differences among people, differences influenced by role and status. A manager may view a change in work hours as much less important than do the subordinates, who believe that no one was concerned about them when making the decision. The manager sees the change as necessary to accommodate a new schedule, whereas the workers are convinced the company never takes them into consideration. These perceptual differences affect the amount of attention given to the message and the interpretation of its meaning. They also influence the ability of the manager and members of the group to transmit the message to others. In addition to role, status, experience, values, and personal style, numerous other influences contribute to perception and how individuals knowingly or not distort organizational messages.

Finally, the very language of the message is subject to distortion. Definitions of terms and concepts vary throughout the organization. An excellent example of this phenomenon occurred in a small East Coast manufacturing company involved in introducing computer-assisted manufacturing processes. The president of the company announced the "entry of Cooper Manufacturing into the information age." Training classes were scheduled for all personnel working in areas where the new systems were being installed. Instead of the expected positive response, management was amazed when the director of personnel reported employee concern that the training programs were designed for people to fail and were really a way to push them out of jobs.

The Functional Approach—Summary of Essential Characteristics

The Functional approach helps us understand organizational communication by describing message function and structure. Based on a view of organizations as complex communication systems, the Functional approach identifies organizing, relationship, and change functions for messages and describes message structure as the movement of messages through formal and informal networks. Network members use diverse channels that transmit messages in lateral, vertical, and less structured directions. The load of these messages on the networks is the capacity measure of the organizational communication system. Finally, the Functional approach suggests that all messages are subject to numerous and predictable types of distortions—distortions that affect both message movement and meaning.

Can you now answer the questions asked at the beginning of the chapter? Could you use the Functional approach to help advise Bill Drake about Coronado Manufacturing? More important, can you describe your school as an organizational communication system? The case that follows gives you an opportunity to describe an organizational communication system from a Functional perspective and to suggest improvements by using the concepts of the Functional approach.

The United Concepts Advertising Agency Dilemma Case

Jane Peters was having the best morning of her career. Since coming to United Concepts Advertising as an account executive she had been successful in acquiring new business, but nothing as big as the Raven Furniture account. Raven was the largest chain of furniture stores in the West and landing the account meant something not only in the West Coast offices of United Concepts but in Chicago and New York as well.

Jane knew that her creative team, John and Chris, were largely responsible. The close working relationship among the three was the best Jane had experienced in her fifteen years in the advertising industry. In fact, Jane began to think of ways to make John and Chris more visible to her boss, Frank Donnell. After all, Frank was pleased that the agency got the Raven account. Perhaps he could be persuaded to promote John and Chris to senior creative positions.

Three Weeks Later

Jane was exhausted. Getting the Raven account up and going was not only requiring long hours but also complicated by the resistance of some of the top management at Raven. She had never imagined there was resistance at Raven to changing agencies and considerable disagreement about the United Concepts proposal. In fact, dealing with the various people at Raven was taking too much time. Her other accounts were not getting the service they needed and Chris had just made a major error in the Raven ad scheduled to run this weekend. Jane caught the mistake as it was about to go to the printer. Although it was costly to adjust the error at that point, she was relieved but shaken at how close they had come to a major problem. Jane considered approaching Frank Donnell for more help on the account.

One Week Later

The creative meeting wasn't working. John and Chris were angry with each other and could not agree on an approach for Raven's Christmas promotion. They complained Jane was too busy to work with them the way she used to and blamed her for rushing the creative process. Jane was sympathetic but told John and Chris they didn't understand her current pressure. The meeting ended with the first real tension the group had experienced. Jane went to see Frank Donnell and asked for help—additional people and promotions to recognize the real efforts of John and Chris.

Two Weeks Later

Jane was angry as she read her memo from Frank Donnell. Yes, her request for one additional staff person would be honored, but no promotions for Chris and John. Company policy prohibited the creation of additional senior creative positions in the West Coast office. Jane began to draft an angry response. Raven people were just beginning to appreciate their work—how was she going to continue to motivate Chris and John? Would they resent the new person? Was the Raven account worth all this trouble?

1. Describe the United Concepts Agency as a communication system.
2. What are the communication inputs, throughputs, and outputs?
3. Can you find examples of organizing, relationship, and change communication?
4. Describe Jane's communication links or networks.
5. Are communication channels and direction of message flow appropriate?
6. What about communication load?
7. How would you advise Jane? What would you tell Chris and John? Frank Donnell?

THE MEANING-CENTERED APPROACH

The second major approach for understanding organizational communication is the **Meaning-Centered approach.** This approach asks what communication is—not how and why it works. The Meaning-Centered perspective is concerned with how organizational reality is generated through human interaction. As such, message purposes (functions) and message movement (structure) are secondary to understanding communication as the construction of shared realities (human interaction). Specifically, the Meaning-Centered approach describes organizational communication as the process for generating shared realities that become organizing, decision

Meaning-Centered approach—way of understanding organizational communication by discovering how organizational reality is generated through human interaction. The approach describes organizational communication as the process for generating shared realities that become organizing, decision making, influence, and culture.

making, influence, and culture. Figure 3.5 summarizes key assumptions of the Meaning-Centered perspective.

Think back to Coronado Manufacturing. Proponents of the Meaning-Centered approach would have Bill Drake ask questions about which human interactions contributed to the shift away from the company's quality culture. They would encourage him to discover why his perception of the values of the company seem not to be shared either in manufacturing or sales. They would advise him to understand his present problem by reviewing Coronado's organizing and decision-making activities.

Communication as Organizing and Decision Making

Organizing

Organizing—bringing of order out of chaos with organizations as the products of the organizing process; described as almost synonymous with the communication process.

In Chapter 2 we described **organizing** as bringing order out of chaos and organizations as the products of the organizing process. The Meaning-Centered approach to organizational communication describes communicating and organizing as almost synonymous processes. Decision making, or the process of choice from among uncertain alternatives, also is viewed as essentially a communication phenomenon and part of the organizing process.

What do we mean when we say that communicating, organizing, and decision making are essentially similar processes? Karl Weick in his important book *The Social Psychology of Organizing* (1979), provides helpful

---

FIGURE 3.5
Basic Assumptions of the Meaning-Centered Approach

1. All ongoing human interaction is communication in one form or another.
2. Organizations exist through human interaction; structures and technologies result from the information to which individuals react.
3. Shared organizational realities reflect the collective interpretations by organizational members of all organizational activities.
4. Organizing and decision making are essentially communication phenomena.
5. Identification, socialization, communication rules, and power all are communication processes that reflect how organizational influence occurs.
6. Organizing, decision making, and influence processes describe the cultures of organizations by describing how organizations do things and how they talk about how they do things.
7. Organizational culture reflects the shared realities in the organization and how these realities create and shape organizational events.
8. Communication climate is the subjective, evaluative reaction of organization members to the organization's communication events, their reaction to organizational culture.

insight for answering our questions. Weick proposes that organizations as such do not exist but rather are in the process of existing through ongoing human interaction. In other words, there is no such thing as an organization, only the ongoing interactions among human activities—interactions that continually create and shape events. As we have previously discussed, all ongoing human interaction is communication in one form or another.

The Weick perspective suggests that Coronado Manufacturing can be better understood as fifty years in the process of existing rather than as an organization that was founded and structured fifty years ago. Bill Drake's father and uncle initiated the ongoing process, and Drake is part of the continuing stream of interactions. Put another way, the Weick model contends that organizations do not exist apart from the human interactions of members. As Weick has described, communication is "the substance of organizing."

Weick focuses on the organizational environment as the communication links and messages that are the basis of human interaction. He is not as concerned with the physical or technical structure of organizations as he is with the information to which individuals react. Weick contends that human reactions "enact" the organizational environment through information exchanges and the active creation of meanings. Thus, organizational members are continually processing equivocal messages or messages susceptible to varying interpretations. The process of organizing is an attempt to reduce equivocality—ambiguity—to predict future responses to organizational behaviors.

Supervisors reduce equivocality for their subordinates by the organizing of work assignments and the communication of task requirements. The supervisor gives a subordinate an assignment (desired action); the subordinate attempts the assignment (response); the supervisor evaluates the assignment (feedback). This interaction reduces equivocality for both the supervisor and subordinate. The supervisor understands what the subordinate believed the assignment to be by evaluating what was accomplished. The feedback to the subordinate (often in the form of rewards or punishment) reduces uncertainty about the adequacy of the performance. This cycle—repeated at all organizational levels—is the organizing process. As Phillip Tompkins and George Cheney (1983b) have pointed out, "This double interact of control—directing, monitoring, and reward/punishing— simultaneously provides us with the basic act of organizing and demonstrates why communicating and organizing are nearly synonymous."

Bill Drake is processing equivocal messages. He is attempting to determine if the consultant's report is accurate. He is more concerned with the impact of quality defects than specific technical problems. Even if assembly-line improvements are needed, it is through human communication that problems will be identified and solved. Drake does not understand how the company values of quality and customer service have changed. He is uncomfortable with the equivocality (ambiguity) of his interactions with sales and manufacturing management. He needs to figure out what his alternatives are and what to do next.

Decision Making

The process of choosing from among numerous alternatives (decision making) is the organizing process of directing behaviors and resources toward organizational goals. **Decision making,** as with other organizing efforts, is accomplished primarily through communication. Decision making is the process in which Bill Drake and his staff must engage.

A practical example will help illustrate decision making as an organizing process. When you work with a group of students on a major class project one of your goals may be a high grade from your instructor. There are numerous ways to approach this goal. Choosing from among these alternatives (decision making) is the first step toward assigning individual responsibilities within the project and deciding what resources the group will need (organizing). This choosing or decision making results from the communication interactions of the group. The quality of the group's decisions will influence the quality of the project and whether the group reaches its goals.

But what influences the way this decision making occurs? Each member of the group brings different experiences, abilities, and expectations to the group. Each member is operating with a set of premises or propositions about what he or she believes to be true. Decision making is the attempt to merge these individual premises into more general ones (shared realities) that most members of the group can accept.

Think for a moment about a group of students working on an assignment. One student may be operating from the premise that group projects are not worth much time and effort. Others may believe the project is important for the course grade and needs careful planning and attention. Another may believe his or her idea for the topic is superior. These premises (propositions about what is true) influence individual behavior and the types of alternatives the group will consider. Also, some members may identify (experience a sense of "we") with the efforts of the group, whereas others feel no sense of belonging or commitment. Those individuals who identify with each other are more likely to attempt a decision that most members of the group believe is appropriate than are those members who identify elsewhere.

Organizational decision making is the process that sets in motion much of the "doing" of the organization. Decision making reduces message equivocality by choosing from among numerous alternatives. These choosing activities occur through human communication.

Communication as Influence

The Meaning-Centered approach proposes that **influence** is a necessary process for creating and changing organizational events. In other words, who and what are viewed as influential and the way people seek to influ-

Decision making—process of choosing from among numerous alternatives; the part of the organizing process necessary for directing behaviors and resources toward organizational goals.

Influence—organizational and individual attempts to persuade; frequently seen in organizational identification, socialization, communication rules, and power.

ence others contribute to organizing and decision making. Questions about the influence process in organizations focus on how individuals identify with their organizations, how organizations attempt to socialize members, how communication rules emerge to direct behavior, and how power is used. Identification, socialization, communication rules, and power all are essentially communication processes that help us understand how organizational influence occurs. From the Meaning-Centered perspective the influence process is fundamental to the development of shared organizational realities and ultimately to creating and shaping organizational events. Indeed, it is fair to say that from a Meaning-Centered approach organizational communication is the process through which organizational influence takes place.

Identification

We are more likely to be receptive to influence attempts in organizations where we *identify* or have a sense of "we" or belonging. **Identification** or the lack of it results from a variety of organizational relationships (supervisors, peers, subordinates). As such, identification can be understood as an active process to which both individuals and organizations contribute. Tompkins and Cheney (1983b) have described organizational identification as part of the unobtrusive control processes of organizations. According to Cheney (1983), "Identifications are important for what they do for us: they aid us in making sense of our experience, in organizing our thoughts, in achieving decisions, and in anchoring the self. Perhaps most important for students of communication, identifying allows people to persuade and to be persuaded."

> **Identification**—perception of a sense of belonging; usually associated with the belief that individual and organizational goals are compatible.

Most organizations encourage members to identify with the organization. Chances are when you entered school you were encouraged to join various organizations, attend sporting functions, and oppose your school's most important rivals. Although most of these activities are enjoyable in and of themselves, they also develop a sense of "we" with the school. This sense of "we" means that our school's interests become our own and are influential in choices.

It is this relationship between identification and choices that illustrates the relationship identification has to organizing and decision making. Tompkins and Cheney (1983b) describe this relationship: "A person identifies with a unit when, in making a decision, the person in one or more of his/her organizational roles perceives that unit's values or interests as relevant in evaluating the alternatives of choice."

It is likely that when someone perceives the goals of an organization as compatible with their individual goals, they are identifying with the organization. The person who identifies is likely to accept the organization's decisional premises or reasoning. We can say, therefore, that the person who identifies is more likely to be positively influenced by the organization. A subordinate, for example, is more likely to be persuaded that a need for operating changes is favorable if the subordinate identifies with the organization and his or her supervisor. On the other hand, the subordinate who does not identify with the organization may view the same decision with resistance and suspicion. Practically speaking, we can all see how identification works by looking at our personal and organizational lives. The chances are we are more likely to be influenced by individuals and groups with whom we feel a strong sense of "we" than by those with whom we feel no such relationship.

Socialization

Socialization—active organizational attempts to help members learn appropriate behaviors, norms, and values.

Closely associated with identification is the influence process of **socialization,** or active organizational attempts to help members learn appropriate behaviors, norms, and values. The socialization process attempts to help new members understand how their interests overlap with that of the organization. As Mary Brown (1985) stated, "During the socialization process, new members internalize role-related and cultural information about a variety of organizational influences." Raymond Falcione and Charmaine Wilson (1988), in reviewing recent research on socialization, described stages or phases of socialization, namely, anticipatory socialization, encounter socialization, and the metamorphosis stage. *Anticipatory socialization* begins before individuals enter organizations and results from past work experiences and interactions with family, friends, and institutions such as schools, churches, or social organizations. Anticipatory socialization is shaped by preentry information about the organization and the anticipated work role. Anticipatory socialization is the readiness an individual brings to the "reality shock" of organizational entry. The *encounter* stage involves new employee training, supervisor coaching, peer groups, and formal organizational documents. Newcomers learn tasks, develop relationships, and reduce uncertainty about most aspects of organizational life. Finally, the *metamorphosis* phase of socialization occurs when the newcomer begins to master basic organizational requirements and adjusts to the organization. The phases, however, should be considered only general descriptions of the socialization process with full realization that differences in individuals and influence atttempts generate very different socialization experiences.

In her research on socialization, Brown (1985) found that organizational stories were an important part of the process and that as members were more socialized into the organization, story use became more associated with organizational values and cultures. In other words, the more individuals were exposed to organizational socialization attempts and the more they identified with the organization, the more likely they were to tell stories supporting overall organizational values. Presumably, as with the identification process, the greater the degree of socialization the more likely individuals will respond favorably to organizational persuasion. In fact, little doubt remains that socialization is related to organizational commitment, decision making, perceptions of communications climate, and overall job satisfaction.

Communication Rules

Communication rules are general prescriptions about appropriate communication behaviors. Rules operate to influence behavior, are specific enough to be followed, and occur in particular contexts. In other words, communication rules are informal norms about what type of communication is desirable in a particular organization. Rules tell us, for example, whether disagreement is encouraged or discouraged, how we are expected to contribute our ideas, and whether in a particular organization we should ask for a raise or never mention the subject of salary. Rules aid in socialization and therefore are likely to be used by those high in organizational identification, those who want to exhibit a sense of "we" with the organization. Generally, rules are learned through informal communication such as organizational stories, rituals, and myths.

Communication rules are of two general types—thematic and tactical. *Thematic rules* are general prescriptions of behavior reflecting the values and beliefs of the organization. *Tactical rules* prescribe specific behaviors as related to more general themes. Several tactical rules may evolve from one general thematic rule. A major Midwest computer company has a strong thematic rule of "Communicate your commitment to the company." Several tactical rules have developed that relate to that theme. "Come in on Saturday to finish up—but make sure you tell someone." "Complain about how tough the challenge really is." "Use the term *family* to refer to the company." These examples illustrate the contextual nature of thematic and tactical rules. Although the preceding statements are not only acceptable but also desirable in one particular company, they make little or no sense outside of that context. Compliance with thematic and tactical rules indicates that an individual has received socializing information and identifies, at least to some extent, with the organization.

Communication rules—general prescriptions about appropriate communication behaviors. Thematic rules are general prescriptions of behavior reflecting the values and beliefs of the organization, whereas tactical rules prescribe specific behaviors as related to more general themes.

Power

An additional communication dynamic that influences behavior is the use of power. In its most general sense **power** has been defined as attempts to influence another person's behavior to produce desired outcomes. As such, *power* is a neutral term subject to positive use as well as abuse. The power process occurs through communication and is related to resources, dependencies, and alternatives.

A *resource* is something owned or controlled by an individual, group, or entire organization. Resources are materials, information, knowledge, money, and a variety of other possible assets. Either owning or controlling resources allows individuals or organizations to influence interactions with others. A manager may control budget allocations within a department. Individual department members control important technical information not known to the manager. Both are resources influential in interactions between the manager and subordinates. Resources are closely linked to *alternatives*. A resource is more valuable if few alternatives to the use of the resource are available. Generally speaking, the individual controlling

Power—attempts to influence another person's behavior to produce desired outcomes. The process occurs through communication and is related to resources, dependencies, and alternatives.

scarce resources is in a more influential (higher-power) position than the individual who controls resources with ample alternatives.

Although it is an outmoded notion, many believe power is a fixed commodity rather than a process of human interaction. In other words, many individuals behave as if the more power they have, the less is left for others. In reality power is not a commodity but an influence process that permits all involved to gain more power, lose power, or share power. Therefore, when influence attempts result in abuse, evidence suggests we will seek other alternatives and lessen our *dependency* on the power abuser. Communication between supervisors and subordinates can illustrate this phenomenon. Supervisors and subordinates both have resources. The supervisor has the formal authority established by the chain of command. The supervisor controls information flow and performance evaluation. Subordinates control technical performance and have vital firsthand information about the progress of work. Both are dependent on each other—the supervisor directs, but without compliance and performance, no work is accomplished. If the supervisor becomes abusive in directing the work, a subordinate group may seek other alternatives by withdrawing from interaction with the supervisor or withholding information the supervisor needs to make good decisions. At an extreme the subordinate group may complain to others in management, transfer to other departments, or leave the organization.

Communication as Culture

Culture—unique sense of the place that organizations generate through ways of doing and ways of communicating about the organization; reflects the shared realities in the organization and how they create and shape organizational events.

Organizing, decision making, and influence processes, when taken together, help us describe the **culture** of organizations by describing how organizations do things and how they talk about how they do things. Put another way, organizational culture is the unique sense of the place that organizations generate through ways of doing and ways of communicating about the organization. Organizational culture reflects the shared realities in the organization and how these realities create and shape organizational events. Organizational culture is the unique symbolic common ground that becomes the self-definition or self-image of the organization.

Metaphors help us understand the differences between the Functional and Meaning-Centered approaches to organizational cultures. Metaphors are ways of describing the likeness of one concept or person to another concept or person by speaking of the first as if it were the second. We say "She is the life of the party" or "He is the salt of the earth." Managers are referred to as quarterbacks, coaches, or lions in battle, with organizational decisions described as game or battle plans. These metaphors give us underlying assumptions for understanding behavior or concepts based on our knowledge of what we say something is like. We use our knowledge of what quarterbacks do, for example, to understand what managers do. Organization-wide metaphors used for the Functional and Meaning-Centered approaches work in much the same way.

When we described the Functional approach to organizational communication we talked about communication systems with inputs, throughput, and outputs. We described subsystems, suprasystems, and boundaries to external environments. We were using the organic metaphor of the dynamic system taken from the study of biology for conceptualizing or understanding organizational communication. The systems metaphor gave us a distinct and descriptive set of assumptions about the way organizational communication works. Culture, in the systems metaphor, is one of many organizational variables. As Figure 3.6 illustrates, the Functional approach suggests that culture as a variable can be compared and contrasted with other variables within the organization.

The Meaning-Centered and Functional approaches differ in the metaphors used to understand organizational communication. The systems metaphor of the Functional approach is replaced in the Meaning-Centered perspective with the cultural metaphor. This culture metaphor describes communication as culture rather than describing culture and communi-

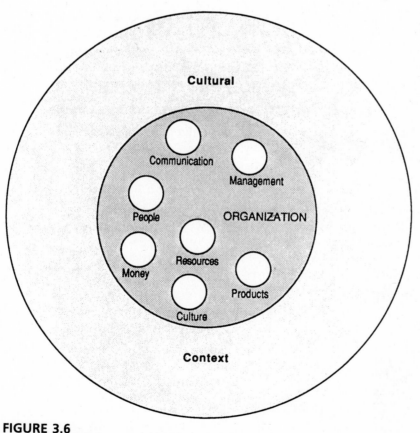

FIGURE 3.6
Culture as a variable of the organization.

cation as separate. The culture metaphor promotes understanding communication as a process for generating shared realities, which in turn we call organizational culture.

When we use culture as a metaphor for organizational communication we attempt to understand communication by understanding the uniqueness or shared realities in particular organizations. We explore how organizations use language, the symbols, jargon, and specialized vocabulary used by people working together. We examine behaviors exhibited in rituals and rites of organizational life and listen for the general standards or values of the organization as described in stories, legends, and reminiscences. We focus on how communication activities generate uniqueness or symbolic common ground. Researchers Michael Pacanowsky and Nick O'Donnell-Trujillo (1983) suggest that we can understand this process of generating shared organizational realities or developing uniqueness when we view organizational communication as cultural performances.

Cultural Performances

Pacanowsky and O'Donnell-Trujillo (1983) describe performances as "those situationally relative and variable interactions by which organizational members construct organizational reality." In other words, individuals in organizations are choice-making people who continually adapt to changing situations. The choices made in changing circumstances construct the reality of the organization. This view is closely related to Weick's (1979) concept that organizations as such do not exist but are in the process of existing through human interactions.

The choices organizational members make in ever-changing situations are *cultural performances* with several specific characteristics.

1. Communicative performances are *interactional*. Members of organizations do not work in isolation. Decisions are made through human interaction, work is accomplished in groups, and all organizational behavior can be understood through the relationships of organizational members. Observing who is involved in important decisions, how influence takes place, and how people treat each other helps us understand the "uniqueness" of an organization.

2. Communicative performances are *contextual*. Human interactions occur within ever-changing situations or contexts. Interactions both create and shape these contexts and are influenced by them. Thus, interactions cannot be understood apart from specific situations or contexts. Autocratic or participative decisions, for example, cannot be evaluated for effectiveness without understanding the circumstances in which they occurred.

3. Communicative performances are *episodic*. Organizational life is characterized by "episodes" or communication events that can be distin-

guished from one another. Staff meetings, performance evaluations, and informal socializing all can be distinguished from each other. Although these episodes relate, they form discrete experiences that taken together contribute to organizational reality. Episodes or events differ from organization to organization and therefore contribute to the uniqueness of a particular organization.

4. Communicative performances are *improvisational*. The interactions of organizational members are not tightly scripted. Choice-making individuals improvise based on past experiences and present context. At times the "script" or organizational expectation is tighter than others, but performances continue to exhibit both uniqueness and variability. In other words, people react differently in different situations. These differences—the lack of being able to predict or control exact responses from organizational members—contribute to continually changing organizational realities.

Taking these four characteristics together, the Pacanowsky and O'Donnell-Trujillo (1983) view suggests that organizational culture or uniqueness is generated as organizational members regularly communicate with one another. Communication events (episodes) help organizational members share similar experiences and realities and help others understand how a particular organization works. These realities, however, are constantly subject to change as organizational members react to new information and circumstances.

In addition to characteristics of performances, Pacanowsky and O'Donnell-Trujillo describe some of the types of performances found in organizations. They contend that *rituals* are an important performance contributing to shared reality. Whether personal, task, social, or organizational, rituals help us define what is important or the values of the culture and provide a communication process to transmit those values. Awards ceremonies, Friday afternoon picnics/beer busts, graduation, and numerous daily routines are all rituals that both provide regularity and signify importance in organizational life.

Organizational *storytelling* is described as a way to infuse "passion" or interest into everyday activities. Stories generate a sense of history about organizational existence and identify values through descriptions of success and failure. In the Coronado case, stories about the founders transmitted important information about the Coronado values of quality and customers. The Meaning-Centered approach suggests we can describe Coronado's manufacturing problem partly in terms of a shift in culture or values.

Bill Drake is faced with understanding the communication interactions that have contributed to a change at Coronado in what is considered quality. Stories about his father and uncle have not been sufficient to maintain the earlier focus on customers. Bill Drake needs to understand what the new unique sense of Coronado really is. Can you suggest ways he might find out? How can his perception of the values of Coronado be different from others in the company? What should Drake do to determine what the culture of Coronado Manufacturing really is?

Communication Climate

We have said that the culture of an organization describes the unique sense of the place and how that organization describes itself. The reaction to an organization's culture is the organization's **communication climate**. Marshall Poole (1985) suggests that communication climate consists of "collective beliefs, expectations, and values regarding communication," which are generated as a result of organizational members continually evaluating their interactions with others.

Communication climate—reaction to the organization's culture; consists of collective beliefs, expectations, and values regarding communication that are generated as organizational members continually evaluate their interactions with others.

We are used to thinking of climate in geographic terms. We think about temperature, humidity, winds, and rainfall and react somewhat subjectively to what we believe is a desirable climate. So it is with a climate for communication. The climate is a subjective reaction to organization members' perception of communication events. The subjective reaction is shared to a great extent either by individual groups or the entire organization.

W. Charles Redding (1972) proposed that the collective beliefs that become the communication climate are associated with five communication factors: supportiveness; participative decision making; trust, confidence, credibility; openness and candor; and high performance goals. In other words, the more supportive the communication environment—the more people participate in decision making, have trust and confidence in their co-workers, can be open, and understand organizational goals—the more likely there will be positive collective attitudes about the communication climate. Underlying this notion is the assumption that the more positive the climate the greater the satisfaction of individual employees.

Research has related communication climate to morale, job satisfaction, perceptions of organizational effectiveness, and actual organizational effectiveness. However, critics of this research suggest that the subjective nature of climate makes it a difficult concept to relate definitively to organizational outcomes. Nevertheless, most researchers agree that communication climate is an important factor influencing organizational behavior.

Think for a moment about the culture of your school. By now you probably have learned the ropes and know how things are supposed to work. You know who holds power, what some of the rituals are, and how socializing generally takes place. You can describe the unique sense of the place to others. But your description does not necessarily tell us whether you think it is a good place. Your attitude—climate evaluation—is your reaction to the culture, not a description of the culture itself.

Identify the organizations of which you are a member. How would you describe their climate? How does a positive view of climate influence your behavior? What are the differences when your view is negative?

The Meaning-Centered Approach—Summary of Essential Characteristics

The Meaning-Centered approach to organizational communication understands communication as a complex process that creates and shapes organizational events. As such, communication is organizing, decision making, influence, and culture. Organizing is viewed as an ongoing process of human interactions attempting to reduce message equivocality. Decision making is part of organizing and is the process responsible for moving individuals and resources toward accomplishment of organizational goals. Influence is the process in which individuals and organizations engage to generate desired behaviors and is, therefore, closely related to organizing and decision making. Culture, as a metaphor for organizational communication, is the unique sense of a place that reflects the way things are done and how people talk about the way things are done. Finally, communication climate is the subjective reaction to the communication events that contribute to uniqueness or culture. The Meaning-Centered approach makes only limited distinctions among organizing, decision making, influence, and culture. All are seen as processes of communication and all help us understand how organizations create and shape events through human interaction.

Now return to the beginning of the chapter. Can you answer each of the questions about the Meaning-Centered approach? How does it differ from the Functional approach? What are the similarities? Earlier you described the communication system of your school. Now describe the culture of your school. Are there particular stories or rituals that come to mind? What are the communication rules? The following case gives you an opportunity to apply the Meaning-Centered approach to an organizational problem and to suggest improvements from the Meaning-Centered perspective.

The "Newcomers Aren't Welcome Here" Case

Joe and Henry have worked for Temple Air Conditioning and Heating for over twenty years. Both men are competent workers who were hired by Temple's founder, Bernie Jones. In fact, Joe, Henry, and Bernie still have an occasional beer together on Friday nights after work. Bernie is always complaining that the good old days are over and that nobody should have so much paperwork to run a heating and air-conditioning business. Joe and Henry don't think things have really changed all that much except the houses keep getting bigger and fancier. Joe and Henry have worked as a team for the last fifteen years without a supervisor. They are part of the reason Temple has a good reputation for quality work and fast service. Joe and Henry don't spend time with other installation teams and don't see any reason why they should.

Early Monday Morning

Bernie's announcement was a blow. He was bringing in a college guy to supervise the installation teams. Joe and Henry could hardly believe what they were hearing. They should have known something was up when Bernie called everyone together before the trucks went out on a Monday morning.

JOE: Who does he think he is, bringing in some college guy—what do we need another guy for?

HENRY: Yeah, Bernie is losing it. He knows how this place got built—off our backs. I am not going to work for anybody, let alone a guy with a fancy degree.

JOE: I always looked up to Bernie—and I thought he felt the same way about us. Obviously we were wrong. After twenty years, to be wrong about a guy makes you feel stupid.

HENRY: What do you think we should do?

JOE: How would I know?

HENRY: Well, I'm not going to take this lying down. Are you with me?

JOE: Sure, we can make Temple fall apart.

1. How would you describe Temple's culture?

2. How would you describe the identification of Joe and Henry with Temple? Before the announcement? After the announcement?

3. What are Joe and Henry's communication rules? Are they the same as for the rest of the organization? Do we know?

4. Can you identify any shared realities for Joe and Henry?

5. What should Joe and Henry do?

6. Could Bernie have handled the announcement in a manner that would not have alienated Joe and Henry?

7. What do you think is going to happen?

The Functional and Meaning-Centered approaches for understanding organizational communication help us ask questions important for analyzing organizational problems. Figure 3.7 identifes key questions from each perspective. These questions can be used throughout the text as we analyze a variety of organizational problems.

SUMMARY

The Functional approach describes organizations as dynamic communication systems with the parts of the system operating together to create and shape events. Communication input, throughput, and output deter-

---

FIGURE 3.7
Analyzing Organizational Problems

The Functional Approach

1. How effective are organizing, relationship, and change messages?
2. What types of formal and informal communication networks exist? What network roles can you identify? Are they adequate?
3. Is channel use appropriate for effective communication?
4. Is the load on the communication system part of the problem?
5. What types of communication distortion exist?
6. Does the organization get good input communication from its environment? How effective is throughput and output communication?
7. Is this an open or closed system?

The Meaning-Centered Approach

1. Do organizing activities help reduce message equivocality?
2. How effective is decision-making communication?
3. Do most organizational members identify with the organization? How do you know?
4. What attempts are made at organizational socialization? Are they appropriate and effective?
5. How does power relate to the problem?
6. Do organizational stories, rituals, and events provide important information?
7. What type of culture exists? Is it effective? How do you know?
8. How can the communication climate be characterized? Is this appropriate? What should change?

---

mine whether the system is open or closed. The Functional perspective describes communication as a complex organizational process that serves organizing, relationship, and change functions. Message structure transmits these functions through the organization. Structure is characterized by networks, channels, direction, load, and distortion. Organizing messages establish rules and regulations and convey information about how work is to be accomplished. Relationship messages help individuals define roles and assess the compatibility of individual and organizational goals. Change messages generate innovation and adaptation and are essential to an open system. Communication networks, the repetitive patterns of interactions among individuals, are both formal and informal. Network members use a variety of oral and written channels that carry messages in vertical, horizontal, and less structured directions. The amount and complexity of messages—communication load—contributes to a variety of types of distortion.

The Meaning-Centered perspective describes organizational communication as organizing, decision making, influence, and culture, which when taken together explain how organizations create shared realities. Organizing is described as communication interactions that attempt to reduce ambiguity or equivocality. Decision making, also accomplished through communication, is the organizing process of directing behaviors and resources toward organizational goals. Influence is communication to generate desired behaviors from others and is evidenced in the identification of individuals with their organizations, in organizational attempts at socialization, in communication rules, and in the way power is used. As a metaphor for organizational communication, culture is the unique sense of place that organizations generate through ways of doing and ways of communicating about the organization. Cultural performances are interactional, contextual, episodic, and improvisational. Rituals and stories are important examples of these performances. Finally, communication climate is the subjective, collective attitude or reaction to an organization's culture or the organization's communication events.

Although viewing communication from different perspectives, both the Functional and Meaning-Centered approaches see organizational communication as a primary and vital process for organizations. Both approaches provide ways to analyze communication situations and both provide background important for developing communication competencies.

WORKSHOP

1. Form groups of four to six members each. Using your school as an organization with which all class members are familiar, identify organizing, change, and relationship messages. Groups should compare lists. How much agreement and disagreement exist? What accounts for the differences?

2. The Meaning-Centered approach to organizational communication describes communication as culture. The following exercise, The Empty Chair, is designed to help you identify communication you believe describes the culture of your school. (See page 75.)

3. Networks represent the repetitive patterns of communication interactions in which organizational members engage. Networks, therefore, influence how organizations solve problems and make decisions. The following exercise, Communication Networks and Problem Solving, is presented to help you better understand the influence of networks on the efficiency and effectiveness of problem-solving communication. (See pages 75–76.)

4. All members of your class make conscious and unconscious evaluations of your school's organizational climate. Evaluating an Organizational Climate is a climate-assessment activity. Individually com-

plete the assessment questions and fill out the scoring form. Comparison of climate evaluations can be discussed in small groups, or your instructor can graph scores from various class members for a general class discussion. (See pages 76–78.)

The Empty Chair

The class should divide into groups of six members each. A circle, with an empty chair in the middle, should be formed by each group. The empty chair is to be considered occupied by a newcomer to your school and a stranger to all class members. Group members are to take turns describing communication examples that will help the stranger understand the culture he or she is entering, know what types of behaviors are generally expected, and become aware of any special traditions or customs unique to this new environment. The empty chair should be addressed for fifteen minutes. At the end of that time group members should discuss how adequately they were able to describe their organization and how they learned the communication behaviors they attempted to describe to the stranger.

Communication Networks and Problem Solving

Your instructor (or a team of process observers) has developed a problem you will attempt to solve in groups structured to illustrate different types of communication patterns and networks. The problem will be the same for each group; the only difference will be how the communication networks are structured for problem solving. Problems require five elements per problem set for each group member, or twenty-five total elements for each network. Of the twenty-five elements, five and only five must be identical. Commonly used problem sets are developed from decks of playing cards (e.g., five spades, one distributed in each hand of five cards; five face cards, one distributed in each hand of five).

The instructor forms groups of five participants each and a process observer for each group. Network structures are shown in Figure 3.8.

The groups should be seated as the diagrams illustrate and should be permitted to use only the communication lines illustrated by the arrows. Each group should have three empty chairs that can be moved from person to person. The instructor distributes a problem set of five elements to each group member. (Only one element is common to all five group members.) The goal is to identify the element all group members hold in common. Each group must try to solve the problem while communicating in their assigned network structure. The rules are as follows:

1. The instructor decides who begins communication in each network.
2. The person who begins must go to the "office" of the person with whom he or she wishes to confer to talk privately without being

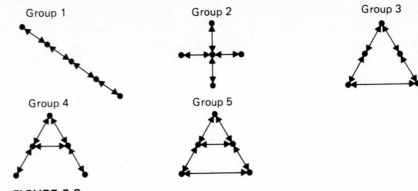

FIGURE 3.8
Network Structures

overheard. (The empty chairs are used for this movement.) The "office" choice is determined by the arrows in the network structure.

3. Any member of the group can notify the instructor when he or she believes the problem is solved. The instructor will verify the solution or ask the group to continue working toward a solution.

4. The process observer is instructed to watch all communication behavior, both verbal and nonverbal.

When all problems have been solved, process observers should discuss their observations with each group. Group members should discuss the strengths and weaknesses of their particular network structure. General experiences should be shared among groups. Specifically, groups should identify which network structure solved the problem most quickly. Which network was the slowest? Which network contributed to the most mistakes? What were the most frustrating and satisfying parts of the problem? What does this exercise illustrate about organizational communication?

Evaluating an Organizational Climate

Read each of the following statements, in numerical order, marking an X on the numbered square of the following answer sheet that corresponds to the number of the statement if you think the statement about your school is generally true. If you think the statement is not generally true, leave the square blank. Work from left to right, beginning with the top line. Be careful not to miss any statements.

1. Lines of responsibility are clear and easy to understand.
2. Students can influence decisions that affect them.
3. Faculty, staff, and students are interested in their work.
4. Students are encouraged to be creative.

5. Competition among students and between departments is discouraged.
6. Jobs and services are clearly defined.
7. The administration makes effective decisions.
8. Faculty are excited about teaching and helping students learn.
9. New ideas are encouraged.
10. Groups work well together.
11. The services and offices of the school are organized effectively.
12. Information is readily available to help make decisions.
13. Students are committed to excellence.
14. Most students are bright and capable of quality work.
15. Students help each other.
16. Class scheduling is well organized.
17. Decisions are made in a timely fashion.
18. Faculty are committed to excellence.
19. Innovation and change are encouraged.
20. Faculty cooperate with one another.
21. Enrollment procedures, advising services, and library systems are well organized.
22. Grievances and problems are well handled.
23. The faculty and staff create an environment in which students want to succeed.
24. Classes contain new and exciting information.
25. Competition among students is handled fairly and constructively.

	Structure	Decision Making	Motivation	Creativity	Teamwork
	1	2	3	4	5
	6	7	8	9	10
	11	12	13	14	15
	16	17	18	19	20
	21	22	23	24	25
TOTAL X's					

You have been evaluating your school's organizational climate in five areas: structure (how the school is organized), decision making (who is involved and how effective are their choices), motivation (the degree of commitment among faculty, students, and staff), creativity (the school's emphasis on quality and innovation), and teamwork (the ability of students, faculty, administration, and staff to work together).

Your score in each category can range from 0 to 5, with 0 indicating a negative evaluation and 5 the most positive evaluation. Discuss the similarities and differences in class members' profiles. Is your assessment consistent with your general feelings about your school?

Based on the climate assessment scores in your group or class, describe the organizational climate of your school. What are the strengths? The weaknesses?

SUMMARY OF COMPETENCY COMPONENTS:

KNOWLEDGE, SENSITIVITY, SKILLS, VALUES

KNOWLEDGE

Functional approach describes organizations as communication systems.

Functional approach identifies message functions and structure.

Meaning-Centered approach is concerned with communication as the focal process for creating and shaping organizational events.

Meaning-Centered approach identifies communication as organizing, decision making, influence, and culture.

SENSITIVITY

Human communication is described as shaping all organizational activities.

Shared realities are generated through organizational communication.

SKILLS

Analysis frameworks are developed for Functional and Meaning-Centered approaches.

Analysis skills are practiced through case study and exercises.

VALUES

Effective organizational communication is viewed as necessary for organizational survival.

Communication is described as the fundamental organizational process.

REFERENCES AND SUGGESTED READINGS

Allport, G., and L. Postman. 1947. *The psychology of rumor*. New York: Holt.
Baird, J. E., Jr. 1977. *The dynamics of organizational communication*. New York: Harper & Row.

Barnett, G. 1988. Communication and organizational culture. In *Handbook of organizational communication*, eds. G. Goldhaber and G. Barnett, 101–30. Norwood, NJ: Ablex Publishing.

Brown, M. H. 1985. That reminds me of a story: Speech action in organizational socialization. *Western Journal of Speech Communication* 49: 27–42.

Cheney, G. 1983. On the various and changing meanings of organizational membership: A field study of organizational identification. *Communication Monographs* 50: 342–62.

Conrad, C. 1985. *Strategic organizational communication: Cultures, situations, and adaptation*. New York: Holt, Rinehart & Winston.

Cummings, H. W., L. W. Long, and M. L. Lewis. 1983. *Managing communication in organizations: An introduction*. Dubuque, IA: Gorsuch Scarisbrick.

Dahle, T. L. 1954. An objective and comparative study of five methods of transmitting information to business and industrial employees. *Speech Monographs* 21: 21–28.

Davis, K. 1967. *Human behavior at work*. New York: McGraw-Hill.

Donnellon, A., B. Gray, and M. Bougon. 1986. Communication, meaning and organized action. *Administrative Science Quarterly* 31: 43–55.

Eisenberg, E., and P. Riley. 1988. Organizational symbols and sense-making. In *Handbook of organizational communication*, eds. G. Goldhaber and G. Barnett, 131–50. Norwood, NJ: Ablex Publishing.

Falcione, R., L. Sussman, and R. Herden. 1987. Communication climate in organizations. In *Handbook of organizational communication*, eds. F. Jablin, L. Putnam, K. Roberts, and L. Porter, 195–227. Newbury Park, CA: Sage.

Falcione, R., and C. Wilson. 1988. Socialization processes in organizations. In *Handbook of organizational communication*, eds. G. Goldhaber and G. Barnett, 151–69. Norwood, NJ: Ablex Publishing.

Farace, R. V., P. R. Monge, and H. M. Russell. 1977. *Communicating and organizing*. Reading, MA: Addison-Wesley.

Goldhaber, G. M. 1986. *Organizational communication*. 4th ed. Dubuque, IA: Brown.

Greenbaum, H. H. 1976. The audit of organizational communication. In *Communication in organizations*, eds. J. L. Owen, P. A. Page, and G. I. Zimmerman, 271–89. St. Paul, MN: West.

Jablin, F. 1982. Formal structural characteristics of organizations and superior-subordinate communication. *Human Communication Research* 8(4): 338–47.

Katz, D., and R. Kahn. 1966. *The social psychology of organizations*. New York: Wiley.

Koehler, J. W., K. W. Anatol, and R. L. Applbaum. 1976. *Organizational communication: Behavioral perspectives*. New York: Holt, Rinehart & Winston.

Kreps, G. L. 1986. *Organizational communication*. White Plains, NY: Longman.

Level, D. A., and W. P. Galle. 1980. *Business communications: Theory and practice*. Dallas: Business Publications.

McPhee, R. D., and P. K. Tompkins, eds. 1985. *Organizational communication: Traditional themes and new directions*. Beverly Hills, CA: Sage.

Mehrabian, A. 1971. *Silent messages*. Belmont, CA: Wadsworth.

Mintzberg, H. 1973. *The nature of managerial work*. New York: Harper & Row.

Monge, P., and E. Eisenberg. 1987. Emergent communication networks. In *Handbook of organizational communication*, eds. F. Jablin, L. Putnam, K. Roberts, and L. Porter, 304–42. Newbury Park, CA: Sage.

Pacanowsky, M., and N. O'Donnell-Trujillo. 1983. Organizational communication as cultural performance. *Communication Monographs* 50: 126–47.

Pace, R. W. 1983. *Organizational communication: Foundations for human resource development*. Englewood Cliffs, NJ: Prentice-Hall.

Poole, M. S. 1985. Communication and organizational climates: Review, critique, and a new perspective. In *Organizational communication: Traditional themes and new directions*, eds. R. D. McPhee and P. K. Tompkins, 79–108. Beverly Hills, CA: Sage.

Poole, M. S., and R. D. McPhee. 1983. A structural analysis of organizational climate. In *Communication and organizations: An interpretive approach*, eds. L. Putnam and M. Pacanowsky, 195–219. Beverly Hills, CA: Sage.

Putnam, L. 1983. The interpretive perspective: An alternative to functionalism. In *Communication and organizations: An interpretive approach*, eds. L. Putnam and M. Pacanowsky, 31–54. Beverly Hills, CA: Sage.

Putnam, L., and M. Pacanowsky, eds. 1983. *Communication and organizations: An interpretive approach*. Beverly Hills, CA: Sage.

Redding, W. C. 1964. The organizational communicator. In *Business and industrial communication: A source book*, eds. W. C. Redding and G. Sanborn, 29–58. New York: Harper & Row.

Redding, W. C. 1972. *Communication within the organization*. New York. Industrial Communication Council.

Redding, W. C. 1983. Stumbling toward identity: The emergence of organizational communication as a field of study. In *Organizational communication: Traditional themes and new directions*, eds. R. D. McPhee and P. K. Tompkins, 15–54. Beverly Hills, CA: Sage.

Riley, P. 1983. A structurationist account of political culture. *Administrative Science Quarterly* 28: 414–37.

Rogers, E., and R. Agarwala-Rogers. 1976. *Communication in organizations*. New York: Free Press.

Schall, M. S. 1983. A communication rules approach to organizational culture. *Administrative Science Quarterly* 28(4): 557–81.

Smircich, L. 1983. Concepts of culture and organizational analysis. *Administrative Science Quarterly* 28: 339–58.

Smircich, L., and M. Calas. 1987. Organizational culture: A critical assessment. In *Handbook of organizational communication*, eds. F. Jablin, L. Putnam, K. Roberts, and L. Porter, 228–57. Newbury Park, CA: Sage.

Thayer, L. 1968. *Communication and communication systems*. Homewood, IL: Irwin.

Tompkins, P., and G. Cheney. 1982. Toward a theory of unobtrusive control in contemporary organizations. A paper presented at the Speech Communication Association Convention, November, Louisville, KY.

Tompkins, P., and G. Cheney. 1983a. Account analysis of organizations: Decision making and identification. In *Communication and organizations: An interpretive approach*, eds. L. Putnam and M. Pacanowsky, 123–46. Beverly Hills, CA: Sage.

Tompkins, P., and G. Cheney. 1983b. Communication and unobtrusive control in contemporary organizations. In *Organizational communication: Traditional themes and new directions*, eds. R. D. McPhee and P. K. Tompkins, 179–210. Beverly Hills, CA: Sage.

Tortoriello, T., S. Blatt, and S. DeWine. 1978. *Communication in the organization: An applied approach*. New York: McGraw-Hill.

Weick, K. 1979. *The social psychology of organizing*. 2d ed. Reading, MA: Addison-Wesley.

Wilson, G. L., H. L. Goodall, Jr., and C. L. Waagen. 1986. *Organizational communication*. New York: Harper & Row.

CHAPTER

~ F O U R ~

Communication Implications of Major Organizational Theories

Developing competencies through . . .

KNOWLEDGE

Describing Scientific Management theories for organizations
Describing Human Behavior theories for organizations
Describing Integrated Perspectives theories for organizations

SENSITIVITY

Awareness of communication implications of Scientific Management theories
Awareness of communication implications of Human Behavior theories
Awareness of communication implications of Integrated Perspectives theories

SKILLS

Applying theory to familiar organizations
Practicing analysis capabilities

VALUES

Understanding Scientific Management, Human Behavior, and Integrated Perspectives theories in contemporary organizations
Clarifying the importance of values in successful organizations

The Davis Instrument Company's Manufacturing Crisis

Pam Martin was not surprised that the three supervisors in her section were disagreeing about how to train on the new MCF system. Joan, Henry, and Ralph rarely agreed about how to solve section problems. Even though Pam had been their manager for over two years and knew each of them to be highly competent, the three seemed to view their work at Davis very differently. The problem for today's staff meeting was no exception. The new MCF system was being installed throughout all of Davis Instrument Company's manufacturing areas to computer-automate and control assembly work previously done by highly skilled workers. The system would not replace any existing employees but would require training on new machines and computer controls. Over time, productivity would be expected to increase and those employees who had early training on the system would be in positions for rapid advancement. All three of Pam's subordinates had supported acquiring the new system and felt it was in the best long-term interests of Davis. But Joan, Henry, and Frank did not agree about how to select employees for training on the MCF and how to restructure work teams to implement the new process.

Joan argued that Pam and the supervisors should just decide. After all, early training on the system should fit the best workers with the highest aptitudes for computers to the new jobs. Yes, of course that means that other good workers would not have as much chance for advancement, but tough decisions are what management gets paid to make. Joan contended that the supervisors were in the best position to judge how to restructure the work teams. She proposed that the supervisors draw up a list of new job assignments, announce them to the group, and develop a timetable for system implementation.

Henry strongly disagreed. He voiced concern that his work team was worried about the new assignments. Henry believed that the affected workers should have some say in the assignment decisions. He supported letting each work team give their supervisors a plan for reassignment that the supervisors then would use for final decisions. He contended that individuals were more likely to be motivated and accept the changes willingly if they had a part in determining how the changes were to be implemented.

Frank thought that both Joan and Henry represented extreme positions that really did not serve the best interests of Davis. He proposed that the three supervisors draw up overall criteria for the new positions and the job assignments needed for each work team. They should then present the reorganization plan to their work teams and have individual meetings with each worker to determine interest and skill fit for each of the new positions. Frank agreed with Joan that some tough decisions about particular individuals would have to be made. He also agreed with Henry that better motivation would result if each individual had some input about the future assignment.

Pam knew all three wanted the project to succeed. The question was how to get Joan, Henry, and Frank to agree on an approach.

1. Joan, Henry, and Frank are all competent supervisors. What accounts for their differences?
2. Is it possible that they have different types of people in their work teams?
3. Can you describe how each of the three views the role of supervisor?
4. How do you think they view their work groups?
5. Do they have different theories of how organizations work?

INTRODUCTION

The disagreement of Joan, Henry, and Frank is a good example of individuals with different views about how organizations should operate. Joan, Henry, and Frank all agree that the MCF system is a needed change but disagree about how that change should be made. Their disagreement can be traced, at least in part, to the differing ways in which they view workers and organizations.

In Chapter 3 we established two major perspectives for studying organizational communication—the Functional and Meaning-Centered approaches. In this chapter we will identify and describe major organizational theories and evaluate their communication implications from Functional and Meaning-Centered perspectives. We will look at how researchers describe the ways in which organizations should work, what types of assumptions are made about people in organizations, and what these descriptions and assumptions mean for organizational communication.

We will examine three major perspectives or schools of organizational thought—the Scientific Management, Human Behavior, and Integrated Perspectives schools. The three can be distinguished from each other by the questions researchers representing each viewpoint ask about organizations. Theorists representing the Scientific Management school ask questions about how organizations should be designed, how workers can be trained for maximum efficiency, how the chain of command works, and how division of labor should be determined.

Human Behavior theorists are concerned about the influence of individuals in organizations, what motivates workers, and how motivation affects the organization. These theorists believe organizational design and structure reflect basic assumptions about human behavior. They describe organizational relationships and people as resources. Human Behavior approaches frequently are discussed as human relation and human resource theories.

Finally, the development of what we call the Integrated Perspectives school can be traced to criticisms of Scientific Management and Human Behavior approaches. In the Integrated Perspectives approach, researchers ask questions about how structure, technology, and people relate to their environments. They are concerned with relationships among organizational design, employee motivation, communication participation, and organizational values as these factors relate to the organization's ability to function in its environment. In some respects the Integrated Perspectives approach reflects a merger of much of the thinking developed by Scientific Management and Human Behavior researchers.

This chapter is designed to contribute to *knowledge* competencies by describing major organizational theories representing Scientific Management, Human Behavior, and Integrated Perspectives. *Sensitivity* competencies are fostered by examining communication implications found in theory. Analysis *skills* are developed by combining *knowledge* and *sensitivity* competencies for application to familiar organizations and case studies. Finally, *knowledge, sensitivity*, and *skill* competencies will influence *values* through evaluation of Scientific Management, Human Behavior, and Integrated Perspectives theories in contemporary organizations and by examining the importance of values for successful organizations.

THE SCIENTIFIC MANAGEMENT SCHOOL

The Scientific Management school was well described by Frederick Taylor when, in his classic work *Principles of Scientific Management* (1913), he attempted to convince readers that the inefficiency in most organizations is caused by a lack of systematic management and that "the best management is a true science, resting upon clearly defined laws, rules, and principles, as a foundation." This foundation, from the Scientific Management point of view, rested on "scientifically" designed organizations characterized by carefully developed chains of command and efficient division of labor.

Three men—Frederick Taylor, Henri Fayol, and Max Weber—were largely responsible for developing the major concepts of the Scientific Management approach. All three were contemporaries living and writing during a period from the middle of the nineteenth century to World War I. The approaches of Taylor, Fayol, and Weber will be used to describe the **Scientific Management perspective.**

Scientific Management perspective—theoretical approach to organizations that emphasizes organizational design, worker training for efficiency, chains of command, and division of labor. The perspective rests on the assumption that work and organizations can be rationally or "scientifically" designed and developed.

Major Scientific Management Theories

Principles of Scientific Management: Frederick Taylor (1856–1915)
Frederick Taylor is often referred to as the father of Scientific Management. Taylor's work experience, ranging from common laborer to chief engineer, served as the basis for the development of the four essential elements he

viewed as the foundation of scientific management: (1) careful selection of workers, (2) inducing and training the worker by the scientific method, (3) equal division of work between management and workers, and (4) discovering the scientific method for tasks and jobs.

Taylor (1913) held management responsible for devising the scientific method of work. He contended that inefficiency is fostered by allowing workers to determine how tasks should be performed. Furthermore, he believed management is responsible for identifying "one best way" to perform tasks and that management should be exacting in teaching workers this scientific method for task performance. Taylor advised managers that "each man should daily be taught by and receive the most friendly help from those who are over him, instead of being, at the one extreme, driven or coerced by his bosses, and at the other left to his own unaided devices. This close, intimate, personal cooperation between the management and the men is the essence of modern scientific or task management." Taylor believed close contact between management and workers would eliminate the necessity for peer communication and what he called "soldiering," the unhealthy influence of the peer group.

Taylor is famous for his introduction in industry of the **time and motion** study. Taylor believed that if tasks were "scientifically" designed and workers extensively trained, the efficiency of production could be determined by timing the amount of work (motion) performed by individuals and teams. His "one best method" of task design was intended to produce the adoption of work standards that could be measured to increase efficiency and overall productivity.

Time and motion—technique for determining the efficiency of production through work observation and time measurements; used to develop work standards that can be measured for efficiency.

To implement scientific task design and measurement in the work place, Taylor recommended that management have sole responsibility for adopting and enforcing work standards. Taylor underscored the importance of the relationship between supervisor and subordinate when he suggested as "an inflexible rule to talk to and deal with only one man at a time, since each workman has his own special abilities and limitations, and since we are not dealing with men in masses, but are trying to develop each individual man to his highest state of efficiency and prosperity." He also considered the possibility that workers might propose improvements in how to complete tasks. When this occurred, Taylor advised management to conduct careful analysis of the new methods, conduct experiments to determine their accuracy, and then revise the existing standard if the new method should prove superior.

Taylor believed scientific management could only be accomplished with a well-defined chain of command and very specific division of labor. He held management responsible for developing the chain of command and organizing a division of labor based on well-defined work standards and measurement of standards to increase efficiency. Taylor's concepts were extremely influential in the early 1900s and continue today to influence how organizations are designed, how performance standards are established, and how work efficiency is measured.

Principles of Management: Henri Fayol (1841–1925)

Henri Fayol is credited with the first known attempt to describe broad principles of management for the organization and conduct of business. A French mining engineer, Fayol spent his working career as an engineer and later managing director of the Comambault, a mining company that was floundering before Fayol assumed leadership. Fayol enjoyed enormous success as director of Comambault and was widely credited with turning a financially troubled company into a stable and thriving institution. Fayol founded the Center for Administrative Studies and, as a leading industrialist, attempted to influence the French government to apply his principles of administration. His early papers on general administrative theory became the influential text *General and Industrial Management*, first published in 1916.

In *General and Industrial Management* (1949), Fayol proposed fourteen principles of administration or management that he viewed as essential for effective organization: division of work, authority, discipline, unity of command, unity of direction, subordination of individual interests to the general interest, remuneration, centralization, scalar chain (line of authority), order, equity, stability of tenure of personnel, initiative, and esprit de corps.

1. *Division of work.* Fayol argued that specialization is the natural order in the universe and as such should be applied to organizations. Specifically, he proposed a division of labor based on task specialization, with individuals having specific and well-defined assignments.

2. *Authority.* Fayol defined authority as "the right to give orders and the power to exact obedience." As did Taylor, Fayol placed responsibility for the exercise of authority with management. He also emphasized a difference between authority as a result of job title versus what he called "personal" authority. He preferred personal authority based on intelligence, experience, moral worth, ability to lead, and past service. Although he didn't describe it as such, Fayol was recognizing the importance of what we now call credibility in leadership.

3. *Discipline.* Discipline can be observed, according to Fayol, in the agreed-upon behavior and the evidence of that behavior between individuals and the organization. In other words, discipline is present when the behavior desired by management is exhibited by the work force. Fayol held management responsible for discipline, although he made no mention of a specific implementation process.

4. *Unity of command.* Fayol's principle of unity of command carried specific recommendations for communication. He contended that orders should come from only one superior and that a bypass of the chain of command would be a source of organizational problems. He believed messages should move from supervisors to subordinates as prescribed by the formal organization chart.

5. *Unity of direction.* Unity of direction was expressed by Fayol as "one head and one plan for a group of activities having the same objective." Unity of direction was achieved by sound structuring of the organization. Unity of direction represented the formal organizational structure, whereas unity of command referred to people functioning within the structure.

6. *Subordination of individual interests to the general interest.* Individual interests were to be secondary to the overall good of the group or the organization, according to Fayol. Specifically, he suggested that this subordination should be brought about by "(1) firmness and good example on the part of superiors; (2) agreements as fair as is possible; (3) constant supervision."

7. *Remuneration.* Fayol called for a fair price for sevices rendered. He believed that pay scales should be just and should motivate workers but should not overcompensate.

8. *Centralization.* In his principle of centralization, Fayol recognized the need for flexibility in management principles. He advised, "Centralization is not a system of management good or bad of itself, capable of being adopted or discarded at the whim of managers or of circumstances; it is always present to a greater or lesser extent. The question of centralization or decentralization, is a simple question of proportion." In discussing centralization, Fayol made direct reference to serial transmission of communication messages. He said, "In small firms where the manager's orders go directly to subordinates there is absolute centralization; in large concerns, where a long scalar chain is interposed between manager and lower grades, orders and counter-information too, have to go through a series of intermediaries. Each employee, intentionally or unintentionally, puts something of himself into the transmission and execution of orders and of information received too. He does not operate merely as a cog in a machine."

9. *Scalar chain.* In his discussion of the scalar chain, Fayol directly referred to messages moving vertically and horizontally throughout the organization. In fact, his discussion of the scalar chain is the only known treatment of horizontal communication found in organizational literature until the writings of Chester Barnard in 1938. Fayol defined the scalar chain as "the chain of superiors ranging from the ultimate authority to the lowest ranks. The line of authority is the route followed—via every link in the chain—by all communications which start from or go to the ultimate authority."

   Fayol described the chain as carrying messages in vertical directions. As such, the chain would have an equal capacity to carry messages vertically, both downward and upward. Fayol admitted that at times the chain required too much time for messages to travel effectively through all the links. He suggested that when the ne-

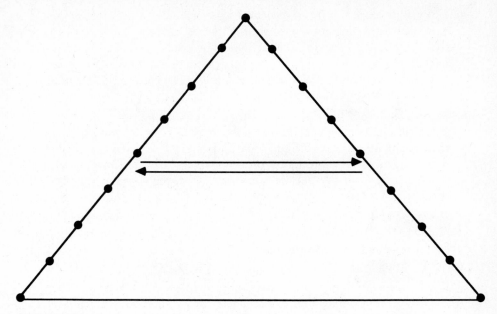

FIGURE 4.1
Fayol's gang plank, or horizontal communication between peers.

cessity for rapid message exchange occurred, it would be advisable to use a "gang plank" whereby peers communicated directly without regard to the scalar chain (see Figure 4.1). This "gang plank" has become known in organization and communication literature as Fayol's **bridge**. Fayol says, "use of the 'gang plank' is simple, swift, sure." He warned that the gang plank should be used sparingly and only in cases where it would serve the general interest. Fayol viewed horizontal communication as task-related and as not carrying the potentially negative influences of "soldiering" as described by Taylor.

Fayol's bridge—horizontal communication between peers.

10. *Order.* Fayol contended that both material and social order should be interpreted so that everything and everybody had a specific place and responsibility. As a principle of administration, the concept of order was to be put into effect through an organization's structure.

11. *Equity.* Fayol valued what he termed "equity," or a combination of kindliness and justice toward all members of the scalar chain. He viewed equity as necessary to encourage workers to carry out duties with devotion and loyalty.

12. *Stability of tenure of personnel.* Fayol recognized the cost to organizations of training workers and the amount of time it took for a person to become competent in a given position. Thus he believed

a work force that was relatively stable across time was in the best interests of the organization.

13. *Initiative.* Fayol saw initiative, as a principle of administration, as the ability to think through and execute plans. Furthermore, initiative was needed at all organizational levels, according to Fayol. He considered the manager who permitted the exercise of initiative within a work group to be superior to the one who could not.

14. *Esprit de corps.* Fayol's concept of esprit de corps was based on his belief that the strongest organization exhibited union of purpose. Fayol suggested that esprit de corps could be achieved by implementing his principle of unity of command. In advising managers about establishing esprit de corps, Fayol warned against dividing and ruling and the abuse of written communication. He suggested that when giving an order that required explanation, "usually it is simpler and quicker to do so verbally than in writing. Besides, it is well known that differences and misunderstandings which a conversation could clear up, grow more bitter in writing."

In addition to his fourteen principles of administration, Fayol identified five basic activities of management. These activities—planning, organizing, commanding, coordinating, and controlling—encompassed all of the fourteen principles of administration and served as a summary of Fayol's view of the overall responsibility of management.

Planning was described by Fayol as the development of operational plans for the organization and the forecasting of future needs. *Organizing* was the use of people and materials to implement the organizational plan or goals. *Commanding* was the management function of obtaining maximum or optimum return for the organization from human and material resources. *Coordinating* was the function of integrating the efforts of all organizational members. Finally, *Controlling* required management to establish how closely to its plan the organization was operating. To successfully accomplish these five activities of management, managers were to use all fourteen of Fayol's principles of administration. Although Fayol was writing early in the 1900s, his activities of management and principles of administration continue to receive extensive attention and are influential in the operation of contemporary organizations.

Principles of Bureaucracy: Max Weber (1864–1920)

Max Weber, a German sociologist, is frequently referred to as the father of bureaucracy. Heavily influenced by socialist philosophy, Weber developed his theory of **bureaucracy** as a response to the abuses of authority he believed to be present in early patrimonial (advancement by inheritance) systems. To Weber, the bureaucratic model for organizations should be based on authority relationships that emphasize depersonalization and task competence.

Bureaucracy—organizations based on formalized rules, regulations, and procedures, which make authority rational as opposed to charismatic or traditional.

Weber (1947) identified three types of authority: charismatic, traditional, and bureaucratic. *Charismatic authority* is based on the specific characteristics of the person exerting authority. Personal attributes of the individual inspire others to follow. This authority is nonstructural (does not go with specific jobs) and usually nontransferrable from person to person. In other words, charismatic authority is individually based, and when the charismatic leader leaves the organization, the authority or ability to influence leaves with him or her. Weber believed charismatic authority contributed to unstable organizations and disorderly transition of power from one person to another.

Traditional authority, according to Weber, is associated with the customs of a group or society. Although generally more stable than charismatic authority, traditional authority passes from individual to individual based on custom or tradition rather than ability or task competence. A family-owned company, for example, traditionally remains in the family from one generation to another, regardless of the abilities of others who might want to head the organization. Outsiders are simply not members of the family.

Weber believed *bureaucratic authority* represented the ideal for organizations. Bureaucratic authority was to rest on formalized rules, regulations, and procedures that made authority "rational-legal," not based on personal charisma or tradition. Bureaucratic leaders were to be selected according to rules and regulations designed to promote the most competent for the particular job. This ideal bureaucracy, with its "rational-legal" authority mode, was designed to counteract nepotism, favoritism, and unbalanced decision making. As did Taylor and Fayol, Weber called for division of labor and for task specialization. He supported a formal **chain of command** and hierarchical structure. Impersonality in interpersonal relations was valued and employment selection and promotion were to be based on competence.

Chain of command—formal authority and reporting structure of an organization.

Weber's ideal bureaucracy can be described as having a hierarchy of authority with a scalar chain of command. This chain of command would be organized according to task specialization and should represent division of labor appropriate to the required tasks. Also, the chain of command should operate with standardized rules and procedures designed to emphasize "rational" decision making and task competence. The rules and procedures of the bureaucracy should emphasize the employment of qualified personnel—not necessarily those who have family or personal connections or whom tradition might select, but personnel with the best task competencies for a particular job. To secure qualified personnel, detailed definitions of job expectations and responsibilities would have to be developed in accordance with the rules and procedures of the organization. Communication in the bureaucratic system should be formal and follow the chain of command. According to Weber, the ideal bureaucracy should place primary emphasis on the goals of the organization and put individual interests secondary to organizational productivity.

Communication Implications of Scientific Management Theories

Communication, from the Scientific Management point of view, was to be a tool of management designed to facilitate task completion and, as such, was to operate as one of many organizational variables. Communication activities were to be specialized, as were tasks and jobs. Specifically, communication was required to train workers and give daily instructions concerning job requirements. Communication activities were to be formal, and interpersonal communication of a social or personal nature was to be discouraged, particularly among peers. Horizontal communication was to occur infrequently and only when following the chain of command was too time consuming and cumbersome. Scientific Management theorists envisioned more messages flowing from supervisors to subordinates than from subordinates to supervisors. Status differences between managers and workers were to be encouraged and were believed essential for enforcing organizational rules and regulations.

Taylor, Fayol, and Weber all viewed communication as rational and functioning to reduce uncertainty about task expectations and measurement. Thus, the communication activities of the organization were developed and implemented by management as a natural reflection of their planning, organizing, commanding, coordinating, and controlling responsibilities.

We can use the Functional approach to organizational communication to describe communication implications from the Scientific Management viewpoint. Specifically, Taylor, Fayol, and Weber viewed organizational communication as functioning to organize task performance and to clarify rules and regulations. The relationship function of communication was relatively unimportant, although managers were advised to treat subordinates fairly and justly. Social or personal messages were to be discouraged. Although the Scientific Management theorists did not emphasize organizational change, management was to be responsible when change was necessary. Thus, any change communication would result from management decisions and would be initiated and implemented by management. Worker involvement in change messages was to be minimal.

In terms of message structure, Scientific Management theorists described messages as flowing via the chain of command primarily in a downward direction. Limited upward communication was desirable, and only in particular types of situations should horizontal "bridge" communication occur. Communication networks were formal and prescribed to follow the chain of command, with the supervisor/subordinate communication link of particular significance. Informal networks were described as undesirable, and load in the system was expected to be moderate with minimal distortion.

The Meaning-Centered approach to organizational communication provides yet another way to analyze and evaluate communication implications from the Scientific Management viewpoint. Taylor, Fayol, and Weber did not describe communication as processes of organizing, decision making, influence, and culture. Communication was described as a variable of the organization controlled by management. Organizing and decision making were management responsibilities that were to be carried out with bureaucratic authority. Culture was not a primary consideration, although culture contributed to the undesirable customs (traditions) of Weber's traditional authority mode or Taylor's concept of soldiering.

Even though Taylor, Fayol, and Weber did not envision communication as organizing, their works have implications for message equivocality. Specifically, the Scientific Management theorists prescribed messages low in equivocality with high degrees of definition in both task expectations and performance meansurement.

The Scientific Management theorists viewed decision making as an organizational variable. They did not envision decision making as an ongoing process, much less a communication process. The decision-making variable was management-controlled, with the primary premise for all decisions the efficient use of both human and material resources for goal achievement. Influence also was described as management-controlled and -executed. Management was responsible for organizational identification and the use of power to direct the organization. Ideally, power was the bureaucratic power of the Weber description rather than influence of personal characteristics (charisma) or the authority of tradition and custom. Although culture was not directly considered in the Scientific Management point of view, the emphasis on management responsibility and control implied a "management" culture that established the norms of the organization. Figure 4.2 summarizes communication implications of the Scientific Management viewpoint from Functional and Meaning-Centered approaches to organizational communication. The left column lists major components of each perspective and the right column assesses how Scientific Management theorists described these components.

Scientific Management Theories in Contemporary Organizations

By looking at the dates of the writings of Taylor, Fayol, and Weber, we are tempted to believe that the Scientific Management viewpoint is outdated and may provide limited usefulness in understanding today's organizations. Dates, however, can be misleading. A careful examination of most contemporary organizations reveals numerous Scientific Management principles still in operation. The Davis Instrument Company from the beginning of this chapter is a prime example. Davis has a chain of command for its manufacturing units. Pam is a manager responsible for three supervisors, who in turn each direct a team of workers. Davis can be described as having a division of labor that is in the process of change because of the introduction of the new MCF system. This change will re-

---

FIGURE 4.2
Communication Implications:
The Scientific Management Viewpoint

Functional Approach

Message Function
    Organizing: Important—tasks, rules,
                                            performance measurements

    Relationship: Relatively Unimportant—superior/
                                          subordinate

    Change: Relatively Unimportant—
                                            management-controlled

Message Structure
    Direction: Vertical, primarily downward
    Networks: Formal
    Channels: Written and oral
    Load: Moderate
    Distortion: Minimal

Meaning-Centered Approach

Organizing
    Equivocality: Low

Decision Making
    Individual Premises: Individual goals secondary to
                                            organizational goals

    Organizational premises: Efficient use of people and
                                            resources
                                        Decision making a management-
                                        controlled variable

Culture
    Performances: Not considered/probably
    Rituals/stories: inappropriate

Influence
    Identification: Management-controlled and
                                          -executed
    Socialization: Superiors train subordinates
    Communication rules: Management structures
    Power: Bureaucratic authority

---

quire extensive task instruction and the careful selection of the "best" workers for the new jobs. Davis holds management responsible for determining
how the system is to be implemented. Furthermore, Joan is exhibiting a
Scientific Management perspective when she argues that Pam and the supervisors should decide about job assignments without worker input. She

believes managers should be responsible for work design and for structuring their teams for maximum efficiency. Based on what we have learned about the principles of administration proposed by the Scientific Management theorists, Joan's proposal represents their views.

Our local, state, and national governments have been organized with many of the principles from the Scientific Management school. Not only do these organizations have hierarchies and chains of command, but also the transfer of power is governed by rules and regulations similar to those proposed by Weber. Although our votes for officials may be based on their personal charisma, the successful candidate assumes office only after following the prescribed election rules. Both state and federal civil service have detailed job descriptions for most positions, with promotions governed by rules and regulations designed to eliminate favoritism and emphasize overall ability. Obviously, we can argue with how well these principles work in actual practice, but their design is a distinct legacy from the Scientific Management theorists.

Think about your school from the Scientific Management viewpoint. Are "scientific" principles reflected in admission policies and the rules and regulations that govern the granting of degrees? How would you characterize the division of labor between students and teachers? Is there a chain of command? Do "scientific" principles influence communication? Attempt to characterize the effectiveness of the "scientific" principles you identify and extend your analysis to other organizations to which you belong. For most organizations, you will be able to identify at least some of the principles first described by Taylor, Fayol, and Weber.

THE HUMAN BEHAVIOR SCHOOL

The Human Behavior school shifts the emphasis from the structure of organizations, work design, and measurement to the interactions of individuals, their motivations, and influence on organizational events. The **Human Behavior perspective** assumes that work is accomplished through people and emphasizes cooperation, participation, satisfaction, and interpersonal skills. Theorists representing this viewpoint see organizational design and function as reflections of basic assumptions about human behavior. The work of three men—Elton Mayo, Douglas McGregor, and Rensis Likert—will be used to describe important characteristics of the Human Behavior approach to organizations.

Human Behavior perspective—theories of organizations that emphasize the interactions of individuals, their motivations, and their influence on organizational events.

Major Human Behavior Theories

The Hawthorne Effect: Elton Mayo (1880–1949)

Elton Mayo (1945) did not intentionally begin the Human Behavior point of view. As an influential Harvard professor he was interested in expanding the understanding of the work environment as described by Frederick Taylor. When the famous Hawthorne studies began, he was experimenting with the alteration of physical working conditions to increase productivity.

The Chicago Hawthorne plant of the Western Electric Company was the site of the research. In 1927, Mayo led a research team from the Harvard Graduate School of Business Administration in a series of experimental studies designed to improve the physical working environment for increased productivity. Management at the Hawthorne plant was aware that severe dissatisfaction existed among workers, and previous efforts by efficiency experts had failed both to reduce tension and to increase productivity. Mayo and his colleagues began to experiment with altering physical conditions to determine a combination of conditions that would increase productivity. They worked with factors such as lighting, noise, incentive pay, and heating. As the studies progressed they found little support for the expected relationship between improved working conditions and improved productivity. They became aware that other unexpected factors were interacting with physical factors to influence work output. During their study of changes in lighting intensity, Mayo and his colleagues observed that work output increased when lighting intensity increased. That was a result that could be interpreted in terms of Taylor and the Scientific Management viewpoint. But they also observed that work output increased when they decreased lighting intensity. That was a result that was counter to not only Taylor but also any previously established principles of Scientific Management. In fact, output increased no matter how the physical variables were changed. Mayo and his colleagues came to understand that a powerful and previously unrecognized influence in the experimental setting was the attention the researchers were paying to the workers. The attention encouraged a group norm that emphasized increased production no matter how the physical environment was altered. This effect, widely known as the **Hawthorne effect**, was the first documentation in industrial psychological research of the importance of human interaction and morale for productivity. The Hawthorne studies became the first organized attempts to understand the individual worker as key to the overall production process. As a result of the Hawthorne research, production could no longer be viewed as solely dependent on formal job and organizational design.

Hawthorne effect—group norms that influence productivity apart from the physical production environment.

Theory X and Theory Y: Douglas McGregor (1906–1964)

In his famous work *The Human Side of Enterprise* (1960), Douglas McGregor proposed his **Theory X-Theory Y** concept as a way to distinguish between the Scientific Management and Human Behavior perspectives. A former president of Antioch College and Massachusetts Institute of Technology professor of management, McGregor was interested in the basic assumptions about human nature inherent in both scientific and humanistic theories of management and organization.

McGregor presented Theory X as a summation of the assumptions about human nature made by those favoring the Scientific Management ideas of

Theory X-Theory Y—McGregor's description of management assumptions about workers. Theory X characterizes assumptions underlying Scientific Management theory, and Theory Y is associated with assumptions common to Human Behavior perspectives. Theory X managers assume that workers dislike work and will avoid responsible labor. Theory Y managers believe that workers can be self-directed and self-controlled.

Taylor, Fayol, and Weber. McGregor believed that hierarchical structure, management control of influence and decision making, close supervision, and performance measurement were based on assumptions about how to motivate human behavior. Specifically, McGregor proposed that Theory X managers believe the average person dislikes work and will avoid responsible labor whenever possible. Management must respond to this dislike of work with controls that are supported by punishments if workers fail to perform adequately. Theory X managers also assume that most people actually prefer to be directed in order to avoid responsibility for their actions. This direction allows workers to maintain job security without having to exhibit personal ambition.

Although McGregor believed Theory X accurately characterized the assumptions underlying Scientific Management theory, he doubted that these assumptions provided the best evidence of how to motivate workers, contribute to employee satisfaction, or stimulate high levels of productivity. Building on the work of Mayo and others, he proposed Theory Y as an alternative to Theory X and as a way to understand individual motivation and interaction within organizations.

Theory Y managers assume a very different type of worker. The worker characterized by Theory Y finds work as natural as play and as such is self-directed and self-controlled. Employees are personally committed to organizational objectives and do not need close supervision or the threat of punishment to be productive. Individual commitment is a function of feeling rewarded through personal achievement. Unlike workers depicted in Theory X, Theory Y workers actually seek responsibility and have a high degree of innovativeness and creativity for solving organizational problems. McGregor contended that most modern organizations do not realize the Theory Y potential of their work force and therefore only partially use the intellectual potential of their employees.

McGregor has been criticized for what some have called a polarized either/or approach to human nature. McGregor has responded that Theory X and Theory Y are assumptions that may be better understood as ranges of behaviors from X to Y. Managers, as such, can draw on both sets of assumptions depending on the situation and specific people involved (Figure 4.3).

Participative Management: Rensis Likert (1903–1981)

As a professor of sociology and psychology and director of the Institute of Social Research at the University of Michigan, Rensis Likert conducted extensive research to determine how management differed between successful and less successful organizations. His classic work, *New Patterns of Management* (1961), advanced his theory of **participative management** based on comparisons between productive and less productive work groups.

Likert, in *New Patterns of Management*, set forth a new theory—participative management—that rejected many of the assumptions on which Sci-

Participative management— Likert's theory of employee-centered management based on effectively functioning groups linked together structurally throughout the organization.

FIGURE 4.3
Douglas McGregor—
Theory X and Theory Y

Theory X Assumptions

1. People dislike work and will avoid work when possible.
2. Workers are not ambitious and prefer direction.
3. Workers avoid responsibility and are not concerned with organizational needs.
4. Workers must be directed and threatened with punishment to achieve organizational productivity.
5. Workers are not highly intelligent or capable of organizational creativity.
6. Organizations have difficulty in using human resources.

Theory Y Assumptions

1. People view work as natural as play.
2. Workers are ambitious and prefer self-direction.
3. Workers seek responsibility and feel rewarded through their achievements.
4. Workers are self-motivated and require little direct supervision.
5. Workers are creative and capable of organizational creativity.
6. Organizations have difficulty in using human resources.

---

entific Management was founded. His employee-centered management was based on effectively functioning groups linked together structurally throughout the entire organization. In other words, Likert proposed that the management process should depend on participative groups formed to have overlapping individual membership among groups. Figure 4.4 illustrates how an organizational chart using the Likert concept might look.

Likert supported his participative management theory with extensive research in high- and low-production situations. He believed that proper understanding of the differences or variability in human performance could help build productive organizations. Frederick Taylor had interpreted variability in performance as a need to establish specific procedures and production standards; Likert's interpretation called for an increase in participation by organizational members at all levels.

In an attempt to demonstrate the importance of participative management, Likert offered an extensive comparative analysis of management systems, which he identified as Systems I–IV. System I (exploitive authoritative) is similar to McGregor's Theory X assumptions. System I finds management closely controlling and directing work with little reliance on workers for problem solving. A general atmosphere of distrust discourages communication from flowing freely in all directions. System II (benevolent authoritative) is still characterized by hierarchical management control.

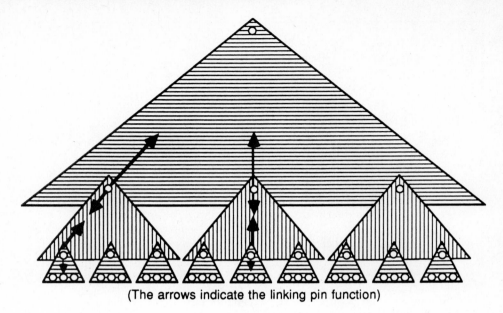

(The arrows indicate the linking pin function)

FIGURE 4.4
Likert's linking pin concept.
R. Likert, *New Patterns of Management*, © 1961, p. 113. Reproduced with permission of
McGraw-Hill Book Company, NY.

However, some trust and confidence is placed in workers. A System II organization generally has more communication from employees than its System I counterpart. System III (consultative) finds management actively seeking input from employees. Important decisions still are made at the top but with much greater worker involvement than in Systems I and II. System III even permits some decisions to be made at lower levels within the organizations.

System IV, Likert's ideal of participative management, is characterized by trust between management and employees and by decisions being made throughout the organization. Accurate communication flows in all directions and people are motivated because of their participation in organizational events and in shaping their own futures. Goal setting takes place at all organizational levels as well as appraisal of how well goals are being met and the overall effectiveness of the organization.

To support his participative management theory, Likert conducted extensive research comparing high- and low-performance groups. He contended that advances in the behavioral sciences made it possible to measure organization dimensions such as motivation, communication, and decision making. On the basis of this work, Likert contended that general supervision produces better results than close supervision and that employee-centered versus job-centered groups were more productive. Both findings are in direct contrast to basic principles from the Scientific Management school.

As had Mayo and his colleagues, Likert believed the influence of the peer group was important. Unlike Taylor, who called for the elimination of peer group influence, Likert believed the peer group could assist in building an effective organization. Furthermore, Likert's research indicated that higher productivity came from groups with high peer loyalty and a group sense of responsibility for getting work done.

Likert's (1961) attitude toward communication was clear when he stated, "Communication is essential to the functioning of an organization. It is viewed widely as one of the most important processes of management." Likert believed that confidence and trust throughout the organization were essential for effective communication. He also commented on research that indicates most managers view downward messages as the greatest communication problem in organizations. He contended that deficiencies in upward communication were probably more serious than in downward messages.

Likert's research also indicated that productivity was high in groups in which the supervisor and subordinate shared reasonably accurate perceptions of each other. Likert concluded from this finding that good communication and high performance go together.

Likert's participative management system was based on cooperation and motivation. Participative management was considered most appropriate when the work was varied, thereby creating a greater need for decision making throughout the organization. (Likert admitted that worker attitude was not as highly correlated to productivity in highly mechanized and routine work situations.) To disperse decision making throughout the organization, supportive relationships had to exist. Leadership and all other processes of the organization were to be exercised so that individuals would feel supported and affirmed in their personal worth and importance. This supportive climate could only be achieved, according to Likert, through the interlocking of effectively functioning groups.

Likert's theory of participative management was based on his research and assumptions about what happens in groups. Specifically, he contended that groups with high loyalty and attraction communicated more and were more receptive to communication from others than groups where loyalty and attraction were not high. Members of effective groups also tended to communicate more accurately and relevantly than did individuals using the scalar chain.

Likert's participative management system was put into practice through a structure of interlocking groups with members having multiple group memberships. These multiple group memberships provided "links" among groups, or what is now known as the famous "linking pin" function. This system of organization underscored Likert's commitment to broad participation at all organizational levels. Likert (1961), in describing the benefits of linked groups, predicted "fuller and more candid communication throughout the organization—upward, downward, and between peers." In sum, Likert's concept of participative management rested on his contention that the supportive atmosphere of the effective group promoted creativity, motivated people to use the communication process as both senders and receivers, and exerted more influence on leadership than in other types of systems.

Communication Implications of Human Behavior Theories

Effective communication was a cornerstone of the Human Behavior perspective. Management was to trust employees, and employees were to feel free to discuss job-related concerns with their supervisors. Peer-group interaction was not only recognized but also viewed as a potentially positive influence for productivity. The human behavior theorists recognized both formal and informal communication networks carrying task and social support messages. Interactions at all levels were expected to be extensive and friendly with substantial cooperation throughout the organization. From the Human Behavior viewpoint, communication was vital to the use of human resources and good organizational decision making.

When we use the Functional approach to describe communication implications from the Human Behavior viewpoint, we see a more complex role for communication than the Scientific Management theorists envisioned. As in the Scientific Management viewpoint, communication was seen as performing an organizing function providing task instruction, information, rules, and regulations. Unlike the Scientific Management viewpoint, the relationship function of organizational communication was considered significant. Mayo and Likert, in particular, recognized the importance of peers and how peer interactions contributed to integration within the organization. Also, Likert believed supportive relationships that were developed through effective communication were crucial for organizational productivity. Finally, the change function of communication was everyone's responsibility. Human Behavior researchers believed employees at all levels capable of participation in decision making and creating new directions for the organization.

The Human Behavior theorists described messages moving in all directions—through both formal and informal networks. These theorists emphasized oral channels, with little emphasis on written modes of communication. With both formal and informal messages moving in multiple directions, Human Behavior theorists described a communication load that was moderate to high and predictably distorted.

When we use the Meaning-Centered approach to identify the communication implications of Mayo, McGregor, and Likert, we again come to the conclusion that communication was better understood in the Human Behavior perspective than in the Scientific Management approach. For example, communication was described by Likert as part of the organizing process. Likert also encouraged increased communication participation throughout the organization. Decision-making responsibility rested with all organizational members based on the belief that individual workers were capable of creative organizational input and that organizations were more productive with broad participation.

Culture was not specifically considered by Mayo, McGregor, and Likert, although Likert did talk about supportive climates and described the types of groups he believed contributed most to productivity. Culture, however, was alluded to by the Human Behavior theorists when they discussed influence and power. They described the influence processes of identification and socialization as occurring primarily within peer groups, with power dispersed widely throughout the organization. Figure 4.5 summarizes communication implications of the Human Behavior perspective from Functional and Meaning-Centered approaches to organizational communication. The left column lists major components of each perspective, and the right column assesses how Human Behavior theorists described these components.

Human Behavior Theories in Contemporary Organizations

Most contemporary organizations include not only Scientific Management ideas but also much of the thinking generated from the Human Behavior theorists. Again we can return to the Davis Instrument Company as an example. Davis is structured according to many of the principles of Scientific Management, but Davis also exhibits the influence of men like Mayo, McGregor, and Likert. Pam Martin is making decisions about the new MCF system with participation from her subordinates. She is using a group process to address issues and solve problems. Earlier we identified Joan as articulating a Scientific Management approach. We can expand our analysis and describe Henry as representing the Human Behavior viewpoint when he calls for extensive involvement from the various work teams in determining their new training and job assignments. Both Henry and Frank reflect Theory Y assumptions about people when they contend that workers are more motivated when involved in decisions that directly affect them. In fact, when we thoughtfully analyze the Davis case, it is possible to conclude that both Scientific Management and Human Behavior ideas are in evidence and that both will contribute to the success or failure of the new MCF system.

Most contemporary organizations are similar to Davis in their combined usage of Scientific Management and Human Behavior ideas. Committees, project teams, quality circles, and work units all are examples of the use made of groups in modern organizations. Training for managers and supervisors emphasizes developing interpersonal skills for working effectively with subordinates. New employees attend orientations designed to help them understand and become a part of the organization. Awards honor a variety of creative contributions, and profit-sharing and merit-pay

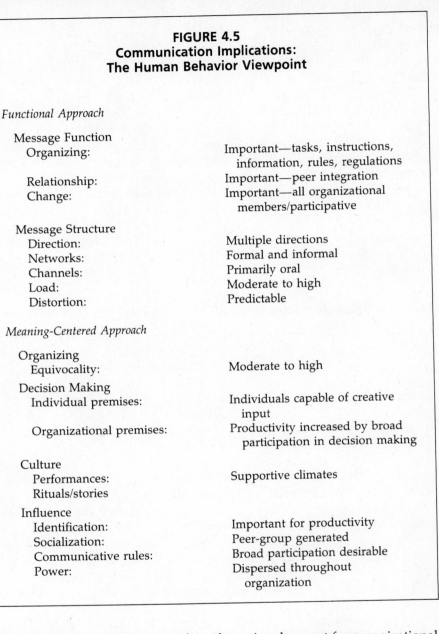

FIGURE 4.5
Communication Implications:
The Human Behavior Viewpoint

Functional Approach

Message Function
    Organizing: Important—tasks, instructions, information, rules, regulations

    Relationship: Important—peer integration
    Change: Important—all organizational members/participative

Message Structure
    Direction: Multiple directions
    Networks: Formal and informal
    Channels: Primarily oral
    Load: Moderate to high
    Distortion: Predictable

Meaning-Centered Approach

Organizing
    Equivocality: Moderate to high

Decision Making
    Individual premises: Individuals capable of creative input
    Organizational premises: Productivity increased by broad participation in decision making

Culture
    Performances: Supportive climates
    Rituals/stories

Influence
    Identification: Important for productivity
    Socialization: Peer-group generated
    Communicative rules: Broad participation desirable
    Power: Dispersed throughout organization

plans attest to the importance of employee involvement for organizational success. These examples and many others exist side by side in today's organizations with hierarchical structures, division of labor, chains of command, and final management responsibility in decision making.

Earlier you described your school from a Scientific Management point of view. Now think about that same organization from the Human Behavior viewpoint. What assumptions are made about the basic nature of students? Is there an honor code for academic achievement or are exams tightly monitored and cheating vigorously punished? Is creativity expected from students? Is there a supportive atmosphere that contributes to effective communication among students and with teachers? Attempt to characterize your school in terms of Theory X and Theory Y. Does one work better than the other? If so, why? If not, how do they work in combination? Finally, describe which of the Human Behavior concepts you believe to be the most influential for effective communication.

THE INTEGRATED PERSPECTIVES SCHOOL

Both Scientific Management and Human Behavior approaches have been criticized for their failure to integrate organizational structure, technology, and people with the larger environment in which organizations exist. The Scientific Management theorists concentrated on organizational structure and work design with little attention to people and organizational environments. The Human Behavior theorists were concerned with people but also tended to ignore influences beyond organizational boundaries. In reaction to these criticisms, a number of organizational researchers have developed what we will call the **Integrated Perspectives** viewpoint. These theorists attempt to explain how people, technologies, and environments integrate to influence goal-directed behavior. Specifically, we will examine the process and environmental approaches of Herbert Simon, Eric Trist and Kenneth Bamforth, Joan Woodward, Paul Lawrence and Jay Lorsch, and Daniel Katz and Robert Kahn, and the cultural approaches of Terrance Deal and Allen Kennedy, William Ouchi, and Thomas Peters and Robert Waterman.

Integrated Perspectives—theories that attempt to explain how people, technologies, and environments integrate to influence goal-directed behavior.

Major Integrated Perspective Theories: Process and Environmental Approaches

Process and environmental approaches to organizational theory attempt to describe how complex processes such as decision making influence the internal operation of organizations and are influenced by external environments. Researchers using these perspectives seek to explain how human and technical systems interact with the broader environments in which organizations operate and, in so doing, seek to test basic assumptions from both Scientific Management and Human Behavior viewpoints. To describe process and environmental approaches, we will discuss the decision-making approach of Herbert Simon, sociotechnical integration as described by Trist and Bamforth, contingency theory as introduced by Joan Woodward and Lawrence and Lorsch, and Katz and Kahn's systems theory.

Decision-Making Approach: Herbert Simon (1916–   )

In 1947, Herbert Simon offered a description of organizations that differed from both the Scientific Management and Human Behavior viewpoints. Simon (1957) proclaimed that organizational behavior is a complex network of decisions with decision-making processes influencing the behavior of the entire organization. According to Simon, organizations can be understood in terms of what types of decisions are made at various organizational levels and with what types of information. As such, Simon viewed the **decision-making approach** as the essential organizational process.

Understanding the limitations of human decision making was important to Simon's model. Along with James March and Richard Cyert (1958, 1963), Simon introduced the concept of **bounded rationality** as a way to understand information processing and decision making. Specifically, the concept of bounded rationality assumed that people intend to be rational, but with limited information-processing capacity human decision making is based on selective perception and therefore exhibits "limited" rationality. Simon argued that individuals often make organizational decisions while realizing that their decisions are based on partial information. Simon called this process "satisficing," or the making of decisions with partial information in the hope the decision will be good enough, if not the best.

Simon clearly challenged the "one best way" of the Scientific Management theorists. He also largely ignored the descriptions of human behavior as offered by Human Behavior theorists in favor of an explanation of human behavior based on the concept of bounded rationality. He described decision making as the fundamental organizational process. Decision making, he said, occurs through the communication behaviors of individuals who intend rationality but can only approach rationality because of limited information-processing capacity.

Sociotechnical Integration: Eric L. Trist (1909–   ) and Kenneth W. Bamforth*

The concept of **sociotechnical integration** rested on two assumptions first described by Eric Trist and his student Kenneth Bamforth (1951) as a result of their work with a British coal-mining operation: (1) Organizational production is optimized through optimizing social and technical systems, and (2) a constant interchange exists between the work system and the broader environment.

The sociotechnical approach attempted to balance human social-psychological needs with organizational goals. Communication in the sociotechnical approach related to work, to the needs of the environment, and to the personal needs of workers. Trist and Bamforth tested the sociotechnical concept in a British coal-mining operation. Workers were trained to rotate as necessary through all of the tasks required by new machines. This cross-training was designed to introduce variety and interest into the

Decision-making approach— Simon's concept that organizational behavior is a complex network of decisions, with decision-making processes influencing the behavior of the entire organization.

Bounded rationality— assumption that people intend to be rational, but with limited information-processing capacity human decision making is based on selective perception and therefore exhibits "limited" rationality.

Sociotechnical integration— theoretical attempt to balance human social-psychological needs with organizational goals; an assumption that organizational production is optimized through optimizing social and technical systems.

* Birthdate unknown.

work environment. Also, each work team was permitted to set its own rate of production and was responsible for handling its own problems and conflicts. The output of these autonomous groups was compared to groups with more traditional and "scientifically" designed assignments. In the Trist and Bamforth experiment, the sociotechnical groups outperformed their scientific group counterparts by approximately 34 percent, or 1.8 tons per shift.

These experiments led Trist and Bamforth to conclude that meaning in work could be established through group assignments that permit individuals to be included in entire task cycles rather than working on isolated parts of a job. The autonomy of groups in setting their own standards and making decisions about their own problems could give individuals a sense of self-determination that closer supervision and control could not achieve. This emphasis on group-set goals and responsibilities could contribute to a solidarity of purpose that could help integrate individual and organizational goals. This integration would be productive for both individuals and organizations.

Contingency Theory: Joan Woodward (1916–1971), Paul Lawrence (1922–   ), and Jay Lorsch (1932–   )

What we call **contingency theory** began when Joan Woodward (1965) researched 100 British manufacturing firms in an effort to develop a list of characteristics that would indicate differences in organizational structure. Her classification included organizations with little technological complexity and those with extensive reliance on complicated technologies. Her findings relating differences in technology to differences in organizational structure became the foundation of modern contingency theory, or the realization that differences in organizations are due to differences in goals and environments.

Contingency theory rejects the "one best way" to organize as described by Scientific Management's theorists. Contingency theory also finds the Human Behavior approach lacking an explanation of the complex relationships among units within the organization and the larger environment in which the organization operates.

Lawrence and Lorsch (1969) describe contingency theory as the establishment of internal organizational operations contingent or dependent on external environmental needs and individual needs. Lawrence and Lorsch view organizations as having three primary relationships that determine how organizations operate and respond to their environment. Specifically, organizations have what Lawrence and Lorsch call "interfaces" at the organization-to-environment, group-to-group, and individual-to-organization levels. They suggest that organizational design and operation should be based on these three "interfaces," which differ for all organizations.

Proponents of the contingency view suggest there is no specific set of prescriptions appropriate for all organizations. Organizations must adapt to changing circumstances and the needs of individuals and the environ-

Contingency theory—approach that rejects the "one best way" to organize in favor of the view that no specific set of prescriptions are appropriate for all organizations. As such, organizations must adapt to changing circumstances and the needs of individuals and the environment in which the organization operates.

ments in which the organizations operate. As such, organizational designs based on Scientific Management concepts may be appropriate in certain circumstances. The concerns of the Human Behavior theorists also can be valuable when matched to specific situations. In other words, contingency theory suggests that considerable judgment is required to understand effective organizational operation because that operation "all depends on the situation."

The Systems Approach: Daniel Katz (1903–   ) and Robert Kahn (1918–   )

Systems theory—describes organizations as made up of subsystems, which take in materials and human resources, process materials and resources, and yield a finished product to the larger environment.

Closely related to contingency theory, **systems theory** grew in direct response to criticisms of both Scientific Management and Human Behavior philosophies. The systems approach emphasizes interaction with the larger environment, and as Katz and Kahn (1966) suggest, "is basically concerned with problems of relationships, of structure, and of interdependence rather than the constant attributes of objects."

Katz and Kahn contend that most formal organizations operate with five basic subsystems: productive subsystems dealing with work accomplished; supportive subsystems dealing with relationships and needed materials support; maintenance subsystems to integrate people into their functional role; adaptive subsystems geared for change; and managerial subsystems for coordination and control of the various subsystems.

In systems theory, the organization takes in materials and human resources (input), processes materials and resources (throughput), and yields a finished product (output) to the larger environment. Along with input, throughput, and output, the ideal system should have a self-corrective mechanism whereby feedback or input from the environment can be processed into adaptation of throughput and, potentially, output. The system's self-corrective mechanism is called the system's cybernetic, which in the ideal system is the management team. In systems theory the law of equifinality attests to the multiple-action courses possible for the achievement of a goal. Equifinality rejects the concept of a single course of action to reach a single goal.

Katz and Kahn and other systems theorists advance a principle of optimization, or looking for maximum output in return for minimum input. Maximum return for minimum input is affected by feedback from the environment and management's ability to adjust. Thus, systems may be described as open or closed, mechanistic or organic. An open system exchanges information with its larger environment. A closed system limits exchange with the environment and seeks to operate as a self-contained unit. Systems theorists relate the closed organizational system to a closed thermodynamic system, contending they both will approach a condition of maximum entropy with no further possibility of useful work. The open system, on the other hand, fights entropy and seeks a dynamic equilibrium among input, throughput, and output. The open system exhibits the law of equifinality and has a sound self-corrective mechanism.

The organic system is suited to change, whereas the mechanistic system functions best in stable conditions. The mechanistic system frequently exhibits much of the prescriptive structure of Scientific Management with its rigid hierarchy and specialized differentiation of tasks. The organic system is characterized by greater emphasis on individuals and their capacities for unique contributions. Hierarchy may exist in the organic system but authority is exercised more by consent than coercion or legitimate right of office. The organic system compares favorably with descriptions of open systems, whereas the mechanistic system may be compared to closed systems.

Major Integrated Perspectives Theories: Cultural Approaches

Cultural approaches to organizational theory describe how organizational members collectively interpret the organizational world around them in order to define the importance of organizational happenings. In other words, cultural approaches to organizational theory explain organizational behavior in terms of the influence of cultures that exist both internally and externally to the organization. Cultural research attempts to identify how a unique sense of the place (culture) contributes to individual behavior and organizational effectiveness.

Cultural approaches—theories that describe how organizational members collectively interpret the organizational world around them in order to define the importance of organizational happenings. Approaches to theory that explain organizational behavior in terms of the influence of cultures that exist both internally and externally to the organization.

Cultural theories are the newest additions to the Integrated Perspectives approach, although the importance of culture has been recognized for many years. Deal and Kennedy, Ouchi, and Peters and Waterman are only a few of the current researchers interested in how cultures influence organizational effectiveness.

Elements of Culture: Terrence Deal (1939–   ) and Allen Kennedy (1943–   )

Deal and Kennedy, in their book *Corporate Cultures: The Rites and Rituals of Corporate Life* (1982), identify five basic elements of organizational culture: business environment, values, heroes, rites and rituals, and the cultural network. Each contributes to managing behavior and, according to Deal and Kennedy, "helps employees do their jobs a little better." Essentially, a strong culture contributes to managing the organization by spelling out in general terms how people are to behave while helping people feel better about what they do, enabling hard work and excellent productivity.

Deal and Kennedy suggest that the business environment is "the single greatest influence in shaping a corporate culture." What companies do in their competitive environments shapes the reality of how organizations manage activity and whether or not they are successful. Values emerge that help individuals determine where the emphasis of their efforts should be placed. In other words, organizational values help people become dedicated to a cause, which in turn guides decisions about all types of behaviors. These strong values are not, however, without their dangers. Strong organizational values may limit change and encourage obsolescence when organizational values come in conflict with changing environments requiring new decisions and approaches. Regardless of whether their impact is positive or negative, values, according to Deal and Kennedy, are the core of corporate culture.

Deal and Kennedy contend that heroes are the "real live" human successes who become role models for the culture's values. Stories and myths about the behaviors of heroes help organizational members determine what they have to do to succeed and what is valued by the organization. Rites and rituals also serve this function. Deal and Kennedy identify management rituals such as formal meetings, where rituals develop about the number held, the setting, the table's shape, who sits where, and who is in attendance. Recognition rituals, ranging from formal events honoring outstanding service to informal traditions, also identify what the organization holds to be important and help to integrate individual and organizational goals. Finally, Deal and Kennedy suggest that informal organizational communication is the cultural network and as such is the only way to understand what is really going on. From the Deal and Kennedy perspective, culture is the organizational process that most contributes to shaping organizational outcomes. The communication of culture, therefore, both shapes behavior and reflects the operating reality of the organization.

Theory Z: William Ouchi (1943–   )

Among the more popular of the new cultural approaches is William Ouchi's *Theory Z* (1981). As Douglas McGregor characterized human behavior with Theory X and Y, **Theory Z** proposes that organizations must adapt to the key elements of the culture in which they operate. In other words, Theory Z makes assumptions about culture as Theory X and Y made assumptions about individuals.

Theory Z—Ouchi's theory derived from comparisons between Japanese and American organizations. Theory Z organizations retain individual achievement and advancement as a model but provide a continuing sense of organizational community not typical of many American organizations.

Ouchi's work begins by contrasting what he calls Type A American with Type J Japanese organizations. He contends the two types differ in seven defining characteristics appropriate to each culture. Type A American organizations are characterized by short-term employment, individual decision making, individual responsibility, rapid promotion, formal control, specialized career paths, and segmented concerns. Type A organizations reflect cultural values of individuality over group membership and assume that broad social needs are supported by institutions such as churches, schools, and neighborhood groups rather than formal employment groups.

On the other hand, Type J Japanese organizations can be characterized by lifetime employment, consensual decision making, group or collective responsibility, slow advancement, informal control, generalized career paths, and holistic concerns. The Type J organization reflects a culture in which loyalty to groups is more important than individual achievement and in which individuals gain identity from long-term affiliations with the companies for which they work. Japanese culture supports an organizational structure that actually reduces employees' incentives to leave the work group and does not reward desires for rapid advancement.

Ouchi argues that American culture is changing, requiring a rethinking of some of the elements of the Type A organization. Although individuality is still valued, increased geographic mobility has generated a void in the social needs of workers who previously could have been expected to have those needs met from long-term, stable affiliations in their home communities. Ouchi proposes a Theory Z organization that retains individual achievement and advancement as a model but provides a continuing sense of organizational community not typical of Type A organizations. He sees the Theory Z organization as adapting to the changing needs of a mobile society and adapting to those needs in ways that support important cultural values—individuality—while adjusting to the evolution of new values, beliefs, and needs.

In Search of Excellence: Thomas Peters (1942–   ) and Robert Waterman (1936–   )

In their famous best-seller, *In Search of Excellence* (1982), Peters and Waterman report the results of their study of sixty-two successful representatives of U.S. industry. Peters and Waterman attempted to understand how these large, successful companies were adapting to their changing environments. They worked from the premise that organizational structure cannot be understood apart from people. Indeed, they suggest that "any intelligent approach to organizing had to encompass, and treat as interdependent, at least seven variables: structure, strategy, people, management style, systems and procedures, guiding concepts and shared values (i.e., culture), and the present and hoped-for corporate strengths or skills."

Peters and Waterman studied Hewlett-Packard, Digital Equipment, Frito-Lay, Delta Airlines, McDonald's, Boeing, Exxon, and numerous other companies selected because of their prestige in the business world, overall financial performance, industry position, and innovativeness as measured by their ability continually to bring new products and services to changing markets. They were testing their assumption that excellent companies "not only are unusually good at producing commercially viable new widgets: innovative companies are especially adroit at continually responding to change of any sort in their environments."

As a result of their work, Peters and Waterman have identified eight cultural themes that most nearly characterized excellent, innovative companies. These themes suggest that "excellent companies were, above all, brilliant on the basics."

The eight themes as identified by Peters and Waterman are as follows:

1. *A bias for action.* Excellent companies made decisions. They were analytical but not paralyzed by too much information. When they had a problem, they took action.

2. *Close to the customer*. Service, reliability, innovative products, and continual concern for customer needs were fundamentals for the excellent companies. The close-to-the-customer value also resulted in new product ideas and served as the basis for innovation.

3. *Autonomy and entrepreneurship*. Excellent companies wanted leaders in all types of organizational activity. They encouraged risk taking and innovation and gave people responsibility for their own ideas. People were not so tightly controlled as to lose creativity.

4. *Productivity through people*. Workers at all organizational levels were the source of quality and the source of productivity. Excellent companies fought against a we/they management/labor attitude.

5. *Hands-on, value-driven*. The basic philosophy and values of the organization contributed more to achievement than any specific technology or material resource. Values were seen to influence behavior and were considered the core of excellence.

6. *Stick to the knitting*. Excellent companies stayed in the businesses they knew. They did not diversify beyond what they understood in terms of either technology and service or customers. They grew by doing what they did extremely well.

7. *Simple form, lean staff*. None of the excellent companies was run with complicated organizational structures. In fact, many of the top corporate staffs were running multibillion-dollar organizations with fewer than 100 people.

8. *Simultaneous loose-tight properties*. These companies were both centralized and decentralized. Autonomy and entrepreneurship were encouraged at all levels within the organizations. Decision making was often decentralized, yet core values were very centralized and rigidly supported.

As Peters and Waterman suggest, "The excellent companies live their commitment to people, as they also do their preference for action—any action—over countless standing committees and endless 500-page studies." But above all, "the intensity itself, stemming from strongly held beliefs, marks these companies."

As Ouchi discusses the broad influence of culture, Peters and Waterman describe how specific cultural themes contribute to excellence and organizational abilities to adapt to changing markets. Interestingly enough, much of what Peters and Waterman suggest the excellent companies do in terms of people support and encouragement is similar to what Ouchi suggests the Theory Z organization does in providing recognition for individual achievement while meeting social support needs.

Communication Implications of Integrated Perspectives Theories

The Integrated Perspectives theories we have been discussing present a diverse set of implications for organizational communication. Simon, Woodward, Lawrence and Lorsch, and Katz and Kahn all describe organizations with changing needs and environments. Thus, the effectiveness of communication is related not only to what happens within the organization but also to how the organization communicates with its environment—its customers and community. The cultural approaches, on the other hand, are more specific about the importance of communication in carrying messages about the culture and influencing behavior through cultural expectations.

When we examine the communication implications of the Integrated Perspectives ideas from our Functional framework, we see a different picture from either the Scientific Management or Human Behavior approaches. The rejection of the "one best way" concept and the emphasis on the external environment require a communication system in continual adaptation to changing circumstances. Communication fulfills organizing, relationship, and change functions; however, the balance among these functions depends on the needs of the specific organization based on its goals and environment. Likewise message structure depends on what the organization does, who its members are, and how the organization relates to its public. Message direction, load, channels, networks, and distortion all can be described as contingent or dependent on specific circumstances.

The decision-making and cultural concepts of the Integrated Perspectives viewpoint take on particular significance when viewed from a Meaning-Centered approach to organizational communication. Both these concepts are based on how organizational members generate shared meanings and how these meanings influence behavior and organizational effectiveness. Although Integrated Perspectives theorists do not describe communication as synonymous with organizing, decision making, and culture, they do view rich, intense, informal communication as the foundation for influence and for the network that carries organizational culture. The major premises underlying the cultural approaches are that organizations are more effective with strong cultures, and strong cultures require effective communication. Organizational identification and socialization are fundamental to a strong culture and as such are important managerial responsibilities.

The cultural theorists also underscore the importance of values for excellent organizations and the need for values to become part of the shared realities of organizational members. This concept of developing shared realities is the essence of the Meaning-Centered approach to organizational communication. Thus, cultural theorists can be said to understand that the generation of shared realities contributes to creating and shaping organizational events. Figure 4.6 summarizes the communication implications of

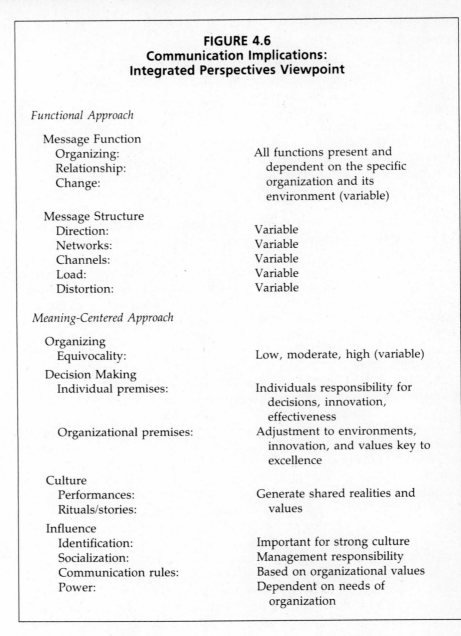

FIGURE 4.6
Communication Implications:
Integrated Perspectives Viewpoint

Functional Approach

Message Function
    Organizing:
    Relationship:
    Change:

    All functions present and dependent on the specific organization and its environment (variable)

Message Structure
    Direction: Variable
    Networks: Variable
    Channels: Variable
    Load: Variable
    Distortion: Variable

Meaning-Centered Approach

Organizing
    Equivocality: Low, moderate, high (variable)

Decision Making
    Individual premises: Individuals responsibility for decisions, innovation, effectiveness

    Organizational premises: Adjustment to environments, innovation, and values key to excellence

Culture
    Performances: Generate shared realities and
    Rituals/stories: values

Influence
    Identification: Important for strong culture
    Socialization: Management responsibility
    Communication rules: Based on organizational values
    Power: Dependent on needs of organization

Integrated Perspectives from the Functional and Meaning-Centered approaches to organizational communication. The left column lists major components of each perspective, and the right column assesses how Integrated Perspectives theorists describe these components.

Integrated Perspectives Theories in Contemporary Organizations

With the contributions of theorists like Simon, Woodward, Lawrence and Lorsch, Katz and Kahn, and Trist and Bamforth, we talked about the importance of the external environment and began to merge much of the thinking from the Scientific Management and Human Behavior approaches. Also, with the advent of the cultural approaches proposed by Integrated Perspectives theorists, communication was described as the process through which shared realities are generated and through which values, identification, and socialization occur.

We can find numerous examples of the importance of organizations adjusting to their external environments. Big American cars of the 1950s and 1960s lost their competitive market position to foreign competition. The introduction of personal computers for a home market found several hundred companies scrambling to introduce new and better products in an attempt to gain market share. The "back-to-basics" emphasis in education has been in response to concerns that students are not developing competencies needed for our information society. And the list could go on. The contribution of Integrated Perspectives theorists in describing the need to acknowledge the influence of the external environment has improved our ability to think comprehensively about organizations and how people and technology relate to larger environments.

Concern for organizational culture is readily apparent in contemporary organizations. Organizations publish philosophy statements, conduct training programs that identify the values of the organization, and hold annual events of special cultural significance. Schools have graduation ceremonies; sales organizations have annual awards banquets; and special traditions emerge to celebrate promotions, achievements, and a variety of other organizational events.

The significance of the Integrated Perspectives approaches can be seen when we return to the Davis Instrument Company's manufacturing changes. The introduction of the new MCF system is in response to market pressure to remain cost competitive. The concern for how to reassign and train workers illustrates essential sociotechnical relationships among environmental needs for change, human needs during change, and the changing requirements of new technology. What happens next at Davis will depend on some factors not readily apparent in the case. What are the general expectations of the Davis work force regarding change? What does the "culture" suggest is going to happen? The decisions Pam Martin's supervisors make will be accepted or resisted, at least in part, based on their cultural fit to the shared realities of Davis and to the organizational values held by Davis employees. To advise Pam Martin and the supervisors effectively, we would need to know more about "how things really work" at Davis.

Think for a moment about organizations with which you are familiar. How have they adjusted to their environments? Is your school state-funded or dependent on private revenue? For either case, think about environmental influences school administrators must consider when planning programs and asking for monetary support. Now describe the shared values of your school. How are they communicated? Can you identify some of the rites and rituals that influence student identification and socialization? Finally, attempt to define what you would say to a new student about what it takes "to be successful around here."

SUMMARY

In this chapter we have described Scientific Management, Human Behavior, and Integrated Perspectives theories for studying organizations and discussed their communication implications. The Scientific Management stance was described by Frederick Taylor, Henri Fayol, and Max Weber as a "scientific" approach to the design of organizations. Organizational design was based on a carefully developed chain of command and efficient division of labor. Taylor described how the scientific method of work was to be established and became famous for the introduction of time and motion studies. Fayol organized the first general set of principles for management and identified five basic activities of management: planning, organizing, commanding, coordinating, and controlling. Fayol also introduced the concept of horizontal communication with the use of his famous "bridge." Max Weber, the father of bureaucracy, established criteria for evaluating an organization based on merit and productivity. Weber's system included bureaucratic authority, standardized rules and procedures, "rational" decision making, task competence, and qualified personnel. In the Scientific Management point of view, communication was viewed as management's responsibility, with task- and rule-related messages moving along formal networks in a downward direction. As such, messages were expected to be low in equivocality. Decision making was a management-controlled variable of the organization, as was influence. Culture was not considered and probably would have been viewed as inappropriate.

The Human Behavior viewpoint shifted the emphasis away from the structure of organizations, work design, and measurement to the interactions of individuals, their motivations, and influence on organizational events. The work of Elton Mayo, Douglas McGregor, and Rensis Likert was used to describe this viewpoint. Elton Mayo's famous Hawthorne studies demonstrated the importance of peer influence for productivity. Douglas McGregor described the assumptions we make about human nature and how they contribute to what we view as appropriate organizational behavior. McGregor proposed that Theory X managers believe the average person dislikes work and will avoid responsible labor whenever possible; the Theory Y worker, on the other hand, was characterized as self-directed and self-controlled and as finding work as natural as play.

Rensis Likert, as Weber had done for the Scientific Management viewpoint, described systems of management and proposed a new theory—participative management. Likert's systems—exploitive authoritative, benevolent authoritative, consultative, and participative—reflect how management uses information from employees. Likert's ideal of participative management was based on trust between management and employees, with decisions made throughout the organization. Groups and links among groups were a central focus of his approach. The Human Behavior theorists described communication as performing organizing, relationship, and change functions, with all organizational members participating. Networks were both formal and informal, and message equivocality could be characterized as higher than the Scientific Management theorists envisioned. Decision making occurred throughout the organization particularly if the organization demonstrated a supportive climate. The peer group was viewed as a primary source of influence.

The approaches of Herbert Simon, Trist and Bamforth, Joan Woodward, Katz and Kahn, William Ouchi, Deal and Kennedy, and Peters and Waterman grew out of criticisms of both the Scientific Management and Human Behavior viewpoints. These viewpoints, according to their critics, had failed to integrate organizational structure, technology, and people with the larger environments in which organizations exist. The Integrated Perspectives approaches attempted to explain how people, technology, and environment interact to influence goal-directed behavior. Herbert Simon introduced the concept that decision making could be viewed as the essential organizational process. To Simon, organizational behavior was a complex network of decisions that created and shaped organizational events. The process was "bounded" in rationality by the limits of human information processing. Trist and Bamforth described the necessity for integrating social and technical systems to maximize productivity, and Joan Woodward and Lawrence and Lorsch rejected any "one best way" to organize in favor of what they called contingency theory. Contingency theory was described as the establishment of internal organizational processes and states contingent on external environmental and individual member needs. Although closely related to contingency theory, the systems approach, as described by Katz and Kahn, emphasized the relationships among subsystems of the organization for the taking in of materials and resources (input), the processing of materials and resources (throughput), and the yielding of a finished product (output) to the larger environment.

Cultural approaches attempted to explain organizational behavior in terms of the influence of culture. Deal and Kennedy identified five basic elements of organizational culture: business environment, values, heroes, rites and rituals, and cultural network. Ouchi described a new Theory Z organization that adapts to the American culture through emphasis on both individual achievement and social support. And Peters and Waterman identified eight cultural themes dominant in successful American organizations. These themes, according to Peters and Waterman, emerge from the strongly held beliefs or values that mark successful companies. The communication implications resulting from the work of the Integrated Perspectives theorists are diverse, with communication viewed both as a central process for organizational effectiveness and as dependent on the needs of a particular organization.

WORKSHOP

1. Form groups of four to six members each. Identify organizations in your community with which group members have some familiarity. Discuss whether these organizations represent Scientific Management, Human Behavior, or Integrated Perspectives viewpoints. Do any of the organizations represent combined approaches? How effective is communication in the various organizations?

2. An invited essay, "One or Two Aspects of Communication in the Scientific Environment," by Charles Zalabak, retired NASA physicist, provides a personal perspective influenced by the requirements of a scientific career. As you read the essay think about your own personal perspective for organizational communication. Does the Zalabak essay represent a Scientific Management, Human Behavior, or Integrated Perspectives view? What would your own essay reflect? (See pages 118–120.)

3. A Guide to Case Development and Analysis, which follows Zalabak's essay, should be used as you begin to examine increasingly complex organizational cases and prepare cases from personal interviews and experiences. (See pages 120–122.)

4. Using the Guide to Case Development and Analysis, analyze the "What Do You Mean I'm Not Going to Graduate?" and "We Never Had to Advertise Before" cases and propose ways to approach the problems identified in the cases. (See pages 122–123.)

5. In teams of two or working individually, interview an organizational member for his or her description of an organizational event or events that contributed to communication problems or the need for new communication policies. Following your interview, use the Guide to Case Development and Analysis to write a "case" and prepare it for class presentation. In addition to presenting the facts of the case, present recommendations for solutions for class discussion.

One or Two Aspects of Communication in the Scientific Environment

Charles Zalabak*

In desperation I begin this essay with the hope that, once the writing is finished, I will again be able to eat and drink without the ulcerative ten-

* Charles Zalabak, a NASA research scientist for twenty-four years, also served with the Peace Corps at the University of Science and Technology at Kumasi, Ghana, West Africa.

dencies, that I will be able to breathe without palpitations. To free myself of the anxiety over getting it done prompts me to action. I am sure that by doing so those who are awaiting the completion will no longer point an accusing finger and I will recover a modicum of self-respect.* After all, I feel that a few of my experiences may be noted, with benefit, by a student interested in communication in the technical world.

Graduating with a bachelor's degree in engineering physics (communication requirement: one semester of public speaking) I went to work for the National Advisory Committee for Aeronautics (NACA) as a research scientist. When the NACA became a part of the National Aeronautics and Space Administration (NASA), I was more concerned with product development. The working conditions were very good by my evaluations. Resources were adequate (a researcher will almost always claim a better job could be done with more money and what it can buy in simulations, manpower, supplies, and time), the environment was stimulating (exciting fields of inquiry, capable and generally compatible people), and a review process by which the research projects were maintained was consistent with needs.

To examine the process of communication as I experienced it at NASA, let me describe several assignments and leave the detail of communication analyses to the student and to those better qualified than I.

As a new employee just out of school, one might expect to do menial tasks, of course. One of my first assignments in the research environment was the plotting of curves, whereby it is possible to deduce a mathematical relationship or to check how closely the experimental data fit the theoretical curve. Today, of course, electronic curve plotters eliminate the tedium, except as it applies to the programmer. Whether an assignment is individually completed or performed with sophisticated technology, the scientist is concerned with determining what are meaningful data. What should be accepted and what should be rejected? How accurate are the standards we use for judgment? I have frequently asked myself the questions: What about data that were rejected on the basis of such situations as instrument error or nonstable set point? Were some of those data also meaningful? If so, what was the impact of discarding those data?

As in most research environments, we were constrained in design by a variety of limitations. I was assigned to create mechanical designs to convey concepts, materials, and dimensions for needed equipment such as a furnace capable of high-temperature materials testing. Did the need for limitations provide equipment (and resulting data) that could be misused by persons not fully understanding the limitations?

Report writing—formal communication—was the culmination of a research effort. After progress and findings had been reviewed by supervisors and agreement had been obtained that the results merited distribution, a draft report was prepared for supervisor approval. Corrections

---

* The author is obviously familiar with Maslow's Hierarchy of Needs. Chapter 5 will make this plain.

made, the report was submitted to an editorial committee that included a checker (responsible for accuracy of formulas, calculations, and references), a co-worker or two (not directly on the project), and a person attempting to ensure the report would be comprehensible to technical persons not in the same specialty area (described as a *mean* intelligence). The author of the report could expect sessions with the editorial committee to be lengthy and somewhat combative. Following additional corrections/approvals, the grammarians made their recommendations. Final corrections, duplication, distribution, and cataloguing were the responsibilities of the author(s). Communicating the results was part of the research assignment.

The communication examples, questions, and concerns I have described were basics to most of my assignments. Additionally, technical reviews as presenter or participant were common at various levels in both group and interpersonal settings. Again, the responsibility to examine and critique was as much a part of the job as actual manipulation of data.

Throughout, I found a pervasive, honest, ethical relationship among people, a sincere attempt to present findings with full disclosure of the limitations. And yet, we have witnessed a space-mission failure resulting in death. And digressing to other areas of science, we remember Nobel felt compelled to fund a commemoration of peace efforts because his discovery of dynamite was so devastating. We note the pollution of air, water, and land due to accidents arising from nuclear fission and the potential pollution from fission residues that require disposal. Disposal of toxins from manufacturing processes poses increasing problems, as does the use of toxins by inadequately informed people. The list can be continued. However, the point is that in each case the initial product was to improve the lot of the human race—from dynamite as a source of concentrated energy to pesticides that improve agricultural productivity and facilitate distribution.

So what about communication (besides the fact that a lack of communication contributed to the above-cited problems)? I see work being done to advance the discipline. As cause and effect become better defined, the potential for abuses grows. Can the student of communication help establish a course of action to forestall these abuses, as well as guide the technical community so they may better convey the totality of information?

QUESTIONS FOR DISCUSSION

1. How does Zalabak see human communication influencing scientific progress?

2. Can you identify other examples of scientific problems related to human communication?

3. How should scientists be trained in human communication?

A Guide to Case Development Analysis

Case studies help close the gap between reading about organizations and theory and knowing what to do in an actual organizational situation. Cases are examples or illustrations of organizational problems to which we apply the theory we study to determine how best to solve problems.

A case gives information about the organization, its people, and its problems. Information is used to analyze what contributed to the problems and determine how the problems presented in the case might be treated. When preparing an original case, your personal business experiences or interviews with organizational members can be used to identify interesting communication problems. Problems are usually presented (either orally or in writing) in story or narrative forms with enough clarification so others can generate solutions. Case development and analysis can be approached by a three-step process. The process begins by asking questions and developing answers in each of our competency areas: knowledge, sensitivity, skills and values.

1. Identify and Describe the Situation or Problem

KNOWLEDGE

What are the major and minor problems in the case?

What communication theories apply to these problems?

What organizational theories or perspectives are apparent?

What information is missing?

What assumptions are we making about the organization, its people, and their problems?

SENSITIVITY

Who or what appears to be most responsible for the communication problems?

What are the "shared realities" in the organization?

Are the principal individuals good communicators? If not, what are their limitations?

Are the principals in the case assuming responsibility for their communication behaviors?

SKILLS

What skills do the case principals exhibit?

What additional skills are needed?

How could these skills be developed?

What overall organizational skills are lacking?

What are the major organizational strengths?

VALUES

What is important or valuable to the involved individuals?

Do they share similar values?

How would you describe the culture of the organization?

Are individual and organizational goals compatible?

2. Develop Alternatives and Test the "Reality" of Possible Solutions

What should be done?

How many alternatives can be generated?

Can alternatives be combined?

What can be done?

Are the people involved willing to change?

3. Propose Solutions and Suggest Implementation Plans

Explain your reasoning for solution selection.

Identify who is responsible for what?

Determine a timetable for implementation.

Suggest how your solution might be evaluated.

The "What Do You Mean I'm Not Going to Graduate?" Case

Central University is a large midwestern school noted for its fine undergraduate liberal arts programs. All students entering the university are required to complete humanities, social science, mathematics, natural science, and foreign language requirements. The foreign language requirement has been strengthened in the last two years, and all students are required to complete four semesters of a language or pass a competency examination.

The foreign language requirement has not been received favorably by the student body. Petitions to the university's committee on academic progress often are requests for exceptions to the requirement in order to graduate in a desired semester. To minimize these complaints and better inform the student body about the nature of the requirements, the committee has asked that admissions and records revise Central's bulletin to place the requirements section in a more prominent position. The advising service also has been asked to name all juniors and seniors who have not completed the requirement.

Jane Jordan is one of the students who, in her second semester of her senior year, has received a notice from the advising office that she will not graduate on schedule because of a one-semester deficiency in Spanish. Jane is furious and goes to the head of the committee on academic progress with her complaint. Jane claims she was admitted to Central before the requirement was put in place and, although she had to drop out for two semesters to work, she should be graduated under her original admission requirements. Jane admits she was advised of the new requirement when she returned to Central but was assured by an advisor that she could get out of it because of her original admission date and generally good academic record. Jane further contends that she has a job waiting at the end of the semester and will be harmed if required to stay at Central another term. The head of the committee on academic progress ponders what to do.

QUESTIONS FOR DISCUSSION

1. What are the communication problems in this case?
2. Who is responsible?
3. Is Jane approaching the problem correctly?
4. What should the head of the committee do?

The "We Never Had to Advertise Before" Case

John Murphy and his father, Al, are arguing again. In fact, it seems they argue most of the time now. Today's argument is over whether or not to begin radio advertising for their appliance repair shop.

Al Murphy founded Murphy's Appliance Repair some twenty-five years ago. John literally grew up in his father's business and had been eager to finish college and prepare to take over daily operation when his father retired. Neither man had anticipated their numerous differences of opinion.

Al felt he knew the business better than anyone, that John's ideas were too new and costly for any successful operation. John, on the other hand, believed there was increasing competition in their part of town and that resting on past success was dangerous. John wanted to add additional automated machinery and advertise, as two of their competitors were doing. John saw the changes as progressive and necessary to the long-term survival of the business.

John had never had trouble communicating with his father before. He wondered what he could say to make his point. After all, the business had to support not only his father and mother but John's family as well. He had every right to make decisions if he was to have so much responsibility. Al felt much the same way. How could this be happening? He had looked forward to John's entrance into the business. Had college ruined his understanding of business? Wasn't it supposed to be just the other way around?

QUESTIONS FOR DISCUSSION

1. What is happening between John and Al?
2. Is advertising the real issue?
3. Are their values different?
4. What would you suggest that John do?
5. What can Al do?

SUMMARY OF COMPETENCY COMPONENTS:

KNOWLEDGE, SENSITIVITY, SKILLS, VALUES

KNOWLEDGE

Scientific Management viewpoint is concerned with bureaucracy, work design, and measurement.

Human Behavior viewpoint emphasized importance of individuals and peer groups.

Integrated Perspectives viewpoint merged both Scientific Management and Human Behavior assumptions with environment and culture.

SENSITIVITY

Assumptions about people influence assumptions about organizations.

Individual behavior is influenced by informal communication and culture.

SKILLS

Analysis skills are developed through application of Functional and Meaning-Centered approaches to Scientific Management, Human Behavior, and Integrated Perspectives ideas.

Analysis skills are practiced through case study.

VALUES

Cultural beliefs/values are important in organizations.

Values influence behavior.

REFERENCES AND SUGGESTED READINGS

Barnard, C. 1938. *The functions of the executive.* Cambridge, MA: Harvard University Press.

Cyert, R. M., and J. G. March. 1963. *A behavioral theory of the firm.* Englewood Cliffs, NJ: Prentice-Hall.

Deal, T., and A. Kennedy. 1982. *Corporate cultures: The rites and rituals of corporate life.* Reading, MA: Addison-Wesley.

Fayol, H. 1949. *General and industrial management,* trans. C. Storrs. London: Pitman & Sons.

Katz, D., and R. Kahn. 1966. *The social psychology of organizations.* New York: Wiley.

Lawrence, P., and J. Lorsch. 1969. *Developing organizations: Diagnosis and action.* Reading, MA: Addison-Wesley.

Likert, R. 1961. *New patterns of management.* New York: McGraw-Hill.

Lorsch, J., and P. Lawrence. 1970. *Studies in organization design.* Homewood, IL: Irwin.

McGregor, D. 1960. *The human side of enterprise.* New York: McGraw-Hill.

March, J. G., and H. A. Simon. 1958. *Organizations*. New York: Wiley.

Mayo, E. 1945. *The social problems of an industrial civilization*. Boston: Graduate School of Business Administration, Harvard University.

Ouchi, W. 1981. *Theory z*. Reading, MA: Addison-Wesley.

Pasmore, W. A., and J. J. Sherwood. 1978. *Sociotechnical systems: A sourcebook*. San Diego: University Associates.

Peters, T. J., and R. H. Waterman, Jr. 1982. *In search of excellence*. New York: Harper & Row.

Roethlisberger, F. J., and W. J. Dickson. 1939. *Management and the worker*. Cambridge, MA: Harvard University Press.

Simon, H. A. 1957. *Administrative behavior*. New York: Macmillan.

Smith, A. 1937. *The wealth of nations* (Cannon ed.). New York: Modern Library.

Taylor, F. W. 1913. *Principles of scientific management*. New York: Harper & Brothers.

Trist, E. L., and K. W. Bamforth. 1951. Some social and psychological consequences of the longwall method of coal-getting. *Human Relations* 4: 3–38.

Weber, M. 1947. *The theory of social and economic organization*, trans. A. Henderson and T. Parsons. New York: Free Press.

Woodward, J. 1965. *Industrial organization: Theory and practice*. London, New York: Oxford University Press.

PART ~II~

Organizational Communication: Roles/Relationships/Responsibilities

In Part One we described the need for communication competency in an information society. We went so far as to claim that organizational excellence depends on human communication and that organizations of today and tomorrow need a work force with communication knowledge, sensitivity, skills, and values. We discussed the Functional and Meaning-Centered approaches to understanding organizational communication and applied the two approaches to a variety of organizational problems. We also explored major organizational theories and their implications for communication. Part One was designed to develop *knowledge* about the process of communication and how that process can be observed in organizations. *Sensitivity* was developed through self-analysis and by exploring a variety of assumptions about human behavior. Analysis *skills* were practiced through self-examination and case studies. Finally, Part One attempted to contribute to *value* development by emphasizing the importance of communication for organizational excellence.

In Part Two, we change our focus from the organization as a whole to individuals and how they relate to organizations. We also identify individual competencies needed for organizational excellence. Part Two is designed to apply competencies you developed in Part One to your own participation in organizations. We will seek to develop knowledge, sensitivity, skills, and values important in supervisor, subordinate, and group relationships. We will also explore the important subjects of organizational conflict and leadership and management communication.

~ F I V E ~

Individuals in Organizations

Developing competencies through . . .

KNOWLEDGE

Describing the diversity in the work force

Describing intrapersonal and interpersonal experiences of individuals in organizations

Describing theories of motivation

Identifying elements of effective organizational messages

SENSITIVITY

Relating motivation to communication behaviors

Being aware of communication apprehension in organizational experiences

Understanding how perceptions of communication competencies affect work satisfaction

Distinguishing between barriers and positive attitudes for valuing diversity

Distinguishing between effective and ineffective message strategies and tactics

SKILLS

Valuing diversity

Practicing active listening

Critiquing and developing organizational messages

Practicing analysis capabilities

VALUES

Relating individual communication experiences to organizational identification, work performance, communication, and job satisfaction

Identifying personal needs in work settings

Relating valuing diversity to interpersonal effectiveness

Dave Green's First Real Job

Dave Green was excited. Today was his first day in the Human Resource Department of AMX Corporation, one of the best known management training firms in the country. Landing a job with AMX had not been easy. On his campus alone, ten candidates had interviewed with the AMX recruiter. He had been told AMX had over 200 total applications from which to choose.

Dave knew his degree in organizational communication was a good choice. Even so, he had been apprehensive about finding just the right job. The training position in the Human Resource Department was perfect, and working for Sally Johnson—one of the best trainers in the Midwest—was a real opportunity. Of course, he still worried about exactly what would be expected and whether he really was ready.

Dave's initial assignment was to work with a team of three experienced researchers and trainers to locate materials for a new training program Sally was developing. Although Sally had assured him that the three wanted more help, Dave wondered about his reception into the group. After all, they had been with AMX for several years and had worked together for Sally for more than two years. How would they feel about him becoming a member of the team?

As Dave prepared for his first meeting with Sally and the group he began to think about what he might say and ask. How should he describe his skills? What techniques could he use to best understand their expectations of him? What were his goals in this job?

As we study Chapter 5, we will follow Dave's experiences with AMX Corporation. We will try to understand his experiences as they might relate to our attempts to develop communication competencies important for working with supervisors, subordinates, and peers.

INTRODUCTION

It is not unusual to be both excited and apprehensive when we begin a new semester, a new job, or join a new volunteer group. We aren't completely sure what to expect. What will the people be like? Will our competencies meet the expectations of others? As individuals we bring skills and abilities to organizations and expectations about what we hope will happen. We want to be successful, but like Dave Green, we wonder if our communication competencies are appropriate to the task.

Think for a moment about the organizations of which you are a member. How did you feel when you first enrolled in your school, were hired for your job, or joined a new church? How do you feel now? How would you describe your organizational experiences? Which give you the most satisfaction?

In previous chapters we have described perspectives for understanding organizational communication and have studied major organizational theories. Now we will relate what we know about organizations as a whole to how individuals experience organizational life. Although we view organizations as entities where many people work together for goal achievement, all of us experience organizations as individuals. Understanding our individual experience is important for developing communication competencies that contribute to personal satisfaction as well as to overall organizational effectiveness.

This chapter is designed to contribute to our *knowledge* by defining and describing concepts of motivation and identifying primary characteristics of supervisor-subordinate and peer relationships. *Sensitivity* competencies are developed through awareness of individual predispositions for organizational communication behaviors and by identifying effective and ineffective message strategies and tactics. *Skills* are developed by applying *knowledge* and *sensitivity* competencies to case and transcript analysis, practicing active listening, and designing effective organizational messages. Finally, *values* are developed through awareness of the relationship of communication and organizational identification, work performance, and communication and job satisfaction.

INDIVIDUALS IN ORGANIZATIONS

Working in organizations is an important fact of life for almost everyone—so important, in fact, that for most of us our organizational experiences influence how we evaluate our individual self-worth and achievements. But how do we understand these experiences? How do they relate to developing communication competencies for organizational excellence?

An individual's organizational experiences result from the attitudes, beliefs, preferences, and abilities the individual brings to the organization, how the organization seeks to influence the individual, and what types of organizational relationships the individual develops. Each person brings to an organization his or her personal needs, predispositions for behavior, communication competencies, expectations, and skills. Individuals also develop relationships with supervisors, peers, and subordinates that become primary information sources about all aspects of organizational life. The organization, in turn, establishes goals, policies, procedures, and reward systems that influence individual expectations and job experiences.

An individual's relationship with his or her supervisor is one of the most important of the primary communication experiences in organizational life—so important, in fact, that the quality of this relationship usually determines how the individual identifies with the organization and determines the individual's job and organization satisfaction. Peers also are an important source of information and support. Communication experiences with supervisors and peers are so influential that they contribute to the quality and quantity of an individual's work. The research of J. David Pincus (1986) has related quality and quantity of work—job performance—to perceptions of organizational communication experiences. In particular, quality of supervisory communication and information exchange within peer groups has been significantly related to revenue and work load measures of the overall organization.

An individual's communication satisfaction, according to Cal Downs and Michael Hazen (1977), is really a "summing up" of individual experiences in organizations, particularly experiences with information flow and relationships. Communication satisfaction is important to individuals, as evidenced by numerous studies that have linked communication satisfaction to job performance and job satisfaction. In other words, individuals who are satisfied with organizational communication experiences are more likely to be effective performers and to be satisfied with their jobs than those who have less positive communication relationships.

Figure 5.1 illustrates the primary communication experiences of individuals in organizations and relates these experiences to organizational outcomes such as communication and job satisfaction. The next sections of this chapter explore intrapersonal and interpersonal experiences in organizations and identify strategies and tactics for increasing individual communication effectiveness. Chapter 6 discusses individuals and small-group experiences.

THE INTRAPERSONAL EXPERIENCE

Intrapersonal experience— comprises our personal needs, predispositions for behavior, communication competencies, and expectations.

Most of us want to identify with the organizations for which we work. We want to be thought of as good performers with high work standards. Certainly most of us want to be satisfied with organizational communication as well as other aspects of our jobs. Earlier we found that people's work satisfaction is related to a variety of organizational relationships. If this is true for us, it becomes important to understand what contributes to these relationships. Among the primary influences on our relationships with supervisors, peers, and subordinates are the individual characteristics we possess—characteristics that can be described as our **intrapersonal experience.** Our intrapersonal experience comprises our personal needs, predispositions for behavior, communication competencies, and expectations. Before we discuss ways of understanding the intrapersonal experience, we will return to Dave Green and his "first real job." We will look at what Dave brings to AMX as a way of understanding individual intrapersonal experiences within organizations.

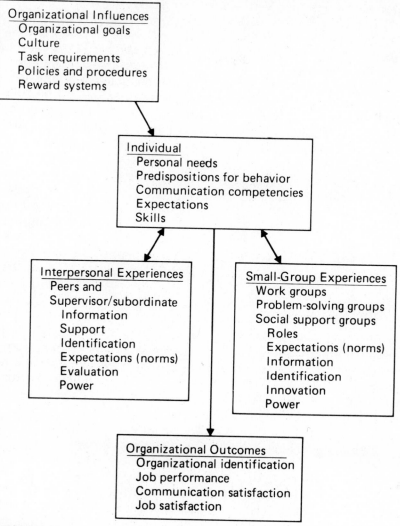

FIGURE 5.1
Individuals in organizations; primary communication experiences

Dave Green—The Intrapersonal Experience

Dave knows the AMX job will be a test of what he has learned. He has always been a top student. He was proud to be listed on honor rolls, and he graduated in the top 10 percent of his class. He has thought a lot about the AMX interview questions concerning his strengths and weaknesses and ultimate career goals.

Dave knows he has good verbal skills and has been able to work effectively in groups. In fact, on most group projects during his university days he volunteered to do the oral presentations—something many of his fellow students dreaded. In return, Dave has not always done his share of the research and writing. He remembers describing himself to the AMX interviewer as a leader, yet he wonders if that will be at all appropriate when he is the new member of an experienced work team. As Dave thinks about his new job he is inclined to wait and let others take the lead until he has more experience. After all, he wants the people at AMX to think he is competent and worthy of their decision to hire him.

As Dave begins his new job, he expects his work to be very different from his four years of college. He believes AMX is a top company with highly competent people. He is somewhat apprehensive about his ability to produce in a team of experienced researchers and trainers. Also, he believes his new boss will have high expectations of his abilities—abilities that as yet have not been thoroughly tested.

Motivation

Motivation—term to describe intrapersonal experiences that influence behaviors.

Dave Green would say he is beginning his new job at AMX with high **motivation.** He wants to succeed and looks forward to the chance to demonstrate his abilities. Chances are the AMX interviewers offered him the job because they, too, believed he was motivated to achieve. But what exactly is motivation and how does motivation relate to our intrapersonal experience and communication competency?

Put simply, *motivation* is the term we use to describe intrapersonal experiences that influence behavior. We don't see the motivation, but we see behavior. We infer that unseen internal reactions have motivated that behavior. Dave Green, for example, tells the interviewer he is eager to work for such a well-respected management training firm. Dave's statement is observable behavior. The interviewer, however, infers that Dave's statement of eagerness reflects his motivation to succeed at AMX. Taking the interview and Dave's qualifications as a whole, the interviewer decides Dave is positively motivated to behave in a way desirable to AMX. As a result, Dave gets the job.

Chances are all of us can recall times when we were highly motivated to do a good job and other times when we were not motivated at all. We recognize what "feeling motivated" is and can understand that in some way that feeling influenced our behavior. But what causes that internal experience? What happens to motivate us?

Social scientists take many different approaches to describe the somewhat ambiguous concept of motivation for behavior. Abraham Maslow, for example, contends that behavior is influenced by internal needs. He feels needs such as safety and security, prestige, and self-actualization are more important in understanding an individual's behavior than influences in the external environment. Frederick Herzberg, on the other hand, describes behavior as a result of both internal and external motivators, and B. F. Skinner views reinforcement from the external environment as the primary influence for behavior. In their criticism of need satisfaction theories, Gerald Salancik and Jeffrey Pfeffer provide an important link between motivation and communication theory when they propose that workers' job attitudes are a function of their communication activities.

Abraham Maslow (1908–1970)

Abraham Maslow (1954) is famous for what has been described as his **Hierarchy of Needs** theory, which proposes that human behavior seeks either to increase need satisfaction or to avoid a decrease in need satisfaction. According to Maslow, individuals focus attention on needs that are not met and are motivated to seek satisfaction of those needs. Maslow describes needs in an ascending hierarchy beginning with physiological needs, followed by safety and security needs, love and social belonging, esteem and prestige, and self-actualization (see Figure 5.2).

Physiological needs are the basic body needs of food, sleep, sex, and survival. Although these needs vary from individual to individual, Maslow contends that until these needs are reasonably well met, individuals do not focus their behavior on higher-level needs. From an organizational perspective, many physiological needs are met by the regularity of a paycheck, which provides food and basic physical survival.

Maslow believed that the satisfaction of *safety* and *security needs* also varied from individual to individual. What constitutes freedom from physical harm and security to one individual may not represent that same safety to another. Individuals in organizations satisfy their safety and security

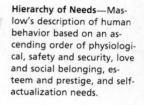

Hierarchy of Needs—Maslow's description of human behavior based on an ascending order of physiological, safety and security, love and social belonging, esteem and prestige, and self-actualization needs.

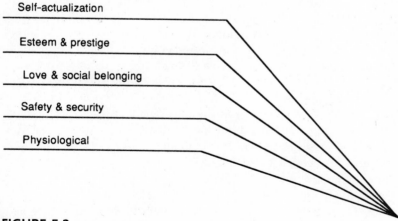

Self-actualization

Esteem & prestige

Love & social belonging

Safety & security

Physiological

FIGURE 5.2

Illustrates the need levels in Maslow's Hierarchy of Needs.

needs when they believe their jobs are relatively secure and when working conditions are free of physical harm.

Love and *social belonging needs* are met through family affiliations, friendships, and a variety of peer groups that provide social support and affection. As with all other needs, the degree to which individuals seek love and social belonging varies. Social belonging needs in organizations are generally thought of as being satisfied through peer and supervisory and subordinate relationships and through similarities between the organization's values and the values of individual members.

Maslow describes *esteem* and *prestige needs* as the desire for self-respect and the respect of others. Esteem and prestige are both internally defined and influenced by perceptions of what is prestigious to others. In organizations, esteem and prestige needs are satisfied through performance evaluation, job titles, status symbols, and the pride individuals feel in their work contributions.

Self-actualization is at the top of Maslow's hierarchy. According to Maslow, self-actualization is the belief that one has satisfied his or her full potential and is engaged in activities for which he or she is uniquely suited. As such, self-actualization cannot be explained in terms of a specific organizational responsibility or recognition but in terms of how an individual believes his or her abilities are used within the organizational setting.

Maslow's Hierarchy of Needs has several important implications for communication behavior. The theory implies that individual communication behavior in some way reflects an assessment of need satisfaction. Observation of individual communication behavior, therefore, can provide important evidence about what is motivational to an individual at a given time. The individual who communicates an insecurity about his or her acceptance in a work team may be focusing on low fulfillment of love and social belonging needs. A supervisor, according to Maslow, is unlikely to be able to motivate this individual by describing the prestige associated with a new job assignment that further removes the individual from peer approval.

Maslow's theory implies that it is not motivational to communicate about needs that are reasonably well met. Although money and fringe benefits are important, communication designed to motivate at these lower-level needs frequently does not accurately assess the love and social belonging, esteem and prestige, and self-actualization needs of individuals. Maslow's theory also suggests that if communication behavior in the organization does not meet the perceived needs of the individual, the individual will continue, in what is essentially healthy behavior, to seek need satisfaction. Thus, complaints and conflict that are often viewed as counterproductive organizational behaviors may be healthy individual behavior in pursuit of personal need satisfaction.

As Dave Green begins his job at AMX he is concerned about his acceptance in an experienced work team. Using Maslow's concepts we would say that Dave is concerned about his love and social belonging needs. He is likely, therefore, to pay particular attention to communication with his peers and to behave in ways he believes appropriate for their acceptance.

Frederick Herzberg (1923—   )

The **Motivation-Hygiene theory** of Frederick Herzberg (1966) emphasizes the influence of both internal and external factors in explaining human behavior. Herzberg's theory proposes that satisfaction and dissatisfaction are not polar opposites. In other words, what produces dissatisfaction in the work environment, if corrected, will not necessarily produce satisfaction or motivation. His research suggested that environmental factors (hygiene factors) such as status, interpersonal relations, supervision, policies, working conditions, and salary all influenced whether workers were dissatisfied. For example, if salaries were too low, dissatisfaction was predictable. However, if salary adjustments were made, satisfaction or motivation would not necessarily occur, although dissatisfaction might be lessened. The factors he found to be motivational were work itself, achievement, growth and responsibility, recognition, and advancement. Herzberg concluded that many organizations attempt to motivate workers through hygiene factors, when hygiene factors can only be expected to relate to whether workers are dissatisfied, not whether they are truly motivated. From a communication perspective, Herzberg's Motivation-Hygiene theory suggests that dissatisfaction can be relieved by satisfactory communication and action directed toward hygienic work factors. Motivation, however, will not be achieved by such communication. Motivational communication is more likely to be effective when directed to achievement, recognition, challenging work, increased responsibility, and growth and development.

Herzberg's concept of motivation, applied to Dave Green, suggests that Dave will be motivated by his desire to be competent (to achieve) in his new work setting. From the Herzberg perspective, Dave's apprehension about joining an experienced work team is based on his motivation for challenging work and growth and development.

B. F. Skinner (1904—   )

Skinner, in contrast to both Maslow and Herzberg, proposed that human behavior can be motivated and is influenced by **rewards** in the individual's environment. According to Skinner (1953), behavior reinforced through positive feedback or tangible rewards will be perpetuated, whereas behavior that does not receive positive reinforcement will be unlikely to continue. When applied to the organizational setting, the paycheck is a form of feedback that reinforces behavior expectations. Supervisors provide feedback on behavior to subordinates, and peer groups develop norms of expected behaviors that when exhibited by individuals, are rewarded with continued group membership. Skinner's theory does not take into account individual needs, as Maslow's does, or admit to complex relationships between satisfaction and dissatisfaction, as does Herzberg's Motivation-

Motivation-Hygiene theory—Herzberg's description of human behavior based on the influence of both internal and external factors. The theory proposes that satisfaction and dissatisfaction are not polar opposites and what produces dissatisfaction with work when corrected will not necessarily produce motivation.

Rewards—positive feedback or tangible reinforcements for organizational behaviors.

Hygiene theory. Skinner's theory does suggest that communication about rewards will be motivational only as long as "rewards" are linked to specific behaviors. In other words, if behavior is to be influenced, communication must be directed at specific behaviors and linkages must be understood by people the organization seeks to influence.

Skinner's theory of what motivates behavior suggests that Dave is joining AMX because of what he knows about the organization and his belief that he has landed a "prize" job. His "reward" in obtaining the job will probably influence his attempts to exhibit behaviors that support the norms of his new work team. According to Skinner, these norm-conforming behaviors, if supported by positive feedback or tangible rewards from his peers and supervisor, will motivate Dave to perpetuate their use and become one of the group.

Gerald Salancik (1943–   ) and Jeffrey Pfeffer (1946–   )

Social Information Processing—theory that proposes that a person's needs and attitudes are determined by the information available to them at any given time.

Salancik and Pfeffer (1978), in criticizing need satisfaction theories, propose that a person's needs and attitudes can be understood in terms of the **Social Information Processing** theory. This theory proposes that people's needs and attitudes are determined by the information available to them at any given time. Salancik and Pfeffer suggest three basic determinants of attitudes or needs: (1) the individual's perception of the job or task characteristics; (2) information the social environment provides to the individual about what attitudes are appropriate (i.e., social information); and (3) the individual's perception of the reasons for his or her past behaviors. Thus, Salancik and Pfeffer describe needs differently from the internal-drives portrayal of Maslow. Salancik and Pfeffer conceptualize needs as the results or outcomes produced by an individual's perceptions and by the social information available in the work environment.

Salancik and Pfeffer identify four ways in which social information influences attitudes: (1) overt, evaluative statements of co-workers directly shape individual worker attitudes; (2) frequent talk among co-workers about certain dimensions of the job and work environment focuses attention on what is considered to be important or salient in the work setting; (3) information from co-workers, or social information, helps interpret and assign meaning to environmental cues and events in the work setting; and finally, (4) social information influences the way an individual interprets his or her own needs. Thus, Salancik and Pfeffer argue that job attitudes are a result of social information in the work setting coupled with the consequences of past individual choices. The organization, then, can be viewed as having influence on attitudes by contributing information to the attitude formation process. The Social Information Processing theory challenges notions that individuals have stable, relatively unchanging internal needs. Salancik and Pfeffer propose that the communication activities of an organization act as a primary influence on attitude formation, which in turn is influential in understanding human behavior.

Dave Green's transition from school to AMX will help us understand the somewhat complex relationships proposed by Salancik and Pfeffer. Dave Green expresses a positive attitude about his experiences during college. The same Dave Green also expresses uncertainty about his ability to meet the expectations at AMX. Salancik and Pfeffer contend that the individual's perception of the job or task characteristics shape attitudes or needs. Thus, it is expected that Dave's perception of his competency will differ based on his understanding of the differences between college and AMX.

During college Dave made effective use of his verbal skills and ability to work in groups by volunteering to organize and make oral presentations researched and written by other classmates. Chances are Dave considered this an appropriate use of his abilities (the approach met his needs) at least in part because his classmates approved of his efforts in the group and made known their dread of doing the presentations themselves. In other words, they influenced Dave with social information: (1) overt, evaluative statements about Dave's positive contributions and (2) frequent talking about certain important dimensions of the project (oral presentations).

Also, Dave told the AMX interviewer he was a leader, yet we see that he is inclined to let others "take the lead" until he has more experience at AMX. From the Salancik and Pfeffer perspective, Dave's attitude probably is shaped by his assignment of meaning to environmental cues—specifically, the competence of the experienced team he is joining as a junior member. The Social Information Processing concept suggests that Dave does not have a stable "need to lead" and that the difference in this need between college and AMX is based on the social information available to him about the differences in the expectations and realities of the two environments.

Relating Communication and Motivation

Regardless of their differences in perspective, the theories of Maslow, Herzberg, Skinner, and Salancik and Pfeffer relate motivation and attitudes to communication experiences and behaviors. Research conducted by H. Wayland Cummings, Larry Long, and Michael Lewis exploring the relationship between communication and motivation also supports this strong link. Specifically, Lewis, Cummings, and Long (1983) found that individuals have a complex mix of intrinsic (internal) and extrinsic (external) motivators that, depending on their importance in a particular situation, influence how the individual responds to managing information, problem and solution identification, conflict management, and behavior regulation. Cummings, Long, and Lewis go so far as to suggest "that a highly motivated worker will be productive when the worker's communication preference (associated with the worker's motivational patterns) matches the managerial communication environment of the organization."

Earlier we inferred from Dave Green's communication behavior that he was highly motivated as he began his new job at AMX. To further illustrate the communication and motivation relationship, the statements in Figure 5.3 have been taken from transcripts of conversations with workers asked to describe what motivates them in their work. The statements have been categorized as they reflect the motivational theories of Maslow, Herzberg, Skinner, and Salancik and Pfeffer.

Predispositions for Organizational Communication Behaviors

Predispositions or preferences for organizational communication behaviors are an important part of an individual's intrapersonal organizational experience. *Predispositions* are personally held preferences for particular types of communication situations or behaviors. These preferences are a result of intrapersonal needs (motivation), past experiences, current information, and self-perception of communication competency. Predispositions for oral communication, for example, have been found to be related to our occupation choice, job satisfaction, productivity, advancement, and job retention. Thus, we infer that communication predispositions and preferences influence behavior and are therefore important for individual organizational experiences.

Communication Apprehension

Communication apprehension—predisposition for behavior described as an individual's level of fear or anxiety associated with either real or anticipated communication with others.

One of the most frequently researched of all communication predispositions is what James McCroskey (1982) has described as **communication apprehension** (CA). Generally defined as an individual's level of fear or anxiety associated with either real or anticipated communication with others, CA has been found to be meaningfully associated with such important organizational outcomes as occupation choice, perception of competence, job satisfaction, advancement, and job retention. In other words, individuals with high communication apprehension are more likely than others to be in jobs with low communication requirements, to believe themselves less competent than others, to exhibit lower job satisfaction than their counterparts, and to not advance in their organization as their technical skills might suggest they could. They will also spend less time than others with the organization.

Dave Green does not appear to be high in communication apprehension. His past experiences in groups suggest he will volunteer for public speaking situations and is generally comfortable with his verbal skills. He can be expected, more than a person with higher communication apprehension, to integrate with his work group and successfully use his abilities at AMX.

Leadership and Conflict Preferences

In addition to differing levels of apprehension, individuals differ in their desire to lead others and in their perception of what is effective leadership. Individuals also differ in how they approach conflict. *Leadership* and *conflict*

FIGURE 5.3
Worker Examples of Personal Motivation

Maslow's Hierarchy of Needs Theory

1. Physiological needs. "I work because I have to put food on the table."
2. Safety and security needs. "I like to work here because there is a real commitment to no layoffs. The last place I worked wasn't like that."
3. Love and social belonging. "The people I work with are my best friends; we would do anything for each other."
4. Esteem and prestige. "This job has given me the visibility I need to advance."
5. Self-actualization. "My work is ideally suited for my talents—in some ways it doesn't seem right to take money for doing what I love to do."

Herzberg's Motivation-Hygiene Theory

Hygiene Factors:
1. Salary. "The pay here is good and I give them a good return on their money."
2. Supervision. "I like my supervisor. We were really unhappy with the previous guy."
3. Status. "I like having my own office and a secretary. I never had that before."

Motivation Factors:
1. Achievement. "I really feel a sense of accomplishment in this job."
2. Work content. "The work is challenging and I think we are putting out a good product."
3. Responsibility. "They let us take real responsibility here. People expect the best but they don't always look over your shoulder."

Skinner's Positive Reinforcement Theory

1. Rewards. "We get a bonus if we outproduce our quota."
2. Rewards. "My supervisor was really complimentary about the design of the new system. I believe my efforts are recognized."

Salancik and Pfeffer's Social Information Processing Theory

1. Social information. "My boss really helped me identify what was important for this job. I think I have responded with efforts that are recognized by the organization."
2. Social information. "My co-workers really helped me learn the ropes. You can make a lot of mistakes in this job if you don't learn what your work team needs and wants."

preferences have been theorized to influence choice of communication strategies and tactics in leadership and conflict situations. Numerous researchers have described both leadership and conflict predispositions or preferences in terms of an individual's combined concern for tasks or goals and people relationships. These two concerns combine with past experiences and an assessment of the present situation to influence behavior. Various predispositions for leadership and conflict behaviors are generally described as preferences for collaboration, compromise, avoidance, competition, or accommodation. For example, an individual with a strong *competitive* predisposition may not cooperate with the ideas of others in the same manner as an individual with a *collaborative* or *accommodative* predisposition. And the individual with strong *avoidance* predispositions may attempt to avoid leadership responsibilities and conflict situations as would the person with high communication apprehension. These preferences will be described in detail in Chapters 7 and 8, and you will be provided with an opportunity to assess your individual predispositions for leadership and conflict.

Communication Competency

Individuals' perceptions of their communication competencies—knowledge, sensitivity, skills, and values—influence their organizational experiences. When individuals believe their competencies are lower than others, it may well limit the responsibilities they will accept. On the other hand, individuals who assess their competencies as comparable to others may willingly accept new responsibilities as challenging and worthwhile. Perception of competency is, of course, related to communication apprehension and leadership and conflict preferences. But it is also related to past experiences, the presence or absence of particular skills, and deliberate attempts to improve competencies. As such, perception of competency can be described as a summing up of preferences and predispositions for organizational communication behavior.

INTERPERSONAL EXPERIENCES

Much of our time in organizations is spent interacting with other people. A variety of interpersonal communication relationships is important for individual job satisfaction. This variety is important in our understanding of yet another dimension of how individuals experience organizations. As you might expect from our discussion of the intrapersonal experience, predispositions and preferences influence the types of interpersonal relationships individuals establish. However, preferences are inadequate to explain fully what happens in what we call *primary dyadic relationships* in organizations. The relationships supervisors and subordinates and peers establish are governed not only by individual predispositions but also by important task and social considerations as well as increasing diversity in the work place. Before we explore the primary interpersonal relationships of supervisors and their subordinates and individual peer interactions, we will return to Dave Green and observe some of his early **interpersonal experiences** at AMX.

Interpersonal experiences— descriptions of important one-on-one organizational relationships such as supervisors and subordinates and peer to peer.

Dave Green—Interpersonal Experiences

Dave was pleased that John, the senior writer on the team, had asked him to lunch. Dave had worried that John might treat him like a kid because John did remind Dave a bit of his own father. He could learn a lot from John and certainly wanted John to think he was doing his job. Maybe John could fill him in on what his boss, Sally Johnson, really expected. The first few weeks of Dave's job at AMX had left him both elated and confused. Sally was friendly and seemed anxious for him to succeed, yet he wasn't sure what her expectations were. She had assigned him to do some research for part of the new project, but organizing and presenting the material was left up to Dave. Dave wasn't comfortable with asking her just what she wanted for the end product. He wasn't sure if Sally wanted a particular approach or didn't care as long as the material was good. John had told him yesterday that Sally would listen to a variety of approaches if the information was interesting and important. Dave was somewhat apprehensive about what Sally would find interesting. This lunch with John was timely. Maybe he could run some ideas past him and get a better feel for what he should do.

Dave's dilemma about his assignment is not unusual. Establishing expectations in supervisor-subordinate relationships can be difficult, especially in the beginning of a job. Dave is fortunate to have a peer like John who can help him define Sally's expectations and give him support as he adjusts to new challenges and ways of doing things.

We say Dave is fortunate to have John's support because research tells us that primary dyadic relationships are important to overall job satisfaction. Successfully meeting Sally's expectations will influence not only how Sally feels about Dave, but also Dave's entire organizational experience. As researchers Sue DeWine and Frank Barone (1984) have suggested, "perceived organizational communication relationships are considered to be the most important contributor to job satisfaction as an organizational outcome." Additionally, Gerald Goldhaber, Michael Yates, D. Thomas Porter, and Richard Lesniak (1978) reported that the most important organizational relationships are those closest to the individual and that "maintaining an effective relationship with an employee's immediate supervisor is, thus, the most important correlate of job satisfaction." Given these findings, we can see why it is important to understand how we form relationships in a diverse work force, and in particular how supervisor and subordinate and peer-to-peer relationships influence our organizational experiences.

A Diverse Work Force

Most organizations employ men and women of differing ages, ethnicity, race, and values. The paid work force of today and tomorrow is characterized by a diversity of people that is only expected to increase as we approach the year 2000. Most of us will form as many interpersonal relationships in organizations with people who are different from us as with those with whom we have much in common. William Johnson (1987), in the Hudson Institute's famous *Workforce 2000* report, describes **work force diversity** by five demographic "facts": (1) The population and overall work force are growing more slowly than at any time since 1930; (2) the number of younger workers is declining as the average age of the work force and population rises; (3) women will continue to enter the work force in record numbers; (4) minorities will be a larger proportion of the new labor force; and (5) immigrants will increase their participation as workers at the highest level since World War I. Johnson refers to these trends as "facts" because everyone who will be working in the year 2000 has been born, and over 60 percent already are in the paid work force. Johnson reports, "The cumulative impact of the changing ethnic and racial composition of the labor force will be dramatic. The small net growth of workers will be dominated by women, blacks, and immigrants. White males, thought of only a generation ago as the mainstays of the economy, will comprise only 15 percent of the net additions to the labor force between 1985 and 2000."

The work force is increasingly diversified by women, minorities, immigrants, the overall aging of workers, and the increased participation by the physically challenged. The resulting differences in communication styles and values all stimulate our abilities to form effective interpersonal relationships. Diverse people bring different intrapersonal attitudes, experiences, expectations, and competencies to organizations. These differences can contribute to organizational effectiveness when those with differing styles and values work together in interpersonal relationships characterized by mutual understanding and satisfaction. As Dave Green enters AMX he will experience what diversity can contribute in generating new and better training designs. Part of his experience will come from understanding how interpersonal relationships are formed.

Forming Interpersonal Relationships

Most relationships in organizations begin on a relatively impersonal basis. We base our understanding of people on what we know about their membership in a specific group, culture, or role and make predictions about communication on general versus individual, specific information. Our effectiveness in impersonal relationships is related to our awareness of

Work force diversity—description of workers that emphasizes differences in age, sex, race, ethnicity, and values.

differences and similarities in groups and our willingness to test the accuracy of our understanding. Additionally, effectiveness is related to our ability to accept differences as legitimate and important for organizational effectiveness. Dave Green begins his relationship with Sally Johnson based on his understanding of professional women and his expectations of what managers do. As Dave becomes acquainted with Sally, the relationship becomes more interpersonal, with Dave and Sally responding to each other not just as members of groups but also as unique individuals. Joseph DeVito (1988) describes this process of relationship development: ". . . in impersonal encounters the social or cultural role of the person tells us how to interact, while in personal or interpersonal encounters the psychological role of the person tells us how to interact." In general we can say that as relationships develop we gather information that helps us establish the general norms or rules of how our interactions will progress.

Interpersonal relationships in organizations are formed for important task and social considerations. Unlike our personal relationships, the organization actually structures for us many interpersonal encounters necessary for task accomplishment. To become effective in these diverse relationships, it is important to understand how we are attracted to others and how the impressions we form influence our communication behaviors.

We are attracted to others by physical and personality characteristics. We attribute, for example, more positive characteristics to those we identify as physically attractive than to their less attractive counterparts. Research also indicates that we are most likely to find as attractive those individuals who are similar to us in attitudes and beliefs and in relatively close physical proximity. The influences of similarity and physical proximity often prove problematic when establishing interpersonal relationships in organizations. The organizational requirement to work with those very different from us and in both close and distant proximity challenges us to examine how we form impressions and how we evaluate the competencies of others. In other words, do we evaluate as more competent and worthy of trust those organizational members who are most like us and with whom we have frequent contact? What are the implications of such an evaluation?

In addition to evaluations based on similarity and physical proximity, we tend to like most those individuals who reward or reinforce us. We prefer people who compliment rather than criticize. Again this pattern of impression formation, while certainly understandable, can limit the amount of developmental feedback we solicit or accept from diverse organizational members. Positive feedback, although comforting, does not always stimulate the growth necessary to increase our competency.

Although research does suggest that we are most comfortable with those similar to us and those who reinforce us, for certain of our characteristics we form positive impressions of those who have complementary rather than similar characteristics. For example, talkative individuals may form their most satisfying relationships with less talkative peers, and some supervisors may prefer submissive to more dominant subordinates. In general, however, research suggests that we are most likely to form positive impressions of those whom we find physically attractive; have similar attitudes to ours; and are of the same race, religion, age, and general social class.

We are more likely to establish satisfying interpersonal relationships based on similarity than relationships characterized by diversity. The implications for organizational effectiveness are obvious. Fully competent organizational members must not limit themselves only to the familiar but must be open to establishing satisfying and effective interpersonal relationships with both similar and dissimilar others. Dave Green will face this challenge as he joins members of a team differing in age, sex, and ethnicity.

Supervisors and Subordinates

The *supervisory-subordinate relationship* can be described as the primary interpersonal relationship structured by the organization. Because it is formed to support task and job requirements, almost everyone in an organization—except perhaps at the very top of the hierarchy—is involved in such a dyad. Dave Green and Sally Johnson form the supervisor-subordinate dyad of our AMX case.

Both supervisors and subordinates bring a wide variety of personal characteristics and predispositions to their relationships. The interaction of these characteristics influences the satisfaction each person has with the other and helps determine the overall effectiveness of the relationship. A supervisor, for example, who thinks a subordinate shares similar values is more likely to view that subordinate as competent. Subordinates, on the other hand, are more likely to be satisfied with both work and supervision if they perceive a high degree of communication competency in the relationship. Specifically, the work of Anthony Smith and Susan Hellweg (1985) found that "a subordinate's satisfaction with his work and supervision is correlated with the communication competence of both the subordinate and supervisor as perceived by the subordinate." A subordinate's perception of the supervisor's ability to listen, respond quickly to subordinate messages, and be sensitive and understanding was the strongest predictor of satisfaction with both work and supervisor. Subordinates' satisfaction with their supervisors also was found to be directly related to their perception of their own personal communication competence.

Other studies support the importance of communication competency for the supervisor-subordinate relationship. Numerous studies report that supervisors who are high in communication apprehension are not as well liked as those lower in apprehension, and highly apprehensive subordinates are not as likely as others to seek supervisory positions. Furthermore, Gary Richetto (1969) has found that the credibility of the supervisor is more important than organizational status in determining who is approached for task, political, and social information.

What is the nature of communication between supervisors and subordinates? For one thing, it is frequent and time consuming. Supervisors may spend from one-third to two-thirds of their time communicating with subordinates. These interactions are face to face for the most part, with supervisors initiating mostly discussions concerning task requirements and performance expectations. The effectiveness of these messages contributes to subordinates' job satisfaction and quality of work. Subordinates want interaction with their supervisors and in fact are more likely to seek informal help from their supervisors than from peers or their own subordinates.

Research on supervisor-subordinate communication reports a "positivity bias" in upward communication. Paul Krivonos (1982) has summarized many of the findings about upward communication in the following four categories: (1) Subordinates tend to distort upward information, saying what they think will please their supervisors; (2) subordinates tend to filter information and tell their supervisors what they, the subordinates, want them to know; (3) subordinates often tell supervisors what they think the supervisor wants to hear; and (4) subordinates tend to pass personally favorable information to supervisors while not transmitting information which reflects negatively on themselves.

John Athanassiades (1973) has found that upward distortion is more likely to occur if the subordinate has advancement aspirations and has some degree of insecurity in his or her job. In a classic study, William Read (1962) reported that trust was a major factor supporting accuracy in upward communication. Furthermore, subordinate mobility aspirations and supervisory ability to influence mobility aspirations lowered trust levels and interfered with accurate upward communication. Karlene Roberts and Charles O'Reilly (1974) have reported that trust in a supervisor is the most important factor for open, upward communication—more important than mobility aspirations of the subordinate or perceptions of the influence of the supervisor. In more recent work Janet Fulk and Sirish Mani (1986) have suggested that the perception of supervisors' downward communication, or the extent to which supervisors are perceived as actively withholding information, influences the accuracy of upward messages. The more the supervisor withholds, the more subordinates withhold and distort. In general, we can say that if trust levels between supervisors and subordinates are low and if subordinates have mobility aspirations that they believe their supervisors can influence, there is likely to be a positivity bias that distorts upward communication.

We can certainly see why individuals want to be positively perceived by their supervisors. But we can also readily understand that a bias for positive upward communication may not be effective for the organization. When a positivity bias distorts upward communication, supervisors may not receive timely information about problems. Thus, needed information about innovation and change may be slow in coming, particularly if the supervisor is perceived as resistant to new ideas. Trust between supervisors and subordinates is the key to improving accurate communication and reversing the possible negative effects of a positivity bias. And trust is established through the communication competencies both parties bring to relationships. In other words, the knowledge, sensitivity, skills, and values exhibited by both supervisors and subordinates contribute to the quality of relationships and to ultimate effectiveness.

The relationship between a supervisor and subordinate is influenced not only by the amount of openness and support between the two but also by the amount of influence the supervisor has in satisfying the subordinate's needs. Much research supports the notion that subordinates base upward influence messages on their perception of how their supervisor attempts to influence them, the ability or power of the supervisor to influence others positively on behalf of his or her subordinates, and the perception on the part of subordinates about whether or not upward influence will indeed affect organizational decisions.

One of the important characteristics of supervisor-subordinate communication is the frequent gap in information and understanding between what the supervisor perceives and what a subordinate believes to be true. Supervisors and subordinates frequently differ on such important issues as basic job duties, performance expectations, amount and quality of communication exchange, and desirability of subordinate participation in decision making. John Hatfield, Richard Huseman, and Edward Miles (1987) reported that supervisors overestimate, according to subordinates, the amount of positive verbal recognition they give. Additionally, supervisors report giving less negative feedback than their subordinates report receiving. Finally, the greater the perceived gap in verbal recognition, the lower the subordinate's satisfaction with supervision and overall job satisfaction. Additionally, Eric Eisenberg, Peter Monge, and Richard Farace (1984) have reported that supervisors and subordinates are more likely to evaluate each other highly when agreement or similarity between personal attitudes and predicted attitudes about the communication rules of others is high.

After being exposed to some significant findings from the research on supervisor-subordinate relationships, how would you advise Sally and Dave? Describe the adequacy of the performance expectations she has established. How can she build trust with Dave? What should Dave do? Think about any supervisor-subordinate relationships in which you have been involved. How candid were you in upward communication? Describe what trust means to you.

Peers

Although secondary in importance to supervisor-subordinate relationships, *peer relationships* are an important part of an individual's organizational experiences. Relationships with peers are characterized by both task and social interaction: Peers communicate job information, advice, evaluation of performance, and personal feedback. Peers help us "learn the ropes" and identify with the organization.

Few research studies have focused on the one-to-one aspect of peer relationships. The studies that do exist, however, support the importance of peer interactions for providing integration, or a sense of belonging, in organizational life. For example, individuals who are high in communication apprehension are less likely than others either to send or to receive integrative messages at the peer level. These same individuals also report less communication participation overall than their peers and lower overall communication satisfaction. On the other hand, individuals who have been promoted to management and those who expect vertical mobility are more likely than others to have developed a sense of belonging with their peers and organization.

In recent work, Beverly Davenport Sypher and Theodore Zorn, Jr. (1987) described how peers evaluate each other in terms of liked and disliked co-workers. Liked co-workers were most frequently depicted as considerate, personable, and exhibiting integrity-related behaviors. The higher in the organization the employee and the more he or she had mobility aspirations, the more ability to influence was wanted from liked peers. Lack of integrity led the list of descriptors for disliked co-workers followed by self-centered and insecure behaviors. The Sypher and Zorn research specifically addresses the importance in peer relationships of the sensitivity and value components for communication competency.

Peers exchange information about job requirements and are in a position to give advice without formally evaluating performance. They can help each other solve problems and determine what approaches are best with particular supervisors. Dave Green, for example, hopes that John will be able to clarify his first assignment from Sally. Dave has positive expectations about his interactions with John. Peer relationships, however, are not always as positive as the one Dave and John share.

Peers can withhold important information from each other, contributing to a variety of problems. In an exit interview conducted in a highly successful West Coast research and development lab, one computer engineer claimed that both of his peers were aware that the line of reasoning he was using for his design had been rejected previously by their manager. Neither peer shared that information, permitting the engineer to pursue six months of research with a high likelihood of failure. When asked why the manager did not know of the line of inquiry the engineer was pursuing, the engineer replied that his peers had advised him to be somewhat vague with his manager, a man who rarely examined the specifics of the projects under his direction. Was the engineer set up to fail? We are not sure from the interview but are convinced that his peer relationships were destructive and probably contributed to an organizational performance that did not reflect his abilities or the needs of the company.

INCREASING INTERPERSONAL EFFECTIVENESS

Thus far we have examined intrapersonal and interpersonal experiences common in organizational life. We have attempted to understand how motivation influences communication behavior and how dyadic relationships are formed and shaped through communication. We have described the importance of our own personal communication competency and our perception of the competency of others as it relates to satisfaction with interpersonal relationships and overall job satisfaction. We have not, however, identified specific skills individuals can use to improve communication effectiveness. Now we will discuss the importance of valuing diversity, describe active listening, identify descriptive message strategies, and discuss a process for designing effective organizational messages.

Valuing Diversity

Barriers and Positive Approaches

Understanding that the work force is diverse does not automatically give us the ability to relate effectively to that diversity. In fact, most of us have had uncomfortable interactions with people who seemed to discount us and our abilities. We, in turn, probably have left others with that same sense of uneasy concern. As we consider our personal communication competency, we can increase our effectiveness by understanding barriers to **valuing diversity** and positive approaches helpful in increasing understanding.

Valuing diversity—ability to understand and appreciate the contributions that differences in people can make to organizations.

There are several important barriers to valuing diversity that help explain problems that frequently occur among men and women of differing ages, ethnicity, race, and values. For each barrier there are positive approaches that can improve effectiveness. The following discussion of barriers and positive approaches will help us examine our personal behaviors and better understand others.

Barrier One: Preconceptions and beliefs that foster inaccurate information and confusion between perceptions of behaviors and actual behaviors.

Carl Carmichael (1988) described the impact of beliefs that foster inaccurate information when he discussed cultural communication, which "has perpetuated myths of aging that have become so widely accepted they are all but impossible to change, even in the face of recent scientific evidence to the contrary. Consider a few salient examples and check your own beliefs in each case: When people get old, they can expect increased memory loss. You can't teach an old dog new tricks. Intelligence declines in old age." Carmichael goes on to explain that these beliefs persist despite gerontological research that disputes their accuracy. And these beliefs have obvious implications for organizations with a growing number of workers past age forty. Are training classes populated with people of all ages or are younger workers given preference? Who has the most opportunity to influence decisions? How might beliefs and preconceptions about aging block organizational effectiveness?

Judy Pearson (1988) has illustrated how we confuse perceptions and reality when males and females behave similarly in organizations but are evaluated differently. Specifically, Pearson stated, "we may view a given behavior of a woman as negative, but we may judge the same behavior to be positive when a man exhibits it. For instance, a businesswoman may be labeled 'aggressive, pushy, and argumentative,' whereas her male counterpart who exhibits the same behavior may be viewed as 'ambitious, assertive, and independent.' Countless studies have demonstrated that when women and men engage in identical behavior, the behavior is devalued for the woman."

Positive Approach: Personalize knowledge and perceptions.

We can learn to separate our preconceptions, beliefs, and attitudes from actual behaviors. We can continually open our awareness to new information and new ways of understanding others. We can understand that knowledge is individual in nature and that others may legitimately view what is factual or correct very differently from us. As Brent Ruben (1988) has so aptly suggested, "People who recognize that their values, beliefs, attitudes, knowledge, and opinions are their own—and not necessarily shared by others—often find it easier to form productive relationships than persons who believe they know *The Truth*, and strive to 'sell' their own perceptions, knowledge, skills, and values to others." In our organizational relationships we can learn to describe what is accomplished, the merit of an idea, or the quantity of work performed. We can consciously separate, or personalize, these descriptions from beliefs about people of a given age, sex, race, or ethnic group.

Barrier Two: Stereotypes that limit the potential contributions of individuals based on their membership in a group or class.

Stereotypes simplify our ability to understand the world by making predictions about people based on the group or class to which they most obviously belong. Stereotypes emerge from basic, widely believed characteristics of a given group. Although stereotyping in a diverse environment makes the world more predictable and deceptively approachable, in and of itself stereotyping invites inaccuracy and undervalues diversity. Stereotypes emerge not only about specific groups or classes of people but also about who should be more powerful, exhibit dominance in interrelationships, and generally engage in social control. Edith Folb (1988) has described the "top dog" stereotype of our society: "Within the United States, those most likely to hold and control positions of real—not token—power and those who have the greatest potential ease of access to power and high status are still generally white, male, able-bodied, heterosexual, and youthful in appearance if not in age." Put simply, stereotypes give us a false aura of similarity and predictability that limits individual potential.

Positive Approach: Tolerance for ambiguity.

Learning to tolerate and value ambiguity is the positive counterpart to the negative effects of stereotyping. An attitude of tolerating ambiguity accepts as normal an environment that requires us to know people as individuals, not as members of a group or class. A tolerance for ambiguity is a sensitivity competency important as we enter new situations of all types. Frustration and discomfort may be normal reactions to ambiguity, but the "sorting through and making sense" of diverse relationships is an essential characteristic for interpersonal effectiveness. Brent Ruben (1988) has suggested that tolerance for ambiguity and tolerance for the lack of control one senses in new situations substantially assist efforts to integrate into new environments successfully.

Barrier Three: Prejudices that produce negative emotional reactions to others.

According to Richard Brislin (1988), "when people react negatively to others on an emotional basis, with an absence of direct contact or factual material about the others, the people are said to behave according to prejudice." Prejudice arises from beliefs that given groups of people are generally inferior or that a given group is interfering with important basic values. Prejudice is associated with discomfort about the unfamiliar and associated with behaviors we personally find offensive. The chances are we have all had prejudices at one time or another. We react emotionally and negatively to others without accurate information or even direct personal contact. Prejudiced behavior can be overt, as in refusal to work with a given group of people, or subtle, as in appearing to accept an individual as equal while carefully controlling the amount of influence he or she can exert in any given situation. Prejudice limits interpersonal relationships by arbitrarily devaluing groups of individuals based on negative emotional reactions. And as we have previously discussed, anything that hampers effective communication limits organizational effectiveness.

Positive Approach: Nonjudgmentalness.

All of us want to feel valued as individuals. Prejudice, or prejudging on the basis of the group to which we obviously belong, robs us of our individuality and limits effective interpersonal relationships. Nonjudgmentalness, or the positive opposite of prejudice, is exhibited by people who give others an opportunity to explain themselves. Nonjudgmental people base their reactions—whether positive or negative—on explanations, not group membership. Nonjudgmentalness requires active listening (a skill we will dicuss later in this chapter) and a willingness to base our evaluations on what Brent Ruben (1988) has described as "a reasonably complete understanding of the other's point of view. When persons believe they have been fully and attentively listened to, they are generally much more receptive to hearing reactions—whether positive or negative. In addition to being of use in improving the fidelity of information transmission, non-evaluative postures seem likely to increase the receiver's regard for the source of nonevaluative messages, and thereby improve the quality of the relationships.''

Barrier Four: Stylistic differences in personal communication that inhibit interpersonal relationships.

We all have style, personal and individual expressions of attitudes about ourselves and our culture. We speak, dress, and behave nonverbally with personal style influenced by culture. We develop vocabulary, syntax, idioms, slang, and dialects reflecting both our past and our present. Our speech style has been developed within the context of our background. What we view as appropriate and effective is a result of our evaluation of our past and present experiences. The same is true for our dress and nonverbal behaviors. Although we may recognize how our style develops, many of us remain uncomfortable with others who have differing styles. Some people appear aggressive and threatening when they are reflecting their own culturally acceptable behaviors. Others physically stand too close, invading our personal space. We move away, signaling a form of disrespect we do not intend. When others are enthusiastic in speech we may consider them illogical, based on our preference for details. We become uncomfortable with each other and thereby limit our interpersonal effectiveness. Style differences frequently block the substance of what we can contribute to each other.

Positive Approach: Display of respect.

A display of respect for differences begins with the attitude that differences are desirable. Respect includes specific recognition that although stylistic differences are normal, they are a possible source of misunderstanding. A display of respect includes active listening and nonverbal behaviors that encourage interactions with others. A display of respect also includes monitoring our own behaviors to minimize misunderstanding of our intentions. A display of respect is a sensitivity competency based on a genuine valuing of diversity.

The barriers and positive apporaches we have just discussed are obviously not the only ones important for interpersonal effectiveness. What other barriers have you observed? How might they be applied to the organizational setting? Next we will consider some of the specific communication skills necessary for valuing diversity and establishing effective interpersonal relationships within organizations.

Active Listening

Myths and Barriers

Listening is as fundamental to effective communication as talking. It is important in organizations. Supervisors talk and incorrectly assume subordinates are listening; groups engage in lively debate, hearing each other but not arriving at similar meanings; organizational members argue without understanding that they support essentially the same position.

Active listening—processes of hearing, assigning meaning, and verifying our interpretations. Increases the accuracy of message reception, enabling responses based on what was said, not on what might have been said.

There are several important myths about listening and barriers to **active listening** that help explain the ineffectiveness described in our examples. The following discussion of myths about listening and barriers to active listening will help us understand our personal listening habits and the listening habits of others.

Myth One: Listening and hearing are the same thing.

Fact: Hearing is the physiological process in which sound waves strike the eardrum, creating vibrations for transmission to the brain. Listening extends the physiological process to the assignment of meaning to sounds. Listening is therefore essential for message decoding.

Myth Two: Listening and hearing are physiological processes.

Fact: Hearing is a natural physiological process, but effective listening extends the physiological process of hearing into the skill of accurate decoding and assignment of meaning. In fact, more people speak well than listen well, although what we choose to say in most situations is a result of our listening skill.

Myth Three: Everyone listening to the same message receives the same message.

Fact: Because listening involves individual decoding and assignment of meaning, listening will be different for everyone.

In addition to myths that confuse listening and hearing, several important barriers to effective listening (the act of receiving and interpreting communication) have been identified. First described by Ralph Nichols (Nichols and Stevens, 1957), listening barriers are important for understanding individual habits that interfere with accurate message reception.

Barrier One: Labeling communicators and subjects as uninteresting or unimportant.

Although at times these labels may be accurate, many of us determine early in an interaction or presentation that we don't understand the subject, don't like the person, or find little of interest or importance in the message. We then tune out the speaker and spend our time thinking about other matters. By not listening to the message we have no way to assess accurately the value of what we might have heard.

Barrier Two: Emotionally resisting messages.

Often we react quickly to emotionally charged words or subjects. Internally we think of ways to respond to the speaker and argue our position. In this process we often quit listening to what is being said. We make judgments and respond to those judgments as if the speaker's position was accurately known to us. Criticisms from supervisors and peers often are met with emotional listening resistance. We hear only the negatives and do not attend to offers of help or ways to improve our performance. We are overstimulated and do not accurately receive messages that could help us grow and develop.

Barrier Three: Criticizing personal style rather than messages.

We often find ourselves criticizing the way a message is presented and ignoring its content or value. We don't like the message being "read" to us, we find the speaker lacking in experience, or we don't care for the negative tone of our boss. Our listening focuses on delivery and approach. Stylistic elements rather than content capture our attention.

Barrier Four: Failing to identify listening distractions.

Believe it or not, listening for facts can be distracting. Trying to listen accurately for a series of facts is not only difficult but also frequently distracts from the overall meaning of the message. Taking notes can distract from meaning, as can attempts to memorize what we are hearing. Physical noise, interruptions, and unidentified sounds also contribute to ineffective listening.

Barrier Five: Faking attention.

Many of us get into the habit of faking attention whether the speaker is interesting or not. We have a lot on our minds and use our listening time for reflecting. We develop behaviors such as head nodding and eye contact that are designed to make the speaker believe we are listening. In reality we have tuned in to our own special world. At times we are not even aware we have begun to fake attention. Most of us can recall a time when we intended to listen and suddenly realized that we had not heard a word. Obviously, we miss most of the message and reduce our chances for accurate communication.

Barrier Six: Misusing thought speed and speech speed differential.

We can think three to four times faster than we talk. Thus, we have time for our minds to wander as we attempt to listen. For most people, the thought speed and speech speed difference is not used to increase listening effectiveness but to think of other subjects while another person is speaking. We sometimes think of our own response, we think of subjects unrelated to the speaker's message, and we use the time to jump from subject to subject. Listening experts tell us our time would be better spent in internally restating the speaker's message, drawing analogies and examples related to the subject, and determining what questions to ask. In other words, effective listeners use the differential time to make sure they understand the message.

Guidelines for Good Listening

Active listening includes the processes of hearing, assigning meaning, and verifying our interpretations. Skill in active listening supports effective communication by increasing the accuracy of message reception. Accurate message reception, in turn, enables better responses—responses based on what was said, not on what we think might have been said.

Active listening begins with an atittude about our role in the communication process. A positive active listening attitude begins with a genuine concern for understanding messages as others intend—to sense meaning from another person's point of view. This attitude includes empathy for others and a willingness to control our emotions to facilitate mutual understanding. Skillful active listeners control mental arguments, avoid jumping to assumptions and conclusions, and are careful not to stereotype others.

Active listeners stop talking long enough to hear what others have to say. When others have finished talking, active listeners frequently paraphrase or feed back what they have understood. They allow people to verify the accuracy of those perceptions or to explain what inaccuracies exist. Active listeners use questions for meaning clarification and do not interrupt attempts to explain ideas or positions.

Active listeners summarize main points and evaluate facts and evidence before responding. Thus, the skill of active listening is as important for disagreements as for agreements. This skill is practiced to foster understanding of another's position—not necessarily to generate agreement with that position. In fact most communication scholars would argue that an individual is in a better position to disagree if he or she has accurately understood the meaning of another's ideas. Figure 5.4 summarizes skills for effective active listening.

Descriptive Messages

By now you are aware that none of us ever fully experiences another person's meaning—we interpret that meaning through communication. The message strategies and tactics we adopt are our attempts to make our meanings understandable to others. Thus, it is important to develop message skills that help others accurately interpret our meanings.

Descriptive messages can help us accurately exchange information with others. In organizations we frequently communicate with people with whom we have little in common and little or no personal relationship; they don't know us and we don't know them. Yet our ability to be understood is crucial to our performance and contributes to the functioning of our organization. Descriptive messages can help us accurately exchange information with supervisors, peers, and subordinates as well as with those with whom we have little regular contact.

Descriptive messages—messages characterized by ownership of perceptions and conclusions and language that presents facts, events, and circumstances all parties in communication are likely to observe or experience personally.

Descriptive messages are characterized by two basic tactics: message ownership and descriptive language. *Message ownership* refers to the ability to "own" our perceptions and conclusions without undue reference to others or attempts at blame. *Descriptive language* describes rather than evaluates, and does so in language that presents facts, events, and circumstances all parties are likely to observe or experience personally.

Message Ownership

Message ownership—attempts to communicate verbally individual perceptions and feelings without attempting to establish blame or find unnecessary corroboration.

When I "own" my own messages I verbally communicate my personal perceptions and feelings without attempting to establish blame or find unnecessary corroboration. The use of the pronoun *I* replaces the *you* message so often associated with blame. The pronoun *I* also replaces vague ownership references such as *we*, *some*, and *they*. Figure 5.5 illustrates effective and ineffective **message ownership** tactics.

FIGURE 5.4
Skills for Active Listening

Self-Control

1. Gain positive attitude for listening
2. Stop talking
3. Control own emotions
4. Empathize with others
5. Avoid mental arguments
6. Avoid assumptions, conclusions, stereotypes

Mental Processing

1. Summarize main points
2. Identify and evaluate facts and evidence
3. Prepare questions
4. Avoid interruptions

Verbal Skills

1. Paraphrase others' positions
2. Question for clarification
3. Summarize main points and meanings

Descriptive Language

Descriptive language is used to describe what all parties to the communication can reasonably be expected to observe. Those using descriptive language avoid evaluation by choosing facts and observable behavior over interpretations of facts and behaviors. Descriptive language users talk about facts, events, and behavior—not attitudes, blame, or other subjective and vague concepts. In other words, descriptive language use tells us what is needed, what happened, what is in question. This is not to say that effective communication never evaluates behavior; rather, descriptive language use is based on the assumption that it is difficult to exchange accurate information about the adequacy (good or bad) of facts and behaviors until all parties understand the specific facts or behaviors of reference. For example, when an important report is late and departments are in conflict, chances are the conflicting individuals can agree that the report must have a new due date. It is less likely that these same individuals will similarly interpret who caused the delay and who should bear the most responsibility and blame. From an organizational point of view, completion of the report is the primary goal of the communication. Of secondary consideration is agreement on blame for the failure.

Descriptive language—language choice based on facts, events, and behavior as opposed to language choice describing attitudes, blame, or other subjective and vague concepts.

FIGURE 5.5
Message Ownership Tactics

Effective	*Ineffective*
I am angry with you.	You always make me mad.
I don't understand the technical terms you're using. They seem to me to be specific to engineering. I am not an engineer.	You're talking like an engineer.
I am responsible to do this job as part of our contractual agreement.	You have problems with authority.
I am telling you directly and honestly what my findings are.	You are being a bit paranoid.
I need this specific information in order to complete this report.	How do you expect me to do my job without adequate information?
I am concerned about the level of costs on Project X.	We think costs are running wild on Project X.
I am worried about the mistakes in your last report.	Some of us think you haven't been yourself lately.

Descriptive messages combine tactics of message ownership with selection of descriptive language and can be both statements and questions. They are useful for summarizing during active listening. Figure 5.6 presents effective and ineffective examples of descriptive messages.

Designing Effective Organizational Messages

Effective organizational messages can be developed with a four-step process: objectives, channels, structure, and feedback. Each step is necessary for effective organizational communication, whether the communication is instruction, reward for good performance, necessary disciplinary action, or recommendation for a procedural change. Although the process is certainly adaptable to informal exchanges, we will discuss it as it relates to generating task-related messages.

The first step in the process, the **objective**, is what the sender hopes to accomplish. Effective objectives are measurable, contain facts, and describe the desired result. For example, a supervisor who needs to discuss an absenteeism problem with John J. might develop an objective to communicate that if he is absent more than five days a year, John J. will lose his job. Many supervisors would make the mistake of simply telling John J. that excessive absenteeism will result in problems. John J. and the su-

Objective—what the message sender hopes to accomplish. Effective objectives are measurable, contain facts, and describe the desired result.

pervisor may have two entirely different opinions about what is "excessive" and what is meant by "problems." The specific objective describes in measurable quantity—number of days—exactly what results from absenteeism.

One of the difficulties in developing effective objectives is that we often have multiple and conflicting objectives. John J. may have a supervisor who desires the absenteeism problem "fixed" but also wants to maintain a friendly relationship with John. The supervisor may engage in a trade-off between clarity (five days of absenteeism in a year will result in loss of job) and ambiguity (excessive absenteeism will result in problems) in an attempt to reconcile conflicting objectives. Frequently, these attempts result in marginal achievement of either objective. Effective communicators seek to resolve their personal conflicts before communicating with others.

The second part of the process is **channel** selection. As we discussed in previous chapters, channels are written, oral (face to face, telephone, private meeting, group meeting), official-directive (both written and oral), and nonverbal. Channel selection may be as important to the success of the message as is the objective. It requires consideration of the person or persons to whom the message is being sent and the message content itself. Is the message complicated? If so, should it be sent in both written and oral form? Is a group meeting the best setting or should the information

Channel—transmission means for messages. Channel selection becomes a message as well as a means for transmission.

FIGURE 5.6
Descriptive Messages

Effective	*Ineffective*
I need information for cost overruns for _____ product in order to finish my audit report by _____ date.	You were to have provided me all the information necessary to finish this report on the costs.
Which part of the cost overrun data is not being submitted? Can you tell me why that particular information seems inappropriate to you?	Why don't you understand my request? What do you mean my request for information is not appropriate?
I do not have a response to my memo of _____ date requesting _____ data.	You are not being straightforward with the agency.
My position suggests I need A, B, and C in order to prepare the report. I understand you are willing to give me A and C but no B. Is that correct?	I know what I need in order to finish the report and so do you, but you are not willing to give it to me.

be transmitted individually? If the message is critical or negative, how can privacy be assured? Which channel gives the greatest chance for understanding? Needless to say, these questions have no definite answers, but they are questions competent communicators learn to ask in considering organizational communication approaches.

Message structure—organization of the message.

The third step in developing an effective organizational message is the **message structure.** How is the message organized? Are the facts in logical order? Is the first step of the instruction understood before the second is explained? In other words, is the behavior that I want to have changed completely described before I ask for change? Am I sure we are talking about the same things? Descriptive message tactics are important here. Is the message "owned" and does its language reflect circumstances or events all parties can reasonably be expected to understand? Message structure should be specific, in logical order, and complete, and it should include time frames if applicable. It should also include a statement of how feedback will occur or whether it is desired.

Feedback—responses to messages; means for determining how messages have been received and understood.

The last step in an effective message is soliciting **feedback.** How do I know if my message has been received? How can I determine if my instructions have been understood? It is often too late to wait until the task is completed. Can I learn to ask questions as I go along that help me to determine whether my message is being understood? Feedback must be timely and must support mutual understanding. It must be specific—getting a description of the task or problem is better than getting a yes or no answer. In sum, feedback needs to be appropriate to the message.

Competent organizational communicators realize that all four components, objectives, channels, structure, and feedback are important. Figure 5.7 summarizes the steps for designing effective organizational messages and is useful as a checklist when sending important messages.

SUMMARY

An individual's organizational experiences result from the attitudes, beliefs, preferences, and abilities the individual brings to the organization, how the organization seeks to influence the individual, and the types of relationships an individual develops. An individual's communication experiences are related to quality and quantity of job performance, job satisfaction, and communication satisfaction.

The intrapersonal experience of individuals in organizations comprises personal needs, predispositions for behavior, communication competencies, and expectations. Personal needs, commonly referred to as *motivation*, have been described by Maslow, Herzberg, Skinner, and Salancik and Pfeffer. Maslow (1954) contended that individuals behave in order to increase or avoid a decrease in need satisfaction. Maslow described needs in an ascending hierarchy beginning with physiological needs and followed by safety and security needs, love and social belonging, esteem and prestige,

FIGURE 5.7
Effective Organizational Messages

OBJECTIVES

> are measurable
> contain facts
> describe the desired result

CHANNELS are

> Oral
>> face to face
>> telephone
>> private meeting
>> group meeting
>
> Written
>> official policy statement
>> memo
>> letter
>> bulletin board

MESSAGE STRUCTURE should

> be specific
> be in logical order
> be complete
> include time frames (if applicable)
> ask for feedback

FEEDBACK should be

> timely
> specific (not yes or no but descriptive of the task or problem)
> appropriate to the message

and self-actualization. Herzberg (1966) contended that satisfaction and dissatisfaction are not polar opposites—that what produces dissatisfaction in the work environment, if corrected, will not necessarily produce satisfaction or motivation. His research suggested that environmental factors (hygiene factors) influence dissatisfaction and that motivational factors are work itself, achievement, growth and responsibility, recognition, and advancement. Skinner (1953) believed that behavior is motivated or reinforced through positive feedback or tangible rewards. Salancik and Pfeffer (1978) proposed that needs and attitudes are determined by the information available to people at the time they express the attitude or need.

Predispositions for organizational communication behaviors are personally held preferences for particular types of communication situations or behavior. Communication apprehension—an individual's level of fear or anxiety associated with either real or anticipated communication with others—influences a wide variety of organizational outcomes, as do preferences for leadership and conflict behaviors. Perceptions of communication competency can be described as an overall summation of preferences and predispositions for organizational communication behaviors.

The paid work force of today and tomorrow is characterized by a diversity of people that is only expected to increase as we approach the year 2000. Not only is the work force increasingly diversified by women, minorities, and immigrants, but also the overall aging of workers, the increased participation by the physically challenged, and the resulting differences in communication style and values all stimulate our abilities to form effective interpersonal relationships. Interpersonal relationships in organizations are formed for important task and social considerations. Unlike our personal relationships, the organization actually structures for us many interpersonal encounters necessary for task accomplishment. We are attracted to others based on both physical and personality characteristics. As fully competent organizational members, we must not limit ourselves only to the similar but must be open to establishing satisfying and effective interpersonal relationships with both similar and dissimilar others.

The relationship an individual develops with his or her supervisor is one of the most important of the primary communication experiences in organizational life. In certain circumstances this relationship is subject to a positivity bias in upward communication. Peers also are an important source of information and support. Communication experiences with supervisors and peers are related to how well individuals perform and their overall measures of satisfaction.

Interpersonal effectiveness can be achieved through valuing diversity; active listening; message ownership and descriptive language; and the development of effective organizational messages including objectives, channels, structures, and feedback. These skills contribute to communication competency for interpersonal communication.

WORKSHOP

1. Write a letter to a hypothetical new employer describing how best to motivate you. Describe the working environment that you would find personally motivational. After your letter is completed, compare it to the various motivational theories described in Chapter 5. Which theory or theories can be applied to your letter?

2. You and another member of your class (preferably someone you do not know well) should take turns describing what you find important in a work environment. This exchange should take ten minutes. Each

of you can ask questions of the other. At the end of ten minutes complete the following What Do People Really Want? rankings. Rank your preferences and what you believe to be the preferences of your partner. After both rankings are complete, you and your partner should exchange ranking sheets and discuss on what basis rankings are made. (See pages 165–166.)

3. The following essay, "Are We So Different We Can't Work Together?" provides a thought-provoking description of cultural differences that influence how individuals are accepted in work environments. The essay helps us think about the characteristics of our own culture that influence our relationships with those of another culture. (See pages 166–168.)

4. To build skills and practical experience with the technique of active listening, select a controversial issue appropriate to the class (an issue that students raise or one that relates directly to work problems is recommended). Form groups of six students each. Two volunteers from each group should represent opposing opinions on the issue. The remaining group members should form a circle around the two volunteers. The only rule that must be followed is that before either volunteer responds to the other, the listener must state to the other's satisfaction what the speaker has just been saying. In other words, no replies are allowed until the speaker is satisfied that the listener can restate the original message.

   With the group observing, the two members should proceed to discuss the issue. Group members are to act as monitors and may intervene if the rule has been violated.

   After ten minutes of discussion, the class should describe how active listening influenced the issue under consideration. (Alternative exercise form: All members of the class can participate in the activity by forming pairs of participants for issue discussion.)

5. Carol Porter, a professional communication consultant, provides guidelines for effective written messages. (See pages 168–172.) Her suggestions should be studied before Exercise 6 is completed.

6. Effective organizational messages have objectives, appropriate channels, are well structured, and develop a plan for feedback. To practice developing effective messages, a message-structuring exercise asks you to critique and improve messages of organizational policy, job information, relationships, and creativity. (See pages 172–176.)

What Do People Really Want?

For the following ten work-related items you will develop a ranking (1–10) of their importance to you and project how the person with whom you have been interacting will rank the items. You will then compare your self-rankings to your partner's projection of your rankings and compare your projections to his or her self-rankings. Discuss the similarities and differences in rankings.

Remember, rank what is important to you and what you believe is important to your partner in a work environment.

	MY PERSONAL RANKING	MY PARTNER'S RANKING OF ME
1. Sensitivity to personal problems	_____	_____
2. Interesting work	_____	_____
3. Salary	_____	_____
4. Job security	_____	_____
5. Loyalty of company to employees	_____	_____
6. Tactful and constructive criticism	_____	_____
7. Appreciation for work	_____	_____
8. A sense of belonging	_____	_____
9. Good working conditions	_____	_____
10. Opportunities for advancement	_____	_____

	MY RANKING OF MY PARTNER	MY PARTNER'S SELF-RANKING
1. Sensitivity to personal problems	_____	_____
2. Interesting work	_____	_____
3. Salary	_____	_____
4. Job security	_____	_____
5. Loyalty of company to employees	_____	_____
6. Tactful and constructive criticism	_____	_____
7. Appreciation for work	_____	_____
8. A sense of belonging	_____	_____
9. Good working conditions	_____	_____
10. Opportunities for advancement	_____	_____

Are We So Different We Can't Work Together?

Adelina M. Gomez, Ph.D.*

John Smith, a black supervisor of predominantly white employees, in response to the question "How do you think your subordinates see you as a manager?" said, "In this particular agency, they see me as being low on

* Adelina M. Gomez, assistant professor of communication at the University of Colorado, Colorado Springs, holds B.A. and M.A. degrees from Western New Mexico University and a Ph.D. in communication from the University of Colorado. Her research and teaching interests include intercultural communication, comparisons of management behaviors across cultures, family communication, and public speaking. Dr. Gomez is an active consultant for both public and private sector organizations.

the power chain even though I am their supervisor. They know they can challenge certain things I ask them to do because there are certain higher-level supervisors who are white and who will listen to them and often countermand my decisions, even though they have disregarded the chain of command. This has caused me some supervisory problems in terms of controlling the employees and it has an impact on respect. I do not believe that they feel they have to be as loyal to me as they are to those above me. Therefore, I am ineffective as a supervisor. So I personally feel they see me as a convenience-type supervisor, someone they tolerate probably because I am black."

———————

Leo Marquez is a Hispanic manager who complains that the cultural differences among his subordinates often create problems in work-related situations when he has to talk to any of them about deficiencies in their work. He explained, "It is easier for me to talk to other Hispanics and Anglos than it is for me to talk to blacks. They usually become defensive when I bring to their attention the mistakes in their work. I try to talk to them in a manner that is not construed as offensive or racist. I have learned to be careful that a black does not feel that I am singling him out because he is black."

———————

Manager Maria Torres has expressed serious concerns about the problems that arise in managing culturally diverse groups. She argues that because 98 percent of the top-level managers in her agency are white males, they are not sensitive to the needs and concerns of minorities, much less those of women. She indicated that there are few, if any, minorities who are in top-grade management levels that are the policy-making positions. She explained, "A few male minorities are promoted to a certain grade level where they are usually dead-ended; women seldom are promoted. I am an exception, and although I am as capable as any male here, I believe mine was a token promotion. There is a strong need to remind white males about this inequity because it seems that no women or minorities will be promoted soon. I address the issue every chance I can. I do it in oversight reports and in supervisory and sensitivity training. I try very hard to get it across to them but to no avail."

She explained that there are serious problems because the buddy system and the selection process work predominantly for white males as they climb the ladder. She concluded, "These men seldom take minority males under their wing and we know they will certainly not take women!"

———————

These three real-life case studies demonstrate some serious organizational problems that often go unrecognized even today. While management programs have made great strides in preparing employees to be effective managers, significant weaknesses exist when these programs fail to recognize that we all have cultural identities and that culturally diverse groups may experience stressful working relations because of those cultural differences.

When people have little understanding of their own culture, it is unlikely they will understand other cultures, thus increasing the chances of communication barriers developing. All cultures have unique values that influence how individuals of those cultures interpret the world around them. It is from these values that attitudes and beliefs are derived that influence the communication process.

When people begin to understand who they are, culturally speaking, then they can proceed to the next stage of increasing their knowledge of other cultures. They can begin to understand how cultural differences influence such dimensions of an individual's working experiences as conflict management, leadership, and decision making. They can begin to make more sense of another person's behavior that may be strongly influenced by his or her culture.

While some cultures share more similarities than differences, it is the differences that are misunderstood and precipitate culturally related problems. For this reason, we should focus on the problems that can occur in the overgeneralizations often made with regard to cultures. These overgeneralizations usually result in patterns of stereotyping, especially with regard to behaviors. Effective communication training supports the need for flexible attitudes and behaviors based on acknowledgment of healthy cultural diversity. In reality, effective communication training recognizes that cultural differences within our organizations are as important to sound relationships as they are to our society as a whole.

QUESTIONS FOR DISCUSSION

1. Select one of these case studies and analyze the problem by addressing the role of cultural differences and how they may have contributed to the existing situation.

2. "Equality," "wisdom," and "a comfortable life" are examples of cultural values. What attitudes do you have that stem from these values and where did they originate?

3. List four characteristics about your own culture that help you to understand the behaviors of someone from a different culture.

A Guide to Writing Effective Business Messages

Carol M. Porter*

Whether you are writing a letter of application, making a proposal, requesting information, or any number of other business messages, there are certain guidelines you can use to make your writing more effective.

* Carol Porter holds a B.A. in business education from the University of Tulsa and an M.A. in human relations from the University of Oklahoma. She has worked as a secretary, administrative assistant, and adult education instructor. Presently, she is partner and administrator in the communication consulting firm of CommuniCon, Inc.

Waldo Mara, a longtime communications consultant, estimates that the average business letter will capture only forty-five seconds of the reader's time and attention. That being the case, your presentation must be well organized, clear, concise, and correct in order to make your point in less than a minute.

Getting Organized

Some people believe there is little to learn about writing and tackle the job with no thought and planning. Others are intimidated by the sight of a blank sheet of paper and don't know where to begin. Remember, writing is a learned skill upon which we can all improve with knowledge and practice.

One of the most important requisites to good writing is to operate with a plan. Most of us think planning is a good idea, but too few of us really do it. To clarify your thinking about any writing task, ask and answer the following questions before proceeding:

1. Why am I writing?
   Am I writing to inform?
   Am I writing to persuade?
   Am I writing to sell good will?

2. What point(s) do I want to make?
   What is the logical sequence of ideas?

3. To whom am I writing?
   What are they like?
   What are their needs?
   Will they understand technical language?
   What is their anticipated reaction?

4. How do I get the desired effect?

Inexperienced writers will need to answer these questions on paper and make an outline. With practice, though, some writers become proficient enough to work through the writing process in their heads.

A well-written letter or report should act as a road map for your reader, leading him or her to the final destination without detours and side trips. Sentences within a paragraph should be related. Paragraphs should logically follow one another, moving in the same direction. If you have carefully considered your journey on paper, your reader should still be on board at trip's end.

Achieving Clarity

Clear writing means being specific and communicating all the details. The writer must anticipate all the questions the reader might ask. Contrary to face-to-face communication, which provides the speaker with immediate feedback, you have no opportunity to evaluate the way your written message is being received. Your letter must say exactly what you want it to the very first time in a way that is easily understood by your reader.

Use appropriate punctuation. Incorrect usage of words and punctuation can create confusion. Can you get three different meanings from the following statement?

Example: The supervisor said the subordinate is inept.
Do you see how different punctuation changes the meaning?

Example: "The supervisor," said the subordinate, "is inept."
Finally, a third meaning can be derived:

Example: The supervisor said, "The subordinate is inept."
What a difference punctuation makes!

Choose the most precise word. Knowing subtle differences between and among words of similar spelling or meaning reflects upon the knowledge of the writer. Would you be able to select correctly "adapt," "adept," or "adopt" in the following example?

Example: The school _____ a new procedure for recruiting new instructors who are _____ at teaching more than one subject.

Be aware of the connotation of words. Some words have a positive effect while others have a negative effect. A single sour note can ruin the effect of a beautiful song just as a negative word can spoil the tone of a letter. The positive side of cheap is inexpensive; stingy is economical; extravagant is generous. Think carefully about your choice of words. You won't be present to correct any misunderstandings the reader might get from a poorly chosen word or negative idea.

Being Concise and Complete

Conciseness means being brief but complete. All deadwood words and ideas should be eliminated while retaining necessary details and common courtesy. Most letters can be reduced by one-third and still convey the message completely and courteously.

CHANGE THIS	TO THIS
For the purpose of	For
For the simple reason that	Because
At the present time	Now
In the amount of	For
In spite of the fact that	Despite/although
Due to the fact that	Because
Enclosed please find	Enclosed is
In the near future	Soon
We wish to thank you	Thank you

If a word doesn't add to the meaning, get rid of it. Take the time to polish a letter to its most concise form.

For greater understanding, generally use short conversational words and short sentences. A long word should not be used when a short one will do. Be aware that long sentences make a reader's job more difficult. If your sentence is too long, break it up so that each main idea has a structure of its own. Each sentence should contain only one main idea and be pruned of all unnecessary words. Don't be guilty of using inflated, outdated phrases:

Examples: As per our conversation . . .
Herewith enclosed you will find . . .
If you have any questions regarding the above, please contact the undersigned.

Your letter will be more effective if it sounds like you. Use your normal vocabulary, but use it more precisely than in normal conversation with a degree of formality appropriate for your reader.

Making It Accurate

The accuracy and appearance of your letter makes a statement about the competency of you and the organization you represent. If your writing is slipshod and messy, your reader may reasonably question the quality of your work and the services you offer.

Correctness implies checking for accuracy in spelling, punctuation, grammar, computations, facts, and enclosures. Proofreading twice, proofreading aloud, or even proofreading backward will help you to catch errors. If you are a poor speller, make sure your work is checked by someone who doesn't have the same handicap.

Putting the Reader First

The best way to get and keep someone's attention is to show your interest in them. Here are some suggestions for putting the reader first:

1. Place yourself in your reader's shoes and imagine how he or she might react to your words.

2. Be sensitive to sexist language. Use nongender pronouns and non-sexist terms and verbs. Also, use "Ms." when addressing women, especially in business. Avoid "girl," "gal," and "lady," when talking about an adult woman.

3. Personalize your letters by being human, pleasant, and caring. Too often writers forget that they are writing to a person with feelings rather than an inanimate machine. Even bad news, such as a collection letter for a long overdue account, should be packaged pleasantly, though with firmness. Hostility and sarcasm never belong in a business letter, and the organization's good will is always at stake.

To summarize, it takes good planning with the objective in mind to write an effective business message. It is safe to assume that your reader is a busy person who will spend a minimum amount of time understanding your message. Writing with clarity, conciseness, and accuracy will enhance your chances of success. If you expect to achieve your goals, you must develop the skills and attitudes to express your ideas effectively in writing.

Message-Structuring Exercises*

Instructions. Read the following messages carefully. Consider their objectives and the channels available to you for message sending.

Evaluate each message for achievement of its objective. Consider improvements you would make. Then

1. Restructure/rewrite each message in order to effectively accomplish communication objectives.

2. Choose the channels you would use to communicate these messages.

3. Outline how you would seek feedback for each message.

I. Structuring an Effective Organizing Message
MESSAGE OBJECTIVE

. . . to reduce abuses of the company's phone policy in an organization of thirty-five employees.

MESSAGE STRUCTURE

. . . "This announcement is to advise you that the Personnel Department has received numerous complaints regarding violations of company policy for phone usage. The complaints relate to how incoming phone calls are being answered. Some employees are not identifying themselves by name and company or department name. Some phones are being used for more personal calls than they should be. The Personnel Department has requested that all employees reread their employees' policy manuals regarding phone usage and abide more closely by those regulations."

The above message is __ very effective __ effective __ ineffective. Why? What improvements would you make?

IDEAS FOR RESTRUCTURING THE MESSAGE

---

* Message-structuring activities were prepared by Sherwyn P. Morreale.

AVAILABLE CHANNELS

————— telephone   ————— individual conversation

————— official directive   ————— bulletin board notice

————— staff meeting   ————— company newsletter

————— memorandum   ————— formal report

————— letter   ————— group meeting

————— other _____

                                                (describe)

PLAN FOR FEEDBACK

II. Structuring An Effective Organizing Message
MESSAGE OBJECTIVE

. . . to inform fifty employees of a new system for dispensing company supplies.

MESSAGE STRUCTURE

. . . "This notice is to inform all employees of the immediate relocation of the 'Supply Closet' from Room 507 in the Main Building to Room 108 in the Annex. With this change of location, some different procedures regarding supplies are now in order. Only draw on those supplies that are marked for your department. Each department will have a separate shelf for supplies. Second, any large withdrawal of supplies should be charged off to your department. Third, when a withdrawal brings a supply item below a reasonable level, put in a reorder for that item."

The above message is ___ very effective ___ effective ___ ineffective. Why? What improvements would you make?

IDEAS FOR RESTRUCTURING THE MESSAGE

AVAILABLE CHANNELS

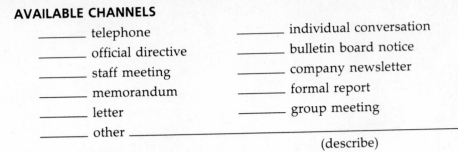

_____ telephone	_____ individual conversation
_____ official directive	_____ bulletin board notice
_____ staff meeting	_____ company newsletter
_____ memorandum	_____ formal report
_____ letter	_____ group meeting
_____ other	_____
	(describe)

PLAN FOR FEEDBACK

III. Structuring an Effective Relationship Message

MESSAGE OBJECTIVE

. . . to involve all one hundred employees in a company-sponsored recreational activity.

MESSAGE STRUCTURE

. . . "The baseball season and annual company picnic are coming up again. As in past years, the season will be kicked off with a company-wide potluck picnic. There are openings on the baseball teams for all the player positions and for cheerleaders also. For the potluck picnic, the company will supply beverages and paper products. We, the employees, will be responsible for the food. It is recommended that last names A to H bring a meat dish, I to R bring a salad, and S to Z, bring a dessert, bread or snack. Let's get out there, have a good picnic, and PLAY BALL!"

The above message is __ very effective __ effective __ ineffective. Why? What improvements would you make?

IDEAS FOR RESTRUCTURING THE MESSAGE

AVAILABLE CHANNELS

———— telephone   ———— individual conversation

———— official directive   ———— bulletin board notice

———— staff meeting   ———— company newsletter

———— memorandum   ———— formal report

———— letter   ———— group meeting

———— other ———————————————————
                                    (describe)

PLAN FOR FEEDBACK

IV. Structuring An Effective Change Message

MESSAGE OBJECTIVE

. . . to encourage suggestions from all employees, in an organization of two hundred, for improving the information system.

MESSAGE STRUCTURE

. . . "Although our company traditionally has done a good job of keeping all employees well informed, a good job can always be done better. As company president, I'd like to call on all of you to think about our company, your job in it, and what you need to know about your job. I'm concerned about what information you need to know and how you might know it better. I'll be holding informal meetings in each department to discuss this. Come to your meeting with any creative suggestions you have to improve our communication system. Thanks in advance for any thoughts you may have. My door and ear are always open to your ideas."

The above message is —— very effective —— effective —— ineffective. Why? What improvements would you make?

IDEAS FOR RESTRUCTURING THE MESSAGE

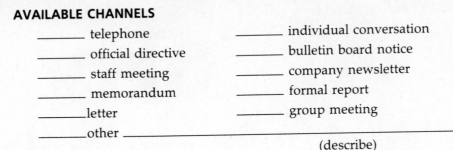

AVAILABLE CHANNELS

_____ telephone	_____ individual conversation
_____ official directive	_____ bulletin board notice
_____ staff meeting	_____ company newsletter
_____ memorandum	_____ formal report
_____ letter	_____ group meeting
_____ other _____	
	(describe)

PLAN FOR FEEDBACK

SUMMARY OF COMPETENCY COMPONENTS:
KNOWLEDGE, SENSITIVITY, SKILLS, VALUES

KNOWLEDGE

Motivation consists of intrapersonal attitudes that influence behavior. Maslow, Herzberg, Skinner, and Salancik and Pfeffer present contrasting approaches.

Communication apprehension, leadership and conflict preferences, and self-perception of communication competencies are influential in organizational communication behaviors.

People diversity is an important work force characteristic.

Supervisor-subordinate and peer relationships are primary interpersonal relationships in organizations.

SENSITIVITY

Motivation influences communication behaviors.

Impersonal and interpersonal relationships are formed in a diverse work force.

People with high communication apprehension experience organizations less positively than their counterparts with lower apprehension.

Perceptions of communication competencies contribute to work and supervisor satisfaction.

Valuing diversity is important for interpersonal effectiveness.

Hearing and listening are not the same process.

Listening is critical for message reception.

SKILLS

Valuing diversity is developed through positive approaches.

Active listening is developed through analysis and practice.

Ownership messages are identified and practiced.

Descriptive language is identified and practiced.

Effective organizational messages are identified and practiced.

Analysis skills are developed through case and essay evaluation.

VALUES

Individual communication experiences relate to organizational identification, work performance, communication, and job satisfaction.

Motivation is important for communication behaviors.

Valuing diversity, active listening, verbal ownership, and descriptive language contribute to effective organizational messages.

REFERENCES AND SUGGESTED READINGS

Athanassiades, J. 1973. The distortion of upward communication in hierarchical organizations. *Academy of Management Journal* 16: 207–26.

Baird, J. E., Jr. 1977. *The dynamics of organizational communication.* New York: Harper and Row.

Booth-Butterfield, M., and S. Butterfield. 1986. Effects of evaluation, task structure, trait-CA, and reticence on state-CA and behavioral disruption in dyadic settings. *Communication Monographs* 53(2): 144–59.

Brislin, R. W. 1988. Prejudice in intercultural communication. In *Intercultural communication: A reader,* eds. L. Samovar and R. Porter, 339–44. Belmont, CA: Wadsworth.

Carmichael, C. W. 1988. Intercultural perspectives of aging. In *Intercultural communication: A reader,* eds. L. Samovar and R. Porter, 139–47. Belmont, CA: Wadsworth.

Cummings, H. W., L. W. Long, and M. L. Lewis. 1983. *Managing communication in organizations: An introduction.* Dubuque, IA: Gorsuch Scarisbrick.

Daly, J. A., and J. C. McCroskey. 1975. Occupational desirability and choice as a function of communication apprehension. *Journal of Counseling Psychology* 22(4): 309–13.

Dansereau, F., and S. Markham. 1987. Superior-subordinate communication: Multiple levels of analysis. In *Handbook of organizational communication,* eds. F. Jablin, L. Putnam, K. Roberts, and L. Porter, 343–88. Newbury Park, CA: Sage.

DeVito, J. A., 1988. *Human communication: the basic course.* 4th ed. New York: Harper & Row.

DeWine, S., and F. Barone. 1984. Employee communication and role stress: Enhancement or sabotage of the organizational climate? Paper presented to the Organizational Communication Division of the International Communication Association Convention, May, San Francisco.

Downs, C., and T. Hain. 1982. Productivity and communication. In *Communication yearbook 5,* ed. M. Burgoon, 435–53. New Brunswick, NJ: Transaction Books.

Downs, C. W., and M. D. Hazen. 1977. A factor analytic study of communication satisfaction. *Journal of Business Communication* 14: 63–73.

Eisenberg, E., P. Monge, and R. Farace. 1984. Coorientation of communication rules in managerial dyads. *Human Communication Research* 11: 261–71.

Falcione, R., J. McCroskey, and J. Daly. 1977. Job satisfaction as a function of employees' communication apprehension, self-esteem, and perceptions of their immediate supervisor. In *Communication yearbook 1*, ed. B. D. Ruben, 363–76. New Brunswick, NJ: Transaction Books.

Folb, E. A. 1988. Who's got the room at the top? Issues of dominance and non-dominance in intracultural communication. In *Intercultural communication: A reader*, eds. L. Samovar and R. Porter, 121–30. Belmont, CA: Wadsworth.

Fulk, J., and S. Mani. 1986. Distortion of communication in hierarchical relationships. In *Communication yearbook 9*, ed. M. McLaughlin, 483–510. Newbury Park, CA: Sage.

Goldhaber, G., M. Yates, D. Porter, and R. Lesniak. 1978. Organizational communication. *Human Communication Research* 5(1): 76–96.

Hatfield, J., R. Huseman, and E. Miles. 1987. Perceptual differences in verbal recognition and relative job satisfaction. *Communication Research Reports* 4: 8–13.

Herzberg, F. 1966. *Work and the nature of man*. Cleveland: World.

Jablin, F. M. 1978. Message-response and openness in superior-subordinate communication. In *Communication yearbook 2*, ed. B. D. Ruben, 293–309. New Brunswick, NJ: Transaction Books.

Johnston, W. 1987. *Workforce 2000*. Indianapolis: Hudson Institute.

Krivonos, P. D. 1982. Distortion of subordinate to superior communication in organizational settings. *Central States Speech Journal* 33(1): 345–52.

McCroskey, J. C. 1982. *An introduction to rhetorical communication*. 4th ed. Englewood Cliffs, NJ: Prentice-Hall.

McCroskey, J. C., and V. P. Richmond. 1979. The impact of communication apprehension on individuals in organizations. *Communication Quarterly* 27(3): 55–61.

Maslow, A. 1954. *Motivation and personality*. New York: Harper & Row.

Miller, K. I., and P. R. Monge. 1985. Social information and employee anxiety about organizational change. *Human Communication Research* 11(3): 365–86.

Nichols, R., and L. Stevens. 1957. *Are you listening?* New York: McGraw-Hill.

Pace, R. W. 1983. *Organizational communication: Foundations for human resource development*. Englewood Cliffs, NJ: Prentice-Hall.

Pearson, J. C. 1988. Gender and communication: Sex is more than a three-letter word. In *Intercultural communication: A reader*, eds. L. Samovar and R. Porter, 154–62. Belmont, CA: Wadsworth.

Pincus, J. D. 1986. Communication satisfaction, job satisfaction and job performance. *Human Communication Research* 12(3): 395–419.

Read, W. 1962. Upward communication in industrial hierarchies. *Human Relations* 15: 3–15.

Richetto, G. M. 1969. Source credibility and personal influence in three contexts: A study of dyadic communication in a complex aerospace organization. Unpublished doctoral dissertation, Purdue University, Lafayette, IN.

Richetto, G. M. 1977. Organizational communication theory and research: An overview. In *Communication yearbook 1*, ed. B. D. Ruben, 331–46. New Brunswick, NJ: Transaction Books.

Roberts, K., and C. O'Reilly. 1974. Measuring organizational communication. *Journal of Applied Psychology* 59(3): 321–26.

Ruben, B. D. 1988. Human communication and cross-cultural effectiveness. In *Intercultural communication: A reader*, eds. L. Samovar and R. Porter, 331–39. Belmont, CA: Wadsworth.

Salancik, G., and J. Pfeffer. 1977. An examination of need-satisfaction models of job attitudes. *Administrative Science Quarterly* 22: 427–56.

Salancik, G., and J. Pfeffer. 1978. A social information processing approach to job attitudes and task design. *Administrative Science Quarterly* 23: 224–53.

Scott, M. D., J. C. McCroskey, and M. F. Sheahan. 1978. Measuring communication apprehension. *Journal of Communication* 28: 104–11.

Shockley-Zalabak, P., and D. Morley. 1984. High apprehensives within the organization: How and with whom do they talk. *Communication Research Reports* 1(1): 97–103.

Skinner, B. F. 1953. *Science and human behavior*. New York: Macmillan.

Smith, A. F., and S. A. Hellweg. 1985. Work and supervisor satisfaction as a function of subordinate perceptions of communication competence of self and supervisor. Paper presented to the Organizational Communication Division of the International Communication Association Convention, May, Honolulu.

Smith, P. C., L. M. Kendall, and C. L. Hulin. 1969. *The measurement of satisfaction in work and retirement*. Chicago: Rand McNally.

Snavely, W., and J. McNeill. 1985. A path analytic study of the impact of organizational and interpersonal stressors on job tension, satisfaction, and turnover propensity. Paper presented to the Organizational Communication Division of the International Communication Association Convention, May, Honolulu.

Snyder, R. A., and J. H. Morris. 1984. Organizational communication and performance. *Journal of Applied Psychology* 69(3): 461–65.

Sypher, B. D., and T. E. Zorn, Jr. 1987. Individual differences and construct system content in descriptions of liked and disliked coworkers. Paper presented to the Organizational Communication Division of the International Communication Association Convention, May, Montreal.

Tompkins, P., and G. Cheney. 1983. Account analysis of organizations: Decision making and identification. In *Communication and organizations: An interpretive approach*, eds. L. Putnam and M. Pacanowsky, 123–46. Beverly Hills, CA: Sage.

CHAPTER

~ S I X ~

Groups in Organizations

Developing competencies through . . .

KNOWLEDGE

Describing small-group experiences of individuals in organizations

Describing group development

Identifying types of groups in organizations

SENSITIVITY

Relating individual communication behaviors to effective participation in groups

Understanding positive and negative participation behaviors

Evaluating personal skills for group participation

SKILLS

Practicing effective group participation

Practicing analysis capabilities

VALUES

Relating group effectiveness to individual participation behaviors

Identifying responsibilities for self-managing groups

Dave Green's Small-Group Experiences

Dave had been at AMX for over three months. He would be glad when his first presentation to Sally and the group was behind him. Not that they had not been helpful. The weekly planning meetings Sally held with the team were useful, and he was beginning to get more familiar with what to expect. John was clearly the leader. He talked more than any of the others, at least when Sally was present. The staff meetings usually began with an overall progress report of the week's activities, with some attention given to any problems encountered since the last meeting. Dave had observed that few serious difficulties were aired during the meetings. He wasn't sure if the others approached Sally for individual problem solving. As for him, he had not experienced a serious problem, except not knowing what Sally expected. And John had helped with clarifying expectations on more than one occasion. The staff meetings were the forums for formal presentation of researched materials. Dave had observed two such presentations in the last three months. Next week was his turn, and he expected the group would be supportive.

In addition to the staff meetings, the research team met informally about once every two weeks. Again, John seemed to call and run the meetings. Dave was not sure how the others felt about John's leadership but assumed both Ralph and Susan supported him. At two of these meetings Dave had been a little uncomfortable with being assigned some work from John. He wasn't quite sure what if anything, to do about the assignments. After all, John seemed an accepted informal leader and John had been personally supportive of Dave.

INTRODUCTION

Peer relationships are more frequently discussed as small-group rather than as one-on-one organizational experiences. Most individuals in organizations spend considerable time in groups. Membership in work, problem-solving, and social support groups is common and influences how we experience organizational life. Dave Green is the new member of his team. His new job gives him formal membership in the group. He hopes he will become part of an informal social group, but AMX as an organization won't make that happen. Dave's social support network will depend on his informal relationships at AMX.

Small-group experiences—individual involvement in the formal and informal groups formed within organizations for task or social support.

Most of us have memberships in multiple groups. Families, work organizations, athletic teams, friendships, and volunteer groups are only a few **small-group experiences** in which most of us are involved. We join these groups in different ways and for different reasons. In our organizational lives, our jobs often define membership in certain groups. Our skills and visibility within the organization may determine membership in other types of groups, and our interpersonal relationships determine the extent of our membership in social support networks. Before we explore the types of primary groups relationships in organizations and the roles individuals play in these groups, we will examine Dave Green's reflections on his early group experiences.

This chapter is designed to contribute to our *knowledge* competencies by identifying individual experiences in groups, describing group development, and discussing groups common to most organizations. *Sensitivity* competencies are fostered by relating individual participation to group effectiveness, distinguishing between positive and negative participation behaviors, and evaluating personal communication skills for participation. *Skills* are developed by practicing positive participation behaviors and analyzing transcripts and group participation. Finally, *values* are developed by relating group effectiveness to individual participation behaviors and by identifying responsibilities for self-managing groups.

SMALL-GROUP EXPERIENCES

Dave Green became a member of Sally Johnson's staff by virtue of his new job assignment. His first three months on the job have helped him learn about how the group works, what the expectations are, how issues are handled, and what his role or roles will be. Dave is also a member of an informal work group unofficially led by John. This group also has informal rules and operating procedures. He is less clear about his responsibilities to John but in general finds the group supportive and helpful. Dave's AMX experiences are common to most organizations. Some of the groups to which we belong are formally structured with specific goals, rules, and procedures. Others are more informal, blending task and social roles, and still others serve a purely social support function.

Organizations have many different types of formal and informal groups. Work teams, quality circles, sales teams, problem-solving groups, management teams, and unions are only a few examples of formally structured organizational groups. Informal groups come together for social events, athletic competition, coffee breaks, gripe sessions, and a variety of other purposes. Both types of groups are important for individual task accomplishment and social support.

We talk about groups as if they are easily described and recognized. But what exactly is a group? How do we identify group members and the types of activities in which groups actually engage? John Baird (1977) has defined a group as "a collection of more than two persons who perceive themselves as a group, possess a common fate, have organizational structure, and communicate over time to achieve personal and group goals." This definition places communication relationships at the core of group activity. As such, groups can be understood in terms of how they are formed and structured, how individuals understand their dependence on one another, and how members communicate.

Organizations form groups to fulfill a variety of organizational needs. Work groups are formed for maximum task efficiency and effectiveness. Problem-solving groups address ongoing organizational issues as well as emergencies. Groups meet regularly to review organizational operations and make future plans, to negotiate labor-management agreements, to respond to financial crises or unusual pressure from competition; and groups such as quality circles are formed to examine systematically new and better ways of doing things. The underlying assumption is that the efforts of numbers of individuals exceed individual efforts requiring energy and creativity for either completing tasks or examining issues.

Groups also contribute to establishing the shared realities of the organization. Expectations about member conduct can be found in most groups. Members communicate expectations to new members and evaluate behavior as either conforming or disregarding the group rules. Dave is learning the communication rules of his work team. For example, he is learning that John expects to be the informal leader and that apparently Ralph and Susan accept this situation. Dave is attempting to determine whether the lack of problem discussion in staff meetings is a communication rule or the absence of any real problems during his tenure with AMX. He is also trying to determine what the group expects to be discussed in group settings and what should be handled privately with Sally. These rules and others become the realities Dave shares with his work team.

The next several sections of this chapter will help us understand Dave's experiences by describing individuals in groups, how groups develop, and the types of groups commonly formed in organizations. Finally, we will describe how we can increase effective group participation by working individually and cooperatively.

Individuals in Groups

When we discussed how individuals experience organizations we described predispositions or preferences for organizational communication behaviors that are related to occupation choice, job satisfaction, productivity, and a variety of other organizational outcomes. We talked about the importance of communication apprehension, leadership and conflict preferences, and perceptions of communication competencies. As you might expect, these predispositions or preferences for communication also are influential as we work in groups.

John Brilhart and Gloria Galanes (1989) have suggested that "the most important resource a small group has is its members: their knowledge, attitudes, and skills. How well they work together toward a common goal depends partly on the attitudes they have toward themselves, each other, the group, and the information and ideas presented." Brilhart and Galanes have contended that the sense of responsibility for the success of the group that each individual brings to group efforts is what promotes group effectiveness.

Generally speaking, the more positive we feel about our personal communication competencies, the better able we are to work in groups successfully. Moreover, when we respect the competencies of others we consider the time and energy invested in group experiences to be worthwhile. All of us have attended a meeting or served on a committee that we evaluated as a waste of time. Think for a moment about that group and the commitment of individual members. Think about the knowledge, sensitivity, skills, and values each brought to the effort. What conclusions can you draw from your experience? Now recall a more positive group effort. What made the difference? How were your individual contributions affected?

Brilhart and Galanes have suggested that the concept of rhetorical sensitivity is important for group communication. Broadly defined, rhetorical sensitivity is the ability of an individual to monitor personal communication behaviors with regard to potential consequences for other group members. Five components of rhetorical sensitivity are identified by Brilhart and Galanes as especially relevant to group communication: (1) acceptance of personal complexity, (2) avoidance of communicative rigidity, (3) interaction consciousness, (4) appreciation of the communicability of ideas, and (5) tolerance for inventional searching.

Acceptance of personal complexity is a sensitivity competency that recognizes and values the diversity of people in a group. When individuals value diversity they are likely to avoid communicative rigidity and to use a variety of speaking and interacting patterns based on the needs of the situation. Dave Green is an excellent example. In the past Dave has been a leader in most of his school groups. He has frequently contributed ideas and set directions. At AMX Dave is the junior member of an experienced group. His participation patterns are different because of his sensitivity to the needs of the new situation. He realizes that he does not fully understand the personal complexity of his new work team although he values their willingness to help him.

Interaction consciousness refers to the awareness an individual brings to the process of interaction. How can ideas be presented? What support do others need? What is the balance between aggressiveness and passivity or argumentativeness and acquiescence? Along with sensitivity to interactions comes appreciation for the communicability of ideas or an awareness of when expressing ideas and feelings facilitates goal achievement. All of us have been in situations when an idea, although valuable in and of itself, made no real contribution to the issue at hand. The **rhetorically sensitive** individual weighs the appropriateness of expressions as they relate to the purpose of the situation. Finally, the rhetorically sensitive individual understands that many approaches may be effective in the expression of an idea or feeling and, based on this belief, attempts to en-

Rhetorically sensitive—individual acceptance of personal complexity, avoidance of communicative rigidity, interaction consciousness, appreciation of the communicability of ideas, and tolerance for inventional searching.

gage others in interactions. This sensitivity is referred to as tolerance for inventional searching.

We have been discussing important sensitivity competencies for group participation. In the next several sections of this chapter we will develop knowledge competencies by describing group development and common types of organizational groups. We will build communication skills for effective group participation. However, before we proceed, it is important to examine our value competencies as they relate to information and ideas generated within groups. Are we open-minded to new information? How do we view opinions that differ from ours? Do we support what Brilhart and Galanes have described as skeptical inquiry, or are we more dogmatic in resisting changes in existing beliefs or ways of doing things? Do we genuinely value a dialectic process, the search for truth in the form of the best possible answer to an issue, problem, question, or challenge? It is easy to respond that we are open-minded and supportive of skeptical inquiry. That is certainly the socially desirable answer. However, for many of us, our beliefs and opinions at times have influenced dogmatic behaviors. To become fully competent organizational communicators, we must continually assess our values, which will make important contributions to the types of knowledge we use, the sensitivity we display, and the actual communication behaviors in which we engage.

Group Development

Previously we have said that the organization actually structures many of the groups to which we belong. Although certainly accurate, this notion of group formation only begins to help us understand how groups evolve and develop. We can be more effective group participants when we become familiar with stages of group development and how groups generate norms and roles. Additionally, it is important to consider specific influences on group participation such as prestige and climate.

Group Stages

Groups have both socioemotional and task concerns. Group members must become acquainted, learn about each other, and usually move from impersonal to somewhat interpersonal relationships. Group members also recognize that there is a job to do or an assignment to accomplish. These socioemotional and task concerns need attention as groups form; move through production, performing, or decision phases; and adjourn or recycle to new issues or problems.

Researchers generally suggest that groups progress through a series of **group stages** that begin with formation. During formation members work out interpersonal concerns or tensions and establish relationships necessary for enough stability to permit task efforts. Groups move from formation to production phases, that is, an emphasis on task-related behaviors such as idea generation or problem solving. These production phases have

Group stages—concept that groups progress through sequences such as formation, production, resolution, and dissolution; frequently described as forming, storming, norming, performing, and adjourning.

been variously referred to as decision emergence, confrontation, compromise and harmony, and performing. The labels are not as important as the concept that as the group matures, a variety of communication processes—idea generation, conflict, problem solving, decision making, compromise—become typical of group interactions. The effectiveness of these interactions is directly related to the effectiveness of group outcomes—both task and socioemotional. Following production, groups move toward resolution, the phase when problems are more readily resolved and the group is productive with less overall expenditure of energy than in earlier phases. Resolution can precede the actual dissolving of groups formed for a specific and not ongoing purpose.

Bruce Tuckman and Mary Ann Jensen (1977) have provided a frequently used five-stage description of task group development. Their first stage, forming, includes the establishment of new relationships and the tension associated with entering new situations. The second stage, storming, is characterized by individuals reacting to the demands of the situation, questioning authority, and developing enough comfort to be themselves. Norming is described as the third stage, in which the group establishes general ways of doing things that are particular to the group and can be described as rules for behavior. The next stage, performing, finds group members working on the task as they have previously worked on relationship formation. Finally, when the task nears completion, group members, in what is called the adjourning phase, bring closure to both task and interpersonal issues.

It is important to understand that these stages or phases, regardless of the labels associated with them, are meant to describe groups moving through a developmental process. As with any other type of development process, the stages are not distinct and do not necessarily progress in a fixed sequence. However, they do provide an overall model to help us understand the variety of communication behaviors we experience in the numerous organizational groups in which we are likely to become members.

Dave Green is joining a work group that has been together for some time. In a very real sense his membership may influence the group to re-form to include the new member. Obviously, the others know each other well. Their sense of tension with one another is predictably less than the tension of coming to know Dave. Dave, on the other hand, must establish new relationships with Sally, John, Ralph, and Susan. His tension is probably the highest in the group as he attempts to absorb the most new information. Dave is experiencing the reality of group membership in organizations. Often we will find ourselves the new member of a long-standing group. At other times we will be assigned to group projects in which all members are new. And at times we will be responsible for forming groups for important task and social considerations.

Dave is anxious to understand the expectations of Sally and the others in his work group. He has observed that very little conflict is voiced in group meetings. He is attempting to know whether this is a behavior expectation of the group—a norm—or whether few potentially conflicting issues have come before his group in the short period of his membership. Dave is concerned, as we all are in new groups, about the expectations the group holds and how the members will evaluate him. Simply put, Dave is concerned about AMX norms.

Group norms are unwritten behavior rules, ways of doing things, that groups develop over time, usually through tacit rather than explicit approval. Norms reflect what the group deems desirable, and they can be said to be cultural beliefs about effectiveness or appropriateness. Groups have general norms that apply to all members and role-specific norms that apply to individual members in such roles as leader, secretary, information collector, and critic. Generally speaking, group members disapprove and sometimes punish members who violate norms. We can only imagine what might occur if Dave Green openly disagreed with John in one of Sally's staff meetings. We don't know if the absence of conflict is an AMX norm, but we suspect that based on his observations, Dave will be cautious in initiating conflict. Dave is essentially attempting to establish his role in the group by understanding its norms or expectations. Based on the competencies Dave brings to the group, that role will emerge and will be worked out in relationship to other group members.

Group Communication Roles

We have previously described organizational communication as the construction of shared realities and the culture of organizations. We can also observe communication activities in groups as they contribute to shared group realities and culture. One way is by examining the roles group members enact and how these roles are encouraged or discouraged in the group.

Individuals assume different roles in groups. As a newcomer to the AMX team, Dave has a task role but also a newcomer role. Probably at first Dave's group will expect less from his task role because he is a newcomer who does not yet know the ropes. Dave can probably get more help from the group while he is still a newcomer than when the group believes he has had enough time to become socialized and make an equal contribution.

Dave also brings to his group predispositions for a variety of communication behaviors. His predispositions and his communication roles will interact with the predispositions and roles of other group members to create the "shared realities" of the group.

Kenneth Benne and Paul Sheats (1948) have developed three important classifications of **group communication roles:** group task roles, group maintenance roles, and self-centered roles. **Task roles** help groups accomplish goals, whereas **maintenance roles** promote social support among group members. **Self-centered roles** support individual goals and may or may not be compatible with overall group goals and relationships. An understanding of individual communication roles is useful for determining how

Group norms—unwritten behavior rules, ways of doing things, that groups develop over time. Norms reflect what groups deem desirable and can be said to be cultural beliefs about effectiveness or appropriateness.

Group communication roles—task, maintenance, and self-centered categories for description of behaviors that individuals exhibit in groups.

Task roles—communication roles that help groups accomplish goals.

Maintenance roles—communication roles that promote social support among group members.

Self-centered roles—communication roles that support individuals' goals and may or may not be compatible with overall group goals and relationships.

groups work and for identifying personal roles and skills that contribute to improved competency for group interaction.

Following is an adaptation of the Benne and Sheats role classification with examples of role statements taken from transcripts of staff meetings at a major national retailer.

GROUP TASK ROLES

1. *Initiator:* makes suggestions, contributes new ideas, recommends goals and procedures, speculates about approaches.

   "I don't think we should be bound by what we did last year for the Fourth of July sale. After all, the competition knows all that. Let's brainstorm for a few minutes about a new approach."

2. *Information requestor:* asks for facts, asks for experiences and comparisons, asks for new ideas; seeks clarification of expectations and information.

   "Do we know what our three major competitors are planning for the Fourth? I think it's important to find out, especially after our strong showing last year."

3. *Information giver:* submits facts, experiences, identifies relevant data, makes comparisons.

   "We were first in sales over the Fourth. However, we kept locations adjacent to public parks open at least two hours longer than our competitors. Our profit picture was influenced by additional operating overhead."

4. *Procedure facilitator:* takes notes, records ideas, distributes handouts, guides group to agenda.

   "I will gladly record all of our ideas while we brainstorm."

5. *Opinion requestor:* seeks opinions, values, beliefs of others, speculations about courses of action.

   "I know we aren't ready to make a final commitment to a promotion. If we had all the money we need, which of the proposals would fit your best guess of an ideal Fourth promotion?"

6. *Opinion giver:* gives opinions, expresses values and beliefs, gives speculations about courses of action or direction.

   "I think we ought to go with the television campaign. I don't have all the cost estimates but I think that gets us the most overall visibility."

7. *Clarifier:* explains ideas and elaborates; describes expectations, illustrates ideas, coordinates relationships between ideas and information.

   "I want to make sure we all understand. We need to compare cost projections for both types of promotions and then compare with sales projections."

8. *Summarizer-evaluator:* restates ideas and describes relationships, criticizes accomplishments, details agreements and differences.

   "I believe it is fair to say we have agreed on the need for a new promotion for this Fourth of July. We have agreed that it is between the TV campaign and a major celebrity event for the big stores. We will need to have full presentations on both ideas for the next meeting."

GROUP MAINTENANCE ROLES

1. *Social supporter:* expresses togetherness, encourages others, gives praise, suggests solidarity.

    "I think we have a really good group here. Of course, we don't always agree, but our track record is really impressive."

2. *Harmonizer:* mediates and reconciles differences, suggests areas of agreement between disagreeing members, suggests positive ways to explore differences.

    "John and Sally both have good points about possible promotions. Let's ask them both to present their ideas and identify possible ways of combining the best from both promotions."

3. *Tension reliever:* relaxes others, changes subjects, jokes, admits mistakes.

    "Let's not worry so much about this. After all, we can't make as big a mistake as we did for the Thanksgiving promotion. None of us got fired over that—we can take ourselves too seriously if we aren't careful."

4. *Energizer:* stimulates group activity, seeks group action.

    "Look, we need to decide what we are going to do next. Facts are nice, but we can't have a paralysis of indecision."

5. *Leader:* takes personal responsibility, represents group to others, determines agenda.

    "I will take personal responsibility to confront our advertising agency. They need to keep us better informed. I will put them on the agenda for our next meeting."

6. *Follower:* goes along with the group, accepts others' ideas, supports group decisions, listens to others.

    "You senior managers have the experience. Whatever you decide is fine with me."

7. *Compromiser:* seeks a middle position in disagreement, supports both task and people issues, gives up some of own position.

    "I think we can find a middle ground on this problem. It is possible to do TV and have a celebrity at one or two of the big stores. This combination might be better than either idea by itself."

8. *Gatekeeper:* asks opinions of nonparticipants, prevents dominance by others, facilitates overall interaction.

    "We haven't heard from John. Let's be quiet and hear what he has to say."

SELF-CENTERED ROLES

1. *Negative blocker:* negative responses to most ideas, negative about any positive solutions, raises continuous objections.

"Look, I have told you over and over again that what we decide doesn't make any difference. The advertising department controls the promotions; our ideas don't matter."

2. *Dominator:* controls through interruptions, superiority of tone, and length of conversational control.

"What you are saying isn't very important. I believe I know best what we should do."

3. *Attacker:* aggressive to achieve personal status, expresses disapproval, critical of status of other.

"Look, you are only the manager of a small store, and one that isn't all that successful. I would keep my mouth shut if I were you."

4. *Clown:* disrupts with jokes and other diverting behavior, brings up tangents, refuses to take ideas seriously.

"We don't have a problem—we need to let the good times roll. You people take all this much too seriously. When I was with [names a competitor] we really knew how to party when all the managers got together."

Generally speaking, group task and maintenance roles are considered productive for group interaction, whereas self-centered roles are destructive and contribute to ineffectiveness. However, chances are that most of us engage in all of these roles at one time or another. Communication competency for group settings is related to our ability to identify the roles we are likely to use and to analyze group needs in order to use those roles for effective problem solving.

Although the roles we have just described are frequently observed in organizational groups, they by no means represent all the possible communication roles. You can probably add to the list from your group experiences. Which communication roles are you likely to fulfill? Does your answer differ depending on the group in which you find yourself? If so, why? If not, why not? The transcript of a small-group problem-solving session in Figure 6.1 was taken from a staff meeting in the personnel department of a major computer manufacturer. As you read the transcript, try to determine the roles of the individual participants. Try also to determine whether or not these roles contribute to productive group outcomes.

Influences on Group Members

Stages of group development, norms, and group communication roles do not fully explain some of the subtle influences on our group experiences. Why are we more comfortable in some groups than others? What makes one group more prestigious than another? Why is it that certain group memberships help our career and others hinder professional success? How can we determine the difference?

There are no definite answers to these questions. Generally speaking, we are most comfortable in groups in which group goals and our individual

FIGURE 6.1
Group Problem-Solving Transcript

Jane (department manager): I think we had better get started. We have a lot to do to get ready to announce the new training plan.

Sally (senior trainer): Jane, I'm not sure everyone in the group really understands our plans. I think before we decide how to introduce the program to the division we need to make sure everyone in personnel is thoroughly familiar with what we intend to do.

Jane: That's a good point. How much information do the rest of you have?

John (compensation specialist): I just know we are going to plan a training program for each employee, but I have been on vacation and don't know much more than that.

Henry (recruiter): Look, I don't think each of us can be expected to know all the details. I think we should stick to our original plan and decide how a division-wide annoucement should be made. The rest of us are too busy to understand all the details.

Sally to Henry: I think you're very wrong. Especially in your job, you can actually attract people to this company with the type of ongoing training we are proposing.

Kathy (benefits administration): Sally, maybe you could describe the type of training our department will receive. That might help us understand the general concept.

Jane: Sally, I do think an overview of the program would be helpful. We do, however, have to decide on the timing of the division-wide announcement.

[Sally explains the basics of the new training program to the staff (narrative not included).]

Frank (employee representative): I think this sounds like a very impressive program, but I wonder if we can really pull it off—remember the time we decided to computerize all the records and start the year with a new payroll process. We were crazy. Who made that decision, anyway—does anyone remember? Let's not have another Kent Smith [employee who left the company following the record computerization project].

Sally to Frank: This is not another Kent Smith project. I resent you implying that it is—a lot of hard work and planning have gone into identifying training opportunities which will help all our employees. I think you should keep an open mind.

Jane: Does anyone else have any questions about the program?

Kathy: Well, I think we need to move in this direction. What ideas do you need from us to make the division announcement?

Sally: Thanks, Kathy. First of all, we need to know the timing of major communications from your individual areas to all employees. We don't want too much new information going out at once.

Try to identify the roles individuals played in the dialogue (see following list). Can you determine which individuals work more cooperatively than others? Is there a leader? Are important roles missing? How would you describe this group?

Task Roles	Maintenance Roles	Self-Centered roles
Initiator	Social supporter	Negative blocker
Information requestor	Harmonizer	Dominator
Information giver	Tension reliever	Attacker
Procedure facilitator	Energizer	Clown
Opinion requestor	Leader	
Opinion giver	Follower	
Clarifier	Compromiser	
Summarizer-evaluator	Gatekeeper	

goals are compatible. When our personal needs are met, we are more likely to attempt to meet the needs of others and to exhibit cohesive behavior within the group. We are attracted to remain in the comfort of the group.

Most of us are also attracted to groups with high prestige or in which we have prestige. Conventional wisdom suggests that prestige contributes to career success. The culture of an organization communicates which groups are prestigious and which are not. Prestigious groups usually have more authority, responsibility, and risk associated with their efforts. Those with confidence in their communication and task competencies will be attracted to such groups, whereas those with lower estimations of themselves will avoid membership in such visible groups.

Additionally group participation is influenced by the overall climate of a group, the degree of interaction among group members, and the overall size of the group. Rodney Napier and Matti Gershenfeld (1989) have suggested that group members are more attracted to groups in which the climate is characterized by commitment to the group, compatibility among members, more cooperative than competitive behaviors, and expectations that work will be evaluated on a team versus individual performance basis. Finally, groups are more attractive as participation among members increases and the overall size of the group remains relatively small. Additionally, Napier and Gershenfeld have identified influences that they believe block effectiveness: domination of single members; negatively critical norms; vested interests of individual members; changing group membership, resulting in less compatible relationships; and problems of physical space.

Conflict, leadership, and problem-solving processes affect our group experiences. Whether or not conflict is effectively handled may determine whether we wish to continue membership in a given group. Leadership may determine whether any actual work gets done or whether members are recognized for their contributions. And problem-solving processes determine the task effectiveness of organizational groups. Conflict processes in groups, leadership and management communication, and problem solving and decision making are the specific subjects of the next three chapters in this text. In each of these chapters emphasis will be placed on how conflict, leadership, and problem-solving processes affect both individual and group effectiveness.

TYPES OF GROUPS

Earlier we said that organizations have many different types of formal and informal groups for important task and social considerations. We talked about relationships in primary work groups between supervisors and subordinates and among peers. We are aware that most of us will have multiple group memberships in addition to our primary work team. The next section of this chapter identifies some of the specific types of groups common to organizations.

Primary Work Teams

Primary work team—group to which an individual is assigned upon organizational entry.

The first group assigned to us when we enter an organization is our **primary work team.** What we have been hired to do places us structurally within the organization and identifies our supervisor and related peer group. Work teams vary in size and formality. Some will work closely together, whereas others exchange infrequent information. Carl Larson and Frank LaFasto (1989) have identified three common features of competent work team members: (1) the possession of essential skills and abilities, (2) a strong desire to contribute, and (3) the capability of collaborating effectively.

In recent research on effective teams Larson and LaFasto found that effective work teams had members whose technical abilities were relevant to the team's objectives and who valued commitment and contributions to the team. Effective teams were characterized by the understanding of individual members concerning the relationship of their personal efforts to team effectiveness. Finally, Larson and LaFasto reported, "a consistent response . . . was the importance of selecting team members capable of working well with others. The emphasis in their responses was on capability. It was noted, repeatedly, that some people are capable of dealing with others in a collaborative fashion, and some are not. Some people are capable of focusing on issues instead of positions, capable of sharing information openly, capable of listening objectively to fellow team members, and capable of bringing out the best in others. Some people are simply not 'wired-up' that way." Larson and LaFasto concluded that their data collected from effective teams strongly suggested that people who could not collaborate should be removed from team efforts.

John Cragan and David Wright (1986) have identified some of the different types of work teams we are likely to encounter. Their descriptions of long-standing work groups, project teams, and "prefab" work groups help us understand the different team structures organized to meet particular work needs. **Long-standing teams,** for example, are formed when the overall responsibilities of the team change slowly with time and when team membership can be expected to remain relatively stable. Long-standing work teams have well-defined organizational responsibilities, enabling selection of new team members based on qualifications previously identified as important for the group. Dave Green is joining such a group at AMX. The training function is well established and is expected to continue over time. AMX has experience with the types of people who are successful in training and development jobs. As such they have drawn up a list of qualifications they believe new members of the department should possess. Dave Green matches their initial expectations and enters a relatively long-standing group.

> **Long-standing teams**—relatively permanent groups of individuals organized for task accomplishment.

University departments are examples of long-standing teams. Although advances in knowledge change the content of courses, the general responsibilities for teaching, research, and service remain. Our government is another long-standing example. The Congress, state and local governments, the Supreme Court, the presidency, and numerous other entities are examples of groups established by law but supported by the customs of the society as a whole. In most organizations personnel, financial, legal, and overall management responsibilities are carried out by long-standing teams. Long-standing teams develop ways of doing things that not only make qualifications for new members clear but also identify expected behaviors for members. Long-standing teams have the strength of team history and practical experience. However, they can limit creativity and change when group traditions block rapid adaptation to new circumstances.

Project teams are formed with highly specialized individuals to accomplish a specific project in a fixed period of time. These teams have specific goals, such as the design of a new product or the integration of technologies across the organization. Project teams are commonly used in high-technology industries for the research and design of products and processes. Their formation is based on the technical expertise needed for a given line of inquiry. Project teams draw membership from other teams in the organization, and assignments may be viewed as temporary or relatively permanent, depending on the needs of the project. Project teams have been part of the space program for many years and are common in telecommunications, electronic, computer, and research-based industries. Because of the nature of their formation, project teams do not have the history and traditions of long-standing work groups. They must quickly clarify goals, roles, and responsibilities in order to establish working relationships

> **Project teams**—work groups established for the duration of a specific assignment.

necessary to meet project guidelines and timetables. The formation of project teams permits an organization to respond rapidly to changing markets. Team members, however, may have difficulty in establishing trust and mutually satisfying working relationships when pressured by deadlines and the technical complexity of a challenging assignment.

Whereas project teams are associated with high-technology research and development efforts, the **prefab group** is the invention of the U.S. service industry. As Cragen and Wright (1986) have described the prefabricated group, "the job descriptions of this type of work group have been meticulously defined and rigidly structured so that a collection of people with no previous experience of working together can quickly form a work group that will produce a predictable level of productivity. Fast-food chains in the United States are the most obvious examples of industries that use prefab groups. These organizations use a highly fluid work force, yet, despite the high turnover, each neighborhood outlet reliably turns out the same product in about the same time." The prefab group is efficient and predictable. Behavior expectations are specifically and clearly established. The group is designed to produce an average level of production and not expected to solve problems, introduce creativity into the process, or adapt to new situations. Prefab groups are best utilized for the production of goods and services but are not appropriate to meet problem-solving needs.

Prefab group—work group designed and structured for frequent replacement of members. Prefab groups have detailed individual assignments requiring limited experience to produce specified products.

Quality Circles

Quality circles is the name applied to a specific application of group problem solving that has gained popularity in the United States during the last decade. The term *quality circle* is applied to a group that meets regularly to identify and propose solutions to problems affecting product or process quality. Although the utilization of problem-solving teams began as early as the turn of the twentieth century, the emphasis on quality circles as we know it today began after World War II when Edward Deming introduced his statistical quality-control methods to Japanese management. By the early 1970s over 6 million Japanese workers were participating in quality circles or attempts to have line workers and leaders spend voluntary time solving product quality problems. The success of quality circles in Japan and increasing concerns for product quality in the United States have generated intense interest in this participative process of quality control.

Quality circles—voluntary groups charged with responding to quality or quantity problems and to issues raised by management.

Typically, quality circles are groups of volunteers who work in the same general area with the same general technology. Groups are led by supervisors or elected group members and are charged with responding to quality or quantity problems and to issues raised by management. Emphasis is placed on training quality circle members in group dynamics, problem solving, communication, and quality control. Quality circles are formed around the idea that groups can more quickly and effectively identify problems and propose solutions; that workers at all levels want to participate in problem solving, not just task implementation; and that innovations proposed at all levels within organizations can improve quality and productivity. Quality circles have made documented improvements in productivity. However, they must be supported by access to useful information for problem solving and by genuine management responsiveness to change.

Task Force Groups

Task force groups are formed to bring together individuals with technical specialties, and who are members of other organizational groups, to accomplish a specifically designed task or project. Like project groups, task force groups are formed around the technical specialties of their members. Unlike project teams, task force groups generally do not create products or implement processes but plan the initiation of projects or organizational changes. Simply put, task force groups are study groups charged with making recommendations. A task force may research and evaluate how to restructure organizational responsibilities. Recently, for example, a major high-technology firm was unable to recruit successfully approximately 60 percent of the job applicants to whom they made offers. In their concern for recruiting effectiveness, top management formed a task force to study recruiting responsibilities and make recommendations for changes. Membership of the task force was selected from all organizational groups with any recruiting responsibility. The task force was given specific responsibilities by management and a time frame in which to present conclusions. Task force groups have the advantage of focused responsibilities and potential membership from qualified individuals throughout the organization. However, they frequently face challenges because individual members may seek to protect the position of their primary work groups. Task force groups are generally more successful when members agree that change is needed and they work cooperatively for organizational versus subgroup goals.

Task force groups—groups of individuals with diverse specialties and group memberships who are charged with accomplishing a specifically designed task or project.

Steering Committees

Steering committees resemble task force groups in the composition of their memberships. However, what task force groups recommend, steering committees implement. Formed with diverse organizational membership, steering committees implement organizational plans, processes, or change. Whereas the task force might recommend a new recruiting process for the high-technology firm, a steering committee might be formed to implement recommendations and monitor the process of the new plan. Steering committees literally "steer" the progress of a plan, goal, issue, or program. They give organizations the advantage of broad participation in the oversight of a project. Steering committees have been criticized, however, as "rubber stamp" groups in which no one takes definite responsibility, permitting the best-laid plans to miss the mark or actually fail. Research sug-

Steering committees—groups of individuals with diverse specialties and group memberships who are charged with implementing organizational plans, processes, or change.

gests that authority and responsibility to bring about change are critical for successful steering committees.

Focus Groups

Focus groups—collections of individuals who have familiarity with a problem or issue and are asked in a somewhat nonstructured format to describe the issue and make recommendations; formed to discuss problems but not take responsibility for final recommendations or implementation of change.

Like quality circles, **focus groups** represent a technique gaining in organizational use. Focus groups are collections of individuals who are familiar with a problem or issue and are asked in a somewhat unstructured format to describe the issue and any recommendations they might have. Focus groups have been utilized by advertising and marketing organizations to understand consumer preferences, identify effective message strategies, and evaluate potential new products. The successful use of focus groups in advertising and marketing has stimulated their application to numerous other organizational issues. Focus groups are formed to discuss problems, not to take responsibility for final recommendations or implementation of change. Focus groups can be utilized to gather information and get reactions quickly to proposed courses of actions. The groups frequently are formed to identify new types of training needs, assess employee morale, uncover poorly defined problems, and make policy recommendations. They provide excellent information when made up of individuals with adequate concern for or information about the subject for discussion. Focus group members, on occasion, have voiced frustration about not knowing the outcome of their efforts. Forward-thinking companies, when using employee focus groups, are careful to provide feedback mechanisms.

Social Support Groups

Social support groups—formed as subgroups of larger task groups or among people with similar organizational interests; function to stimulate trust and cohesiveness among group members.

Work teams, quality circles, task forces, steering committees, and focus groups all can be **social support groups.** Formed for task considerations, most continuous groups provide informal social support to group members. Social support groups form as subgroups of larger task groups among people with similar organizational interests and among friends. They have few formal task responsibilities as such but often support task accomplishment by stimulating trust and cohesiveness among group members. Social support group membership has been associated with organizational and communication satisfaction and competency. Individuals apprehensive about communication are less likely to be members of diverse social support groups and are more likely than others to work in relative isolation. Those comfortable with their communication competencies are more likely to be involved in diverse groups and are more likely than their more highly apprehensive counterparts to exhibit communication and job satisfaction.

As you can readily see, groups are important for our organizational experiences. In many cases, our competencies will be evaluated through our group participation. The next section of this chapter will describe effectiveness in groups, with a particular emphasis on effective individual participation behaviors.

INCREASING GROUP PARTICIPATION EFFECTIVENESS

We have been discussing the importance of a variety of groups for organizational life. We have described how individuals bring attitudes about themselves, others, groups, and information to group membership. We have examined how groups develop, the group communication roles that emerge, general influences on group members, and the types of groups common in organizational life. We have concluded that effective organizational participation includes participation in groups. The question now becomes how we can evaluate our competencies for group participation. What types of behaviors are most productive? What should be avoided? Are there particular communication skills we should develop for group effectiveness? And finally, can we identify general guidelines for effective group participation? The next section of this chapter seeks to increase our effectiveness by identifying positive and negative group participation behaviors, describing communication skills necessary for effective participation, and concluding with guidelines for effective group participation.

The positive behaviors, skills, and guidelines we will discuss are based on the emerging concept of self-managing groups. In our fast-paced information society, less emphasis is placed on layers of management control and more on innovation and creativity at all organizational levels. The increasing use of project teams, quality circles, focus groups, task forces, and steering committees attests to the notion that organizations are seeking teams of people who can be self-motivated and self-directed. The concept of self-managing teams speaks to the need for broad-based responsibility from all team members and underscores our need to develop effective personal participation behaviors. With fewer managers, more complex decisions, more information, and less time to respond, teams in organizations will increasingly be required to manage information and change while effectively managing themselves.

Positive and Negative Participation Behaviors

Each individual brings to group participation preferences for behavior. Research on effective group participation permits us to generalize about productive and counterproductive individual behaviors.

Positive Behaviors

1. Be prepared and informed when in decision-making and problem-solving groups. Contributions to meetings should be based on knowledge about the topic, agenda, and facts that bear directly on the problem.

2. Exhibit cooperative and open-minded behaviors that encourage participation by all involved. When working in a group setting, group

goals have important priority. Cooperation includes encouraging participation and encouraging listening and the clarification of meanings among group members. Cooperation also includes speaking with receivers in mind (concerning both content and style) to minimize message distortion. Groups tend to work best when all members accept a collective responsibility for productive outcomes.

3. Attempt to remain rational, and thoughtfully evaluate all information. Effective participation includes analyzing our own logic as well as the logic of others. Effective members exhibit enough patience for this examination to be possible. Effective members recognize that good decisions are based on good information subjected to solid reasoning and evaluation.

4. Observe the participation process of the group. Members have not only a contribution responsibility but also a process responsibility for helping all members to participate thoughtfully. Those not speaking are in a position to observe when the group is straying from its goals or when silent members are not being given an opportunity for participation. Observation is also important for subtle cues that suggest some members may be holding important reservations that will ultimately affect their commitment.

5. Actively participate as well as observe. Active participants who seek active participation from others set a tone in the group that encourages good decision making and problem solving.

Negative Behaviors

1. Argue stubbornly for your own ideas, positions, and conclusions. Make sure all members know exactly where you stand and resist modifying or changing your views. Do not bother to listen actively to opposing viewpoints because of the rightness of your position.

2. Suppress differences of opinion and conflict. Use formal techniques such as agendas or majority rule to quiet opposition. Don't encourage others to express controversial opinions and make sure the group considers only safe topics.

3. Work for quick agreement. Extended problem analysis and solution generation may contribute to dissent. Don't worry about "groupthink" because, after all, you are a group and everyone should support the same viewpoint.

4. If a stalemate occurs, pit one person against another so that there are clear winners and losers. This will return the group to action and discourage others from blocking progress.

5. Use your power position to get others to agree with you. Don't hesitate to "pull rank" or threaten sanctions to preserve your ability to influence others.

Communication Skills for Effective Participation

Self-managing group members assume roles and responsibilities in task and maintenance areas. Earlier we described group communication roles in task, maintenance, and self-centered categories. We are now going to examine how, as we assume group roles, we will engage in task and maintenance behaviors utilizing a variety of communication skills. Figure 6.2 lists participation roles and responsibilities in the task and maintenance categories previously discussed. (Self-centered roles are not included because our focus is on effectiveness.) For each role and responsibility area, communication skills that contribute to effectiveness are identified. The list in Figure 6.2 is not intended to be all-inclusive or to suggest that skills needed in one responsibility are not useful in other areas as well. This identification of responsibilities and skills is presented to help focus our thinking on how communication tactics influence task and maintenance processes. Effective group members learn to think strategically about the tactics they use to achieve overall excellence from group efforts. Table 6.1 describes each of the identified communication skills and their desired results. In the Workshop section of this chapter you will have an opportunity to evaluate your own skill development in each of these areas.

Guidelines for Effective Group Participation

The following guidelines for effective group participation have been adapted from the work of John Cragan and David Wright (1986). As you review the guidelines try to decide which are the most important and what additional guidelines you would suggest.

1. Prepare for group participation: Review relevant materials before meetings; ask for additional needed information; formulate ideas; help with physical arrangements; encourage other team members.

2. Value diverse opinions and people: Promote differing ideas; challenge team members to offer alternative views; support disagreement; encourage broad participation.

3. Contribute ideas and seek information: Willingly risk ideas and opinions; ask for criticism; ask for opinions. Support participation; discourage negative evaluation.

4. Stress group productivity: Encourage group members; note past successes; identify group strengths; remember group responsibilities.

5. Avoid "role ruts": Use diverse communication roles; encourage diversity among team members; share roles with others.

6. Avoid self-centered roles: Identify disruptive behaviors; self-monitor behavior; give feedback to those exhibiting self-centered roles.

7. Ease tensions: Facilitate positive expressions of differences; support people; evaluate ideas; stress cooperation.

FIGURE 6.2
Self-Managing Group Responsibilities

Role/Responsibility	*Communication Skills*
Task Roles	
Problem analysis	Initiating
	Questioning
	Interpreting
	Suggesting
	Facilitating
Idea generation	Initiating
	Questioning
	Suggesting
	Facilitating
Idea evaluation	Evaluating
	Giving feedback
	Facilitating
	Questioning
Abstract ideas/vision identification	Initiating
	Clarifying
Solution generation	Initiating
	Suggesting
	Facilitating
	Questioning
	Summarizing
Solution implementation	Initiating
	Facilitating
	Summarizing
	Terminating
Goal setting	Initiating
	Questioning
	Facilitating
	Suggesting
	Evaluating
	Summarizing
Agenda making	Initiating
	Facilitating
	Summarizing
	Terminating
Discussion clarification	Clarifying
	Active listening
	Interpreting
Disagreement identification	Active listening
	Clarifying

	Questioning
	Confronting
	Facilitating
	Blocking
Consensus identification	Active listening
	Clarifying
	Summarizing

Maintenance Roles

Group participation	Active listening
	Clarifying
	Questioning
	Modeling
	Facilitating
Group climate	Confronting
	Reflecting feelings and supporting
	Empathizing
	Blocking
Conflict management	Active listening
	Clarifying
	Questioning
	Confronting
	Reflecting feelings and supporting
	Blocking
	Terminating

8. Support leadership: Help leaders accomplish goals; share leadership when necessary.

9. Build group pride: Create traditions, symbols, and slogans; celebrate work, progress, success; celebrate interpersonal relationships.

10. Produce results: Take responsibility for group outcomes; encourage responsibility from team members; focus on effectiveness.

Think for a moment about groups in which you have been a member. Which of the guidelines for effective participation were used? Which were not? Should they have been? What additions can you recommend? Many effective groups actively establish guidelines for their own effectiveness. Think about the guidelines you might recommend to groups in which you are currently a member.

SUMMARY

An individual's small-group experiences result from the attitudes, beliefs, preferences, and abilities the individual brings to a variety of groups and the overall effectiveness of group participation behaviors. Organizations

TABLE 6.1
Communication Skills, Descriptions, and Results

Skill	*Description*	*Purpose*
1. Initiating	Introduces ideas, directions; calls for action	To increase productivity, include expertise, and pace the group process
2. Questioning	Asks for ideas, analysis and exploration; seeks participation	To generate information, stimulate thinking, and increase overall participation
3. Interpreting	Offers explanations for self- and other verbalizations and behaviors	To provide expanded perspective and clarify meaning
4. Suggesting	Offers ideas, advice, information, and tentative direction	To provide group directions and explore alternatives
5. Facilitating	Asks for participation; reminds of agenda and goals; organizes group activities	To promote effective participation among group members and stimulate good problem solving
6. Evaluating	Appraises and critiques ideas and group process	To stimulate quality decisions/solutions and promote effective group processes
7. Giving feedback	States reactions to ideas and group processes	To open the communication process and develop self-awareness of others
8. Clarifying	Attempts to explain messages for maximum understanding at both the feeling and thinking levels	To improve message understanding for entire group
9. Summarizing	States all important elements of the group process	To give overall direction and facilitate group process
10. Terminating	Brings a group session to a close	To finalize decisions, summarize disagreements and agreements, and establish follow-up responsibilities
11. Active listening	Attends to verbal and nonverbal communication and feeds back to speaker a summary of what was understood	To seek understanding and clarify meaning for self and others
12. Confronting	Challenges others to eliminate discrepancies between words and actions, produce ideas, or manage personal behavior	To promote critical evaluation of ideas, open honest communication, eliminate destructive behavior, and encourage participation
13. Positive blocking	Stops counterproductive individual or group behaviors	To provide for effective overall group process and good problem solving
14. Modeling	Demonstrates through personal behavior desired group behaviors	To give examples of effective behaviors for others to follow
15. Reflecting feelings and supporting	Communicates understanding of feelings and encourages and reinforces participation	To develop trust and an atmosphere in which all feel free to participate and disagree
16. Empathizing	Verbally identifies with the frame of reference of others	To develop trust and encourage group understanding of similarities and differences

form groups to fulfill diverse organizational needs. The underlying assumption is that the efforts of numbers of individuals exceed individual efforts either for completing tasks or for examining issues requiring energy and creativity.

The most important resource a group has is its members. Working relationships in groups result from the attitudes we have about ourselves, our attitudes about others, our beliefs about groups in general, and our concern for inquiry. Generally speaking, the more positively we feel about our personal communication competencies, the better able we are to work in groups successfully. Our rhetorical sensitivity, important for group communication, is related to (1) acceptance of personal complexity, (2) avoidance of communicative rigidity, (3) interaction consciousness, (4) appreciation of the communicability of ideas, and (5) tolerance for inventional searching.

Groups have both socioemotional and task concerns. Researchers generally suggest that groups progress through a series of stages that begin with formation, move to production, and finally to resolution and dissolution. A frequently used five-stage description of task group development is forming, storming, norming, performing, and adjourning. It is important to understand that these stages or phases are meant to describe groups moving through a developmental process generally.

Norms are unwritten behavior rules, ways of doing things, that groups develop over time. Norms reflect what the group deems desirable and can be said to be cultural beliefs about effectiveness or appropriateness. Groups have general norms that apply to all members and role-specific norms that apply to individual members. Individuals assume different roles in groups. Generally speaking we can describe three important classifications of group communication roles: group task roles, group maintenance roles, and self-centered roles. Task roles help groups accomplish goals, and maintenance roles promote social support among group members. Self-centered roles support individual goals and may or may not be compatible with overall group goals and relationships. Most frequently, we are attracted to groups in which our individual goals and group goals are compatible; prestige is high; the climate is characterized by commitment to the group, compatibility among members, and team versus individual work; and the size of the group remains relatively small.

Effective groups have essential skills and abilities, a strong desire by members to contribute, and the capability of collaborating effectively. The first group assigned to us when we enter an organization is our primary work team. Primary work teams have been described as long-standing work teams, project teams, and prefab groups. Quality circles are voluntary teams of workers from the same general area or related technology who meet regularly to identify and propose solutions to problems affecting product or process quality. Task force groups are formed to bring together individuals with technical specialties who are members of other organizational groups to accomplish a specifically designed task or project. Steering committees resemble task forces in composition but are formed for the implementation of projects or to "steer" the progress of a plan, goal, issue, or program. Focus groups help organizations quickly understand issues and programs through use of unstructured formats. Focus groups are not charged with final recommendations or implementation planning. Finally, social support groups form across all types of formally structured groups and in less structured ways. Individuals comfortable with their communication competencies are more likely to be involved in diverse groups and are more likely than their more highly apprehensive counterparts to exhibit communication and job satisfaction.

The concept of self-managing teams, emerging in our fast-paced information society, speaks to the need for broad-based responsibility from all team members and underscores our need to develop effective personal participation behaviors. Positive participation behaviors include preparation for group participation, cooperative and open-minded behaviors, attempts to remain rational, an understanding of participation processes within groups, and active personal participation. Self-managing groups exhibit roles and take responsibility in task and maintenance areas. For each responsibility area, communication skills can be identified that contribute to effectiveness. Finally, guidelines for effective group participation include individual participation requirements, valuing of diverse opinions and people, avoidance of "role ruts" and self-centered roles, and a concern for the group and its results.

WORKSHOP

1. In groups of six, develop descriptions of effective and ineffective groups. Describe what makes the difference. Summarize your findings and compare with other groups.

2. Identifying effective and ineffective communication roles in groups helps us understand our own behavior and the behavior of others. Read the following Group Communication Roles and attempt to identify the communication roles used by John, Henry, Tim, Mary, and Mike. (See pages 207–208.)

3. Form groups of six members each and select a topic of mutual interest for discussion. One member of the group will become a nonparticipating observer. Select a topic for which a group recommendation for action can be made. The group will be given fifteen minutes for discussion. Although consensus is not required, each group should attempt to reach one or two recommendations for the issue that most members can support. During the discussion the appointed observer will fill out the observation form that follows. At the conclusion of the discussion each participating member also should fill out the form from his or her memory of communication skills exhibited by each

group member. The assigned nonparticipant discusses his or her observations with the group, followed by general discussion of all observations.

4. Individually, or in teams of two or four members each, attend a small-group meeting where your presence for observation will not interfere with the work of the group. Attempt to identify the roles enacted by group members and the communication skills they utilize. List all of the behavior norms you can identify for the group. Finally, evaluate whether or not you believe their meeting was effective. Specify why you arrived at your conclusion. Be prepared to report your findings either verbally or in writing.

Group Communication Roles

Read the following transcript of a typical group meeting that could occur in any organization.* Identify the various communication roles used by the group members. Which individuals demonstrate more effective roles? What might members do differently to improve their communication?

The group members: John, Henry, Tim, Mary, Mike

The problem: Planning the development of an improved employee policy manual

Communication roles: Task, maintenance, self-centered

The Transcript

JOHN: I know you'll all agree that it's an honor to be chosen to be on this committee. And as you know, my background is primarily in personnel, so I'll be glad to take primary responsibility for a first rewrite on the manual.

HENRY: That's good of you, John. But before moving too quickly to a rewrite, I'd like to hear some general ideas for improving the manual from all the members of our committee. Policy for the employees is a matter of importance to all of us.

TIM: Hey, you two, either of your suggestions would work well. John, if you want to do a rewrite, it might save all of us plenty of time. But then again, it might also be good to base your rewrite on ideas from other committee members.

MARY: True, Tim, but the main point we want to keep in mind is that we, as a committee, want to write a new manual that will act as a model for other companies; something we can all be proud to have worked on.

* Prepared by Sherwyn P. Morreale.

MIKE: You're right, Mary, that's the spirit. We're all in agreement on doing the best possible job. I'd sure like to hear everybody's thoughts regarding the two possibilities we can now consider. Do you all think we should begin with a rewrite from John? Or should we begin with the manual we've got? Or are there other possible ways to go that we should consider?

JOHN: Listen, since our time is limited today, why don't I go ahead with just a simple rough draft of a rewrite. Then I'll get a copy of it to each group member before our next meeting. We can go from there.

TIM: Sounds great to me. You'll be saving all of us time and energy. When's the next meeting?

HENRY: Saving time is always a good idea. I'm with you 100 percent, Tim. But I'm a little concerned about our committee being a group that forgets to look before it leaps. Before we adjourn today, why don't we go out and come in again on this one. Let's talk it through a little more.

MARY: Okay, Henry, do you think we should take more time right now and have everyone present what they think this rewrite should focus on? I'd like to hear some more ideas from everyone also. It may be our ideas will be a little different; or we may really disagree on just how the rewrite should be done.

HENRY: True, but the best final manual is going to be a product of some friendly disagreeing. So how does everybody see it? Where do we go with this rewrite job?

MARY: I think the best thing to do, at this point, is for each of us to draw up a list of the best things we see in our present manual, plus a list of its weakest points. Then together we can do a summary list of what to keep and what to improve.

JOHN: That sounds good, from a creativity point of view. But time counts here and unless I can get on the rewrite soon, my schedule might tighten up. Then I might not have time to do a rewrite at all.

TIM: Then maybe we need to prepare these lists as quickly as possible and get them right to John. Whichever way, though, it'll work well. We seem to know how to work together on a job like this.

HENRY: We do not need to make a decision here on how to proceed. Let's have each person put their ideas out for, say, five minutes each. Then we can take a vote on what to do.

Identification of Group Communication Skills

SKILLS USED	NAMES OF GROUP MEMBERS					
Initiating						
Questioning						
Interpreting						
Suggesting						
Facilitating						
Evaluating						
Giving feedback						
Clarifying						
Summarizing						
Terminating						
Active listening						
Confronting						
Positive blocking						
Modeling						
Reflecting feelings and support						
Empathizing						

SUMMARY OF COMPETENCY COMPONENTS

KNOWLEDGE, SENSITIVITY, SKILLS, VALUES

KNOWLEDGE

Groups have both task and socioemotional concerns.

Small-group experiences occur in work, problem-solving, and social support context.

Individual group members enact task, maintenance, and self-centered roles.

Groups develop norms that influence member behavior.

SENSITIVITY

Rhetorical sensitivity is important for group communication.

Individuals exhibit both productive and counterproductive roles in groups.

Self-managing teams require effective personal participation behaviors.

SKILLS

Personal communication skills are practiced and evaluated.

Analysis skills are developed through observation and transcript evaluation.

VALUES

Individual attitudes, beliefs, and practices affect group effectiveness.

Group participation behaviors reflect values about inquiry and information generation.

Self-managing groups accept responsibility for participation and effectiveness.

Group experiences influence job and communication satisfaction.

REFERENCES AND SUGGESTED READINGS

Baird, J. E., Jr. 1977. *The dynamics of organizational communication*. New York: Harper & Row.

Benne, K., and P. Sheats. 1948. Functional roles of group members. *Journal of Social Issues* 4(2): 41–49.

Brilhart, J. K., and G. J. Galanes. 1989. *Effective group discussion*. 6th ed. Dubuque, IA: Brown.

Cartwright, D., and A. Zander. 1968. *Group dynamics research and theory*. 3rd ed. New York: Harper & Row.

Cragan, J., and D. Wright. 1986. *Communication in small group discussions*. 2nd ed. St. Paul, MN: West Publishing.

Larson, C. E., and F. M. LaFasto. 1989. *TeamWork: What must go right/What can go wrong*. Newbury Park, CA: Sage.

Napier, R. W., and M. K. Gershenfeld. 1989. *Groups: Theory and experience*. Boston: Houghton Mifflin.

Tuckman, B. W., and M. A. C. Jensen. 1977. Stages of small-group development revisited. *Group and Organization Studies* 2(4): 419–427.

CHAPTER

Photograph courtesy Mountain Bell Company

~ S E V E N ~

Organizational Conflict: Communicating for Effectiveness

Developing competencies through . . .

KNOWLEDGE

Defining and describing organizational conflict
Identifying conflict episodes
Describing contexts for conflict

SENSITIVITY

Understanding individual conflict styles and strategic objectives
Distinguishing between productive and counterproductive conflicts
Identifying supportive communication climates

SKILLS

Assessing communication tactics used during conflict
Developing a problem-solving process for conflict
Practicing analysis capabilities

VALUES

Understanding individual responsibilities for productive conflict
Clarifying ethical conflict behaviors

The Middlesex Insurance Company Case

John Fellows was excited to be named manager of the highly respected claims division for a major midwestern insurance company. John's experience in the insurance business was varied, and at age thirty-three he had just completed extensive training on a new computer system the company hoped would eventually reduce escalating overhead costs. John was aware that at least two members of his new department had applied for the job he was assuming, and he believed the company had placed him in the position partly to avoid making a choice between two competent peers.

John's initial month in the claims office of Middlesex was productive, confirming what he had been told about the competence of department personnel. Even the former applicants for his job, Joan and Tom, were cooperative and helpful. As a result of these early successes, John decided to move forward quickly with a plan to train personnel and install a new computer system. His immediate manager expressed concern that he was moving too fast without being thoroughly familiar with the department.

Following his staff meeting announcement of training schedules for all employees, John was surprised and somewhat irritated when Joan complained that he was moving too quickly before understanding department procedures. John decided Joan probably had not really accepted his promotion into the job she wanted. This seemed to be confirmed when Tom came to John and suggested there was reason to be concerned about the morale of the department with all of the upcoming changes. Tom even hinted that three key people were considering asking for transfers. Although Tom did not say so, John was sure Joan was at the bottom of the trouble.

John decided to confront Joan with her lack of support for this major corporate project. Joan became defensive and denied she was resisting the change—in fact, she claimed that John's misunderstanding of her concerns proved her point. To Joan, John simply was moving too fast and would create problems in systems about which he knew very little. John left the encounter wondering if maybe he had made a mistake about Joan, about Tom, or about his decision.

INTRODUCTION

Are John and Joan engaged in organizational conflict or is this a personal problem? Is the new computer system the issue? Is the issue John's approach? How is Tom involved? More important, what would you do if you were John, Joan, or Tom?

As a new manager, John is faced with a real test of his communication competency. Also, he is dealing with how important and inevitable conflict is in organizational life. What John decides will affect Joan, the entire department, and possibly his future career. How would you help John decide? What does he need to understand to be an effective manager of the claims division?

Although we may not have had John and Joan's specific problem, most of us have been involved in numerous conflicts and have been faced, as John is, with important decisions. Students have conflicts with teachers over grades. Families argue about issues of responsibility or money. Co-workers have negative feelings when particular individuals carry more of the work load than others. All are examples of conflicts that test our understanding and abilities.

It is important before you read further to think specifically about some of the conflicts that have been meaningful to you. What were the issues? Who was involved? What happened? For most of us it is easier to decide what John should do in the claims division than to make decisions when we are directly involved. Yet as John and Joan discovered, conflict is an inevitable part of our daily interactions.

Certainly if we are to be competent organizational communicators we will be confronted with the need to solve problems effectively during conflict. To develop communication competencies for conflict, it is necessary to understand what conflict is, how it works, what role it plays in organizational functioning, and finally how individuals within organizations influence conflict outcomes.

This chapter is designed to contribute to our *knowledge* by defining the concept of conflict, describing its various contexts and causes, and developing an analysis framework for understanding its process. Knowledge competencies, in turn, will help develop analysis *skills* for specific situations. *Sensitivity* competencies are developed by identifying individual predispositions and style preferences for conflict and by becoming familiar with strategies and tactics commonly used in conflicts. Sensitivity competencies influence the use of verbal and problem-solving process skills appropriate for each individual and the conflict at hand.

Value competencies are developed by exploring productive consequences of conflict, identifying supportive climates for conflict, and clarifying ethical conflict behaviors. As would be expected, value competencies are reflected in the use of ethical and supportive skills during conflict.

Finally, all four competencies—knowledge, sensitivity, skills, and values—are applied to the development of a problem-solving process for conflict and to competency practice through case analysis.

DEFINING AND DESCRIBING CONFLICT PROCESSES

Defining Conflict

Conflict can be described as a process that occurs when individuals, small groups, or organizations perceive or experience frustration in attaining goals and concerns. At times this frustration is the result of a struggle over

Conflict—process that occurs when individuals, small groups, or organizations perceive or experience frustration in attaining goals and concerns.

differing values or scarce rewards, while at other times the central issue is the status or power of involved individuals. Regardless of the reasons, for all conflict participants the process includes perceptions, emotions, behaviors, and outcomes.

Contexts and Causes for Conflict

Researchers H. Wayland Cummings, Larry Long, and Michael Lewis (1983) have suggested that conflict can occur in any organizational setting where there are two or more competing responses to a single event. In other words, conflict can occur in any context—intrapersonal, interpersonal, small group, intergroup, organization-wide, or between the organization and its broader environment.

The context in which conflict occurs influences the conflict symptoms, behaviors, and outcomes. *Intrapersonal* conflict, for example, is not readily observable through overt behaviors; an individual experiencing internal conflict may not discuss the problem. Yet he or she may be observed to be under pressure or generally in a bad mood. These observations are indirect symptoms of the intrapersonal conflict. When John begins to wonder about his assumptions regarding Tom and Joan and to doubt his decision about the computer system, he may begin to experience intrapersonal conflict common to all of us when our perceptions differ from those around us and when our judgments are called into question. Furthermore, because John is the manager, it will be difficult for him to take a wait-and-see attitude while letting others resolve the problem.

The conflict between John and Joan is a good example of the *interpersonal* context for organizational conflict. John is excited about his job and the opportunity to put into practice his training on the new system. While he can understand that Joan wanted his job, he isn't prepared for her resistance to change. He believes she is frustrated because she was not promoted and thus discounts her concerns about his lack of understanding of the department. He also links Tom's warning about people leaving the claims area to an attempt by Joan to undermine his efforts. Joan, on the other hand, sees John as another example of a powerful manager moving too quickly without sufficient background. In addition, neither really trusts the other's motives. Chances are that what happens next between John and Joan not only will affect their relationship but also will influence productivity throughout the department.

As in the interpersonal setting, conflict in the *small-group* context can be observed through behaviors during the conflict and by the conflict's lasting effects. The productive or destructive outcomes of conflict often are evidenced in the amount of group cohesion and productivity a team exhibits long after the actual conflict has ended. An example comes from a large West Coast electronics firm where four of ten senior research scientists left the organization within a period of fourteen months. The ten scientists had been together on a successful project for more than six years when two in the group disagreed with the direction a new product was to take.

The two refused to negotiate a settlement and ordered their two principal assistants to pursue a line of research not supported by other team members. The remainder of the team approached project management with the problem and asked for resolution. Management refused to intervene, fearing alienation of the entire group if forced to take sides. Over a period of weeks, a once-productive team ceased to work together, and four key members began to look for new employment. The technical merits of the disagreement were never resolved, and in effect the team ceased to exist.

The contexts for organizational conflict are not limited, however, to interpersonal or small-group exchanges. Two separate organizational units may conflict over priorities in providing resources to one another. Or an entire organization may appear to be in conflict over the fairness of pay and benefit plans. The *organization-wide* context, in actuality, is interpersonal, small-group, and intergroup conflict simultaneously addressing the same event or issue. Finally, the context of the organization's conflict with others—its competition, the public, the stockholders, the government—illustrates both how complex and how necessary conflict is for organizational functioning. American automobiles and foreign competition, airline and oil company mergers, concern for nuclear accidents and hazardous waste disposal, and competitive approaches to advertising and marketing are only a few examples of conflicts between *organizations* and *their environment*.

Daily organizational life is filled with conflicts in a variety of contexts. The results for individuals or entire organizations rest, however, not with whether conflict occurs but with the appropriateness of conflict behaviors and the effectiveness of conflict outcomes.

Conflict Episodes

Knowing what conflict is, why it happens, and in what context it occurs contributes to our understanding of conflict as a complex interaction of both individual and group perceptions, emotions, behaviors, and outcomes. These complex interactions frequently are viewed as a process researchers describe as **conflict episodes.** Scholar Louis Pondy (1967) has provided a particularly useful understanding of episodes as five basic conflict stages: (1) latent conflict, (2) perceived conflict, (3) felt conflict, (4) manifest conflict, and (5) conflict aftermath. These stages are seen as influencing each other, and the total interaction determines whether the conflict is productive or counterproductive. The stages help us visualize conflict as a process and help us analyze specific conflicts from a process perspective.

Conflict episodes—descriptions of the complex interactions of both individual and group perceptions, emotions, behaviors, and outcomes during conflict.

Latent Conflict

Latent conflict refers to underlying conditions in organizations and individual relationships that have the potential for conflict. For example, decisions about responsibility and authority, control of resources, goals, and activities in the pursuit of goals are all necessary for organizational func-

Latent conflict—underlying conditions in organizations and individual relationships that have the potential for conflict.

tioning; however, few, if any, organizations make these decisions with the total agreement of all members. In other words, the daily functioning of the organization generates disagreement and conflict.

When John became the new manager of the Middlesex claims department, his appointment over two qualified applicants—Tom and Joan—can be considered a latent conflict condition. Furthermore, the introduction of the new computer system, as with any organizational change, has the potential for conflict. From the individual perspective, John, Tom, and Joan fulfill multiple roles in the department. These multiple roles may carry different and sometimes incompatible requirements—again, underlying conditions for conflict. A supervisor, for example, may genuinely encourage a subordinate group to be open about mistakes. That same supervisor may work for a manager who is critical of mistakes and harsh in the treatment of those who make them. What the supervisor wants from the subordinate group is very different from what the supervisor, in the role of subordinate, sees as rewarded behavior. These incompatible requirements are underlying, or latent, conflict conditions.

It is important to understand that latent conflict conditions always exist in one form or another, although they may or may not produce conflict. Communication competence develops from being able to recognize latent conditions without assuming that conflict will automatically result.

Perceived Conflict

Although latent conflict conditions always exist, individuals, work groups, or entire organizations may not see goals, individual roles, resources, or authority decisions as conflict producing. When conditions of high agreement and mutual satisfaction exist, organizational members are unlikely to view latent conflict conditions as anything other than routine decisions necessary for smooth organizational functioning. However, most organizations have disagreements about even routine decisions. Who gets a promotion, which approach is best to achieve a sales goal, or how individual performance is to be evaluated are examples of decisions frequently subject to differing viewpoints and misunderstandings. When individuals or groups become aware these differences exist, they are in the **perceived conflict** stage of an episode.

Perceived conflict—awareness of individuals or groups that differences exist.

It is important to recognize that in this stage overt conflict has not occurred—only the perception of significant frustrating differences. Also in this stage, it is possible that only one person in a relationship or situation will perceive a potential conflict. Problems between supervisors and subordinates arise, for example, when a supervisor sees a performance problem that the subordinate does not. Likewise, a subordinate may define the lack of supervisory feedback as a problem, whereas the supervisor believes additional communication is unnecessary. These perceptual differences are characteristic of the perceived conflict stage.

The ability to analyze thoughtfully is very important in this stage. Think about your relationship with a person who is important to you and try to recall a time when you became aware that a significant difference was possible between you. What were the cues to the difference? What assumptions were you making? How did you think the difference might alter your relationship? Was the other person aware of the problem? Were his or her perceptions of the situation similar to yours? The perceptions we form as we face significant differences with others are crucial to the process of conflict because those perceptions shape and influence the next two stages, which hinge on emotions and behaviors.

Felt Conflict

Closely linked to the perceived conflict stage is **felt conflict,** the emotional impact the perception of conflict has on potential conflict participants. This stage precedes actual conflict behaviors and is important to behavior because it represents the merger of our perceptions and emotional reactions. It is at the felt conflict stage that we conceptualize or define probable outcomes should an actual conflict occur; in other words, it is our ego-investment stage.

Our perception of the importance of the problem, our motives and the motives of others, and the varying abilities and relative power positions of those involved all contribute to the emotional impact, or the felt conflict. For most of us, seeing a possible difference with a co-worker is a different emotional experience from seeing that same possible difference with our boss—not that the difference with the boss is necessarily worse, only that the relationships are different. The emotional impact of the problem is linked to the value we place on the specific relationship. Put another way, the felt conflict stage is an expansion of the perceived conflict stage. Perceptions are intensified by our emotional reactions to the potential conflict. Think again about the personal situation you identified for the perceived conflict stage. How did your emotional reaction influence your behavior? What was most important to you as you considered what was going to happen? Were you aware of consciously considering your behavior choices?

Felt conflict—emotional impact the perception of conflict has on potential conflict participants.

Manifest Conflict

The **manifest conflict** stage has been referred to as the "action time" of conflict or the time "when the lid blows off and we really get down to business." The manifest conflict stage consists of conflicting behaviors—problem solving, open aggression, covert action, or numerous other possibilities. In this stage communication behavior is influenced by participants' conflict preferences, perceptions of rules of interaction, power relationships, roles, and skills and abilities. All too often it is this manifest stage that we recognize as "conflict," without realizing the powerful influence of previous stages.

Actual conflict behaviors—manifest conflict—are influential in determining the productivity of the conflict and the way conflict participants will interact in the future. Are all sides of the issue heard? Does power and influence decide what happens? How are people treated when their ideas are rejected? Group conflicts in which all members are treated with

Manifest conflict—actual conflict behaviors: problem solving, open aggression, covert action, and numerous other possibilities; influential for determining the productivity of the conflict and the way conflict participants will interact in the future.

respect, for example, frequently result in decisions group members can support. On the other hand, when groups engage in personal attacks or use coercive power to enforce decisions, a very different result is predictable. Although both groups may reach reasonable decisions related to specific problems, the chances of continuing group support may be reduced if individual members feel discounted or threatened. These discounted members may contribute to future disagreements that are covert and unproductive.

Think about your personal experiences. Recall a conflict that you believe was resolved productively. How did you behave? How did others behave? Was the decision a good one? How did you feel several days later? Next, recall a conflict that left you frustrated and concerned. How did this situation differ from your more productive experience? What can be learned from contrasting the two? What competencies do you think are most important for the manifest conflict stage?

Conflict Aftermath

Conflict aftermath—result of the complex interactions of latent conditions, perceived conflict, felt conflict, and manifest conflict.

The **conflict aftermath** (outcomes) stage is a result of the complex interactions of latent conditions, perceived conflict, felt conflict, and manifest conflict. Put simply, this stage is what happens—in terms of both issues and relationships—as a result of the other four stages. It is the stage in which we evaluate the conflict as productive or counterproductive.

Although most of us fear conflict, contemporary thinking suggests that it can be productive as well as counterproductive. Although the contemporary view acknowledges that conflict outcomes can disrupt communication; produce psychological scars; and disrupt individual relationships, groups, or even entire organizations, the view also holds that conflict permits individuals and organizations to develop new ideas and approaches and to become actively involved in necessary change. In fact, communication scholar Brent Ruben (1978) contends that "conflict is not only essential to the growth, change, and evolution of living systems, but it is, as well, a system's primary defense against stagnation, detachment, entropy, and eventual extinction." When applied to organizations, conflict is an essential process for continued operation. Without conflict, organizations stagnate and die.

From a practical point of view, conflict outcomes influence the quality of decisions in organizations and consume large amounts of organizational resources. A 1976 study for the American Management Association (Thomas and Schmidt) reported that managers spend approximately 20 percent of their time dealing with conflict (chief executive officers, or CEOs, spend 18 percent, and middle managers spend 26 percent). Practicing managers also reported that managing conflict continues to become more important to organizational effectiveness. Although it is certainly obvious from our examination of conflict processes within various contexts, an often underestimated reality is the important role of individual behaviors in organizational conflict.

Many people who communicate effectively under harmonious conditions lose their ability to influence others and contribute to good decision making because they communicate poorly during conflict. And the evidence suggests that personal experiences with organizational conflict influence how satisfied and productive organizational members are. In essence, fully effective organization members must exhibit communication competency under conflicting conditions and must contribute to productive outcomes both for themselves and the organization as a whole.

THE INDIVIDUAL IN ORGANIZATIONAL CONFLICT

Organizations bring together diverse individuals, some of whom approach conflict as you would and others with very different preferences. The various predispositions, skills, and abilities of individuals in organizations influence how organizational conflict occurs. Sensitivity to these differences is central to becoming a competent communicator within a complex environment.

Sensitivity to our own preferences and behaviors helps us develop sensitivity to differences among people. One of the best ways to develop that sensitivity is to examine our own preferences in conflicts that have been important to us. The self-report questionnaire in Figure 7.1 should be completed and scored before you study the material about conflict styles, objectives, and tactics. This questionnaire is designed to increase your awareness of your individual preferences and predispositions for conflict. Scoring forms and profile interpretations are located on pages 243–244. Score your profile before studying the remainder of the chapter.

Upon completion of the questionnaire in Figure 7.1 you will have short profiles of three conflicts you saw as important to you. These profiles are organized around conflict scholar Kenneth Thomas's (1976) basic components of individual conflict behavior: orientation/style, strategic objectives, and tactics. You will want to refer to your profiles as we discuss each of the behavior components.

Orientations, or predispositions, for conflict are the balances individuals try to make between satisfying their personal needs and goals and satisfying the needs and goals of others in the conflict. These orientations or predispositions are commonly referred to as conflict *styles*. *Strategic objectives* are a combination of balancing the individual preferences for conflict styles with what the individual sees as feasible outcomes in a particular situation. Behavior choices, known as *tactics*, are specific communication choices that are influenced by both orientation and style and strategic objectives.

Orientations/Predispositions/Styles

Prominent conflict researchers such as Leonard Berkowitz (1962), Robert Blake and Jane Mouton (1964), Jay Hall (1969), and Kenneth Thomas (1976,

FIGURE 7.1
Personal Profile of Conflict Predispositions, Strategies, and Tactics

Before attempting to answer the following questions about your preferences and behaviors during conflict, list three conflicts that have been important to you.

1. The conflict was with _____
about _____ .
It was generally productive/counterproductive. (circle one)

2. The conflict was with _____
about _____ .
It was generally productive/counterproductive. (circle one)

3. The conflict was with _____
about _____ .
It was generally productive/counterproductive. (circle one)

Based on your memory of these conflicts and others, respond to the following questions about preferences for conflict behaviors.

Circle the number that indicates whether you strongly agree (4), are inclined to agree (3), are inclined to disagree (2), or strongly disagree (1) with each of the following statements.

1. When problems arise I prefer to let others take the responsibility for solving them.	4	3	2	1
2. I believe a middle ground can be reached in most conflicts.	4	3	2	1
3. I like everyone to be able to say what they think even if they don't agree with me.	4	3	2	1
4. I can be firm in pursuing what I think is right.	4	3	2	1
5. I try to reduce tension with others, to take people's minds off their problems.	4	3	2	1
6. Usually it is best to postpone trying to talk to someone when he or she is upset.	4	3	2	1
7. Talking about feelings and issues is important in conflict.	4	3	2	1
8. I like people to be willing to give some if I will also.	4	3	2	1
9. The goal must come first; conflict is inevitable and some people just can't take it.	4	3	2	1
10. When people are upset, I am more concerned about their feelings than any particular problem.	4	3	2	1
11. I don't like to be in unpleasant or tense situations.	4	3	2	1
12. I like to win my points.	4	3	2	1
13. Most conflicts are subject to compromise.	4	3	2	1

14. Everyone should share in the gains and bear some of the losses. 4 3 2 1

15. I will not contradict others if I believe it will make them unhappy. 4 3 2 1

16. I offer solutions and ask others for solutions. 4 3 2 1

17. I prefer to have everyone who is affected involved in solving a conflict. 4 3 2 1

18. Believing disagreements can destroy effectiveness, I encourage others to stay with more agreeable subjects. 4 3 2 1

19. I go after what I want, even if that makes others uncomfortable. 4 3 2 1

20. Differences usually aren't important enough to worry about. 4 3 2 1

21. I don't like to make other people feel bad by disagreeing. 4 3 2 1

22. I think the best solutions come when everyone participates and has concern for others. 4 3 2 1

23. I want others to know where I stand and will convince them of the rightness of my position. 4 3 2 1

24. Confrontation can be managed if we seek middle ground. 4 3 2 1

25. I try to help others be at ease, even if that means not pressing my point. 4 3 2 1

Again remembering the important conflicts you identified, circle a number ranging from 1 (never) to 5 (always) to describe your behaviors during conflict.

	Never		Average		Always
1. Name calling	1	2	3	4	5
2. Postponing the discussion	1	2	3	4	5
3. Proposing compromise	1	2	3	4	5
4. Expressing concern for others	1	2	3	4	5
5. Expressing concern for facts	1	2	3	4	5
6. Proposing areas of agreement	1	2	3	4	5
7. Making threats	1	2	3	4	5
8. Silence	1	2	3	4	5
9. Adding issues to the original conflict	1	2	3	4	5
10. Denying the conflict	1	2	3	4	5
11. Supporting friends even if disagreeing	1	2	3	4	5
12. Proposing solutions	1	2	3	4	5
13. Agreeing to solutions	1	2	3	4	5
14. Using formal rules to suppress conflict (voting, parliamentary procedure, etc.)	1	2	3	4	
15. Overpowering competition	1	2	3	4	5
16. Describing gains and losses	1	2	3	4	5

Orientations/predispositions—behavioral preferences for handling conflict; Frequently described as avoidance, competition, compromise, accommodation, and collaboration.

1988) all support the notion that individuals have behavioral **orientations/predispositions** or styles for handling conflict. Researchers further conclude that individuals have an order of preference among the styles that ultimately influences communication choices. In other words, an individual has a dominant or most preferred style, but when that style seems inappropriate in a given situation or does not work, the individual may go to the next preference in the hierarchy, and so on. The self-assessment you just completed identified the hierarchy you used in the specific conflicts you remembered. Refer back to that hierarchy as we explore what these various styles mean. Think about the accuracy of your profile and whether it is an effective one for you.

Conflict styles frequently are described as five basic orientations based on the balance between satisfying individual needs and goals and satisfying the needs and goals of others in the conflict. Figure 7.2 depicts the five styles—avoidance, competition, compromise, accommodation, and collaboration—on a two-dimensional grid with individual goals/assertiveness and concern for other/cooperativeness dimensions.

Avoidance—individuals, who as a result of their preferences, are unlikely to pursue their own goals and needs or to support relationships during conflict.

Avoidance. Individuals preferring the **avoidance** style are unlikely to pursue their own goals and needs or to support relationships during conflict. Conflict makes them very uncomfortable and often fearful. Although avoiders may have a genuine concern for goals and relationships, they do not see conflict as a positive solution. Avoiders may cope well during times of harmony but refrain—often both psychologically and physically—from participating in conflict situations.

Where was the avoidance style in your personal hierarchy? Can you identify friends or family who have this preference? How would you describe the impact of avoiders on decision making and on long-term relationships? The question of impact is especially important for organizations. Although most people agree that individuals within organizations have important preferences, organizations employ people to use their skills and abilities—the best of their thinking. When an individual avoids participating in decisions subject to conflict, the organization may lose important information that the individual is essentially responsible for contributing.

Competition—preference for emphasizing personal goals and needs without considering the opinions or needs of others in the conflict.

Competition. The individual who prefers **competition** approaches conflict by emphasizing personal goals and needs without considering the opinions or needs of others in the conflict. Competitive individuals often conceptualize conflict as win-lose and prefer to view themselves as winners. This orientation can block good problem solving, particularly if the competitive person needs input on a decision. On a more positive note, when a group is hopelessly deadlocked, competitors often believe it is their responsibility to make a decision and to take responsibility for that decision. Given ability appropriate to the problem, this approach can be organizationally effective.

How often do you use the competitive approach? How effective has it been? Can you visualize a competitor and an avoider in a conflicting

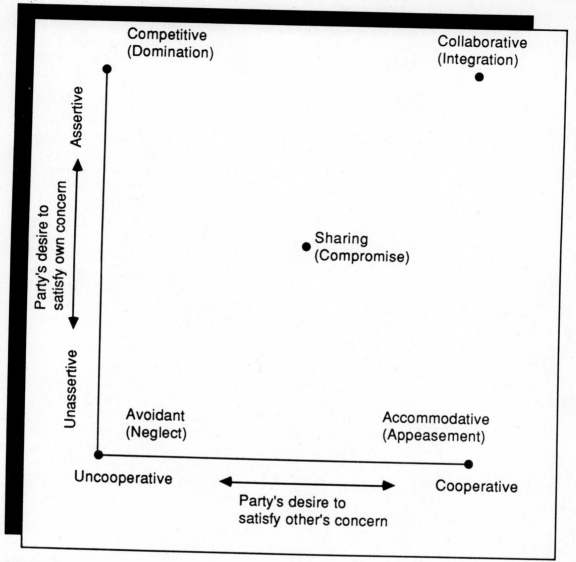

FIGURE 7.2
The Conflict Grid.
K. Thomas, "Conflict and Conflict Management," in *The Handbook of Industrial and Organizational Psychology*, M. Dunnette (Ed.). © 1976, p. 900. Reproduced by permission of John Wiley & Sons, Inc.

situation? What would you predict will occur? Sensitivity to the impact of the competitive approach is especially important because this style can be both abusive or exactly what the organization needs. The strong competitor can be guilty of discounting other good ideas and personally attacking others in order to remain a winner. When an avoider and a competitor disagree, the competitor usually wins, with little or no resistance; but this win is good for the organization only if the competitor was right and had all the appropriate information. Can you think of a time when you really had the best information, even if others disagreed? What type of behavior was needed for an effective decision? How important was it to pursue your point of view? The competitor runs the risk of competing for the sake of competing. However, the competitor can make a decision when others are hopelessly deadlocked. The potential positives and negatives from the competitive style illustrate the need for sensitivity competency in communication. Competent communicators are sensitive to their preferences and the appropriateness of applying them to specific situations. In this case, competency involves knowing when competitiveness is needed and when it is counterproductive.

Compromise. Compromisers prefer to balance people concerns with task issues and often approach conflict with a give-and-take attitude that contributes to negotiation. Most of us can identify numerous times when conflict was managed through **compromise.** Compromise works because all parties can minimize losses while establishing some gains. Indeed, organizations frequently encourage compromise, and it has become a preferred orientation in many decision-making groups.

Compromise—preferences during conflict for balancing people concerns with task issues and exhibiting give-and-take or negotiation behaviors.

However, a word of caution is appropriate. Have you ever been involved in a compromise that didn't really work, and the problem surfaced again? Did the compromise represent good problem solving or was it just a convenient and comfortable way out of conflict? As with the competitive approach, a preference for compromise should be matched to the needs of the situation. Individuals who are willing to compromise can help organizations make a decision from among various conflicting viewpoints. If that decision, however, does not represent thorough problem solving and allows the issue to resurface, the compromise orientation should have been avoided. Look again at your profile. How important is compromise to you? How effective has it been?

Accommodation. People who want to be liked, have high affiliative needs, or genuinely are concerned for the needs of others often prefer an accommodative approach to conflict. **Accommodation** is characterized by the sacrifice of personal goals in order to maintain relationships. This style can provide important support to groups engaged in making difficult decisions, but it also encourages the accommodative individual to abandon issue, goal, or task input when others appear to disagree.

Accommodation—preference for conflict associated with the sacrifice of personal goals in order to maintain relationships.

Naturally, most of us want to be liked. But again, the issue is organizational effectiveness. Is the accommodative individual withholding an opinion to maintain a relationship with his or her boss or coworkers? How important is that opinion to what happens in the work group? Does the accommodative style keep the individual from being a good contributor or is his or her real contribution the support of others? These are difficult questions requiring both sensitivity and good analysis skills. Think again about the conflicts you identified in your profile. Was accommodation a preference for you or others? How did the accommodative approach work? Should it be used again?

Collaboration. When you examine Figure 7.2, the collaborative style is clearly seen as the ideal because this approach influences individuals to work for goals, to examine issues thoughtfully, and to be task oriented while supporting others to do the same. On the other hand, **collaboration** is the most difficult of all the styles to actually use for strategic objectives and tactical behaviors. Individuals who prefer collaboration can only behave collaboratively when others assume a collaborative orientation and have enough task or goal information to solve the problem thoroughly.

Collaboration—preference for ideally balancing people and task concerns during conflict.

Where was the collaborative preference in your hierarchy? Can you see why conflict researchers believe this approach has more merit than avoidance, compromise, competition, or accommodation? Now think back to the specific conflicts you used in your self-analysis. Were these problems handled collaboratively? If these problems were not handled collaboratively, describe what might have been managed differently. Also, return to John's problem at Middlesex Insurance. Try to determine what John can do to establish a collaborative approach to his problem with Joan.

Strategic Objectives

As Kenneth Thomas (1976) has suggested, individuals' strategic objectives in conflict are determined not only by orientations or preferences for conflict styles but also by assessments of the probable outcomes of behavior within particular contexts. Specifically, strategic objectives are determined by matching general preferences for particular conflict styles with assessments of the risks involved in a particular situation. In addition, as Charles Conrad (1985) has pointed out, strategic choices are made not only with individual preferences in mind but also with consideration of the communication strategies used by others involved in the conflict. Organizational role, power positions, previous experiences, and the importance of specific issues all contribute to the strategic objectives adopted by conflict participants.

A strategic choice is, according to Gerald Phillips and Nancy Metzger (1976), a "planned method of conducting operations" in order to structure the conflict in one of four strategic directions: escalation, reduction, maintenance, or avoidance. As Joyce Frost and William Wilmot (1978) have suggested, "strategies are the large, general game plans in conflicts, and tactics are the moves made to advance the conflict in the strategic direction that the participants informally and implicitly work out among themselves."

In the Middlesex Insurance case, as John reflects on his problem with Joan, he is beginning to establish strategic objectives. His personal preferences and decisions will affect whether the conflict escalates, reduces, stays at the present level, or is avoided. For example, if John chooses to escalate the conflict he can announce that his training schedule will be initiated as announced and that those not in agreement can look for work in other departments. If John has good analysis skills he can predict that this action will probably anger Joan and possibly others. He cannot know with certainty what Joan's reaction will be, but he can assume that conflict escalation is the probable outcome. John might attempt to escalate the conflict if he really wanted Joan and the others to leave; however, his analysis ability probably will tell him he may be viewed with suspicion if competent people leave a department soon after he becomes manager.

On the other hand, John might attempt to reduce the conflict by asking Joan to help him understand her objections to the timetable for training. He would then be in a position to decide whether her objections were based on department operations or were primarily due to his promotion.

John could attempt to maintain the conflict at its present level by acknowledging that he and Joan have differences. He can suggest that he will try his new ideas while being willing to listen to her objections if there are problems. John will have difficulty in choosing the strategic objective of avoidance because he and Joan have already voiced opposing views. He can, of course, back off of his training schedule and not make further reference to their disagreement.

Regardless of what John decides, the result is determined by all those involved in the situation. John's strategic objective is based on his desired outcome and his best estimate of the reaction of Joan and others. His individual preferences, past experiences, and overall competency with conflict will influence his decisions and contribute to whether the outcomes are productive for the Middlesex claims department.

Communication Tactics in Conflict

Conflict tactics can be described as communication behaviors that attempt to move the conflict toward escalation, reduction, maintenance at the present level, or avoidance. The tactics adopted are influenced by individual conflict preferences and strategies and by overall organizational values about how conflict is supposed to work. For example, powerful individuals frequently use competitive and confrontational tactics, whereas individuals apprehensive about communicating use more avoidance tactics. Some organizations encourage open debate and disagreement, whereas others insist on disagreement only if there are no personal attacks or displays of anger. Still others discourage overt conflict of any type. In any case, the exchanges of communication tactics among conflict participants illustrate the interactive nature of conflict, with outcomes related to complex tactical interactions as well as orientations and strategic objectives.

Although it is impossible to list or define all of the possible tactics available to conflict participants, it is important for our personal sensitivity and also for our verbal skills to identify frequently used conflict tactics. Figure 7.3 presents excerpts from actual organizational conflicts. Each example is accompanied by a description of the tactic it represents. Tactics are grouped into the following categories: tactics for conflict escalation, tactics for conflict avoidance, tactics for conflict maintenance, and tactics for conflict reduction. Strategic objectives and tactics have been summarized from the research of Joyce Frost and William Wilmot (1978) and Charles Conrad (1985).

Organizational conflicts are characterized by the frequent use of all of these tactics and many more. Furthermore, organizational life brings all of us in contact with individuals who have vastly different conflict styles, strategic objectives, and tactical approaches. These differences can either contribute to productive conflict or be a primary reason conflict is destructive, resulting in bad decisions and ultimately additional conflict.

Figure 7.3 identifies frequently used conflict communication tactics through short excerpts from transcripts of organizational conflict. To further develop your sensitivity and skills for tactic identification, Figure 7.4 provides a more detailed transcript of an organizational conflict. As you read the transcript, try to identify tactics used for escalation, avoidance, maintenance, or reduction. Also, identify and describe any tactics not previously listed in Figure 7.3. Finally, as you read the transcript think about tactics you use and tactics you have observed.

GROUPS IN ORGANIZATIONAL CONFLICT

In Chapter 6 we described the importance of groups for organizational functioning and discussed many of the types of groups we will probably join. Now we will think specifically about some of the reasons for group conflict and describe a variety of approaches for conflict management.

Most of us have been in groups in which tensions and conflict made us uncomfortable or blocked problem solving. It is hoped that most of us also belonged to groups in which conflict contributed to new and better ways of doing things, actually strengthening the group's ability to work together. Think for a moment about these experiences. What made the difference? How did you feel and behave in these differing circumstances?

Individuals in Group Conflicts

Earlier we described a variety of orientations, predispositions, and styles; strategic objectives; and communication tactics for conflict. As you would expect, these orientations, objectives, and behaviors can contribute to conflict when diverse individuals participate in groups. Group members also play task, maintenance, and self-centered roles. In Chapter 6 we discussed the generally negative influence of self-centered roles and the need for

FIGURE 7.3
Communication Tactics for Conflict

Organizational Narrative
Tactics for Conflict Escalation

Conflict Tactic

"You have a bad attitude or you wouldn't do such sloppy and unprofessional work."

1. *Applying evaluative labels* to individuals or issues

"I know you don't want to work this out. Six months ago you weren't willing to give us the extra people for the [manufacturing] line. I can't imagine it is any different now."

2. *Expanding the conflict* at hand to related problems or old unsettled disputes

"It's not just me. Every member of this department thinks you are wrong. We just can't make the deadlines you keep establishing."

3. *Forming alliances* and making them known in an attempt to overpower competitors

"I don't intend to be surrounded by people who make trouble for me. You get this machine fixed this time or you can cause trouble for someone else."

4. *Making threats* with or without control of sanctions or outcomes

"I don't want to work with John on this project. You can give me Mary or Sam but not John."

5. Deliberately *limiting the choices* of others

"I know we agreed to work this out between us—but I went to Ralph [both people's supervisor]. Your team just doesn't have the work load that mine does and he has got to create some justice."

6. *Breaking previously agreed-upon rules* of behavior for the specific relationship

Tactics for Conflict Avoidance

(Supervisor to subordinate not recommended for promotion) "Being upset about Mary getting the job isn't going to help—let's talk about it when you're feeling better—you just need to be patient and wait for another opportunity."

1. *Delaying* or procrastinating in addressing conflicting issues

(Top manager to unhappy employee) "I understand you think your boss is unfair—and I know we have an open-door policy—but when you have a grievance you are to go to personnel and file a formal report. I will look at the issue only after you have followed proper channels."

2. *Using formal rules*, rank, seniority, majority rule and other means of controlling processes to constrain the behavior of conflicting parties

"This is simply not a problem—I am not angry with you and you have no right to be mad at me. I am going to continue to believe nothing is wrong."

3. *Denying* the existence of a conflict

"I know it was important to get two more people on the night shift, and I know you really need them, but I believe you can maintain your production level. More people would help but your group is good and I know they can continue to do the job."

4. *Fogging the issue* by acceptance of part of the concern while ignoring other important concerns

Tactics for Conflict Maintenance

"The only way we are going to meet this deadline is to work together. It doesn't matter right now who got us into this mess— if we don't deliver to the customer on time we will all get blamed."

1. Describing what all parties have to *gain and lose*

(Two managers before a board of directors meeting) "No, I won't make matters worse. I have always supported you in the directors meeting. I will continue to do that even though you know I think this is not the way to go."

2. Agreeing to *honor long-term relationship* rules

"Look, I think the way you have been behaving is inconsiderate of your fellow workers, but maybe I don't have all the facts and I certainly don't know how you are feeling."

3. Combining both *escalation and reduction tactics*

(continued)

"I believe we can agree that this level of budget is all we are going to have to spend between us. I will look at my travel plans if you will consider your expenditures for part-time secretarial support services."

4. *Proposing areas of agreement* and areas for compromise

Tactics for Conflict Reduction

"Now, changing the entire computer system is a major departure from our current operations. I think we need to think first of who has what type of training and how we can approach bringing people up to speed without destroying our work schedules. We then can approach purchasing and installing the new system."

1. Identifying *numerous manageable issues* and suggesting approaching "smaller" concerns

"I know we are upset that John promised we would get these shipments out over the holiday. But if we are to present our case and be listened to we must not personally attack John or remind him that this is the second time in six months that this has happened."

2. Describing *behaviors and outcomes to be avoided* during the conflict

"Obviously the report has to be corrected. I'm concerned about the amount of time that is going to take and how fatigued you must be. But I am also concerned about how we got so much inaccurate information to begin with."

3. Exhibiting concern *for both facts and feelings*

"Perhaps I was wrong to believe we should hire another account executive before secretarial support staff. I will consider a part-time secretarial type along with the new exec."

4. Offering *compromises* from original positions

balance in task and maintenance behaviors. It is easy to understand why self-centered roles and inappropriate balances of task and maintenance roles are a possible source of group conflict. Additionally, although most organizations talk about the importance of teamwork, rewards usually recognize individual versus group efforts. Members of a work team, for example, will be asked to collaborate, yet each knows that merit salary increases will reflect how they compare to each other, not how they produce as a group. This seeming contradiction is another source of work group conflict.

Procedural Conflict

Most types of organizational groups conflict over procedures or ways of doing things. How the group is organized, the process of decision making,

---

FIGURE 7.4
Transcript of an Organizational Conflict

Mary is in conversation with her subordinate, Dan. This is Dan's second warning about tardiness and absenteeism. Dan contends he does more work than others on the maintenance crew. Mary knows Dan is a good worker but cannot tolerate his abuses of company policy.

Mary: Dan, you know why I asked you to come in this morning. We talked about your problem last month, and I thought you intended to improve. But when I checked the monthly time report it shows you were late four times and used two more sick leave days. That tells me you didn't take our conversation very seriously. Dan, your work is good, but your attitude isn't. I can't tolerate any more of this behavior.

Dan: Yeah, I know we talked last month, and I did intend to get here on time, but my car is old, and anyway, I always get all my work done. I work twice as hard as Fred. I wish you would do something about that instead of always being on my back.

Mary: Now, Dan, Fred is not the issue; you are.

Dan: Well, Fred and several of the others should be. I'm in here defending myself when I do better work than most of the crew. You aren't fair!

Mary: Dan, I acknowledge that your work is good but the company policy is important. You can't keep being late and running out of your sick leave by April or May of each year. What am I going to do with you? I really would hate to have to use a formal warning. You do know what that is?

Dan: Yeah, I know about formal warnings. I guess I can watch it a little better. The problem is I still think that the fact that I work harder than the others should count for something.

Mary: Well, Dan, your good work could count for something if you didn't have these other problems. If you ever want to make more money or be a foreman you are going to have to be here on time and support company policy.

Dan: Well, I suppose you're right, but I still don't like it.

Mary: Dan, the choice is yours. If the report next month is not better I am going to put you on warning.

Dan: [Under his breath] Okay, okay—but I still don't think it's fair.

---

who accepts responsibility, or what happens when responsibilities are not carried out can all contribute to tension and conflict within groups. Most of you have experienced this procedural conflict when preparing a project for a class. Some group members preferred majority rule, others worked for genuine consensus, and still others attempted to force their positions or opinions on the entire group.

Interpersonal Issues

One of the most common types of group conflict emerges when all members do not fairly or equally perform their responsibilities or make contributions to the group. The necessity to "carry" a member of the team raises tension and disrupts group cohesiveness. Groups also have interpersonal power clashes between and among members who seek influence and control. Powerful members produce conflict when attempting to force group members to take sides in essentially interpersonal disputes. We have all observed two individuals disagreeing or disparaging one another in front of the group. We often suspect that their disagreements have little or nothing to do with the issues at hand but reflect ongoing difficulties in the relationship. Unfortunately, they introduce tension and counterproductive behaviors into what might otherwise be an effective setting.

Substantive Issues

The very reason for forming groups in organizations can contribute to group conflict. We have said that organizations should utilize the energy of diverse individuals to establish effective ways of doing things or to challenge existing processes in favor of new and better efforts. In effect, we are saying that organizations should encourage conflicts of ideas that contribute to excellence. Individuals normally and productively can differ about positions, interests, approaches, or problems. Groups, therefore, can be expected to have conflicts over issues, ideas, or tasks.

Groupthink

As is true in interpersonal conflict, group conflict can range from highly productive to counterproductive. Most of us have been present at a meeting where displays of anger blocked effective problem solving. However, if we think carefully about our group experiences, we probably can remember a time when surface harmony also blocked problem-solving effectiveness.

Surface harmony, or the absence of productive conflict, can block group effectiveness when critical thinking is absent, resulting in ill-conceived courses of action. Irving Janis (1983) has called the surface harmony frequently associated with highly cohesive groups **groupthink**, or the tendency of groups to suspend critical thinking and to adopt proposed solutions too quickly. Groups in danger of groupthink overestimate their own

Groupthink—tendency of groups to suspend critical thinking and too quickly adopt proposed solutions.

capabilities, seek information that supports their point of view, and avoid or discount contradictory ideas. Have you ever participated in groupthink? What happened? How can group members decide if they genuinely agree or are exhibiting groupthink tendencies? Our discussion of a format for productive conflict will provide some possible answers.

Group Conflict Management Processes

Group conflict is so important in organizations that a variety of processes for management have become commonplace. These processes are typically described as negotiation, bargaining, mediation, forcing, and arbitration. Although this chapter will not describe each of these processes in detail, your awareness that they are frequently used becomes part of your knowledge competency for group participation.

Negotiation is a common process in groups. Generally speaking, negotiation can be understood as a broad process involving discussions between and among individuals who are interdependent and need to come together for a decision or course of action. Groups negotiate procedures and issues with expected give and take among members. The negotiation process is frequently associated with the need to compromise effectively. The next section of this chapter describes a concept of principled negotiation that supports productive conflict.

Bargaining is a more structured form of negotiations. Bargaining usually involves the presentation of fairly specific proposals for the purpose of achieving a working agreement on particular issues. You are probably familiar with collective bargaining as it applies to labor and management group interactions. Yet bargaining has numerous other organizational applications. At budget time, groups may be asked to present very specific proposals for money. Representatives from each group may be asked to negotiate or bargain for fixed resources. In some cases the rules for these exchanges will be well defined, whereas in others the process is more open-ended. Regardless of the formality, bargaining is an established conflict resolution procedure in many organizations.

Mediation is another possible group conflict management process. In mediation a designated individual guides the negotiations or bargaining efforts of the groups in conflict. Mediation is utilized when negotiations are deadlocked or tensions so high that a designated leader is desirable. When mediation fails, the designated leader frequently has to rely on forcing or making a decision that the group must accept. Obviously, for mediation or forcing to be effective, the designated leader must have credibility with the opposing factions and responsibility and authority appropriate to the task. Generally speaking, mediators are members of the group or organization involved in the process.

Finally, when negotiation, bargaining, or mediation fails, organizations can manage group conflict with third-party **arbitration.** Arbitration usually involves an outside negotiator who resolves differences with formally es-

Negotiation—broad conflict management process involving discussions between and among individuals who are interdependent and need to come together for a decision or course of action; frequently associated with the need to compromise effectively.

Bargaining—structured form of negotiations usually involving the presentation of fairly specific proposals for the purpose of achieving a working agreement on particular issues.

Mediation—use of a designated individual for guiding the negotiations or bargaining efforts of groups in conflict.

Arbitration—conflict management process involving an outside negotiator who resolves differences based on formally established procedures.

tablished procedures. Labor-management disputes have been subjects of arbitration, as have a variety of legally related cases. Arbitration frequently results in ill will because of the forced nature of resolving the conflict.

Fortunately most of us will work in groups that manage conflict through collaboration and negotiation. We know from experience that effectiveness is more likely to occur when group members voluntarily solve their own disputes than when leaders or an outside individual must take charge. The need, therefore, is to develop an understanding of how to engage in conflict productively. The next section of this chapter contributes to our competencies by describing supportive climates, ethical behaviors, and principled negotiation for conflict. The section concludes with a recommended format for productive conflict.

PRODUCTIVELY ENGAGING IN CONFLICT

Thus far in this chapter we have been exploring what conflict is, how it works, and what role individuals and groups play in the process. Specifically, we have attempted to develop knowledge, sensitivity, and skills important for communication competence during conflict. The underlying assumption for this development has been that conflict can be productive and can make a valuable contribution to individuals and organizations. In other words, not only is conflict inevitable, but also, when productively managed, it is often desirable.

Before we think specifically about possible positive outcomes of conflict, review again the conflicts you identified earlier in this chapter and the Middlesex Insurance case. Were there positive outcomes from your personal conflicts? What do John and the entire department have to gain from productive resolution of their problem? How was conflict valuable in either your personal experiences or the Middlesex case?

In general we can say that a major value of conflict is its stimulus for creativity. Conflict with others forces us to evaluate and assess issues and problems. When productively managed, this evaluation can stimulate new and creative solutions that may not have emerged without competing perspectives. For example, most of us have habitual or routine ways of doing things. Frequently we do not even think about new approaches until someone challenges our effectiveness. Productive conflict can help keep us from getting in a rut. Conflict can restructure our relationships—a fact many of us fear and resist. Yet conflict can bring relationships up to date and strengthen them by addressing underlying problems and working for solutions. Both individually and organizationally, productive conflict can help us analyze goals and find effective means of achieving them.

When we adopt the perspective that conflict can be valuable, we then begin to focus our knowledge, sensitivity, and skills toward conflict as a productive process. We think about what atmosphere is best for conflict, what contributes to ethical behaviors during conflict, and finally what types of problem-solving processes support productive conflict outcomes.

Supportive Climates, Ethical Behaviors, and Principled Negotiation

Creating an environment in which individuals feel secure and encouraged to seek good solutions is a difficult yet important task. The quality of the problem-solving environment is closely linked to considerations of what constitutes ethical communication behaviors during conflict. This subtle but critical relationship between **supportive climates** and the quality of human interaction is well described by Paul Keller and Charles Brown in their interpersonal ethic for communication. Keller and Brown (1968) suggest that people will be able to reach their potential only when they are psychologically free—not fearful of disagreement—and when their beliefs, opinions, and values are acceptable in their interactions with others.

Organizations annually spend millions of dollars training personnel in problem solving and conflict management with the hope that this training will contribute to productive organizational outcomes. And yet the outcomes from conflict often are influenced not only by the skills and abilities of the individual conflict participants but also by the overall organizational climate, which contributes to either supportiveness or defensiveness.

Organizational climates that produce defensiveness are characterized by inaccurate perceptions of motives, values, and emotions of those in conflict. Jack Gibb (1982), in a classic study of behaviors individuals perceive as threatening, discovered that "increases in defensive behavior were correlated positively with losses in efficiency in communication. Specifically, distortions became greater when defensive states existed in the groups." Gibb concluded that there are characteristic behaviors of defensive groups that are distinctly different from the characteristic behaviors in supportive groups.

Supportive climates—organizational environments in which individuals feel secure and encouraged to seek good solutions; characterized by problem description, problem orientation, spontaneity, empathy, equality, and provisionalism.

Evaluation versus Problem Description

Defensive climates are described by Gibb as being evaluative, whereas supportive environments are characterized by problem description. The supervisor who identifies the "bad attitude" or "low commitment" of a subordinate may not fully understand how this evaluative approach contributes to a predictably defensive subordinate reaction. On the other hand, the supervisor who describes concern for a subordinate's absenteeism is describing a problem both the supervisor and subordinate can readily observe and approach—very different from the subjective assessment of attitudes. In summary, the descriptive approach attempts to fit our words as nearly as possible to our experience of reality through descriptive, nonjudgmental terms and by avoiding strong, emotion-laden words.

Control versus Problem Orientation

Defensiveness also is produced through attempts to control the behavior and responses of others. Although enforcing compliance may get short-term results, it rarely builds long-term commitment. Problem orientation is the supportive climate opposite to control. Specifically, problem orientation assumes a collaborative approach to solutions with particular emphasis on the participation of those being asked to make behavior changes. One of the more difficult tasks for many new managers is to encourage participation from those who either need to make behavior changes or are most affected by them. Inexperienced managers frequently learn that attempts to control subordinate behaviors result in the need for time-consuming behavior monitoring. Their more experienced counterparts have learned that subordinates are more likely to keep commitments in which they participate.

Most of us can understand the problem orientation approach in our own behavior. Try to determine when your commitment is greater—when you participate in a decision or when that decision is made for you. For most of us the answer is relatively simple: We put more time and energy into our own commitments.

Strategy versus Spontaneity

Although we all operate from strategic objectives in conflict, defensiveness is produced when we are perceived by others to be engaging in manipulative behaviors. Organizational strategies for "selling" unpopular decisions often produce a defensiveness based on the belief that manipulation is a fundamental form of disrespect. Spontaneity, the opposite of strategy, is reflected in behaviors that make real motives plain and generate a trust that straightforward and honest interactions are taking place. This trust level is fundamental for long-term effectiveness. In fact, Warren Bennis and Burt Nanus (1985), in their research on leaders, suggest that trust in their constancy is one of the fundamental distinguishing characteristics of highly successful leaders. Furthermore, as Joseph DeVito (1986) suggests, straightforward and honest interactions (spontaneity) facilitate the individual's freedom of choice through accurate information—a requirement in his view for ethical interpersonal communication.

Neutrality versus Empathy

Gibb (1982) found that productive groups empathically supported their members rather than assuming a rational neutrality based on "pure" objectivity. Productive groups also were characterized by the acceptance of others with different values and beliefs. This empathic support is closely related to the Keller and Brown (1968) notion of an interpersonal ethic for communication based on psychological freedom to express opinions and beliefs. Thinking again about our personal behavior, most of us would agree that it is more comfortable to express disagreement when we know we will be thoughtfully heard than when we expect personal attack or discounting. Also, for most of us, constructively expressing disagreement is more likely to occur when we feel supported in our right to do so.

Superiority versus Equality

In general, defensive groups are more likely than supportive groups to have members intent on asserting superiority and exhibiting an unwillingness to participate equally in problem solving. In fact, defensive climates are often characterized by individuals believing they really do not have enough in common with others to make communication possible. Although differences in individuals exist, supportive individuals and groups stress commonalities while respecting numerous and diverse contributions to solutions.

Certainty versus Provisionalism

Defensive groups, more than their supportive counterparts, are likely to have members who are certain and dogmatic about their positions. Supportive individuals are more provisional or open to experimentation in behavior, attitudes, and ideas. The provisional individual is investigative and problem oriented rather than polarized into either-or positions. The provisional approach seeks numerous alternatives in order to find the most appropriate solution to a given problem. Again, this support for the generation of alternatives is fundamental to individual choice and ethical communication.

Ethical Communication Behaviors

The supportive conditions as described by Gibb (1982) are closely aligned to notions of ethical conflict behaviors as described by Gary Kreps and Barbara Thornton (1984). Specifically, Kreps and Thornton believe ethical conflict behaviors are exhibited when the individual stays with the issue at hand without hidden agendas; constructs reasonable, logical arguments rather than arguments designed to discount and devalue others; and keeps an open mind to new ideas while avoiding a win-at-all-costs attitude. In other words, ethical communication behaviors generate an environment in which individuals have freedom of expression and also have adequate information to make free, informed choices. Put another way, the value of productive conflict is to stimulate creativity in individuals, groups, and organizations. That creativity is most likely to emerge if we are personally safe, if we are open to many suggestions and viewpoints, and if we honestly seek the best solution from among numerous alternatives.

Principled Negotiation

Principled negotiation is based on ethical communication behaviors and supportive climates. First introduced by Roger Fisher and William Ury (1983), principled negotiation is a strategy for groups of individuals in conflict both to express their needs and to search for alternatives that meet diverse needs. The strategy supports ethical behavior by separating people from the problem and focusing on interests, not positions. Group members are asked to develop options for mutual gain based on mutual interests. Additionally, objective criteria are used to evaluate options so all parties to the conflict can determine the fairness of decisions.

Principled negotiation is based on the assumption that we should express disagreements and react to them with a spirit of inquiry and supportiveness rather than defensiveness. During principled negotiations group members express concern for one another even when issue and position disagreements are obvious. Groups engaging in principled negotiation describe needs and interests in common and avoid rigid, polarized positions. Utilizing common needs and interests as a basis, groups develop options that can be evaluated with agreed-upon objective criteria. Once evaluation has been completed, groups engaging in principled negotiation can arrive at decisions with a high likelihood of broad support.

A Format for Productive Conflict

Individuals who observe or participate in productive conflicts frequently characterize them as good problem-solving processes. And indeed, that is exactly what productive conflict is. Earlier in the chapter conflict was defined as frustration stimulated by competing responses or alternatives to a particular situation. When that frustration is resolved to the mutual satisfaction of involved parties and to the needs of the issue, good problem solving has occurred. The following format for productive conflict is a basic problem-solving format. Based on the concepts of supportive climates, ethical behaviors, and principled negotiation, it is designed to integrate all of our competencies—knowledge, sensitivity, skills, and values—into a productive conflict management process.

The Format

Self-analysis of the issues. When we are experiencing perceived and felt conflict, the time is right to do an in-depth self-analysis about the problem. Can we describe the conflict in terms that represent observable behaviors or events to all parties? What are the limits of our understanding of the problem? What types of solutions can we propose? Who needs to change or make a decision? What can we support in resolution strategies and what types of results are clearly not acceptable? Also, what are the power issues, roles, and relationships of the parties involved? Finally, what are our personal responsibilities for this conflict?

Setting a meeting to work on the problem. Productive conflict occurs in a climate in which all participants feel supported. The setting of the meeting beforehand and the environment of the meeting itself are critical to this supportive climate. Generally speaking, all parties involved in conflict should be notified in advance about the issue for discussion. Although this will sometimes produce anticipation stress, mental preparation can occur only when everyone knows the agenda. Also, the emotional impact of conflict can be lessened and trust levels increased when people don't feel surprised by a conflict. Commitment to agreements is greater if parties have time to think about the problem and their input and limits. In addition, the meeting environment should be conducive to the free exchange of ideas—usually private and on relatively neutral ground. Individuals using the power position of their private office may actually inhibit real problem solving. Finally, adequate time for full discussion should be allotted, with the timing of the meeting as convenient as possible for all participants.

Defining the problem. Effective conflict outcomes occur in solving the basic problem rather than finding solutions to surface issues or discovering vastly differing descriptions of the problem. Conflict participants should be encouraged to define the problem fully before any discussion of solution strategies. Problems often are poorly described because of underlying tension in the setting and a desire to get the confrontation over with as soon as possible. Clarification of the problem—through self-disclosure and active questioning—is essential to productive problem solving.

Developing solutions. We are often relieved to be "getting through this problem" and neglect to look comprehensively at approaches and solutions. In the development of solutions it is important to think broadly about all alternatives, even those that seem to have little immediate merit. Better and longer-lasting solutions will emerge from broad rather than narrow perspectives of alternatives. All conflict participants should be encouraged to participate in solution generation. In fact, if a critically involved party to a dispute cannot offer a single solution, it may be better to adjourn the meeting temporarily and let that person consider what he or she might suggest. Forcing a decision on a nonparticipative individual may result in little commitment or sometimes actual sabotage of the solution. Ultimately, of course, action must be taken. However, all parties must recognize the potential impact of a decision with varying ranges of agreement and commitment.

Narrowing the choices for action. Decisions should be discussed in light of the defined problem issues. Often decisions made with broad agreement fail because the participants have not linked their intended actions to the actual problem. If behavior change is required on the part of some but not all participants, particular care should be taken that the affected individuals participate in narrowing the choices for action. They should be encouraged to select options to which they can commit, although these options can be rejected by others if they do not meet acceptable standards. When individuals who need to change their behavior make commitments to change that they have helped generate, the long-term possibilities for successful conflict resolution have been enhanced.

Committing to solutions. Agreeing on a solution or approach to the problem should occur only after the parties assess how that solution addresses the identified problem, whether individuals can support the decision, if those most affected have participated in the decision, and whether the solution is workable and can be implemented. Commitment to the solution comes through developing an implementation plan. Who is going to do what and in what time frame? How is the solution going to be evaluated? Is everyone clear about what we think this solution will accomplish and also what it cannot do? Finally, can we predict from this experience whether we have a solution that will work? If so, what were the keys to this outcome? If not, what were the barriers we could not surmount?

Monitoring the process. A real key to long-term conflict management is effective implementation of agreed-upon solutions. Effective conflict outcomes are encouraged when participants establish how they will monitor the implementation plan and when they will meet again to assess how it is working. This follow-up builds accountability into the process and also allows for celebration when solutions are working and meeting problem needs. This closure on the process also establishes a framework for revisiting an issue for which the solution—even if faithfully implemented—still does not satisfy the real needs of the conflict.

Although no process, set of skills, or body of knowledge will free individuals, groups, or entire organizations from the reality of conflict, the knowledge, sensitivities, skills, and values of conflict participants directly influence the productivity of conflict outcomes. Effective organizational communicators know they bear responsibilities to monitor continually their own abilities and support that process for others. In particular, effective conflict outcomes help individuals improve their organizational relationships and are an important organizational mechanism for good decision making and adaptation to change.

SUMMARY

Conflict occurs when individuals, groups, or entire organizations perceive or experience frustration in the attainment of goals. Described as an episode, the conflict process has the stages of (1) latent conflict, (2) perceived conflict, (3) felt conflict, (4) manifest conflict, and (5) conflict aftermath. Conflict episodes occur in intrapersonal, interpersonal, small-group, organization-wide, and organization-to-environment contexts. Regardless of context, participants interact in conflict with their individual preferences or styles, strategic orientations, and tactical communication behaviors. Conflict styles are described as five basic orientations based on the balance between satisfying individual needs and goals and satisfying the needs and goals of others in the conflict. These five most commonly referred to styles are avoidance, competition, compromise, accommodation, and collaboration. Strategic objectives are determined by preferences for conflict styles and by assessment of the probable outcomes of behavior within particular contexts. Strategic objectives structure the conflict in one of four strategic directions: escalation, reduction, maintenance, or avoidance. Conflict tactics are communication behaviors that attempt to move the conflict toward escalation, reduction, maintenance at the present level, or avoidance. The tactics adopted are influenced by conflict preferences and strategies and by overall organizational values.

Group conflict is common in organizations. Individual characteristics, procedures, interpersonal issues, substantive issues, and groupthink all contribute to productive and counterproductive group conflict. Organizations manage conflict with negotiation, bargaining, mediation, forcing, and third-party arbitration.

Conflict outcomes are more likely to be productive if parties in conflict foster supportive rather than defensive climates. Supportive climates are characterized by problem orientation, spontaneity, empathy, equality, provisionalism, and ethical communication behaviors. Principled negotiation is a strategy for group conflict based on supportive climates and ethical behaviors.

A format for constructive conflict can be used to integrate all of our competencies—knowledge, sensitivity, skills, and values. The format includes self-analysis of the issues, setting a meeting to work on the problem, defining the problem, developing solutions, narrowing the choices for action, committing to solutions, and monitoring the process. In summary, productive conflict requires competent communicators who can effectively problem solve in a variety of organizational circumstances.

WORKSHOP

1. To put into practice the various competencies this chapter has begun attempting to develop, read The New Career Development Program That Ruins Careers case, which follows. After studying the case, can you describe the events in terms of a conflict episode? What were the predispositions and styles of the principal participants? Did Denise and John have similar strategic objectives? Examine the conflict narrative and establish which tactics were used. Finally—and this is the most challenging part of the assignment—generate for Jane a specific format for productive conflict management. Generate this format with both supportive climates and ethical behaviors in mind. Be prepared to present your format to the class and role-play how Jane should handle her meetings with Denise and John. (See pages 244–247.)

2. Develop a list of outcomes from conflicts that have been important to you. Divide the list into productive and counterproductive outcomes. What kinds of behaviors made the difference? What does this list tell you about your role in conflict?

3. The "Trying to Get What I Want" Negotiations Exercise can be used to build skills in productive confrontation. Dyads or teams can conduct the exercise. (See pages 247–249.)

Personal Profile of Conflict Predispositions, Strategies, and Tactics Scoring Form—Style Predispositions

1. Total your scores from questions numbered 1, 6, 11, 18, 20.

    A. _____

2. Total your scores from questions numbered 2, 8, 13, 14, 24.

    B. _____

3. Total your scores from questions numbered 3, 7, 16, 17, 22.

    C. _____

4. Total your scores from questions numbered 4, 9, 12, 19, 23.   D. _____

5. Total your scores from questions numbered 5, 10, 15, 21, 25.   E. _____

Your scores represent a rank ordering of your preferences or predispositions for five conflict styles: (A) avoidance, (B) compromise, (C) collaboration, (D) competition, and (E) accommodation. Your highest number represents your first preference, and so on down the line. It is possible that you gave two styles the same score. This indicates that you have little difference in preference between the two. List your style preferences in order from most preferred to least preferred.

First choice   _____

Second choice   _____

Third choice   _____

Fourth choice   _____

Fifth choice   _____

These styles will be discussed in detail as you study Chapter 7.

Scoring Form—Strategies and Tactics

1. Total your scores from questions numbered 1, 7, 9, 15 and divide by 4.   A. _____

2. Total your scores from questions numbered 2, 8, 10, 14 and divide by 4.   B. _____

3. Total your scores from questions numbered 3, 6, 11, 16 and divide by 4.   C. _____

4. Total your scores from questions numbered 4, 5, 12, 13 and divide by 4.   D. _____

Your scores represent your average use of a variety of conflict tactics grouped into the four general conflict strategies of (A) escalation, (B) avoidance, (C) maintenance, and (D) reduction. Compare your average use figure to the scale: 1 = Never; 3 = Average; and 5 = Always.

Now return to Chapter 7 where preferences and orientations, strategies, and tactics are discussed in detail.

The New Career Development Program That Ruins Careers Case

The training department of AMEX Corporation was well respected for the quality of programs its staff developed and regularly presented to the over 10,000 AMEX employees. Department members were always ready for new challenges and prided themselves on developing the best training programs in the industry.

Jane Johnson, director of the AMEX training department, was excited that her presentation to top management had been well received. She believed, along with her senior staff, that the AMEX career development program was out of date and needed new materials and a new training format. The changes she and her staff wanted to make would cost around $100,000, requiring management approval and agreement that the program was a top priority for the coming year. The new career development program would be the first such program to be made available to all 10,000 employees.

During her first staff meeting following the management presentation, Jane became aware that although all four senior staff members agreed on the importance of the program, there was little agreement on who should have the lead responsibility and how other work responsibilities should be divided to provide time for program development. Although no open disagreement had been voiced, Jane came away from the meeting with the sense that she had considerable work to do to determine how project assignments might best meet the needs of the entire group.

Jane believed that Denise Giles, her senior staff member in charge of management development programs, had the best experience for the job. Denise had been with AMEX for over seven years and had developed, staffed, and implemented seven new programs for managers at all levels in AMEX. Her program evaluations were consistently outstanding, and top management held her work in high regard. But Jane also knew that John Martin, senior staff member in charge of manufacturing training programs, wanted the assignment. John had less overall program experience than Denise, but the work he had done in quality training was truly outstanding. In fact, he had been asked to lead a workshop describing his program at the International Manufacturers Convention in London. Jane was proud of John and believed he had an outstanding future in training and development. The other two senior staff members, Jill and Roger, had not yet introduced their first programs. Although able trainers and good program managers, neither had the development and writing experience necessary for the career development project.

Jane decided to devote her next staff meeting to a discussion of project allocations for the coming year. She was not prepared for the tenseness she felt as the meeting began.

JANE: As you know, today's agenda deals with our program planning for the next year. Obviously, if we are to undertake the career development project, we will have to evaluate work loads on all of our projects. I would also like expressions of interest in which parts of the career development project each of you would like to be and ideas on what type of team should be established to manage its development. As we talk, please keep in mind not only your own interests but also the strengths and overall work loads of each of your individual staffs.

DENISE: Jane, this is a troublesome issue for us as a group. We all want the career development program to work, but we know it takes one lead person, not all four of us working independently.

JOHN: Denise is right. One of us has to head up the group and be responsible for the lead. I guess I should say right now that I want to take that lead responsibility. I have worked with the largest group (manufacturing) in all of AMEX and believe that experience qualifies me for developing a program that reaches large numbers of diverse people. My manufacturing folks represent almost 6,500 of our total employment.

DENISE (In a tense voice): I don't think we should be declaring who wants the job until we decide how the project might ideally be developed with all of our other responsibilities.

ROGER: Well, I think we need to get down to facts. Neither Jill nor I have the experience to lead the project and we know it. Everyone knows the lead job is between Denise and John. We can't really divide the other work and decide how we can support the project until we choose a leader.

JILL: Roger is right. I would love to lead the project but with about five years more experience.

JOHN: Well, I just stated that I want the lead job and that I think my experience is best suited to the job. What do you think, Denise?

DENISE: I think this is an unprofessional way for us to be entering into this decision. After all, the final decision is Jane's and she should not be forced to choose this way. Her agenda was a discussion of project assignments, not announcing who would take the lead assignment. Isn't that right, Jane?

JANE: Yes, that was the agenda but I am not adverse to hearing what each of you really wants to do. Denise, how do you feel about the lead role?

DENISE: How do I feel? How can you ask me that? I am the senior member of this team. Everyone expects me to lead this project. If I don't get the job it will be a slap in the face. Sure, John has done a great job in manufacturing, but what about the management programs? They may reach fewer people but the people they do reach drive the entire company. What about that experience? Frankly, I resent being put on the spot like this. This is not an issue for general discussion. It is (to Jane) your responsibility to make that decision.

JOHN: Denise, you are doing it again. I have never raised this before but you just won't confront things openly. Sure, you have a good record, but I am willing to say openly that I want the job, not just expect someone to hand me the assignment. This is too important to give it to someone just because they expect it.

JANE: Wait a minute, you are both out of line. We are going to adjourn this meeting right now and I will see both of you individually later in the day. We will meet again as a staff tomorrow morning.

DENISE (Under her breath as she leaves the room): This career development project is alreading ruining some careers.

QUESTIONS FOR DISCUSSION

1. What conflict preferences do we see in the case?
2. What strategies and tactics are in use?
3. What can Jane do to resolve this conflict?

"Trying to Get What I Want" Negotiating Exercise

This exercise can be conducted in dyads or in teams not to exceed three members each. Each individual or team should read the general information that follows.

General Information

RDT, a small training and development company with five branch offices in two states, is currently operating all of its offices with outdated video equipment. Although the equipment is still functional, management of RDT is concerned that its competitors will soon be releasing training tapes with graphics superior to those produced on RDT equipment. United Concepts, a major distributor of video equipment, is holding an inventory of good but somewhat obsolete video equipment that outproduces the RDT equipment but is still substantially below state-of-the-art equipment in the industry. The equipment that United Concepts is inventorying is subject to both interest and warehousing costs. The United Concepts salesperson, Mary Adams, is aware that Al Nodstrom of RDT is in need of new equipment. Her account list at United Concepts includes the RDT account.

Al Nodstrom of RDT is trying to acquire twelve video cameras and two editing units to replace his existing equipment in three offices. Al believes that United Concepts is warehousiing the type of equipment he needs at a substantial annual loss to United Concepts. He believes the equipment to be worth approximately $23,000. Al determines that holding the equipment in the warehouse is costing United Concepts approximately $3,500 per year. United Concepts values the equipment RDT seeks to acquire at $33,000. Mary Adams also realizes there are warehouse and interest costs associated with the equipment. She is not completely sure of the annual amount.

The Position of United Concepts

The individual or team that represents Mary's position will be charged with selling the equipment at the best possible price, keeping in mind that overhead costs are incurred by United Concepts for interest and warehousing of the equipment. Mary also realizes that RDT is a company that cannot afford current state-of-the-art video equipment. She believes RDT is lucky to find a supplier who is in a position to provide somewhat outdated equipment at a reasonable cost.

The Position of RDT

The individual or team that represents Al's position will be charged with buying the equipment at the best possible price, keeping in mind that United Concepts is incurring costs for interest and warehousing of the somewhat obsolete equipment and that RDT cannot afford more state-of-the-art equipment. Al believes United Concepts wants to sell to RDT because of RDT's solid financial reputation. Al believes Mary is authorized to make a deal that is lower than the United Concepts equipment appraisal of $33,000.

Each individual (or team) should spend ten minutes developing their negotiating positions. Each individual or team should then negotiate for a time specified by the instructor. At the completion of the negotiation, the following worksheet should be completed.

NEGOTIATION WORKSHEET

Team members' names (RDT or United Concepts)   ⎯⎯⎯⎯
Objective (ideal sales price) for your team   RDT   ⎯⎯⎯⎯
    United Concepts   ⎯⎯⎯⎯
Starting price for your team   RDT   ⎯⎯⎯⎯
    United Concepts   ⎯⎯⎯⎯
Lowest acceptable price   United Concepts   ⎯⎯⎯⎯
Highest acceptable price   RDT   ⎯⎯⎯⎯
FINAL PRICE   ⎯⎯⎯⎯
(Only if sale is achieved during negotiation)

A class member or your instructor should post the various price positions for the negotiating teams. Specifically, the top of a piece of flip-chart paper or the chalkboard should read NEGOTIATIONS SCORING with lines drawn horizontally for the numbers of teams for the class. Vertical lines will be drawn for the following categories: the Objective Price for RDT and United Concepts, the Starting Price for RDT and United Concepts, the Lowest Acceptable Price for Seller (United Concepts), the Highest Acceptable Price for Buyer (RDT), and the Final Price. The first column on the left will be for the names of the team members. There will also be vertical columns for the Objective Price, the Starting Price, the Lowest Acceptable Price for Seller, the Highest Acceptable price for Buyer, and the Final Price (see example).

NEGOTIATIONS SCORING EXAMPLE

Team	Objective Price	Starting Price	Lowest/ Seller	Highest/ Buyer	Final Sale
Mary and Al	RDT: $28,000 UC: $33,000	RDT: $22,000 UC: $33,000	$27,000	$30,000	$27,500

After the scores of all the teams have been recorded, a general discussion should evaluate the price agreements or lack of agreements between buyer and seller. Questions to be answered include these: What were the predispositions of the negotiation participants? What strategic objectives were used by those representing RDT and United Concepts? What specific tactics did the negotiators use? Which tactics were the most effective? Which the least?

(Another version of this activity includes teams role-playing the negotiations before the entire class. In this version the class attempts to identify the predispositions, strategies, and tactics of the buyer and seller.)

SUMMARY OF COMPETENCY COMPONENTS

KNOWLEDGE, SENSITIVITY, SKILLS, VALUES

KNOWLEDGE

Conflict is described as a process in which individuals experience frustration in goal attainment.

Conflict is caused by self- and other perceptions, scarce rewards/resources, roles, power, and values.

Conflict contexts are identified as intrapersonal, interpersonal, small group, whole organization, and organization to environment.

Conflict process is depicted as an episode with latent, perceived, felt, manifest, and aftermath stages.

SENSITIVITY

Sensitivity is developed to individual conflict orientations/styles, strategic objectives, and tactics.

Conflict styles are described as avoidance, competition, compromise, accommodation, and collaboration.

Strategic objectives are depicted as influencing conflict directions of escalation, maintenance, avoidance, and reduction.

Communication tactics are identified for strategic objectives.

SKILLS

Analysis skills are applied to examination of conflict transcripts and cases.

Analysis and process skills are developed for supportive climates and productive conflict formats.

Process skills are practiced in negotiation exercise.

VALUES

Conflict is described as creative, renewing to relationships, important for good decisions, and necessary for analyzing goals and means to achieve goals.

Supportive climates are characterized as more effective than defensive climates.

Ethical conflict behaviors are related to psychological freedom to disagree; generation of free, informed choices; and commitment to most appropriate alternatives.

REFERENCES AND SUGGESTED READINGS

Bennis, W., and B. Nanus. 1985. *Leaders: The strategies for taking charge.* New York: Harper & Row.

Berkowitz, L. 1962. *Aggression: A social psychological analysis.* New York: McGraw-Hill.

Blake, R., and J. Mouton. 1964. *The managerial grid.* Houston, TX: Gulf.

Brilhart, J., and G. Galanes. 1989. *Effective group discussion.* Dubuque, IA: Brown.

Canary, D., and B. Spitzberg. 1987. Appropriateness and effectiveness perceptions of conflict strategies. *Human Communication Research* 14(1): 93–118.

Conrad, C. 1985. *Strategic organizational communication: Cultures, situations, and adaptation.* New York: Holt, Rinehart & Winston.

Cummings, H. W., L. W. Long, and M. L. Lewis. 1983. *Managing communication in organizations: An introduction.* Dubuque, IA: Gorsuch Scarisbrick.

DeVito, J. A. 1986. *The interpersonal communication book.* 4th ed. New York: Harper & Row.

Fisher, R., and W. Ury. 1983. *Getting to yes: Negotiating agreement without giving in.* New York: Penguin.

Frost, J. H., and W. W. Wilmot. 1978. *Interpersonal conflict.* Dubuque, IA: Brown.

Gibb, J. 1982. Defensive communication. In *Bridges not walls*, ed. J. Stewart, 235–40. New York: Random House.

Hall, J. 1969. *Conflict management survey: A survey of one's characteristic reaction and handling of conflicts between himself and others.* Conroe, TX: Teleometrics International.

Janis, I. 1983. *Groupthink: Psychological studies of policy decisions and fiascoes.* 2nd ed. Boston: Houghton Mifflin.

Keller, P. W., and C. T. Brown. 1968. An interpersonal ethic for communication. *Journal of Communication* 18(1): 73–81.

Kreps, G., and B. Thornton. 1984. *Health communication: Theory and practice.* White Plains, NY: Longman.

Phillips, G., and N. Metzger. 1976. *Intimate communication.* Boston: Allyn & Bacon.

Pondy, L. 1966. A systems theory of organizational conflict. *Academy of Management Journal* 9:246–56.

Pondy, L. 1967. Organizational conflict: Concepts and models. *Administrative Science Quarterly* 12: 296–320.

Putnam, L., and M. Poole. 1987. Conflict and negotiation. In *Handbook of organizational communication*, eds. F. Jablin, L. Putnam, K. Roberts, and L. Porter, 549–99. Newbury Park, CA: Sage.

Ray, E. B., and G. B. Ray. 1986. Teaching conflict management skills in corporate training: A perspective-taking approach. *Communication Education* 35(3): 288–306.

Ruben, B. 1978. Communication and conflict: A system theoretic perspective. *Quarterly Journal of Speech* 64: 202–10.

Shockley-Zalabak, P. 1984. Current conflict management training: An examination of practices in ten large American organizations. *Group and Organization Studies* 9: 491–507.

Thomas, K. 1976. Conflict and conflict management. In *The handbook of industrial and organizational psychology*, ed. M. Dunnette, 889–935. Chicago: Rand McNally.

Thomas, K. 1988. The conflict-handling modes: Toward more precise theory. *Management Communication Quarterly* 1(3): 430–36.

Thomas, K., and R. Kilmann. 1975. The social desirability variable in organizational research: An alternative explanation for reported findings. *Academy of Management Journal* 18: 741–52.

Thomas, K., and W. Schmidt. 1976. A survey of managerial interests with respect to conflict. *Academy of Management Journal* 19(2): 315–18.

Walton, R., and J. Dutton. 1969. The management of interdepartmental conflict: A model and review. *Administrative Science Quarterly* 14: 73–84.

CHAPTER

Picture courtesy of Mountain Bell.

~ E I G H T ~

Leadership and Management Communication

Developing competencies through . . .

KNOWLEDGE

Describing leadership from trait, style, and situational approaches
Distinguishing between leadership and management

SENSITIVITY

Clarifying a personal theory of leadership
Understanding leadership styles, strategic objectives, and tactics

SKILLS

Assessing leadership strategies and tactics
Practicing analysis capabilities and skills using cases, transcripts of meetings, and group activities

VALUES

Relating leadership to organizational excellence
Understanding need for leadership from all organizational members
Describing principled leadership

The Case of the Invisible Manager

John Mitchell was a superior engineer who was widely known throughout Invest Corporation for his ability to solve creatively highly complex technical problems. No one had been surprised when John was promoted approximately a year ago to laboratory manager at Invest's main research and development facility. What was surprising were the complaints from the lab that nothing was getting done. Senior lab members were particularly vocal about John's insistence on knowing every detail of their decisions before letting them move forward. They also complained about their inability to get to see him and the days on end that went by with no word from him about decisions.

Although acknowledging John's technical brilliance, several of the lab management team openly questioned whether John would ever be a leader or even understood the difference between engineering responsibilities and those of management. John responded that his technical abilities were the type of leadership the lab needed. He believed that if intelligent people were doing their jobs they did not need close personal contact with their managers. John viewed leadership as a purely technical contribution and was amazed that some of his top engineers were doubting his contributions. He could hardly believe they had labeled him their "Invisible Manager."

INTRODUCTION

Is John right about leadership? Is superior technical ability the type of leadership a management team really needs? Can both John and his managers be right? How can we define management and leadership responsibilities?

In his new position John is faced with a test of his beliefs about leadership and management. He contends that technical contributions are the essence of his leadership. To make complex technical decisions he requires large amounts of detail, and the sheer volume of work has delayed his response to his managers. He believes delay is justified to improve the technical capabilities of the laboratory. He disagrees that leaders and managers need to stay in close personal contact with subordinates. John, however, is on a collision course with a capable group of senior lab managers. They disagree that his approach is working or that he is even exhibiting leadership. How would you help John and his managers? What does he need to understand to resolve this important problem?

Most of us have seen leadership and management situations similar to the one in which the laboratory is involved. We have been members of a group in which the leader and group members were at odds over the way a project should be accomplished. We have experienced frustration when someone like a teacher or a doctor had information or a service we needed but was not available for an appointment. We have been delayed in making plans while waiting for the decisions of others. We are influenced in all aspects of our lives by leadership or the need for leadership. Most of us act as both leaders and followers in our families, at work, and in the political and social organizations of which we are a part.

Think about the most effective leader with whom you have had direct contact. How did this person behave? What were his or her communication competencies? Now think specifically about an ineffective leader. Describe his or her behavior and communication competencies. Most of us have been influenced by leaders and have fulfilled leadership roles without giving detailed consideration to how leadership works and the competencies necessary for effectiveness. To develop communication competencies for leadership, we need to understand the importance of leadership and management communication, how leadership and management have been described, where leadership and management can differ, the determinants of leadership effectiveness, and constructive communication strategies and tactics for leadership.

This chapter is designed to contribute to our *knowledge* by demonstrating the importance of leadership and management communication; distinguishing between the two; and understanding them by describing trait, style, and situational approaches. *Sensitivity* competencies are developed by identifying individual preferences and styles for leadership and by becoming familiar with commonly used strategies and tactics. Sensitivity competencies also are influenced by self-analysis of leadership experiences. Sensitivity competencies, in turn, influence the use of strategic and tactical communication *skills*.

Value competencies are encouraged by describing the importance of leadership for organizational excellence, identifying determinants of leadership effectiveness, and associating leadership with overall interpersonal communication competency. Value competencies are reflected in the choice of skills for leadership.

Finally, all four competencies—knowledge, sensitivity, skills, and values—are applied to competency practice through self-analysis, transcript analysis, and case study.

THE IMPORTANCE OF LEADERSHIP AND MANAGEMENT COMMUNICATION

Leadership and management communication affect nearly all aspects of organizational life. Leaders help guide individuals, groups, and entire organizations in establishing goals and sustaining action to support goals. Managers fulfill specific organizationally assigned roles designed to direct and evaluate the work of others. Managers are expected to be leaders, although not all managers exhibit leadership behaviors. In fact, leadership communication can come from virtually anyone in the organization, with the effectiveness of leadership and management communication directly relating to organizational success and work satisfaction.

But what exactly do we mean by leadership and management communication? There are literally hundreds of definitions of what leaders do and what is considered to be leadership. Chances are our personal definition of leadership may vary from that of our friends and may even change from situation to situation. We might call an individual a leader, for example, because of the person's election to the presidency of a particular organization. At another time we might say that that same individual is not a leader because he or she does not exhibit leadership behaviors expected from the president. In other words, we expected leadership from the legitimate position of the presidency, but when the president does not exhibit leadership behaviors, we say the president is not a leader.

Leadership—process for guiding individuals, groups, and entire organizations in establishing goals and sustaining action to support goals.

Leadership takes place through communication. Leaders communicate about needed change, translate intentions into reality, propose new strategies, and help sustain action to support decisions. Leadership communication is a process of influence whereby leaders attempt to convince followers to attain specific goals or broad organizational outcomes. The ability to influence is based on the leader's position, credibility to a follower group, analysis and technical skills, and overall communication competence. People can be assigned the position of leader; however, leadership occurs not from the assignment itself but through communication behaviors in interactions with others.

Management—responsibility, specifically assigned by the organization, to direct and evaluate the work of others.

Management fulfills specifically defined roles designed to facilitate work to support organizational goals. Managers are given legitimate power to influence the behavior of subordinates. They are charged with obtaining routine compliance with the operating procedures and expectations of the organization. It is hoped, of course, that managers can exceed routine compliance and instill in subordinates a desire for excellence that goes beyond merely acceptable performance. Whether resulting in routine compliance or a desire for excellence, managerial influence occurs through human communication. Based on the formal superior-subordinate relationships, managerial communication is directed to work assignments, work evaluation, needed changes, and all other aspects of directing organizational action for goal achievement.

Both leadership and management communication are powerful organizational influences. Communication relationships between managers and subordinates influence innovation, decision making, work satisfaction, and perceptions of organizational climate. Leadership communication, whether exhibited by managers or other influential organizational members, becomes the vision of the organization that directs and redirects all organizational activity. As Warren Bennis and Burt Nanus (1985) suggest, "effective leadership can move organizations from current to future states, create visions of potential opportunities for organizations, instill within employees commitment to change, and instill new cultures and strategies in organizations that mobilize and focus energy and resources."

Leadership and management communication is part of the sense-making activities of the organization. It helps members develop priorities and determine what is needed by the organization. It influences decision making, transmits communication rules, and contributes to the shared realities that become the organization's culture. As such, leadership and management communication charts the course of action for the organization. The effectiveness of this communication, therefore, is central to organizational excellence.

THEORIES OF LEADERSHIP AND MANAGEMENT

Thousands of articles have been written about leadership and management. We talk about the need for leadership in our communities, in the organizations in which we work, and in government. Yet trying to describe how leadership and management work and how they should work remains a difficult and often controversial task. Are leaders born with leadership talents? What styles do successful leaders employ? Are some people simply in the right time and place to assume leadership responsibility? What type of leader is John Mitchell (from the beginning of this chapter)? What type of manager? Is there a difference? What can we do to increase our leadership effectiveness?

Theories of leadership and management describe leaders and managers in terms of personal traits or characteristics, preferences for leadership styles or approaches, and responsiveness to leadership requirements in specific situations. Before we explore trait, style, and situational theories of leadership, please complete the leadership experience exercise in Figure 8.1. The exercise will give you a profile of some of your attitudes and experiences with leadership that you can compare with major theories of leadership and management.

You now have before you an assessment of your personal theory of leadership. As you begin to evaluate major theories of leadership and management think about your own personal theory and what is needed for leadership effectiveness.

Trait Approaches

Early theories of effective leadership assumed that leaders had innate traits that made them effective. That is, great leaders were considered to be born with the ability for leadership. This theory of the "great man" first surfaced in the writings of the early Greeks and Romans and is prevalent today among those who believe that leadership cannot be developed—that you either have leadership qualities or not.

FIGURE 8.1
Leadership Experiences

The following twenty-one statements have been used to describe leadership and leaders. Following them are four incomplete sentences that begin "My experience with leadership and leaders has taught me that. . . ." For each of the four incomplete sentences, select from among the following twenty-one statements the five that best reflect your experiences with leadership and leaders. Statements may be used to complete more than one incomplete sentence.

Statements Describing Leaders and Leadership

1. Leaders are *born*.
2. Leadership *ability* can be *developed*.
3. Leaders are high in *intelligence*.
4. Leaders take *initiative*.
5. Leaders *deviate* from norms.
6. Leaders have *good communication* skills.
7. Leaders are in the *right place* at the right time.
8. Leaders are *democratic*.
9. Leaders are *autocratic*.
10. Leaders are *risk takers*.
11. Leaders take a *"hands off"* approach.
12. Leadership is *situation specific*.
13. Leaders *block ideas* and *punish opposition*.
14. Leaders *seek ideas* and *encourage disagreement*.
15. Leaders *ignore conflict*.
16. Leaders *solicit feedback*.
17. Leaders are *outcome oriented*.
18. Leaders *share praise*.
19. Leaders *set goals*.
20. Leaders *blame* those who fail.
21. Leaders *control* their followers.

My experience with leadership and leaders has taught me that effective . . .
    1.
    2.
    3.
    4.
    5.

My experience with leadership and leaders has taught me that ineffective . . .
    1.
    2.
    3.
    4.
    5.

My experience with leadership and leaders has taught me that the most important aspects of leadership are . . .

1.
2.
3.
4.
5.

My experience with leadership and leaders has taught me that the least important aspects of leadership are . . .

1.
2.
3.
4.
5.

What type of person and situation does your personal leadership theory describe? Compare your theory to the ones you will now study in Chapter 8.

Over eighty years of research has attempted to define traits or personality characteristics that best predict the effective leader. Lists of desirable traits have numbered approximately eighty characteristics, but the **trait approach** has failed to define clearly a stable set of characteristics associated with effective leadership. Even the concept of what is effective remains open to question.

Trait approach—theory of leadership that assumed that leaders possessed innate traits that made them effective; commonly referred to as the "great man" theory.

Ronald Applbaum, Edward Bodaken, Kenneth Sereno, and Karl Anatol (1974) suggest that effective leaders are higher in intelligence than other group members, are able to adapt to changing situations, and are willing to deviate more than other group members from traditions and norms, all contributing to the perception of others that the individual is a leader. These researchers suggest that "perhaps leadership is not so much a function of deviancy as it is a function of knowing how much and when to deviate."

Applbaum and his colleagues' observations reflect the findings of Ralph Stogdill and Alvin Coons (1957), which suggest that leaders more than others are higher in intelligence, scholarship, responsibility, participation, and socioeconomic status. Keith Davis (1967) suggests that intelligence, social maturity (being emotionally stable with a good self-concept), initiative, and human relations abilities affect leadership. He does caution, however, that we really do not understand cause-and-effect relationships between traits and effective leadership.

When we study group leaders who emerge on their own rather than being appointed or elected, we find relatively low communication apprehension and a willingness to participate verbally in group activities. Those not emerging as leaders are more likely to exhibit communication behaviors that include rigidity, authoritarian statements, and generally offensive verbalizations.

Despite the importance of intelligence, communication ability, and situational adaptation, the approach of identifying traits has generally failed to explain effective leadership. This approach simply does not provide a comprehensive explanation of how leaders interact with followers and meet the needs of specific circumstances.

To illustrate the difficulty of establishing a trait approach for leadership, identify two leaders you would characterize as effective. Describe their personality traits and characteristics in relation to the groups they lead. Now identify two leaders whose effectiveness you question. What traits and characteristics do they exhibit? Do your effective and ineffective leaders share similar characteristics? How do they differ? What leadership traits do you exhibit? How effective are these characteristics?

Style Approaches

In Chapter 7 we described the importance of predispositions for conflict behavior and how generally recognized predispositions are known as conflict styles. The **style approach** also applies to understanding leadership and management communication. As Wayne Pace (1983) has suggested, "managerial style is, however, quite directly related to three elements over which a manager has some control: (1) a manager's assumptions about people and what motivates them; (2) a manager's perceptions of what he or she can do to influence others; and (3) a manager's views of the resources over which he or she has control."

Style approach—theories that attempt to identify a range of general approaches leaders use to achieve goals. The approaches are thought to be based on the leader's assumptions about what motivates people to accomplish goals.

Style theories for understanding leadership attempt to identify a range of general approaches leaders use to influence goal achievement. These approaches are theorized to be based on the leader's assumptions about what motivates people to accomplish goals. Particular approaches also are thought to reflect complex relationships among the personal characteristics of the leader (i.e., communication competencies, communication apprehension, and internal motivational forces), the requirements of the situation at hand, and the resources over which the leader and followers have control or influence.

Chief among the style theories is the autocratic-to-democratic continuum first proposed by Ralph White and Ronald Lippit (1960). This continuum suggests that leadership can be understood as ranging in behavior from autocratic to democratic. The three primary styles identified are autocratic, democratic, and laissez-faire.

Autocratic—style of leader or manager who makes decisions with little influence from others.

The **autocratic** leader or manager makes decisions with little influence from others. This leader tells others what to do and usually enforces sanctions against those who choose not to comply. The autocratic leader views followers as essential for goal achievement but usually feels little responsibility for subordinate needs and relationships. Some research suggests that autocratically led groups produce more in quantity than democratically led groups but that the quality of output is better when more democracy is practiced.

All of us have been involved with autocratic leaders. Can you identify a successful autocratic leader and one who is not so successful? What makes the difference? Is there a best time for autocratic management? What do you lose in the process of being an autocrat?

Democratic leaders involve followers in decision making. They assume creativity will be greater and there will be more broad-based support for goals if participation is high. Democratic leaders assume followers are able to participate in decision making. These leaders, therefore, attempt to generate a climate in which problem solving can take place while interpersonal relationships are preserved.

Democratic leaders, as do autocrats, both succeed and fail. Now identify a successful democratic leader and one who is not so successful. As you did for the autocrats, attempt to determine the difference. What made the approach work for one and not the other? From your personal leadership profile, attempt to place your theory on the autocratic-to-democratic continuum.

The **laissez-faire** leader is really an example of a nonleader. This leader expects individuals and groups to make their own decisions. The laissez-faire leader takes a "hands off" approach and contributes information only when asked by group members. This leader shows little direct concern for individuals or goals. Groups can succeed with laissez-faire leaders. Their success depends greatly, however, on the abilities of the group and the willingness to work with little or no leadership. Have you ever been in a group with laissez-faire leadership? What happened? How did you feel about that type of working experience?

Robert Tannenbaum and Warren Schmidt (1958) have expanded the concept of the autocratic-to-democratic continuum by describing it in terms of the use of authority by the leader and the area of freedom for subordinates. Figure 8.2 illustrates the conception of what happens when leadership moves through the continuum from autocratic to democratic. As you can see, the autocratic end of the continuum is characterized by the manager using authority to make and announce decisions with little decision-making input from subordinates. As the approach to leading becomes more democratic, more input from subordinates is asked for and utilized.

How would you describe John Mitchell on this continuum? What are his basic assumptions about people? How are those assumptions reflected? If you were advising John, where should he be on the leadership continuum?

Perhaps the best known of the style theories for leadership and management is the one proposed in 1964 and updated through 1985 by Robert Blake and Jane Mouton. The Blake and Mouton Managerial Grid® suggests that leadership styles or approaches are based on two central dimensions: concern for relationships with people and concern for task production. The balances leaders and managers make between these dimensions have become known as the leadership styles of impoverished, middle-of-the-road (organization man), country club, task (authority-obedience), and team management. Figure 8.3 illustrates the Managerial Grid® styles with the two dimensions of concern for people and concern for task.

Impoverished management (1,1). **Impoverished management** is character-

> **Democratic**—style of leader or manager who involves followers in decision making.

> **Laissez-faire**—style of leader or manager who behaves as a nonleader. Individuals and groups are expected to make their own decisions because of a "hands off" approach from the leader.

> **Impoverished management**—leadership style characterized by a low concern for interpersonal relationships and task accomplishment.

Continuum of Leadership Behavior

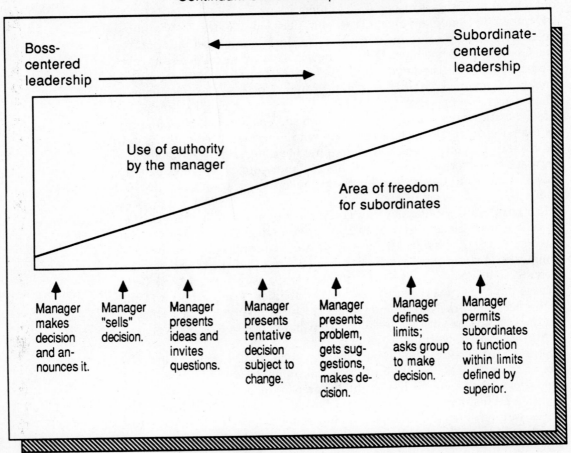

FIGURE 8.2
Illustrates the Tannenbaum and Schmidt Leadership Continuum.
Reprinted by permission of the *Harvard Business Review*. An exhibit from "How to Choose a Leadership Pattern" by Robert Tannenbaum and Warren H. Schmidt (May/June 1973). Copyright © 1973 by the President and Fellows of Harvard College; all rights reserved.

ized by low concern for interpersonal relationships and task accomplishment. The impoverished leader makes few attempts to influence people toward task or goal achievement. This leader frequently dislikes leadership responsibilities and lets others take responsibility that rightfully belongs to the leader. This leader often is uncomfortable with leadership and intellectually resists the need for it. Many impoverished leaders are excellent technically; they have been promoted to supervision or management because of strong technical skills. Technical skills, however, do not prepare them for managing people or letting others accomplish tasks that the leaders themselves have been used to doing. Impoverished leaders may even think that if people would "do their jobs" there would be little real need for leadership. Such leaders are most often found in legitimate or formal leadership positions rather than in emergent positions as the choice of a group of peers. These leaders may be primarily responsible for the failure of a group, yet they can rarely claim much credit for a group's success. Groups with impoverished leaders often succeed despite the leader and through the emergent leadership of other group members.

Middle-of-the-road (organization man) management (5,5). As Figure 8.3 suggests, **middle-of-the-road management** balances task and people concerns. Sometimes referred to as *compromise* leadership, the middle-of-the-road leader negotiates and compromises in order to achieve workable agreements and directions for action. This leader is more concerned with practical versus excellent solutions. The middle-of-the-road leader will seek the

Middle-of-the-road management—style of leader who balances task and people concerns; commonly referred to as compromise management or leadership.

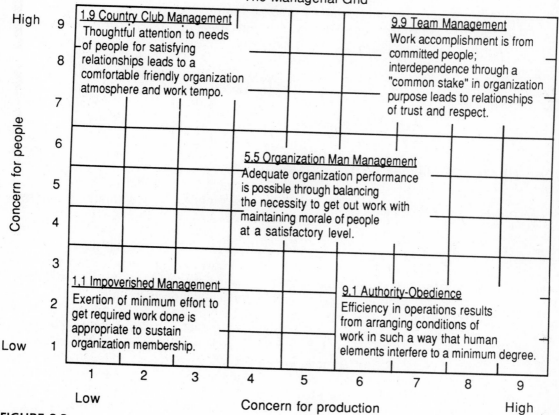

FIGURE 8.3

Illustrates the Blake and Mouton Managerial Grid®.
From *The Managerial Grid III: The Key to Leadership Excellence,* by Robert R. Blake and Jane Srygley Mouton. Houston, TX: Gulf Publishing Company, copyright © 1985, p. 12. Reproduced by permission.

"middle" position to maintain a group where everyone has some stake in the decision. The compromise positions of middle-of-the-road leaders have been criticized as Band-Aids on the wounds of more serious problems. Critics suggest that middle-of-the-road leadership provides short-term solutions guaranteeing long-term problems. Middle-of-the-road leaders frequently are found in middle (or "organization man") management, where compromise between the needs of subordinates and top management seems inevitable. In fact, the difficult position of middle management has often been referred to as the sandwich position because of the pressures from below (subordinates) and from above (top management)—pressures that often result in the need for compromise.

Country club management (1,9). In Figure 8.3, we see that **country club management** places the emphasis on interpersonal relationships at the expense of goal achievement. The country club leader wants to be liked and to have a group of followers who feel supported by the leader. This leader provides an interpersonal relationship bond that is low on task emphasis and high in interpersonal support. Country club leaders may want the task accomplished but will not take steps to emphasize this element to others if group members are not highly task oriented. Country club managers are frequently observed doing the work of their subordinates rather than insisting that their subordinates exhibit high standards of performance. These managers may not develop the abilities of their subordinates. However, they may lead successful groups when group members themselves have high task motivation and only require interpersonal support to maintain motivation.

Task (authority-obedience) management (9,1). Often referred to as autocratic leadership, the **task management** leader is concerned with goals or task achievement and exhibits little concern for personal relationships. This leader makes decisions and expects compliance. He or she often enforces decisions with little subordinate input and is willing to defend his or her position when necessary. Task leaders often exhibit win-lose conflict style preferences. The task leader values efficiency and will make quick and timely decisions. Task leadership, as do other approaches, requires having appropriate information on which to make good decisions; but by showing low concern for people, such leaders may alienate others to the point that they withhold information that might improve decision making. Task leadership, however, may be appropriate when a group is hopelessly deadlocked on an issue and someone needs to take responsibility for making a decision. Furthermore, surveys of top management in leading American companies indicate that task leadership is a prevalent style preference among highly influential managers.

Team management (9,9). As you can see from Figure 8.3, **team management** is the theoretical ideal. Exhibiting high concern for both task and interpersonal relationships, team leaders emphasize goal accomplishment while supporting people. Team leadership fosters a sense of "we" with high performance standards. This leadership shares decision making and

Country club management—style of leader or manager who emphasizes interpersonal relationships at the expense of goal achievement.

Task management—style of leader or manager who is concerned with goals or task achievement while exhibiting little concern for personal relationships; commonly referred to as autocratic leadership.

Team management—team leadership or management is the theoretical ideal. Team leaders exhibit high concern for both task and interpersonal relationships by emphasizing goal accomplishment while supporting people.

strives for problem solving designed to solve rather than postpone problems. Team leaders respect differing points of view and value diversity as long as all contribute to the group effort. Team leaders, however, must have capable and willing team members for successful efforts. Although the style is highly desirable, team leaders depend on team followers for their style of leadership to work. Team members who support each other but who do not have enough ability or information to work on problems will not be able to produce a high-quality decision. In other words, willingness to be a team member does not ensure a solid team, and team leadership only produces excellent results with a capable team.

To better understand the styles approach to leadership, identify a series of leaders with whom you have had contact and who exhibited each of these five approaches. Try to determine how you reacted to each and how effective his or her leadership was. From your own experiences, what determines whether a particular style is effective or ineffective?

Situational Approaches

Both the trait and style approaches failed to describe comprehensively why particular approaches would work in one set of circumstances and fail in another. In response to this difficulty, **situational**, or contingency, **approaches** were developed to understand better how leaders interact with followers and the requirements of a particular environment.

In 1967, Fred Fiedler pioneered understanding leadership styles based on the concept of *contingencies*. He suggested that leader effectiveness could be evaluated only in relationship to how style choices related to contingencies in particular situations. Task and interpersonal relationships were important, but also to be considered were the leader's power position and how rewards and punishment were handled. Sometimes powerful leaders had good follower relationships to accomplish well-defined tasks, a favorable condition for leadership. At other times the leader's power position was in question, with an ambiguous goal to accomplish. In the latter circumstance, leader-member relationships could become strained, generating an overall unfavorable condition. According to Fiedler the approach or style an effective leader chose depended on a combination of task, relationship, power, and situational contingencies.

Building on the work of Robert Blake and Jane Mouton, Paul Hersey and Kenneth Blanchard (1977) proposed a concept of leadership that suggested that the appropriateness and effectiveness of leadership behaviors could not be determined by the specific behavior of the leader but by the appropriateness of the behavior in a particular situation. Hersey and Blanchard's Situational Leadership theory postulated that effectiveness of a particular leader was related to the leader's selection of behavior appropriate to the maturity level of the follower group. Maturity was based on achievement-motivation, ability, education, experience, and the willingness to participate responsibly in goal-oriented activity. In other words,

Situational approaches—leadership theories that explore how leaders interact with followers and the requirements of a particular environment.

the maturity level of the follower group was the primary factor that determined an effective leadership style. Hersey and Blanchard described situational leadership as dependent on concern for relationships, concern for task, and concern for maturity of followers. They saw four general styles of situational leadership: telling, selling, participating, and delegating. Figure 8.4 depicts the Hersey and Blanchard situational grid.

As you can tell from Figure 8.4, the telling style has high task and low relationship emphases and is best used with immature followers. The leader defines what should be done and instructs followers in how to accomplish well-established goals or tasks.

The selling style also has high task emphasis, but it has a higher relationship emphasis than the telling style. The selling style is characterized by the leader's attempt to convince followers of the importance of the goal and the leader's definition of how the goal is to be accomplished. The selling style is appropriate for a follower group mature enough to accept some responsibility for decisions and actions.

Unlike the team style of Blake and Mouton, the participating style in Figure 8.4 has high relationship and low task emphases in order to stimulate the creativity of a mature group of followers. The leader supports relationships and encourages participation in decision making because followers are sufficiently mature to contribute to good decisions and support decisions with appropriate action.

The final style, delegating, has low task and low relationship emphases based on high follower maturity. In other words, the leader lets followers take responsibility for decisions and actions based on a maturity level sufficient for that responsibility. The leader actually passes leadership to the group in the delegating style.

Based on the Hersey and Blanchard description of effective leadership, a mature follower group with considerable experience in a particular set of circumstances may become an immature group when faced with new challenges. An effective leader, therefore, would be required to delegate under the first circumstance and possibly return to the telling style when circumstances change.

As an example of how situational leadership might be applied, consider the case of an advertising account team in transition from one account to another. The creative group—artists, writers, and producers—was very familiar with the products manufactured by their former client. They knew how the products worked, what their advantages were over major competitors, and how to produce budget-effective commercials the client liked. When the client was sold to a major competitor, the needs of the situation changed. The entire creative team was transferred to the new owner's account with only limited responsibility to their old product line. In fact, the assignment was to integrate the old product line with the new owner's products. Quality advantages, pricing structure, client tastes, and budgets all were changed. The talent of the creative staff remained the same, but the changing assignment contributed to less "maturity" in the group. The

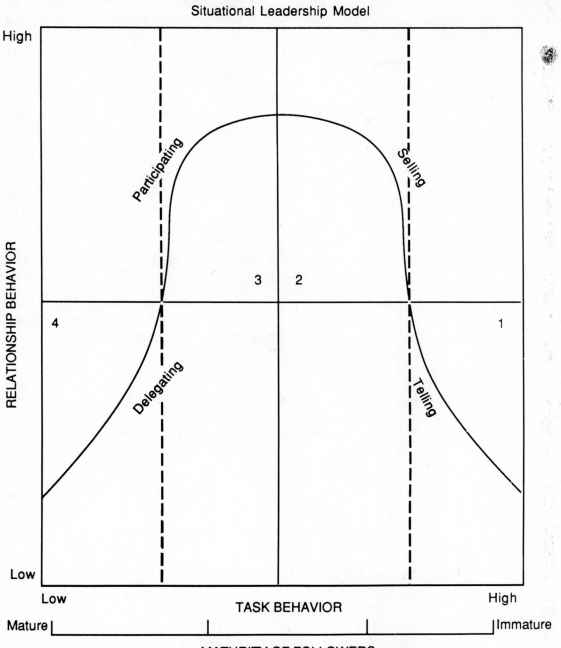

Situational Leadership Model

High

RELATIONSHIP BEHAVIOR

Participating

Selling

3   2

4   1

Delegating

Telling

Low

Low   TASK BEHAVIOR   High

Mature | | Immature

MATURITY OF FOLLOWERS

FIGURE 8.4

Illustrates the Hersey and Blanchard concept of situational leadership.
P. Hersey and K. Blanchard, *Management of Organizational Behavior: Utilizing Human Resources*, 3rd ed. © 1977, p. 322. Adapted by permission of Prentice-Hall, Inc., Englewood Cliffs, NJ.

account executive supervisor could no longer use a delegating style under dramatically changed circumstances. Although not reverting to the extreme of the telling style, the group's supervisor used a selling style in order to bring about quickly needed changes without losing the account to other agencies. The fact that the account stayed with the same creative team despite a change in client ownership attested to the flexibility of the manager and the appropriate application of a leadership style reflecting changing business needs. Leadership effectiveness, from the situational perspective, can be described as style selection appropriate to the needs of followers in a particular circumstance. With this approach, situational analysis becomes as important as task and relationship behavior.

How would you describe John Mitchell's leadership from the style or situational perspective? Describe the assumptions John makes about his subordinates. Also describe the overall situation in which John is expected to provide leadership. If you were advising John, which of the theories would you use? Why?

We have described trait, style, and situational approaches to understanding leadership and management communication. By now you have probably recognized that these approaches are complementary, each building on the other. In other words, our approaches for studying leadership are simply different ways of attempting to describe how leadership occurs. We look at the traits, styles, and the circumstances in which a particular leader influences his or her group. We use our trait, style, and situational approaches together to help us explain why a particular leadership effort was successful or how the effort might have been more effective. We are not trait, style, or situational leaders but leaders who exhibit traits, styles, and reactions to specific situations. The approaches we have just studied should help us evaluate our own efforts and better understand the efforts of others.

Throughout our discussion we have described leadership as a responsibility of managers, as well as an influence process that engages those other than managers. We will now describe important distinctions between leadership and management communication. Keep in mind, however, that whereas managers need to be leaders, excellent organizations require leadership from all organizational positions.

DISTINCTIONS BETWEEN LEADERSHIP AND MANAGEMENT

Warren Bennis and Burt Nanus (1985) make important distinctions between leaders and managers when they suggest that

> the problem with many organizations, and especially the ones that are failing, is that they tend to be overmanaged and underled. They may excel in the ability to handle the daily routine, yet never question whether the routine should be done at all. There is a profound difference between management and leadership, and both are important. "To manage" means "to bring about, to

accomplish, to have charge of or responsibility for, to conduct." "Leading" is "influencing, guiding in direction, course, action, opinion." The distinction is crucial. Managers are people who do things right and leaders are people who do the right thing. The difference may be summarized as activities of vision and judgment—effectiveness versus activities of mastering routines— efficiency.

Bennis and Nanus further contend that the vision leaders provide is the clearest of all distinctions between leaders and managers. To provide vision requires marshalling the "spiritual and emotional" resources of the organization as reflected in its values, commitment, and aspirations. Management, on the other hand, is charged with directing the physical resources of the organization, its people, machines, and products. Competent managers can get work done efficiently, but excellence comes from leaders who inspire followers to emotional involvement with work and their organization. Bennis and Nanus state, "Great leaders often inspire their followers to high levels of achievement by showing them how their work contributes to worthwhile ends. It is an emotional appeal to some of the most fundamental human needs—the need to be important, to make a difference, to feel useful, to be a part of a successful and worthwhile enterprise."

The increasing complexity of an information society places new demands on leaders and managers. The sheer volume of information available for organizational decision making complicates the development of organizational vision and the direction of organizational activities. This volume of information, when coupled with fast-paced technological changes, puts a new emphasis on the need for leadership from diverse organizational positions. In a complicated information society, the development of vision and the generation of emotional commitment to the work and values of an organization can no longer rest solely with leaders at the top of the organization or with the management team that directs organizational activity.

Put simply, the information society requires leadership from diverse organizational positions. Managers will continue to fulfill specific organizational roles for the direction of work. It is hoped that those in the role of manager will also provide leadership and generate commitment to the values of the organization. However, the management role represents the formal organizational hierarchy and, as such, is deeply involved in efficiently planning and implementing what the organization has decided to do. Put another way, managers are responsible for generating enough stability for efficient work to be accomplished. Leaders, on the other hand, are responsible for generating enough change continually to adapt to new circumstances. Thus, the competencies for effective leaders and managers are not the same. Complex organizations need leadership exhibited by those who identify emerging problems and opportunities, whether they fulfill the role of manager or not.

We can readily understand how a manager becomes a leader when inspiring subordinates to excellent performance. What we do not as readily see is the leadership role of the subordinate who identifies a needed work change, a possible new product, or an improved service opportunity and proceeds to influence others to share that vision of an improved organization. This subordinate's assumption of leadership responsibility is highly desirable for the fast-paced information age.

DETERMINANTS OF LEADERSHIP EFFECTIVENESS

Thus far we have discussed whether leaders are born or can be developed, what traits are associated with effective leadership, how leadership styles relate to the maturity of followers and to particular leadership situations, and how leadership contributes to establishing organizational vision. Throughout our discussion we have contended that both leadership and management are enacted through human communication. With this perspective, we will now examine how communication competencies, influence (power bases), and analysis abilities contribute to leadership effectiveness.

Communication Competencies as Determinants of Leadership Effectiveness

A recurring theme throughout this text has been that communication competence is necessary for organizational excellence. Knowledge, sensitivity, skills, and values all must be understood and developed for both individuals and entire organizations to be effective in our emerging information era. Nowhere is communication competency more important than when individuals are attempting to lead and establish vision and direction for organizations.

Research on managerial effectiveness and perceptions of effectiveness supports the importance of communication competence. In the famous works of Chris Argyris (1962), Peter Drucker (1966), and Warren Bennis and Burt Nanus (1985), communication effectiveness is described as a central element for overall managerial effectiveness. Communication encoding, decoding, and interaction capabilities are described as factors necessary for communication and overall managerial competence.

Predispositions for Leadership Communication

As we have previously discussed, the knowledge, sensitivity, skills, and values we bring to particular situations powerfully influence our behavior choices. Whether or not we choose to attempt leadership is related to our assessment of our own competencies, the needs of the situation, the receptivity of a follower group, and our potential ability to influence (power).

Those high in anxiety about communication, for example, are less likely to engage in leadership attempts than those lower in communication apprehension. Highly task-oriented individuals are more likely to adopt leadership styles reflecting task emphasis, whereas those preferring close interpersonal relationships are more likely to adopt styles reflecting their concern for people. Return for a moment to Figures 8.3 and 8.4. Although the grids in these figures represent behavioral approaches used for leadership and management, they can also be understood as preferences individuals bring to leadership and managerial situations. Concern for task and people relationships, when coupled with an assessment of follower maturity, influences behavior choices in specific circumstances. But concerns for task and people relationships, follower maturity, personal assessments of communication competence, and assessments of influence or power positions are also reflected in our predispositions for leadership communication—predispositions that subsequently influence strategic objectives and tactical choices.

Strategic Communication Objectives for Leadership

In Chapter 7, we described strategic objectives for conflict as the general game plans for conducting communication based on preferences or predispositions for conflict and on assessments of the probable outcomes within particular contexts. Communication strategies for leadership can be described in the same way. Tactics, then, are the specific behavior choices made by leaders to influence followers in specific situations and to support overall strategies.

Autocratic strategies are used by leaders who seek to have followers implement decisions with little or no follower input. John Mitchell can decide that the current complaints at Invest Corporation call for autocratic strategies. He can announce that he will continue to determine when decisions will be made and that his technical decisions will not be subject to question. He can choose to ignore complaints that he is "invisible" and continue to view leadership as a technical contribution. These autocratic strategies are possible as long as top management supports him.

John also has choices among more participative strategies. He can encourage senior lab members to suggest ways in which he can work with them in a team atmosphere. He can compromise about the number of details he will handle personally and the amount of time he is taking to make decisions. He can seek to establish more open and supportive relationships in order to become a more "visible" manager. Finally, John can use avoidance or laissez-faire strategies and ignore the complaints he is hearing. He has the avoidance option because of his legitimate power position as laboratory manager. He can ignore much of the discontent as long as he retains the support of senior management.

John's selection of strategies is related to his assessment of what is needed for leadership and his assessment of whether individuals need leadership. As you will recall, John believes leadership is primarily a technical responsibility and that intelligent people do not need close personal contact to do their jobs. These assumptions will influence what happens next at Invest.

In a recent extensive study of some ninety outstanding leaders, Bennis and Nanus (1985) identified four major strategies or competencies that all ninety leaders seemed to exhibit: (1) management of attention through vision, (2) meaning through communication, (3) trust through positioning, and (4) deployment of self through positive self-regard and the Wallenda factor.

The outstanding leaders of the Bennis and Nanus study commanded the attention of their followers and organizations by establishing and communicating a *vision* about where the organization should go, what it should be, and what was needed to achieve it. As Bennis and Nanus suggest, "All ninety people interviewed had an agenda, an unparalleled concern with outcome. Leaders are the most results-oriented individuals in the world, and results get attention. . . . The visions these various leaders conveyed seemed to bring about a confidence on the part of the employees, a confidence that instilled in them a belief that they were capable of performing the necessary acts." Bennis and Nanus further suggested that successful leaders not only caught the attention of others but also paid attention to others, underscoring the essential interactional relationship between leaders and followers.

The second strategy, the management of meaning through *communication*, relates to the conscious effort the leaders made to communicate so their meanings would become the meanings of every organizational level. These excellent leaders were concerned not only with what should be done but also with how to develop messages that conveyed that vision. Bennis and Nanus state, "Getting the message across unequivocally at every level is an absolute key. Basically it is what the creative process is all about and what, once again, separates the managers from the leaders." Management of meaning rests on well-developed communication competencies and an understanding of the process of organizational communication. Without competencies and process of understanding, effective leadership is problematic.

Trust as a strategy is hard to define. Bennis and Nanus describe trust as the "glue that maintains organizational integrity." The leaders in the Bennis and Nanus study were trusted (although not always liked) because they were constant, predictable, and reliable. They positioned themselves as worthy of trust by exhibiting personal stability even while encouraging change and innovation. They helped their organizations develop a sense of identity (culture) and integrity (trust). This sense of direction is considered by Bennis and Nanus to be fundamental to their effectiveness.

Finally, the effective leaders in the study liked themselves and other people. They did not focus on failure but viewed mistakes as learning opportunities and challenges. They were like famed tight-rope walker Karl

Wallenda, who until shortly before the fall that claimed his life, always focused on walking, never falling. Bennis and Nanus contend that the "Wallenda factor" in leadership is the ability to focus on success, not failure, and to frame our behavior in terms of the goal, not every detail of the process.

The strategy of positive self-regard and regard for others is closely related to our description of developing communication competencies (knowledge, sensitivity, skills, and values) for organizational excellence. The relationship between regard and developing communication competencies is made clear when Bennis and Nanus sum up positive self-regard as three major factors: "knowledge of one's strengths, the capacity to nurture and develop those strengths, and the ability to discern the fit between one's strengths and weaknesses and the organization's needs." They continue, "In the case of our ninety leaders, they used five key skills: (1) The ability to accept people as they are, not as you would like them to be. . . . (2) The capacity to approach relationships and problems in terms of the present rather than the past. . . . (3) The ability to treat those who are close to you with the same courteous attention that you extend to strangers and casual acquaintances. . . . (4) The ability to trust others, even if the risk seems great. . . . (5) The ability to do without constant approval and recognition from others."

Recent research by Eric Eisenberg (1984) lends support to the Bennis and Nanus contention that generating vision is an important leadership responsibility. Eisenberg proposes *strategic ambiguity* as an organizational communication strategy that promotes unity while maintaining sufficient individual freedom to ensure flexibility, creativity, and change. Eisenberg argues that divergent organizational goals cannot always be resolved through the development of specific consensus from all organizational members. He proposes that

ambiguity is used strategically to foster agreement on abstractions without limiting specific interpretations. . . . Focusing on organizational symbolism casts leadership in a new light as well. While a primary responsibility of leaders is to make meanings for followers (Pfeffer, 1981; Pondy, 1978; Smircich, 1983) and to infuse employees with values and purpose (Peters and Waterman, 1982; Selznick, 1957) the process of doing so is less one of consensus-making and more one of using language strategically to express values at a level of abstraction at which agreement can occur. . . . Effective leaders use ambiguity strategically to encourage creativity and guard against the acceptance of one standard way of viewing organizational reality.

Organizational goal and mission statements, communication rules, and organizational stories and myths are all examples of strategic ambiguity influenced by leaders. An excellent example of strategic ambiguity (vision) comes from the recurring theme to "do what's right, not what's written" of a certain large computer manufacturer. What's "right" is subject to varying interpretations across the organization. The leadership imperative, however, is to take action and personal responsibility, a value with high consensus even though specific interpretations often vary dramatically. In fact, conflict frequently occurs in this generally healthy organization over "what is right" and "who should decide."

The work of Gail Fairhurst, Stephen Green, and B. Kay Snavely (1984) supports the Bennis and Nanus contention that trust and positive self-regard and regard for others are important leadership strategies. In their study of managerial attempts to control poor performance among subordinates, they found that the strategy of using positive face (maintaining an approval of the subordinate's self-image) was positively related to performance improvement. Also, the involvement (trusting) of subordinates in decisions about performance improvement was positively associated with longer periods of time between problem recurrence. These findings suggest that positive self-regard and regard for others can contribute to improved performance and that trusting subordinates by involving them in behavior change decisions improves the quality of and commitment to solutions.

We have discussed autocratic, participative, and laissez-faire or avoidance strategies for leadership. We have also described strategies for the communication of vision, management of meaning through communication, management of trust, and management of positive self-regard and regard for others. We will now describe specific communication tactics used for each of these strategic orientations.

Communication Tactics for Leadership

Leadership tactics can be described as the communication behaviors used to support authoritarian, participative, and avoidance preferences as well as to establish vision, manage meaning, generate trust, and communicate regard and success orientations. Specific tactics are influenced by individual preferences and strategies, by communication competencies of leaders and followers, and by overall organizational values and expectations about how leadership works. Military organizations, for example, encourage authoritarian leadership, whereas organizations involved in research and development of new products usually stress more participative styles. Still others reflect a mix of leadership approaches representing the diversity of people and personalities who work together. It is important to understand that as with conflict tactics, the choice of specific leadership tactics illustrates the interactive nature of relationships. Both leaders and followers are involved in complex tactical interactions influenced by individual preferences and strategic objectives as well as the needs of a particular situation.

It is not possible to list or define all the communication tactics available to potential leaders. It is useful for our personal sensitivity and our skill development, however, to identify several frequently used communication tactics. Figure 8.5 presents excerpts from group problem-solving situations in which the identified group leader illustrates a particular leadership tactic. Each example is accompanied by a description of the tactic it represents,

FIGURE 8.5
Communication Tactics for Leadership

Organizational Narrative   *Leadership Tactics*

Authoritarian Tactics

"The seriousness of the problem leaves little room for continuing to think about new ideas—I believe I know what we should do and am willing to take the responsibility."

1. *Blocking ideas* by establishing responsibility

"We will first assign new sales territories, then we will put one senior salesperson in each territory, and then we will establish sales quotas."

2. *Controlling the process* of events

"I have decided we will stop development of the Henderson project. I think our direction is in Richardson Heights."

3. *Announcing goals* without consultation

"I expected you to be on my team. You can forget about my support come budget time—and you know you need that."

4. *Punishing opposition* through sanctions or withholding support

Participative Tactics

"To make the best decision we need everyone's ideas. I don't want anyone to think he or she doesn't have a say."

1. *Seeking ideas* from all involved

"We need to make a decision on the budget, and I want everyone to have ample time to participate. Therefore, we will each spend 15 minutes on our initial presentations."

2. *Facilitating group processes* which encourage participation

"Look, I'm glad you will disagree with me. That is the only way we will have a good solution."

3. *Encouraging disagreement* when constructive and solution oriented

"I think opening the store at 3rd and Franklin is a good idea— but I need your honesty with any reservations you may have."

4. *Seeking idea evaluation*

"I believe we all agree that the new product line will work. We can easily say to top

5. *Verbalizing consensus* among group members

(continued)

FIGURE 8.5 (*continued*)

Organizational Narrative

minimum quantity of each
appliance in the group."

Avoidance Tactics

"I don't think we have any real
disagreements in this group."

"Look, we have spent enough
time on this, I don't think it is
as important as you think. Let's
move on."

"Whatever you want to do is fine
with me. You all definitely
know best."

"Look, I shouldn't have to ask
you to do this. It is your job. I
am not going to be a baby
sitter. You can take the
consequences yourself."

Vision-Setting Tactics

"I believe we can make our bowl
game the Super Bowl of college
football.

"I want us to move from number
five to number two during the
next three months. I know with
a sales force like all of you that
it is only a matter of time."

"In order to start performing like
a team we have to start acting
like a team. That's why I called
you here today."

Meaning-Management Tactics

"I have talked about what I see
ahead. I now need to know
how you think that affects each
group represented here today."

"Our course of action is a little
like putting our own man on
the moon. Awe, courage,
pride—all these things are part
of this achievement we have
just experienced."

"I want everyone to hear this
change at the same time.
Schedule me to personally meet
with each shift."

Leadership Tactics

1. *Ignoring conflict* even when
   obvious

2. *Changing subject* when
   disagreements or difficulty
   seem likely

3. *Agreeing with others* to avoid
   conflict or new ideas

4. *Refusing responsibility* for
   motivating others to action

1. *Visualizing abstract ideas* by
   symbolic association

2. *Stating desired outcomes* without
   undue emphasis on details

3. *Articulating reasons* for actions
   and goals

1. *Soliciting feedback* to understand
   message clarity and impact

2. *Generating symbolism* to
   interpret events and
   accomplishments

3. *Managing messages* to support
   exchanges of meaning

FIGURE 8.5 (*continued*)

Organizational Narrative

Trust-Generating Tactics

Leadership Tactics

"I told you the truth about the layoffs. I know it wasn't popular but you can trust what I am now going to say. The layoffs are behind us but we still have considerable belt tightening to do."

1. *Communicating constancy* by linking present messages to past actions

"People are the most important resource this company has. For that reason I am asking all of you and all of the management team to take a 10 percent pay cut so that no one will have to be without a job."

2. *Identifying values* and relating values to needed action

"I am asking each department head to meet with me over the next few months. I want to know what is going on and have people free to come to me."

3. *Encouraging access* through planned communication interaction

Positive Regard and Success Tactics

"I know you consider this a mistake. I consider that you have learned a valuable lesson."

1. *Providing support* for individual effort

"This is the best new product release this company has ever produced."

2. *Offering praise* for efforts

"Look, we are all in this together. It doesn't matter as much whose fault it was as what we need to do next."

3. *Avoiding blame* and seeking solutions

"I know the economy is troubled. But this gives us a chance to really see what we are worth. After all, anyone can be successful when things are going well. The mark of excellence is now."

4. *Identifying challenges and opportunities* when others see problems

and tactics are grouped into authoritarian, participative, avoidance, vision-setting, meaning-management, trust-generating, and positive regard and success categories.

Power Bases for Leaders

Preferences for leadership, strategic objectives, and communication tactics all contribute to how leaders influence followers. Yet behaviors alone do not adequately explain how one individual is recognized as a leader whereas another is not. We have all seen individuals who are recognized as leaders exhibit almost identical behaviors as those who never achieve leadership recognition. Frequently the difference in who is a leader and who is not is a subtle matter of credibility—a credibility that enables one person to be more influential than another. This credibility is commonly referred to as *power* or the **power bases** of the leader.

Power bases—influence an individual has over another as a result of dependency on the powerful person. Power bases are commonly identified as legitimate, reward, coercive, referent, expert, and connection.

The concept of power can best be understood as an interactive process. In other words, power does not exist in a vacuum, but rather as people interact with one another. From this perspective power can be understood as the influence an individual has over another as a result of dependency on the powerful person. To understand this interaction it is helpful to think about some of the power bases available to leaders. John French and Bertram Raven (1968) have given us a useful description of five power types: legitimate, reward, coercive, referent, and expert. We will also discuss connection power.

Legitimate power—power emerging from the positions, titles, or roles people occupy.

Legitimate power comes from the positions, titles, or roles people occupy. Supervisors have legitimate power over subordinates. As such, certain rights and responsibilities are "legitimately" defined and generally understood by group members. Disagreement can surround the ability of the "legitimate" leader, yet most agree that certain leadership responsibilities accompany the position. For example, virtually every president of the United States has supporters and critics, yet despite these diverse opinions few would disagree that the individual is legitimately the president.

Reward power—power based on the leader's control and distribution of tangible and intangible resources.

Reward power is based on the leader's control and distribution of tangible and intangible reward resources. A leader can influence with the promise of rewards only as long as those rewards are within the leader's control and perceived by followers as rewarding. Many people attempt to influence with rewards that others do not find important or influential. Many supervisors believe, for example, that money is the primary reward for good performance, although considerable research suggests that communication contact with supervisors is one of the most sought-after of all subordinate rewards. Interestingly enough, communication interaction is more often controlled by supervisors than money or other tangible benefits.

Coercive power—power based on the sanctions or punishments within the control of the leader.

Coercive power can be understood as the sanctions or punishments within the control of the leader. Coercive power is the ability to punish for not complying with influence attempts. To be effective, coercive power must not be threatened beyond what the leader is willing to administer. All of us have seen people lose credibility by threatening sanctions or punishment that were not within the control of the one making the threats. Although reward power can be exercised by virtually anyone, coercive power is related to the role or legitimate position an individual occupies.

For example, a peer can threaten to get another peer fired, but although unpleasant, the threat is generally not considered coercive power. When a supervisor makes the same threat, the influence attempt takes on an entirely different meaning.

Referent power is a result of others identifying with the leader. It is a power base that is only indirectly related to the leader's overt influence attempts. Referent power comes from the desire of others to use the leader as a "reference" or from others seeking to imitate the leader's behaviors with or without the leader's desire for them to do so. Referent power results from actions of the leader, yet the leader cannot directly exercise referent power—it is assigned by others.

Referent power—power based on others identifying with the leader.

Expert or **information power** rests on what the leader knows as a result of organizational interaction or areas of technical specialty. As such, expert power does not require legitimate power for the expert to be influential. Expert power can be used without coercive power and often contributes to the development of referent power. Expert power is considered to be important for organizational excellence and is ideally the basis of effective influence attempts.

Expert or information power—power based on information the leader knows as a result of organizational interaction or areas of technical specialty.

Connection power is the influence leaders have as a result of who they know and the support they have from others in the organization. Generally conceived of as support from others in power, connection power also comes from followers. Supervisors and managers, for example are generally in better influence positions when follower "connections" are supportive. In turn, group members are more influential when their leaders are "connected" to others in the organization. Connection power is understood by observing communication networks and how individuals are linked throughout the organization.

Connection power—power resulting from who the leader knows and the support he or she has from others in the organization.

Situational Analysis for Leadership

Understanding the situations or circumstances requiring leadership is fundamental for effectiveness. The ability to assess thoughtfully the requirements of the problem and the group attempting its solutions contributes to the selection of effective strategies and tactics for leadership.

The ability to communicate vision is related to the ability to generate vision based on sound problem analysis. Communicating outcomes is related to knowing where an organization should go and having a concept of how it can get there. In other words, good problem-solving and analysis skills are fundamental for effective leadership. Analysis skills help define problems, generate solutions, and contribute to the selection of influence strategies appropriate for leadership. Analysis skills cannot be separated from influence strategies for effectiveness. The individual who thoroughly understands a problem may not be able to influence others if communication strategies and tactics are carelessly chosen. On the other hand, we have concern for individuals who are so adept at persuasive communication that they convince groups to follow courses of action that are ill conceived or ill advised.

John Mitchell's experience at Invest is a good example. Chances are John has the technical expertise to lead the laboratory to significant technical accomplishments. No one doubts his ability to analyze technical problems. Yet John is close to failure as the manager of the laboratory. His situational analysis is only partially complete. He understands the technical direction he wants but has not communicated his vision to others and does not see any need for that type of "sales" pitch. John's communication behaviors do not reflect his technical excellence. His dilemma illustrates what can happen when problem analysis is not coupled with appropriate communication behaviors.

INCREASING LEADERSHIP EFFECTIVENESS

We can describe the communication competencies needed to increase leadership capabilities as an expansion of those competencies necessary for interpersonal and conflict management effectiveness. The knowledge, sensitivity, skills, and values identified and developed in previous chapters are all important for effective leadership, especially if we take the position that organizations need leadership from all position levels.

As we have previously suggested, effective leaders understand the problems facing their group and have skill in helping diverse individuals approach common problems. Effective leaders participate in group efforts and encourage others to participate by being open-minded and exhibiting supportive behaviors. Effective leaders consult others and express sensitivity for disagreement. Effective leaders, however, will help groups make decisions when consensus is unlikely. Finally, effective leaders empower others by sharing success and credit.

Self-awareness is a key to leadership effectiveness. Understanding personal preferences, behaviors, and problem situations is fundamental to discovering why some leadership efforts succeed while others fail. Return for a moment to your personal theory of leadership. What does it tell you about your personal leadership strengths and weaknesses? What competencies need further development? When have you been most successful?

In an effort to help you increase your leadership effectiveness, we will describe an important concept of principled leadership; identify task, procedural, and interpersonal leadership responsibilities; and discuss leadership in group settings by identifying barriers to effective group decision making and by proposing how to plan for leadership in a group setting. Finally, knowledge, sensitivity, skill, and value competencies will be applied in the Workshop section of the chapter.

Principled Leadership

In their extensive study of successful teams, Carl Larson and Frank LaFasto (1989) identified **principled leadership** as one of the core characteristics of why successful teams develop. According to Larson and LaFasto, principled leadership provides a consistent message, has a perspective for unleashing talent, practices ego suppression, and creates leaders.

Larson and LaFasto found that "effective team leaders begin by establishing a vision of the future. In the most common language, this need was articulated as the clear, elevating goal. Such a goal, or vision, is a hallmark of effective leaders. They articulate what an organization can and should become, or what a team can or should accomplish. Furthermore, they articulate the team's goal in such a way as to inspire a desire for and eventual commitment to the accomplishment of the goal. The goal, or vision, is seen as worthwhile, making team members eager to be a part of its achievement." In other words, principled leadership establishes and communicates a vision that creates change by unleashing the talent of team members.

In thinking about increasing our own leadership effectiveness, we question what qualities and behaviors are most likely to generate this commitment to vision and overall leadership success. The work of Larson and LaFasto provides insight:

> *A content analysis of our research data yielded a consistent message that focused on how team leaders generated enthusiasm, a bias for action, and a commitment to the team's objective among team members. The single most distinguishing feature of the effective leaders in our data base was their ability to establish, and lead by, guiding principles. These principles represented day-to-day performance standards. They represented what all team members, including the team leader, should expect from one another on a day-to-day basis. The principles identified by our sample created three natural categories of expectations: (1) what the team should expect of the team leader; (2) what the team leader should expect from each team member, and each team member should expect from one another; and (3) leadership principles that established a supportive decision-making climate in which team members could take risks.*

Figure 8.6 summarizes the principles identified by Larson and LaFasto. Not only did the successful leaders of the Larson and LaFasto work unleash talent through the use of guiding principles, but they also suppressed individual ego displays for themselves and the team. Team members were active participants in shaping the destiny of the team, and this active participation contributed to leadership not only for the team but also within the team. In sum we can say that effective leadership promotes the development of leadership in others. Think for a moment about your own leadership attempts. Which of the Larson and LaFasto principles did you use? Which were missing? Would you add others to the list? Next we will

Principled leadership—leadership that provides a consistent message, has a perspective for unleashing talent, practices ego suppression, and creates leaders.

FIGURE 8.6
Principled Leadership

Team Leader Principles

1. Avoid compromisng the team's objective with political issues.
2. Exhibit personal commitment to our team's goal.
3. Do not dilute the team's efforts with too many priorities.
4. Be fair and impartial toward all team members.
5. Be willing to confront and resolve issues associated with inadequate performance by team members.
6. Be open to new ideas and information from team members.

Team Member Principles

1. Demonstrate a realistic understanding of one's role and accountabilities.
2. Demonstrate objective and fact-based judgments.
3. Collaborate effectively with other team members.
4. Make the team goal a higher priority than any personal objective.
5. Demonstrate a willingness to devote whatever effort is necessary to achieve team success.
6. Be willing to share information, perceptions, and feedback openly.
7. Provide help to other team members when needed and appropriate.
8. Demonstrate high standards of excellence.
9. Stand behind and support team decisions.
10. Demonstrate courage of conviction by directly confronting important issues.
11. Demonstrate leadership in ways that contribute to the team's success.
12. Respond constructively to feedback from others.

Team Leader Behaviors for Decision Making

1. Trust team members with meaningful levels of responsibility.
2. Give team members the necessary autonomy to achieve results.
3. Present challenging opportunities that stretch the individual abilities of team members.
4. Recognize and reward superior performance.
5. Stand behind the team and support it.

---

consider how effective leaders use principled leadership for task, procedural, and interpersonal responsibilities.

Identifying Constructive Communication Behaviors for Leadership

Task Responsibilities

Whether leading a major corporation or leading a group in a class project, leaders have task, procedural, and interpersonal responsibilities. In the task area, leaders are responsible for facilitating problem analysis, idea generation, idea evaluation, solution generation, and decision implementation. Leaders need to stimulate creativity and urge people to push the boundaries of their thinking. Effective leaders encourage team members to listen actively to others and expand good ideas. Leaders are responsible for promoting focused and in-depth investigation of ideas and critically evaluating all aspects of a problem. Leaders help the group address the accuracy of their information, evaluate information sources, apply information carefully to defined problems, and develop solution criteria. Review the guiding principles in Figure 8.6. Which of the principles would you apply to task responsibilities? What types of communication skills are required? Can you understand the importance of communication competency for effective leadership?

Procedural Responsibilities

Leaders also are responsible for procedures such as goal setting, agenda making, discussion clarification, and both consensus and disagreement identification. Leaders must be able to introduce ideas, give directions, and call for action. They ask for ideas and the participation of team members. Leaders remind groups of agendas and goals and generally organize group activities. Leaders actively listen as well as offer explanations for their own and others' verbalizations and behaviors. Recall the description in Chapter 6 of communication skills important for group participation. All of these skills and more apply to leadership responsibilities. In effect, we can say that leaders and team members alike must develop key interaction process skills for effective group efforts. Again review the guiding principles in Figure 8.6. Which of the principles apply to procedural responsibilities? What might you add?

Interpersonal Responsibilities

Finally, leaders make significant contributions to the interpersonal dynamics of groups. Leaders contribute to participation, group climate, and conflict management. As Larson and LaFasto (1989) have suggested, effective leaders generate an environment in which team members can achieve excellence because they have the confidence to take risks. Confidence to take risks comes from the supportive climate of effective interpersonal relationships. Leaders are responsible for reflecting feelings and supporting others, empathizing, and stopping personal attacks or other counterproductive individual or group behaviors. What guiding principles should a leader adopt for interpersonal responsibilities? What skills are most important?

In summary we can say that leaders affect how the task is accomplished, how people are supported within the group, and what processes and procedures the group uses to achieve its objectives. Group members also share these responsibilities, but the leader remains influential in guiding task, procedural, and interpersonal contributions.

Leading the Group Meeting

A frequent test of leadership capability comes in leading meetings. Research tells us that many organizational members spend from 40 to 95 percent of their time in meetings. The results of these meetings are crucial to overall organizational excellence. It is fair to say that meetings are one of the most important communication activities in most organizations. It is also likely that for most people, meetings offer a promising yet underused opportunity to exhibit leadership ability.

But how effective are most meetings? Think about your own experiences. Are the meetings you attend well run and productive? How could they be improved? A recent survey of *Fortune 500* executives listed meetings as necessary but among their top time-wasters in organizational life. A visit to almost any large organization finds individual schedules packed with meetings and complaints that little gets done because people are always in meetings.

With meetings a ripe opportunity for exhibiting leadership, the question is what we can do to contribute to effective meetings. First, it is important to understand what typically goes wrong in meetings and what role leadership can play in preventing and correcting problems. Second, leaders need to understand the basics of preparing for and running effective meetings.

Barriers to Effective Meetings

Leland Bradford (1976) has suggested several barriers to successful meetings. Specifically, he contends that meetings fail to reach their potential because of lack of communication skills; apathy; conflict within the group; and reactions against the task that include avoidance, fear of making decisions, and fear of taking responsibility. Members get impatient, attack the ideas of others, and generally contribute to polarized positions. Although we can argue that these barriers are everyone's responsibility, most would agree that effective leadership is crucial to their elimination.

Preparation for the Group Meeting

Three general stages of the meeting process must be understood for a leader to contribute to productive group outcomes. These stages are meeting preparation, the meeting itself, and meeting evaluation. Each stage requires personal communication competency (knowledge, sensitivity, skills, and values) and the ability to assess the communication competency of group participants.

Preparation for any meeting should first include identifying the purpose of the meeting and the composition of members needed to fulfill that purpose. Many organizational meetings are worthless because the purpose is ill defined and the appropriate organizational members are not present. Questions to ask while establishing the purpose include these: Is a meeting the best way to discuss this problem or disseminate this information? Who should be included for maximum effectiveness? How much can we hope to accomplish at one time? Meeting preparation also includes finding a time and place appropriate for a well-defined purpose. Factors to be considered include convenience, privacy, and appropriate accommodations.

Meeting preparation also includes developing some type of agenda, informing potential members of the reasons for meeting, and preparing such items as handouts and audiovisual materials. But meeting preparation should include communication preparation as well. Thoughtful leaders think about communication approaches, potential problems, and how best to encourage quality participation. Communication preparation may include thinking about successes and failures in past meetings and asking others to critique the effectiveness of past leadership attempts. It also should include any introductory remarks or information for which the leader is responsible.

Conducting the Group Meeting

As stated in the previous section, leadership responsibilities include task, procedural, and interpersonal dimensions. When conducting a meeting, the effective leader is continually assessing tactics appropriate to balance all three. Nowhere in organizational life is there more need for well-developed communication competencies. Leaders are responsible for beginning meetings and establishing focus. Leaders influence the procedures by which the meeting is run, whether those procedures are informal or formal. Although all group members can and usually should be encouraged to take responsibility for the group's climate and interpersonal relationships, leaders influence interpersonal relationships by the type of participation they encourage, by the support they give to differences of opinion, by the manner in which they deal with conflict, and by the control they establish over a variety of disruptive influences. Finally, leaders are primarily responsible for guiding the group to goal achievement or determining why goals cannot be accomplished within the meeting setting.

Leaders are not, however, totally responsible for the success or failure of the group. Success depends on the abilities and willingness of all involved to participate. Leadership can enhance the success of a group but cannot alone generate good problem solving without motivated participation and competent group members.

Meeting Evaluation

Leaders are in a good position to evaluate thoughtfully the results of group meetings. In fact, effective leaders frequently assess themselves, the quality of the group's effort, and the process by which these efforts were achieved. Only through this continuing assessment can leadership excellence be maintained. Effective leaders test the productivity of meetings not simply by whether decisions were reached but also by whether members actually followed through on their commitments. In addition, effective leaders evaluate the quality of group decisions once implemented and tested by time. Chances are all of us have been in groups that reach decisions on problems, only to have no one really take initiative for implementation. These groups appear harmonious but in reality are not effective. Leaders of such groups can easily mislead themselves into thinking they are productive even though the evidence suggests little ever gets done. Effective leaders know the importance of evaluating not only the meeting itself but also the outcomes and results of decisions or commitments.

Following is a transcript of a meeting John Mitchell held with the five section managers in the laboratory. As you read the transcript, evaluate how John is handling task, procedural, and interpersonal responsibilities. Also, identify communication tactics used by John and the other managers.

John Mitchell's Laboratory Management Meeting

JOHN: Look, I think we had better get started. We have several things I want to resolve this morning and we only have forty-five minutes.

HENRY: John, how can we resolve anything in forty-five minutes? I have four matters that need attention and I am sure the others have problems as well. (Addressing the other managers) Don't you all?

TIM: Well, I don't know what's on everyone else's agenda but I do have one major project problem that needs working.

JOHN: I thought I had told all of you that I want to work with you individually on your section problems. I don't see these meetings as needing to discuss each section's problems. I can do that with you individually.

MARY: John, I haven't been able to get in to see you for two weeks. How can we be expected to wait until we can see you individually?

TIM: John, that really is right. You are simply invisible when we need you.

JOHN: That's not fair. Look, I have been terribly busy lately but I'm trying to understand product directions for all sections, not just the ones I was already familiar with. It's going to take time but I know things will get better.

MIKE: Okay, you guys. We only have forty-five minutes and this is getting us nowhere. Where should we start?

JOHN: Well, I want to talk with you about this morale problem personnel says we have. I just do not understand. All of you are capable managers. You don't need me to hold your hands. What is it you really want from me as lab manager?

HENRY: John, we need a sense of leadership from you—that is as plain as I can put it. We know you are the best engineer in this lab, but we never see you and don't get timely responses on the issues we need worked.

JOHN: Henry, I appreciate your concern but I think leadership needs to be technical and not personal. We are all grown individuals with excellent backgrounds. You need me to help set product direction, not hand-hold your decisions.

MARY: John, you asked us about the morale problem. Aren't you the least willing to listen?

Evaluate the effectiveness of John's meeting. How would you advise John in preparing for meetings with his managers? How could he run a more effective meeting? What was missing from his preparation? Is John right about leadership? Although there are no absolute answers, these questions raise important issues for understanding leadership and how communication influences leadership effectiveness. Think of other meetings in which you have recently participated. How were they led? Were they effective? If not, how could they be improved?

SUMMARY

Leadership and management communication affect nearly all aspects of organizational life. Leaders help guide individuals, groups, and entire organizations in establishing goals and sustaining action to support goals. Managers fulfill organizationally assigned roles and are expected to be leaders, but leadership can come from virtually any organizational position. Theories of leadership and management emphasize traits such as intelligence, social maturity, initiative, and human relations abilities. Style theories emphasize authoritarian, democratic, and laissez-faire behaviors and frequently use such categories as impoverished, middle-of-the-road, country club, task, and team leadership. Situational approaches build on style theories by emphasizing an interaction among leadership style, maturity of followers, and needs of a particular situation. Distinctions can be made between leadership and management. Managers need to be leaders, but organizations in the information society need leaders in diverse organizational positions. Strategic objectives for leadership include authoritarian, participative, and avoidance approaches. Research suggests that excellent leaders use strategies that manage attention through vision, meaning through communication, trust through positioning, and deployment of self through positive self-regard and an emphasis on success. In addition, leaders adopt specific communication tactics that support these strategic objectives. The ability to influence others is related to the power bases of leaders. Power bases are commonly described as legitimate, reward, coercive, referent, expert or information, and connection power. Situational analyses along with strategies, tactics, and power bases determine leadership effectiveness. Leadership effectiveness is increased by understanding the guiding principles for principled leadership; understanding leadership responsibilities in task, procedural, and interpersonal areas; and developing expertise in conducting group meetings.

WORKSHOP

1. In groups of six, identify by name examples of effective and ineffective leaders. Describe the behaviors of your effective leaders. Describe the behaviors of those you believe were ineffective. Discuss the similarities and differences in your list.

2. As you know from reading this chapter, there's considerable disagreement among leadership theorists. "What's Wrong With Leadership Theory? . . . Maybe Nothing!" by Sherwyn P. Morreale suggests that these disagreements may be healthy and the best way we can understand leadership. Read her comments and be prepared to discuss them and offer your own opinions. (See page 288–290.)

3. Practicing a variety of communication tactics helps us build both oral and analysis skills. The Leadership Team Exercise that follows is designed for participants to use a variety of communication tactics and then analyze their influence on the decision-making process. (See pages 290–292.)

4. Although we would want our managers to be leaders, we have argued that leadership and management communication are not always the same. Responding to this issue of leadership in management, Therese Kelly offers an essay entitled "Managing for Performance." Kelly's essay reflects her concern for helping managers learn how to "lead" others for good overall work performance. Be prepared to discuss the questions she raises. (See pages 292–294.)

What's Wrong with Leadership Theory? . . . Maybe Nothing!

Sherwyn P. Morreale, Ph.D.*

At the present time, a complete and satisfactory theory of leadership that captures all the complexities of the leadership phenomenon has not been agreed to or evolved. Leadership theory might be likened to a complex kettle of fish with too many chefs or leaders who are trying to include far too many ingredients or factors in their kettle. The result is that no present

* Sherwyn Morreale holds a B.A. and M.A. in communication from the University of Colorado and a Ph.D. in communication from the University of Denver. She is director of the Individualized Assistance Laboratory in the Center for Oral Communication Excellence at the University of Colorado at Colorado Springs.

theory considers all the factors involved in leadership in a manner satisfactory for all the researchers and theorists in the field. Whether this circumstance and lack of all-encompassing theory is seen as problematic depends upon the perspective of the given theorist. Whether there is something wrong with leadership theory is debatable. Yes, there is a lack of a comprehensive, all-encompassing theoretical paradigm regarding leadership; but to judge whether leadership theory is in a state of disarray or merely diverse, we must consider

The evolution of leadership theory over time

The present state-of-the-art of theoretical inquiry that now characterizes the leadership field

Theoretical Evolution

Early writings on leadership can be divided into two major schools of thought. The situational school, the environmentalists, perceived leadership as a product of circumstance and a focus of group activities. According to this school, leadership grows out of group processes and problems and is an instrument of group goal attainment. By contrast, the personalistic school described leadership in terms of personality traits that would enable an individual to obtain respect and obedience. According to this school, a leader emerges because he or she is endowed with abilities and characteristics that are deferred to by group members.

Following World War II, leadership theory became more divergent, with two major lines of research developing. One was concerned with the emergence and maintenance of the leadership role (exchange theories); the other was concerned with the relationship of leader behavior to follower satisfaction and group performance (expectancy-reinforcement theories).

In the 1950s and early 1960s, an additional line of leadership thought developed. These humanistic theories emphasized the human element, maintaining that stratified organizational and leadership structures stifle individuals who are striving for autonomy and self-actualization.

More recent developments in leadership theory also are concerned with the relationship of leadership behavior and group performance and/or follower satisfaction. Both path-goal and contingency theories call attention to the fact that no single pattern or style of leadership will be effective in all situations. Rather, leadership should be a function of and appropriate to the task and situation at hand.

State of the Art

Contemporary writings and approaches to research are highly diverse. There has been no agreement on any one comprehensive theory or definition of leadership. Polarization or diversity of thought has emerged from the natural division between two largely separate bodies of academic literature: leadership theory and managerial behavior. These two bodies of literature have spawned two different perspectives of how to conduct leadership research. One perspective, an "establishment" view, contains scholars who advocate the use of already delineated models or theories of leadership. This use of existing models attempts to apply the scientific method to leadership research and inquiry. This perspective is criticized by a "nonestablishment" view that states that the use of narrow, highly deterministic and rigidly delineated models screens out most potentially interesting and important occurrences of leadership in the real world. The nonestablishment scholars advocate the use of observational techniques and studies of managerial behavior in real-world settings.

Which perspective, which approach to leadership research would bring about reconciliation? Would setting aside of past theoretical foundations or a multiplicity of theoretical models be in order? Is this a time of necessary diversity, a time of transition and evolution—or is it a time of disarray? How might a middle-ground perspective between the nonestablishment and the establishment views be achieved?

QUESTIONS FOR DISCUSSION

1. Do you agree with the nonestablishment or the establishment scholars regarding the appropriate approach to leadership research? Why?
2. Considering the present state of the art regarding leadership theory, what type of research would you propose?

THE LEADERSHIP TEAM EXERCISE

The class is divided into teams of seven members each. The following list of communication tactics used during leadership situations is written on small cards or pieces of paper. Each member of the groups draws a card that assigns a range of tactics the member will use during the decision-making exercise. Individuals are aware of the tactics they personally are to use and do not know what tactic cards others have drawn.

INFORMATION FOR THE TACTIC CARDS

1. You are to use *authoritarian tactics* such as blocking ideas, controlling the process, announcing your goals, punishing opposition.
2. You are to use *participative tactics* such as seeking ideas, facilitating group processes, encouraging disagreement, seeking idea evaluation, and verbalizing consensus.
3. You are to use *avoidance tactics* such as ignoring conflict, changing subjects, agreeing with others, and refusing responsibility.
4. You are to use *vision-setting tactics* such as visualizing abstract ideas, stating desired outcomes, and articulating reasons for actions and goals.
5. You are to use *meaning-management tactics* such as soliciting feedback, generating symbolism, and managing messages to support exchanges of meaning.

6. You are to use *trust-generating tactics* such as communicating constancy by linking present messages to past actions, identifying values, and encouraging access to all group members.

7. You are to use *positive regard and success tactics* by providing support, offering praise, avoiding blame, and identifying challenges and opportunities.

In addition to specific tactic assignments, each group member will attempt to identify the tactics used by other group members during the activity. A group tactics chart is provided for recording impressions during group discussion. The information generated on the chart will be discussed when the exercise is complete.

Group Tactics Chart

Names of Group Members

TACTICS USED

Authoritarian
   Blocking ideas
   Controlling process
   Announcing goals
   Punishing others

Participative
   Seeking ideas
   Facilitating
   Encouraging disagreement
   Seeking idea evaluation
   Verbalizing consensus

Avoidance
   Ignoring conflict
   Changing subjects
   Agreeing with others
   Refusing responsibility

Vision setting
   Visualizing abstract ideas
   Stating desired outcomes
   Articulating reasons

Meaning Management
   Soliciting feedback
   Generating symbolism
   Managing meaning

Trust
   Communicating constancy
   Identifying values
   Encouraging access

Positive Regard/Success
   Providing support
   Offering praise
   Avoiding blame
   Identifying challenges

The Situation

Your group of seven is a policy committee appointed to make a recommendation about the position your company should take on an important issue. The committee has never worked together before and members are unaware of the styles each brings to the group. The problem for the committee is to recommend what type of position the company should take on drug and alcohol abuse by all employees—hourly workers through top management.

The committee will have fifteen minutes to discuss the new policy. When the time is up, committee members will complete their forms, attempting to identify the use of various tactics by group members. Each member also will attempt to identify the general tactic assignments of all other members.

Discussion should follow, comparing the tactic identification forms and relating various tactics to the effective development or lack of development of the policy.

Managing for Performance

Therese Kelley, M.A.*

Managing in today's world is a complex process. The responsibilities seem endless at times. There are budgets to keep balanced, people to answer to, information to absorb, employees to oversee, and projects to attend. Of all the responsibilities, though, probably one of the most important is the employees. They are the most valuable resource a manager can have. Wihout them, accomplishments would go wanting. Anything that valuable requires attention and consideration.

Implicit in the notion of managing people is getting work done through others. And managing for optimal performance requires spending time with those who actually do the work. Knowing what managing is, how-

---

* Therese Kelley is a Phi Beta Kappa graduate of the University of Colorado with an M.A. in organizational communication from the University of Northern Colorado. For nine years she was part of Digital Equipment Corporation's management development team and currently has a private consulting practice. She is also an honorarium instructor in the Communication Department at the University of Colorado, Colorado Springs.

ever, is one thing. Knowing how to do managing is another. Just spending time together is not quite enough. In order to effectively manage human resources, managers must spend time with their employees in a particular kind of way. This way of spending time together is based on an assumption that employees can, and want to, perform.

With that belief in mind, the process of managing for performance involves (1) setting clear expectations about the work to be done; (2) providing feedback about how things are going; (3) pointing out discrepancies in performance-related behavior; (4) coaching to improve performance; and finally, (5) formally reviewing performance against a well-defined job plan.

Employees, to perform optimally and effectively, need to understand what it is that they are supposed to do. Managers have a fairly good idea of what is wanted or needed, and have an obligation to convey that information to employees. This requires more than giving employees a general overview of their areas of accountability. Together, a manager and employee will need to establish some clearly defined goals and areas of accountability. High-quality goals are, first and foremost, realistic and achievable. They always contain some measurable quantity and are designed with an end result in mind. An employee's everyday responsibilities, on the other hand, will need some standards by which to measure the completion of them.

Once explicit job plans have been laid out, both manager and employee will want to consider the type of support needed to carry out those goals and responsibilities. Everything from time to tools to secretarial support to budget must be carefully weighed. In other words, whatever it is that is external to the employee but necessary to the accomplishment of the job plan must be considered.

In addition, managers will want to be mindful of development for their employees. Both should understand the skills and/or knowledge the employee will need in order to make goals and responsibilities happen, and then come up with an action plan for getting that development. Formal training programs are one way to learn skills and attain information. Some other activities could include on-the-job training, job rotation, attendance at committee or staff meetings, and individual help from specialists.

Once the job plan and support and development plans have been completed, a manager's job then becomes one of monitor and coach. The idea here is to observe the performance of employees and provide constructive feedback about how they're doing. Through feedback, a manager lets the employee in on whether or not the job is being done correctly and what results the employee is producing. Occasionally a manager will need to coach an employee to improve performance. But even before that managers will have to access the real causes of perceived performance discrepancies. It's important to do that accurately. There is a real danger in dealing with solutions before problems are clearly understood.

The skill then required in being a successful coach cannot be underestimated. A manager first must get agreement with the employee that a problem in performance does exist. That task is much easier said than done. Once an agreement has been reached, both manager and employee can mutually brainstorm possible solutions and develop an action plan to bring the discrepancy in line with expectations.

Finally, managers have an obligation to officially review the overall performance of an employee. Not only does the official evaluation provide historical documentation of an employee's performance, it also acts as a basis for salary increases and promotions. The quality of this review is a direct result of the quality of the formal job plan. Performance is ideally reviewed against goals and standards for measuring ongoing responsibilities.

From the review, then, both manager and employee establish new goals and responsibilities and consider areas for development. The process is, in effect, a cyclical one, repeating itself throughout the terms of the relationship between manager and employee.

Managing for performance means first believing that one's employees can and will perform to expectations. That, along with a good job plan and high-quality monitoring and coaching skills, greatly enhances the possibility that employees' capabilities will develop and their accomplishments will be many.

QUESTIONS FOR DISCUSSION

1. What is management?
2. What are some examples of support and development activities as they relate to the overall job plan of an employee?
3. What are some reasons for conducting a performance review?
4. What things would be important to you in a performance review on yourself?
5. Why might a manager have difficulty getting an employee to agree that a problem in performance does exist?
6. How would a well-defined job plan assist a manager in managing the performance of employees?

SUMMARY OF COMPETENCY COMPONENTS
KNOWLEDGE, SENSITIVITY, SKILLS, VALUES

KNOWLEDGE

Leadership is described from trait, style, and situational approaches.

Leadership is distinguished from management.

Leadership effectiveness is based on individual preferences, strategic objectives, tactical choices, and situational analysis.

SENSITIVITY

Self-awareness is developed through personal theory assessment.

Leadership styles, strategic objectives, and tactics influence effectiveness.

Leadership is needed from diverse organizational positions.

Credibility for leadership is related to power bases.

SKILLS

Analysis skills are practiced through case study and transcript analysis.

Analysis skills are developed through self-assessment.

Verbal skills are practiced through group activities.

VALUES

Leadership is central to organizational excellence.

Excellence in leadership is related to vision, meaning, trust, positive self-regard, and success orientation.

REFERENCES AND SUGGESTED READINGS

Applbaum, R. L., E. M. Bodaken, K. K. Sereno, and K. W. Anatol. 1974. *The process of group communication.* Chicago: Science Research.

Argyris, C. 1962. *Interpersonal competence and organizational effectiveness.* Homewood, IL: Dorsey Press.

Bacon, C. C., and W. R. Ullmann. 1986. Dimensions of interpersonal communication competence, communication accuracy, as predictors of managerial performance and job satisfaction. Paper presented at the Speech Communication Association Convention, November, Chicago.

Bennis, W., and B. Nanus. 1985. *Leaders: The strategies for taking charge.* New York: Harper & Row.

Blake, R. R., and J. S. Mouton. 1964. *The managerial grid.* Houston, TX: Gulf.

Blake, R. R., and J. S. Mouton. 1985. *The managerial grid III: The key to leadership excellence.* Houston, TX: Gulf.

Bradford, L. P. 1976. *Making meetings work: A guide for leaders and group members.* San Diego: University Associates.

Corey, G. 1985. *Theory and practice of group counseling.* 2d ed. Monterey, CA: Brooks/Cole.

Davis, K. 1967. *Human relations at work.* New York: McGraw-Hill.

Dobbins, G. H., and S. J. Zaccaro. 1986. The effects of group cohesion and leader behavior on subordinate satisfaction. *Group and Organization Studies* 11(3): 203–19.

Drucker, P. 1966. *The effective manager.* New York: Harper & Row.

Eisenberg, E. M. 1984. Ambiguity as strategy in organizational communication. *Communication Monographs* 51: 227–42.

Fairhurst, G. T., S. G. Green, and B. K. Snavely. 1984. Face support in controlling poor performance. *Human Communication Research* 11(2): 272–95.

Fiedler, F. 1967. *A theory of leadership effectiveness.* New York: McGraw-Hill.

French, J., and B. Raven. 1968. The bases of social power. In *Group dynamics*, eds. D. Cartwright and A. Zander, 259–68. New York: Harper & Row.

Geier, J. 1967. A trait approach to the study of leadership in small groups. *Journal of Communication* 17: 316–23.

Hersey, P., and K. Blanchard. 1974. So you want to know your leadership style? *Training and Development Journal* 28(2): 22–37.

Hersey, P., and K. Blanchard. 1977. *Management of organizational behavior: Utilizing human resources*. 3d ed. Englewood Cliffs, NJ: Prentice-Hall.

Kelleher, D., P. Finestone, and A. Lowy. 1986. Managerial learning: First notes from an unstudied frontier. *Group and Organization Studies* 11(3): 169–202.

Larson, C., and F. LaFasto. 1989. *TeamWork: What must go right/What can go wrong*. Newbury Park, CA: Sage.

Pace, R. W. 1983. *Organizational communication: Foundations for human resource development*. Englewood Cliffs, NJ: Prentice-Hall.

Peppers, L., and J. Ryan. 1986. Discrepancies between actual and aspired self: A comparison of leaders and nonleaders. *Group and Organization Studies* 11(3): 220–28.

Skaret, D. J., and N. S. Bruning. 1986. Attitudes about the work group: An added moderator of the relationship between leader behavior and job satisfaction. *Group and Organization Studies* 11(3): 254–79.

Snavely, W. B., and E. V. Walters. 1983. Differences in communication competence among administrator social styles. *Journal of Applied Communication Research* 11(2): 120–35.

Soares, E. J., and L. J. Chase. 1985. Communication elements of managerial competence. Paper presented at the International Communication Association Convention, May, Honolulu.

Stogdill, R. M., and A. E. Coons. 1957. Leader behavior: Its description and measurement. *Research monograph No. 88*. Columbus: Bureau of Business Research, Ohio State University.

Tannenbaum, R., and W. Schmidt. 1958. How to choose a leadership pattern. *Harvard Business Review* 36: 95–101.

White, R., and R. Lippitt. 1960. *Autocracy and democracy: An experimental inquiry*. New York: Harper & Row.

PART ~III~

Organizational Communication: Skills and Applications

In Part One we described the need for communication competency in an information society, discussed Functional and Meaning-Centered approaches for understanding organizational communication, and applied these two approaches to major organizational theories and a variety of organizational problems. In Part Two we shifted our focus from the organization as a whole to explore how individuals experience organizations through supervisor-subordinate and group relationships. We also explored the important subjects of organizational conflict and leadership and management communication.

In Part Three we will attempt to develop competencies for decision making and problem solving and identify career options and professional applications of organizational communication. Specifically, Part Three is designed to develop *knowledge* competencies by describing a variety of problem-solving processes and identifying career options for organizational communication. *Sensitivity* competencies will be encouraged through understanding individual and organizational influences for decision making and problem solving, through awareness of positive individual behaviors in group settings, and by establishing personal criteria important for career decisions. Fact-finding, interaction process, and presentation *skills* will be developed and practiced with case studies, in-baskets, and problem-solving exercises. Knowledge, sensitivity, and skill competencies, when taken together, will contribute to the development of *values* important for relating decision making and problem solving to organizational change and organizational excellence.

Decision Making and Problem Solving: Developing Critical Organizational Communication Competencies

Developing competencies through . . .

KNOWLEDGE

Distinguishing between decision making and problem solving
Describing problem-solving processes
Identifying fact-finding, evaluation, and presentation skills for decision making and problem solving

SENSITIVITY

Understanding individual and organizational influences on decision making and problem solving
Awareness of positive individual behaviors for decision making and problem solving

SKILLS

Practicing fact-finding, interaction process, and presentation skills
Applying analysis capabilities to group interactions, case studies, and in-basket exercises

VALUES

Relating decision making and problem solving to excellence
Understanding effective communication as essential to decision making and problem solving

The Decisions, Problems, More Decisions Case

Joan Murphy has an important and exciting dilemma. She has been offered management training positions by two of the top retailers in the country. When she interviewed, Joan was hoping to get an offer from one of the two—but in her wildest dreams she had not expected to hear from both. The two companies were making similar financial offers; both were in the Midwest, where she hoped to stay; and both were reported to have excellent training programs with fast promotional progress. Both alternatives were attractive. How should she decide?

Joan went to work for Dayton Retailers. The decision had been a difficult one requiring considerable weighing of various alternatives. She felt good about Dayton and hoped they liked her work. Joan did not, however, feel comfortable with some of the behaviors being exhibited by others in her management training group. Joan knew that at least two of her peers in the training program were having other friends at Dayton complete their project assignments. To make matters worse, the two were getting the highest praise in the class and seemed likely to get the best assignments when the courses were over. Joan didn't think that was fair or good for Dayton. She questioned what she should do, especially when others might view her complaints as simply trying to get ahead.

Joan's assignment to the Ridgefield Shopping Center was terrific. To be put in charge of Junior Sportswear in a thriving store was quite a plum. Her only difficulty was caused by department remodeling, which limited space to bring in new, competitive lines. Three new lines had been proposed but space limitations permitted the stocking of only one of the three. Joan had called a meeting of the junior sportswear buyers, the top salespeople from the floor, and the floor manager to attempt to decide which of the three would be best. Joan began to think about how the group should approach the decision.

After several successful months at Ridgefield, Joan was transferred to Glencrest, a store that was struggling. Although she knew this was a real learning opportunity, Joan was sorry to leave Ridgefield and the wonderful group of people with whom she was working. Joan also knew that the staff of Glencrest was anything but happy to have her come. The manager Joan was replacing had been popular and her staff were not pleased at the changes management was making. Joan knew the staff did not dislike her personally but were unhappy about management's statement that the store would have to establish a better track record or suffer staff and merchandise reductions. Joan's first responsibility was to change the sales promotions schedules for the next several months. She needed the cooperation of her new staff and their advice on how to develop a promotions plan that could hope to increase sales in the struggling store. After all, she did not know this market area nearly as well as Ridgefield. Joan thought about the type of group she would form for solving the Glencrest problems.

INTRODUCTION

Joan Murphy is engaged in decision making and problem solving common to all types of organizational situations. She has an individual decision to make when she must choose from among two alternative job offers. She encounters a problem when peers in her training group violate ethical standards of conduct, potentially positioning them for superior job assignments. In her first assignment, Joan must work with a group of people charged with deciding among three competitive lines. Finally, she is responsible for attempting to bring together a team capable of solving a sales problem.

The decisions Joan makes and the effectiveness of the problem solving in which she engages will not only affect her personal career but also will influence the success of Dayton Retailers. Indeed, it is fair to say that decision making and problem solving can be described as guiding processes for all organizational functioning. Both individually and in groups, organizational members continually engage in choosing from among alternatives—decision making—and in attempting to move organizations from undesirable states to more desirable ones—problem solving.

Think about some of the decisions you have had to make, the problem solving in which you have been engaged. What were your alternatives? How did you approach your problems?

With decision making and problem solving a daily part of our lives, questions arise about how to develop communication competencies for effectiveness in these critically important processes. This chapter is designed to develop *knowledge* by defining decision making and problem solving and by identifying a variety of problem-solving processes. *Sensitivity* is encouraged through awareness of individual and organizational influences for decision making and problem solving. *Skills* are increased through decision-making and problem-solving practice, with particular emphasis on fact-finding, group interaction, and presentation skills. *Values* are influenced by relating quality decisions and problem solving to overall organizational effectiveness. Finally, all four competencies—knowledge, sensitivity, skills, and values—interact during analysis and practice opportunities.

DEFINING DECISION MAKING AND PROBLEM SOLVING

Decision making is the process of choosing from among several alternatives, whereas **problem solving** is a multistage process for moving an issue, situation, or state from an undesirable to a more desirable condition. Al-

Decision making—process of choosing from among several alternatives.

Problem solving—multistage process for moving an issue, situation, or state from an undesirable to a more desirable condition.

though problem solving includes decision making, decision making and problem solving are not one and the same process. Decision making depends on individuals and groups choosing from among known alternatives. Problem solving is the process by which individuals and groups generate alternatives and evaluate those alternatives in light of the identified problem. As John Brilhart (1986) suggests, "problem solving is a many-staged procedure through which an individual or group moves from some unsatisfactory state to a plan for arriving at some satisfactory condition. Problem solving usually requires making numerous decisions before the group is ready to choose among several possible solutions to the problem and implement one."

Joan Murphy is engaged in both individual and group decision making and problem solving. Joan and her co-workers have alternatives from which to choose as well as sales problems to attempt to understand and correct. The decision-making and problem-solving processes in which they are engaged require them to take risks. These risks ultimately will contribute to the effectiveness of Dayton Retailers.

All decision making and problem solving involve a level of risk. Decisions, whether as choices from among well-defined alternatives or the result of complex problem solving, are desired courses of action before the results of the action are known. Unknown results represent risk. The level of risk is related to the importance of the decision: More risk generally is associated with more important decisions. In other words, the more that can go well as a result of a good decision, the more that can usually go wrong if that decision fails.

Joan Murphy is faced with a high-risk situation as she moves to the Glencrest store. Sales are down and the manager she is replacing was popular with her subordinates. If Joan is successful the store will have an increase in sales and Dayton management will view her efforts favorably. Joan has a lot to gain, and so does Dayton. If her decision-making and problem-solving efforts are ineffective, the store faces staff and merchandise reductions and Joan's own career may be damaged. A good decision-making process will not guarantee success; however, a poor process will almost certainly contribute to failure. Thus, both individual and group decision-making and problem-solving capabilities influence personal and organizational effectiveness.

John Baird (1982) suggests that some problems should be solved individually, whereas others are better suited to groups. Specifically, Baird believes that "the task can best be done by an individual when: (1) the task has one correct solution; (2) the task is not easily divided; (3) the task has a clear goal; (4) the task has few avenues for solutions." Baird contends that "groups work better than individuals when: (1) the task has no one correct solution; (2) the task can be divided easily; (3) the task has unclear goals; (4) the task has many avenues for solutions."

In Herbert Simon's (1960) view, "decision-making is synonymous with management." Managers, in fulfilling their responsibilities, continually are required to choose from among alternatives and to involve others in coming to grips with problems and establishing courses of action for problem solution. The contemporary view, and the one taken in this text, is that decision making and problem solving are everybody's responsibility. Managers certainly make decisions and engage in problem solving; however, the information age is characterized by crucial information widely dispersed throughout the organization. Thus, both managers and individual contributors must be competent decision makers and problem solvers for organizations to adapt quickly to changing environments.

Gerald Phillips (1982) suggests six basic issues that are commonly considered by problem-solving groups:

1. *How can we best review our goals?*
2. *How can we increase productivity, improve distribution, deploy personnel better, or reduce costs?*
3. *How can we deal with emergencies inside the organization?*
4. *How can we deal with changes in conditions outside the organization that affect the organization?*
5. *How can we plan effectively for the future of the organization?*
6. *How can we take advantage of unexpected opportunities to improve the organization?*

Answers to these important questions require effective involvement from all organizational members. Because decision making and problem solving are carried out through human communication, these important questions require competent communicators at all organizational levels.

The following sections in this chapter describe important influences and methods for decision making and problem solving, discuss a variety of problem-solving processes, and identify communication competencies that form a basis for increasing decision-making and problem-solving effectiveness. Figure 9.1 illustrates how influences, methods, processes, and competencies for decision making and problem solving contribute to the quality of decisions and solutions and to the satisfaction we feel with the results.

INFLUENCES FOR DECISION MAKING AND PROBLEM SOLVING

Four primary factors influence individual and group decision making and problem solving. These factors—organizational culture, decision/problem issues, technical competencies, and communication competencies—influence the methods used for problem solving, the quality of decisions made, and the satisfaction participants feel with decision-making and problem-solving processes.

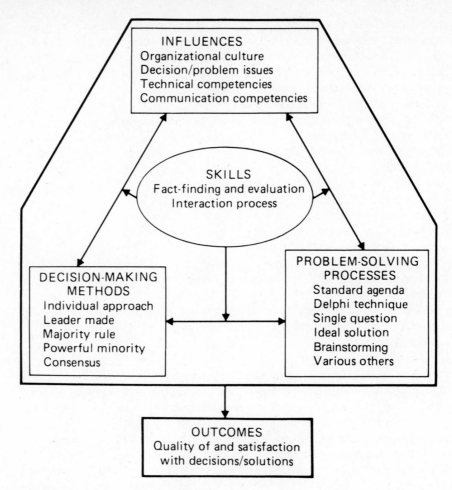

FIGURE 9.1

Components for Decision Making and Problem Solving

Culture

H. Wayland Cummings, Larry Long, and Michael Lewis (1983) underscore the importance of organizational culture for decision making and problem solving when they state, "culture is often conceptualized as the totality of all knowledge, beliefs, values, and attitudes held by a society across time. Although this description is very general, it stresses the importance of all human experiences and values inherent to societies. These factors are particularly important because societies 'train' members to accept and adhere to particular values. As a consequence, organizational and individual problem solving reflects cultural values."

Most scholars agree that central to the notion of organizational culture are the decision-making processes in which organizational members engage. As Phillip Tompkins and George Cheney (1983) have pointed out, "the examination of the decision-making process provides a means of tapping the mutual influences of people and organizations." Indeed, the very activity of organizing can be described as synonymous with the decision-making process. Organizing can be seen as a conscious limitation of alternatives, and therefore decision making. It is this limitation of alternatives (decisions) that becomes the shared realities of the organization, or its culture.

Organizational cultures influence the methods of decision making. Some organizations expect leaders to make and announce decisions. The military, for example, does not depend on majority rule or consensus decision making for determining plans of action. The university, on the other hand, has a long tradition of consensus decision making at all organizational levels. Some organizations expect individuals to make decisions about their job or area of responsibility without notifying others or seeking extensive input. Other organizations emphasize notification of others of intended plans or actions even if such actions are not expected to affect those being notified. Particular organizations may value broad participation in decision making, whereas others may emphasize limited access to decision makers. It is appropriate to conclude that the methods and levels of participation desired for decision making and problem solving are reflections of organizational values and culture.

The Decision/Problem Issue

The nature of a problem also influences decision making and problem solving. Is the problem highly complex? Does the organization have available resources to understand the problem? How important is this decision or solution to organizational effectiveness? Has the organization previously attempted to solve this type of dilemma? Complexity, resources, importance, and previous experience concerning problems all influence how individuals and organizations approach decisions. Complex problems may require more extensive involvement, a higher level of participation, more thoroughness, and greater resources than do less complex problems. The importance of the decision or problem may influence who is responsible and how much time is allocated for decision making.

A sales force reorganization of a large southern insurance company provides an excellent example. Despite an experienced sales force, the company reported three quarters of declining sales as new competitors moved into what previously had been sales territories serviced almost exclusively by company representatives. In the history of the company, top management had never involved themselves in sales territories or sales force organization. Following three quarters of sales declines, top management announced to the vice president for sales that the senior management team would be involved with him in designing a new sales strategy based on new territories and an increased sales staff. The plan was to be complete within thirty days and implemented during an additional sixty-day period. The involvement of top management in the sales reorganization, though unusual to the normal operating procedures of the company, was directly related to the importance of the problem and management's perception of the need for timely action.

Communication Competency

Throughout this text we have continually described the need for communication competency. Many of the competencies we have discussed relate to effective decision making and problem solving. What motivates us and what we believe motivates others influences the quality of our decision-making participation. Our perception of our personal competencies and our predispositions for communication help determine how and when we engage in individual and group decision making. Our interpersonal effectiveness contributes to whether we can influence others during problem solving. Our comfort or discomfort with conflict may determine whether we will contribute information if others are likely to disagree. In addition to our individual participation, the communication competencies of others influence the quality of decision making. Individuals who fail to participate even though they have needed information lower the quality of problem solving. Because decision making and problem solving occur through human communication, the ability and willingness of all involved to engage in quality participation influence the ultimate quality of decisions.

Technical Competency

The final factor to influence decision making and problem solving is technical competency. Do individuals involved in decision making have the technical background or competencies necessary to approach the problem thoughtfully? Are decision makers aware of the best available information on which to base their evaluations? Has the group been formed with a distribution of appropriate technical skills? Excellence in decision making requires a communication process that supports excellence and appropriate technical backgrounds or information. Most of us have attended meetings in which we were willing to participate and yet found that we had no relevant information for the problem at hand. We had to depend on others for our understanding. That dependence probably worked as long as other group members brought appropriate technical competencies to the decision. All too often, however, groups make important decisions without a full range of available information.

METHODS FOR DECISION MAKING
AND PROBLEM SOLVING

Influenced by culture, the issue at hand, and communication and technical competencies, organizational members choose from among a variety of methods and processes for decision making and problem solving. The following methods—individual approach, leader mandate, majority rule, powerful minority, and consensus—will be described to illustrate the diversity of options available for individuals, groups, or entire organizations.

Individual Approaches

Individuals and groups engage in decision making and problem solving with a variety of methods and approaches. Individuals make decisions with a range of involvement from others. At times they come to important decisions without others even knowing a decision is being considered. An individual may decide to apply for a promotion, leave a company, or go back to school based on very private evaluations of alternatives. At other times individual decisions result from extensive interaction with others. An individual, for example, may seek feedback from peers, supervisors, or professional advisors to determine needed skill improvements. A supervisor may have discussions with other supervisors in an effort to solve a performance problem, or a supervisor may work directly with the subordinates in question. In any event, individual decision makers have the option to consider their alternatives alone or with others.

Leader Mandate

Groups also come to decisions with a variety of methods. When a group is hopelessly deadlocked, for example, a leader may make a decision and announce the decision to the group. The authority of the leadership position may be sufficient to enforce the decision without regard to disagreements. Some leaders prefer this method of decision making and only use group members to gather information from which the leader will arrive at the final decision. Decisions made in this fashion may or may not be of high quality. Research suggests, however, that **leader-made decisions** frequently have less group commitment than decisions in which members are more actively involved.

Leader-made decisions— leader of a group makes a decision and announces the decision to the group.

Majority Rule

Majority rule is a common method for decision making. When more than 50 percent of a group agree, a decision is reached. Some groups reach majority agreement informally, whereas others, such as legislative bodies, have operating rules and procedures that govern majority decisions. Al-

Majority-rule decision— when more than 50 percent of a group agree, a decision has been reached.

though faster than moving a group to true consensus, the majority-rule method may not adequately account for the views of the minority. **Majority-rule decisions** can be high in quality but they can also ignore central issues of concern.

Powerful Minority

Powerful-minority decision— process for decision making occurring when group membership is characterized by unequal distribution of power among members. Those members who have the most power (although in the numerical minority) are in a position to assume decision-making responsibility.

Although used less frequently than majority vote, the **powerful-minority decision** is another way groups can make decisions. When group membership is characterized by unequal distribution of power among members, those members who have the most power (although in the numerical minority) are in a position to assume decision-making responsibility. The powerful-minority method can be effective when the minority members have the best information on which to base the decision. This method fails, however, if other-than-expert power drives the decision. Examples of failure of the powerful-minority method can be found in organizational resistance to change. Longtime organizational members who control decision making through seniority and position level may retard needed changes by ignoring the expert opinions of other group members with less organizational power and influence.

Consensus

Consensus— method for decision making that results in all members agreeing on what is best and supporting the group decision.

The **consensus** method results in a decision all members can agree is best and all can support. As John Brilhart (1986) suggests, "When a true consensus has been reached, the result is usually a superior quality decision, a high level of member satisfaction with it, and acceptance of the result." The consensus method may take more time than other methods, unless considerable agreement existed at the beginning of the process. The consensus method does not rest with everyone completely agreeing but with everyone reaching a level of agreement sufficient for decision support. Brilhart states, "Unanimity—the state of perfect consensus in which every group member believes that the decision achieved is the best that could be made—is not at all common. But if all members accept that a consensus may require compromise and collaboration, all will usually support it even though it is not the decision some might have preferred."

BARRIERS TO EFFECTIVE DECISION MAKING AND PROBLEM SOLVING

Throughout our text we have been developing a variety of knowledge, sensitivity, skill, and value competencies important for organizational effectiveness. We have described individual experiences in organizations and identified positive and negative group participation behaviors. We have talked about productive conflict and the importance of leadership and management communication. In general, it is fair to say, we have been exploring the important roles, relationships, and responsibilities that relate to organizational decision making and problem solving, the subject of this chapter.

All of us have participated in groups who made bad decisions or failed to solve real problems. Think for a moment about those groups. Can you identify any particular barriers to effectiveness? What would you do differently if you were to meet again?

Barriers to effective decision making and problem solving can be described in task, procedural, and interpersonal areas. Recall from Chapter 8 a discussion of leadership responsibilities in these categories and the importance for all group members to take responsibility for maximum team effectiveness. It is important for our knowledge and sensitivity competency development for us to understand what commonly goes wrong during problem solving even when individuals have the best of intentions.

Task Barriers

Groups make poor decisions when they short-circuit problem analysis. One of the most important barriers to problem-solving effectiveness is an inadequate description of problems. Group members frequently jump to solutions that appeal to them rather than work toward solutions better suited to the complexity of the issues. Additionally, both individuals and groups have been known to overestimate the positive benefits of a chosen alternative while rejecting accurate or valid information in favor of more popular but flawed data.

Procedural Barriers

Groups also make poor decisions when role ambiguity contributes to confusion about responsibilities, process, or leadership. Who is responsible for what, how decisions are to be made, what authority resides in the group, all are procedural questions that when inadequately answered contribute to ineffective group decisions. The lack of agendas, too much or too little time for meetings, and a variety of other procedural issues are related to low-quality decisions.

Interpersonal Barriers

We have observed or participated in interpersonal conflict that blocked effective decision making. We know from experience that poor leadership or a variety of self-centered or ego-centered behaviors can negatively influence any group. What we may not see is that group cohesion—too much to too little—can influence the quality of decisions. Earlier we described potential dangers from groupthink, or conformity behaviors that suspend critical thinking. It is important also to recognize that too little group cohesion can leave members distrustful and afraid to risk the best of their thinking. Additionally, influential group members have been known to override the logic of others, leading to poor choices.

Needless to say, we have identified only the major barriers to effective problem solving and decision making. What additional barriers can you identify? How can you advise a group to avoid the more serious ones?

PROBLEM-SOLVING PROCESSES

A variety of processes can be identified for both individual and group problem solving. These processes help individuals and groups move from problem identification to determination of action appropriate for problem needs. Although these processes include numerous decision-making activities, they are described as problem-solving processes because of their focus on moving situations, issues, or problems from undesirable to more desirable states. Although decision making occurs during problem solving, problem-solving processes include numerous other stages. Specifically, we will describe the components of problems and present the Standard Agenda, which is known as the rational or scientific model. The Standard Agenda is based on the assumption that problems can be analyzed in component parts with a logical and basically sequential process. The Standard Agenda, in currently popular terminology, depends in large measure on left brain, or logical and rational, thought processes.

We will present brainstorming, the Delphi Technique, Single Question, Ideal Solution, and nominal group process techniques as additional approaches to problem solving. Generally, less complicated than the Standard Agenda, these processes and techniques incorporate logical, sequential information processing with the more intuitive aspects of problem solving popularly associated with right brain functions. Intuition, casual observations, unexpected thoughts or ideas, and sudden insights go hand in hand in these techniques with the more linear cause-and-effect models in the rational approach.

The goal of all of the processes is creative decisions that will contribute to organizational excellence. Which process is most appropriate depends on the needs of the problem, the competencies—both technical and communication—of all involved, the culture of the organization, and a variety of other situation-specific concerns.

Problem Components

Brilhart (1986) suggests that "all problems consist of three major components: (1) an undesirable present situation; (2) a goal, or desired situation; and (3) obstacles to the achievement of the goal. . . . Problem solving is the procedure undertaken to overcome obstacles that stand between a present undesirable situation and a goal." Three primary parts of a problem—an undesirable present situation, goals, and obstacles—are the elements on which the problem-solving process must bear.

We can readily see that people do not always agree on what constitutes a problem. In your class some students will find the examinations challenging and their grades will positively reflect their involvement in the course. Others will be struggling, either finding the material dull or the exams difficult. Depending on which description best fits your situation, you might suggest there is either no problem whatsoever or a problem in need of solving. Organizational members are no different. One supervisor can readily tolerate a capable subordinate who is always late, whereas another considers tardiness an example of poor work habits. One management team may see a short-term decline in profits as reflecting a long-term investment in training new people; another management team, viewing essentially the same situation, might take immediate action to adjust the profit picture.

Goals also are subject to a variety of interpretations. Even when there is high agreement about what constitutes an undesirable situation, defining the goal or the situation's counterpart may remain complex.

Goals often are mistaken for values. Goals are the new or desirable situation that can be measured or compared to the undesirable situation. Values are the underlying belief systems that make the goal worthwhile. Job dissatisfaction can provide a useful example. An individual who finds a job boring and lacking in financial compensation can set a goal to get another job or can erroneously define career success as a goal. The new job represents a goal, but career success is a value. The individual whose goal is the new job enters into a problem-solving process that identifies the obstacles or barriers to the job. Each obstacle or barrier requires a solution in order to attain the final goal. However, the individual who defines his or her goal as career success (and career counselors frequently see people do this) has more difficulty in determining what to do next. Career success is a value difficult to measure against the current undesirable situation. The goal of a new job is, however, measurable and within the reach of the individual's planning process. Career success as a value is the emotional gratification the achievement of the goal is expected to bring.

Finally, an obstacle is anything that prevents the achievement of a goal. For the individual desiring a new job, obstacles may be training, education, work habits, the labor market, geographic location, or a host of other possible factors. The challenge of the problem-solving process is to identify all relevant obstacles and develop a plan of action to eliminate them.

The Standard Agenda: A Rational Model

The **Standard Agenda** is a group application of what John Dewey (1910) identified as reflective thinking necessary for individual problem solving. It can apply to both individuals and groups. Julia Wood, Gerald Phillips,

Standard Agenda—process for decision making based on reflective thinking, beginning with understanding the charge, followed by understanding and phrasing the question, fact-finding, setting criteria and limitations, discovering and selecting solutions, and preparing and presenting the final report.

and Douglas Pedersen (1986) suggest that the Standard Agenda can be described as follows:

1. Understanding the charge. *Why is the group in existence? What is it to do? What form does its output take? Who gets it? What is to be done with it?*
2. Understanding and phrasing the question. *What, precisely, is the group to examine or inquire about? What do the words in the question mean? Are all technical words and issues clear to the members?*
3. Fact-finding. *What are the symptoms of the problem? What is the cause of the symptoms? What is happening that should not be happening? What is not happening that should be happening? Who is suffering from the situation? How badly? What will happen if the situation is not remedied? How must the question be modified in light of fact-finding?*
4. Setting criteria and limitations. *What is possible (as opposed to desirable)? What are the legal, moral, financial, practical, and logistical limits on decision making? What would a solution look like? What would be happening that is not now happening? What will stop happening?*
5. Discovering and selecting solutions. *What are the alternatives? How does each meet the goals? How do they measure up against the limitations? Which provides more of what is wanted with the least new harm? Which one should be selected? Who is to do what about what, when and where, with what projected effect, and how will it be paid for? What evaluation plan can be used to measure the effectiveness of the solution?*
6. Preparing and presenting the final report. *What must be written down? What must be said? When, where, and to whom? How can the final report be most persuasively presented?*

The Diagnostic Phase

All stages of the Standard Agenda require active leader and group member participation to arrive at excellent solutions with a high level of commitment. The first two stages—understanding the charge and understanding and phrasing the question—are crucial steps for establishing a common objective for problem solving. Many groups assume an understanding during these stages that does not exist. The remaining stages in the process can become muddled and ineffective without clarity in these early stages.

During the fact-finding stage, groups often attempt to establish blame rather than engage in obstacle analysis. Even when blame is appropriately placed it does little to eliminate obstacles that contributed to the problem. Blaming also blocks groups from examining the accuracy of information and from identifying causes for the obstacles in question.

When setting criteria and limitations, groups engage in "reality testing" important for discovering workable solutions. This reality testing combats tendencies of some group members to set criteria for the perfect solution as opposed to a solution that is workable. Perfect solutions rarely exist and their pursuit can minimize the effectiveness of the group.

Understanding the charge, understanding and phrasing the question, fact-finding, and setting criteria and limitations can be described as the diagnostic phase of problem solving. During these steps, clarification of problems and the discovery of underlying problem causes and obstacles become the "diagnosis" to which solutions can be applied. This diagnosis is crucial. One of the major reasons problem solving falls short of its potential is inattention to a thorough diagnosis. Groups anxious to solve problems often pay little attention to the details of their diagnosis. Solutions that do not fit the problem cannot be expected to be effective and may even contribute to the problem's recurrence. If you had a sore throat and your doctor did not want to know your symptoms but instead prescribed the flu medicine given at your last visit, you would consider your doctor unprofessional and the prescription (solution) inappropriate to your problem (diagnosis). Yet many of us participate in groups that do essentially that.

The Solution Phase

Throughout the diagnostic stages of the Standard Agenda, groups are required to clarify, find facts, and make decisions. During the phase of discovering and selecting solutions, groups generate and evaluate the feasibility of solutions and decide which best meet the problem. Groups evaluate whether they have considered all possible alternatives and have weighed the assets and liabilities of each. Groups are cautioned to examine thoroughly an alternative for which there seems to be no liability. Usually all alternatives have both strengths and weaknesses. Also, groups are advised to consider combining solutions for maximum assets while establishing the quality of the needed solutions. Effective problem-solving groups make sure they have generated solutions for all identified obstacles and are not ignoring a major barrier simply because its elimination seems difficult. The final criterion for this phase is the reality test of whether the solution can be implemented. Effective groups consider the practicality of implementing their solutions as part of their problem-solving process.

Action Planning

Included in most, although not all, problem-solving group responsibilities is a solution implementation plan. Frequently referred to as an *action plan*, solution implementation includes a description of who is going to do what with which resources and when the plan is to be accomplished. The solution implementation process also includes a feedback plan to determine whether the action plan is working. Important to the feedback plan is identifying information sources and measures to determine the success of the action plan. Will the group evaluate formal reports as feedback? Will the group expect particular individuals to provide feedback on the workability of the solution? What are the criteria by which the group will measure the effectiveness of the solution?

Contingency Plans

Contingency plans also are part of good action planning. They are in place in the event of unexpected failure in the action plan. Let us say, for example, that an action plan has been established for a team of four workers to produce a complicated technical report with a tight but important deadline. Last year the report was late, causing concern about the efficiency of the four workers. The action plan for this year's report seeks to eliminate the previous year's problem. A good action plan will account for contingencies that may not occur but can affect the planned solution. A key group member can become ill or a computer failure could slow the progress of the team. A contingency plan is not an expectation that these events will occur but includes thinking about how the group could adjust. Contingency identification comes from experience with work situations and the types of problems that frequently arise in the pursuit of goal achievement.

Target Dates

Action planning also includes target dates to evaluate the workability of the plan. Many groups are surprised to find that their solutions cannot be implemented within the time constraints of the problem. Target dates help groups avoid establishing carefully laid plans that will be accomplished too late.

Evaluation Dates/Plan Adjustment

Target dates are more likely to be met if evaluation dates are established as checkpoints for the action plan. At evaluation dates, individuals and groups must be able to state specifically which obstacles have been eliminated. Evaluation dates also can be used to determine whether there are new obstacles to the goal. This is important for good problem solving. It is often impossible for groups to consider all eventual obstacles during their initial efforts. Important obstacles may not yet have occurred or their impact may not have been understood earlier. The ability to generate long-term viable solutions rests with individual and group abilities to adjust to changing circumstances.

The example of the insurance company's sales territory problem can be useful here. The original plan for the sales territories was based on available information about the numbers of individuals needed to service accounts in each territory. Sales representatives were well trained and their assignment to specific accounts was based on previous account records and overall sales needs. The individuals developing the original sales territory plan did not have information about major competitor plans for entry into markets they had long ignored. When competition changed, the original plan needed adjustment. The established sales goals were no longer realistic, and only through timely adjustment could the company hope to meet its financial goals. Evaluation dates for progress reports (monthly sales reports) helped management incorporate changing circumstances into their problem-solving process.

Brainstorming

One of the most used and popular processes for generating ideas for problem solving is **brainstorming**. In use for over thirty years, the technique breaks away from linear and controlled processes and seeks creative thinking based on four basic rules: (1) Criticism is not appropriate during idea generation; (2) all ideas are welcome—the more absurd, the better; (3) quantity is wanted—the more ideas, the better; and (4) combinations and alterations of ideas are sought—improve on the ideas of others and combine them. Brainstorming is often used to help understand or diagnose a problem and to elicit ideas when groups are in an alternative- or solution-generation phase. Brainstorming is used as a process in and of itself and often within the framework of the Standard Agenda. It reduces dependency on single powerful or influential individuals by encouraging broad participation without negative evaluation. Brainstorming also encourages a maximum output in a short period of time.

Brainstorming—technique for generating ideas for problem solving based on methods that break away from linear and controlled processes. The process encourages maximum idea generation in a short period of time.

The Delphi Technique

The **Delphi technique** for solving group problems is designed to balance the influence of strong personalities on the problem-solving process. This technique is group problem solving conducted through written response and critique of situations and the responses to those situations. A group leader, referred to as a *charging authority*, forms the group and directs its activities through written correspondence. As Gerald Wilson, H. Lloyd Goodall, and Christopher Waagen (1986) suggest, "By limiting the group communication format to written memos, and by channelling all communication directly between each member and the charging authority, the Delphi technique works through the centralized direction of the charging authority. Group members never know the rest of the group unless the charging authority reveals their identities."

Problem definition or decision alternatives and group membership are defined by the charging authority. Thus, the effectiveness of the Delphi technique rests largely with the leader's understanding of the issues, ability to communicate those issues to others, and capability in selecting competent group members. Once members are selected and the task is defined, each member is asked to respond directly to the leader, describing his or her position or offering solution strategies. The charging authority then responds to members with all of the positions taken by each member. Group members, in turn, respond by continuing support for their original position, modifying that position in light of reviewing the positions of others, or changing their original position as a result of additional information. Written correspondence continues to be circulated until the group reaches a consensus.

The Delphi technique is designed to equalize power among group members and minimize the importance of oral communication skills. Written communication skills, however, replace oral skills in importance and in-

Delphi technique—process of group problem solving conducted through written response and critique of situations and the responses to those situations; designed to balance the influence of strong personalities.

fluence. The Delphi technique is useful for problem solving when group members are in diverse geographic locations. A modification of the technique frequently occurs in organizations when managers circulate for comments correspondence concerning policy changes, new procedures, or a variety of other subjects. This modified Delphi technique is not based on member anonymity, nor does it require responses from all potential participants. The modified Delphi technique is a way of gathering feedback on problems and solutions without seeking full consensus. The major concern with a pure Delphi technique is the responsibility placed on the leader for problem definition and membership selection. This technique, however, does require members to articulate their positions in writing without undue influence from powerful others.

The Single Question Form

Single Question form—process for problem solving consisting of central questions that help groups to narrow topics efficiently by working through questions and subquestions.

The **Single Question form** is Carl Larson's (1969) adaptation of the work of Theodore Harris and Wilson Schwahn (1961) in determining successful and unsuccessful problem-solving approaches. According to Larson, the Single Question form consists of five central questions: "(1) What is the single question, the answer to which is all the group needs to know to accomplish its purpose? (2) What sub-questions must be answered before we can answer the single question we have formulated? (3) Do we have sufficient information to answer confidently the sub-questions? (If yes, answer them. If no, continue below.) (4) What are the most reasonable answers to the sub-questions? (5) Assuming that our answers to the sub-questions are correct, what is the best solution to the problem?"

The Single Question form is efficient in getting the group to narrow the topic by working through questions and subquestions. The process intends that when the group does not have adequate information to answer a question, the question will be handled by the "best guess" approach of members. By the time solution questions are asked, it is assumed that a best solution can be generated from previous answers. The most difficult part of the process is to identify and clarify the initial question. With little fact-finding in the process itself, the Single Question form supports effective problem solving only when group members have considerable knowledge and experience to apply to the question under consideration.

The Ideal Solution Form

Ideal Solution form—process for problem solving that utilizes questions to move a group from agreement on the nature of the problem to a best approximation of the ideal or best solution.

Larson (1969) adapted a Kepner and Tregoe (1965) decision-making process into his **Ideal Solution form**. He suggests the Ideal Solution process answers four essential questions:

1. *Are we all agreed on the nature of the problem?*
2. *What would be the ideal solution from the point-of-view of all the parties involved in the problem?*

3. *What conditions within the problem could be changed so that the ideal solution might be achieved?*
4. *Of the solutions available to us, which one best approximates the ideal solution?*

In critiquing the Ideal Solution form, Stanley Jones, Dean Barnlund and Franklyn Haiman (1980) state, "we can see why this pattern is especially efficient: (1) According to this form, the group formulates the problem in the first step. If no one seems to disagree, the group moves forward to consider the characteristics of an 'ideal' solution. (2) The criteria are not binding. The group can adopt a solution which merely approximates the ideal."

Both the Single Question and the Ideal Solution forms are known for their efficiency. In some respects the Standard Agenda is much less time efficient than either of the question formats. The Standard Agenda, however, is more comprehensive and encourages external fact-finding if group members believe they lack comprehensive information. Thus, success with the Standard Agenda rests more on the process itself than with the comprehensive nature of the knowledge group members bring to the process. In the Single Question and Ideal Solution forms, group member knowledge is fundamental for process success. All three processes can produce effective solutions. Success comes from choosing the process that best fits the problem and available group members.

Nominal Group Process

Nominal group process is a combination of individual and group idea generation. Based on the assumption that both individual and group idea generation has value, a nominal group process begins with individuals silently writing down their ideas. Ideas are reported to the group at large for discussion, clarification, and usually a preliminary vote or decision. Discussion of issues occurs again, and a final decision vote is taken. The process is especially helpful for people who are fearful of free-wheeling discussions of ideas or among groups in which tension levels have previously been high.

Nominal group process— problem-solving process combining individual and group idea generation. Individuals contribute first in writing, and than the group discusses and decides.

INCREASING DECISION-MAKING AND PROBLEM-SOLVING EFFECTIVENESS

Effective problem solving and decision making require individuals and groups to utilize a broad range of communication and technical competencies. In the next section of this chapter, we will focus on two types of skills necessary for problem solving: interaction process and fact-finding and evaluation skills. These communication competencies, coupled with competencies developed in previous chapters, form a basis for increasing our decision-making and problem-solving effectiveness.

Interaction Process Skills

Interaction process skills—skills based on an understanding of the communication process; an awareness of individual predispositions, strategies, and tactics in a variety of circumstances; and knowledge and sensitivity for decision making and problem solving.

We have previously discussed individual strategies and tactics for effectiveness. We have described defensive and supportive climates for interaction as well as the responsibilities participants bring to communication. We have yet to describe, however, **interaction process skills** that relate to effectiveness for decision making and problem solving. Interaction process skills are based on an understanding of the communication process; an awareness of individual predispositions, strategies, and tactics in a variety of circumstances; and knowledge and sensitivity for decision-making and problem-solving processes. Interaction process skills help individuals and groups structure problem-solving discussions, exhibit productive individual behaviors, and avoid behaviors destructive to effective decision making and problem solving.

Brilhart (1986) has identified seven general principles for structuring effective problem-solving discussions:

1. *Focus on the problem before thinking and talking about how to solve it.*
2. *Begin with a single, unambiguous problem question.*
3. *Develop a thorough statement of the problem analysis—map the problem thoroughly (who, what, why, when, where, and how).*
4. *Be sure the group members agree on criteria or ways of measuring the adequacy of decisions/solutions.*
5. *Resist evaluation/judgment when gathering ideas/solutions.*
6. *Avoid "groupthink" (conformity to the beliefs of the group or its leaders) through constructive disagreement.*
7. *Verbally plan for implementation and follow-up solutions.*

These seven principles closely resemble the Standard Agenda discussed earlier in this chapter. There are, however, important distinctions. The Standard Agenda is a process for reflective thinking about problems designed to encourage workable solutions to which groups are committed. The seven principles for structuring group discussion are communication strategies and tactics that support the reflective thinking process. For example, the interaction principle of focusing on the problem before solutions refers to group member and leadership responsibilities to direct conversation toward problem definition and diagnosis without allowing members to jump ahead with recommendations for solutions. Obviously, the principle supports reflective-thinking processes; however, it should be understood as a communication responsibility. Groups can intend to think reflectively about problems and still stray from that goal by engaging in and supporting communication behaviors that make their intended process less than effective. The principle of beginning with a single unambiguous question relates not only to developing a problem statement but also to the use of communication strategies and tactics such as questioning and active listening to determine whether the question contains levels of ambiguity for some group members. The communication skill is not just the formulation of a question statement but the ability to probe to discover what all group members understand as a result of the statement.

Fact-Finding and Evaluation Skills

We make decisions based on our evaluation of the information that bears on the decision. We solve problems based on information about the problem and decisions about the adequacy of our solutions. Furthermore, we base complex decisions on the information available to us, whether or not it is the best information. It is fair to say, therefore, that the quality of information we bring to decision-making and problem-solving processes directly influences the quality of our decisions and solutions.

To illustrate, let's assume for a moment that careful planning has gone into our long-awaited vacation. We've contacted several airlines and have selected what appears to be the best fare. We have asked friends about a possible hotel and selected the one most often recommended. We arrive at our destination and are pleased with our accommodations. But the newspaper in our hotel room is advertising air fares to the resort area, and these fares are at least $100 less than we paid. We also find that while our hotel is very nice, there are other charming inns that give a better view of the mountains. Suddenly, our well-laid plans begin to seem inadequate; we are unsure of our choices. How did this happen with all our careful planning? The answer is relatively simple. We made decisions about our flights and hotel reservations without all the available information. We simply did not have a comprehensive awareness of our alternatives. Our initial fact-finding was inadequate.

Information Criteria

But how can we evaluate the information we need? What criteria are important for our **fact-finding and evaluation skills?** Dennis Gouran (1979) suggests that there are three characteristics of information that should be considered in forming our decision-making rules: relevancy, sufficiency, and plausibility. *Relevancy* refers to the extent to which information bears directly on the matter for decision. In the case of our airline reservations, the fare information acquired was relevant but did not meet the second necessary characteristic, *sufficiency*. Sufficiency refers to the amount of information necessary to establish positions or claims, or to verify what is likely to be correct. The fare schedules acquired were relevant but did not represent all of the possible fares from airlines flying our desired route. Thus, the failure to meet the sufficiency criterion cost us over $100. Finally, *plausibility* or the extent to which information is credible, also influences our decision. Again, our rate information was credible. The airline we chose sold us the ticket for the stated price. However, even though we had rel-

Fact-finding and evaluation skills—skills that assist in the discovery and criticism of information utilized in problem solving and decision making.

evant plausible information, the lack of a comprehensive set of fare schedules (sufficiency) causes us concern about our decision. The same might be said for our hotel selection. We gathered relevant and plausible information but did not have a full set of alternatives from which to choose.

Relevancy, sufficiency, and plausibility of information affect not only individual decisions but also the quality of group efforts. The fact-finding abilities of all involved in decision making influence the effectiveness of decisions and how satisfied individuals and entire organizations are with decision making and problem solving. But what are the abilities needed for successful fact-finding? Three primary capabilities deserve attention: information gathering, data analysis, and observation.

Information Gathering

Information gathering takes place through informational interviews and the collection of data appropriate to the decision. In our vacation example, information gathering was incomplete and failed to meet the sufficiency criteria. Information-gathering skills also can be evaluated by relevancy and plausibility criteria. The adequacy of our information-gathering capabilities is measured by our ability to gather relevant, sufficient, and plausible data from others and to identify sources where needed information is likely to be found.

Interviews are a primary source of information. They are conducted to provide needed information or to verify perceptions of a problem. Ideally, informational interviews are conducted with individuals who can plausibly be expected to have the needed facts and perceptions.

Whether they are informal or highly structured exchanges, informational interviews begin with careful planning. Planning is based on what we want to know, on who has that information, and in what form we are likely to find it. What we need to know emerges during our problem definition and our examination of the limits of our current information. We do not use interviews to gather information the group already has unless there is some disagreement about its credibility.

What we need to know is influenced by our ability to define the limits of what we do not know. Although this sounds like a play on words, the concept is very important to decision making and problem solving. One of the limitations many of us exhibit during information gathering is the tendency to define what is needed in terms of what we know exists. We often do not seek enough open-ended information that may be relevant to our problem. In our vacation example, we knew we needed a nice hotel. We did not even consider our desire for a good view of the mountains in our fact-finding. We limited our fact-finding to what we knew to expect and inadvertently eliminated a highly desirable alternative.

After broadly identifying what we need to know, effective fact-finders locate sources likely to have that information. Fact-finders are faced with deciding who or what source is most accessible and who will be willing to give the needed information. Does one person have the data for our problem? Should we take a representative sample of individuals who can be expected to be affected by the problem? How precise do our sampling techniques need to be? These questions and others help fact-finders focus their efforts to find information sources appropriate for decision making and problem solving.

Once sources have been identified, the fact-finder proceeds to establish a general format for data collection. If an interview is to be conducted, the interviewer thinks about questions to ask and determines how responses will be documented for later evaluation. If written data are to be reviewed, the fact-finder decides how much will be recorded and in what format. This preparation for data collection enables the fact-finder to make better use of time spent with the interviewee or other relevant sources.

When conducting an informational interview with another person, the interviewer must establish rapport and explain the purpose of data collection activities. During this phase of the interview, the fact-finder should establish personal credibility by introducing himself or herself, identifying the organization, and relating facts or circumstances that link the requested information to the purposes at hand. In other words, respondents are more likely to be cooperative if fact-finders introduce themselves with credentials and establish a need for the type of questions to be asked.

Once the interview begins, the fact-finder becomes concerned with framing questions that are clear and will elicit the desired information from the interviewee. Robert Kahn and Charles Cannell (1964) suggest five principles that contribute to success during the questioning phase.

1. *Use language appropriate to the respondent.*
2. *Be sure the questions are clearly related to the purpose of the interview.*
3. *Be certain the informant has the information you want.*
4. *Avoid questions that are overly complex.*
5. *Avoid questions that ask the respondent to violate a social norm.*

These suggestions are similar to numerous other concepts of interpersonal effectiveness. Kahn and Cannell are suggesting that successful interviewers adopt a receiver orientation, continually monitoring whether the interviewee understands the line of questioning and whether the interviewer is placing the interviewee in a situation where truthful response is difficult. A communication consultant seeking information from employees about a supervisory problem, for example, may need to be careful to ensure employee anonymity in order to gather information employees think may not be safe for management to hear. The consultant must understand what employees really think, not a filtered version, to make effective recommendations. Rapport and careful selection of questions are fundamental to gathering this important but sensitive information. Interviewers must know whether interviewees want credit for their remarks or anonymity. Interviewers also must carefully monitor potential bias in the remarks of interview subjects. The ability to evaluate information continually for relevancy, sufficiency, and plausibility is necessary for fact-finders to gather information that supports effective decision making and problem solving.

Effective fact-finders frequently close informational interviews by asking for any additional information the respondent would care to offer. Interviewers also ask subjects what they have not been asking that they should have explored. These questions and others give interviewees an opportunity to add information the fact-finder may not have known existed. This can be as important to effective solutions as information previously identified as important.

Baird (1977) well summarizes an effective atmosphere for an informational interview: "The informational interview should create opportunity and willingness. Respondents give only the information they have an opportunity to give. If our questions do not provide them the opportunity, the information is lost. In addition, respondents give only the information they are willing to give. . . . Through careful selection of topics, questions, and respondents, coupled with skillful questioning, both opportunity and willingness can be maximized."

Fact-finding also includes locating information in files, libraries, archives, reports, and a variety of other documents. Librarians, computer searches, and catalogue files are only a few of the resources used to identify information sources. Much to the surprise of many students, research skills previously applied to term papers and other similar reports are valuable organizational skills when decision making and problem solving require data collection. As we stated earlier, the complex information age brings more potential information to bear on problems than at any previous period in human history. This sheer volume of information complicates the fact-finding process and makes our ability to locate and evaluate data of increasing importance.

Data Analysis

We use the information we gather as proof or support for the ideas we generate or as a way of distinguishing among decision alternatives. As Gerald Phillips (1982) suggests, "proofs are the reasons for understanding, believing, or doing." He further identifies four useful categories of proofs: definitions, examples, statistics, and citations.

Data analysis—evaluation of definitions, examples, statistics, and citations as they support decision alternatives.

To reach good decisions and to solve problems thoughtfully, it is important to develop abilities for **data analysis.** Proofs are found in the information we gather. They are used by other group members to support their positions, and we use them as support for our understanding of ideas and issues.

Phillips (1982) describes his four basic categories of proofs:

1. *DEFINITIONS detail the characteristics by which you can identify a thing, a condition, a state of affairs, or a concept.*
2. *EXAMPLES are concrete illustrations of either definitions or generalizations, sometimes presented as narratives of events.*

3. *STATISTICS are generalizations built out of examples, and phrased in precise numerical form.*
4. *CITATIONS are statements of opinion, generally drawn from people who qualify as authorities.*

Definitions, examples, statistics, and citations all are subject to evaluations of relevancy, sufficiency, and plausibility. The ability to analyze data thoughtfully for these characteristics is a critical decision-making and problem-solving skill.

Definitions. Although individual words have definitions, definitions also describe conditions or situations. In fact, as we have previously discussed, the definition of the problem is the initial step in most problem-solving processes. We may use definitional proofs to determine how experts have defined the problem, how the problem has previously been defined in research literature, and how others in our group define the issue at hand. Let's say, for example, that we are working with a group of supervisors to improve the absenteeism rate among a large number of manufacturing workers. We are attempting to determine causes of the problem and initiate action that will have more people regularly reporting to their assigned shifts. Our report will go to top management for immediate action. One strictly technical definition of our problem is that 10 percent of each manufacturing shift is absent on a given day. That definition helps us understand the magnitude of our problem but provides little or no information about causes. We may contact a variety of experts such as organizational communication specialists, industrial psychologists, or business consultants. Someone in the group may locate articles describing the causes and effects of absenteeism. Chances are these information sources will describe absenteeism as a condition reflecting a variety of potential problems in the work force. We will now begin to consider conditions such as boring, repetitive work; lack of adequate reward systems; or a widely held perception that organizational policies are not seriously enforced when related to absenteeism. This "expert" definition of absenteeism as a condition reflecting work environment dissatisfaction begins to focus our attention on problem solving. Additionally, members of our group may well have individual definitions of the problem, resulting from personal experiences. This range of definitions contributes to our understanding of the problem and our ability to identify obstacles to problem solution.

Examples. We use examples to clarify more general statements. In our absenteeism situation, we may use an example of the problems generated on a particular shift when eight workers failed to report. We might describe the number of product shipments that were missed as a result of the remaining workers having to cover missing positions on the manufacturing line. Our example can help to clarify the measurable impact of our absenteeism problem. When one of our experts begins to give examples of how boring tasks contribute to absenteeism, we make comparisons between the examples being offered and our particular situation. Let's say that the expert describes examples of absenteeism found in manufacturing environments where tasks are highly repetitive and individual workers are never rotated among work stations. Our manufacturing line has individuals cross-trained across four job positions with weekly rotations among those positions. Although the expert may be using a highly plausible example, our use of the expert's example as a proof from which to assume we understand the cause of our absenteeism is suspect. The example is correct but not as relevant to our situation as it needs to be. We must continue to look for examples that better fit our particular circumstance.

Statistics. Statistics are quantifiable generalizations about situations, people, and events. Our 10 percent absenteeism rate is a statistic reflecting the behaviors of a relatively consistent number of our manufacturing work force. Statistics, however, are numbers, not the situation, people, or events they represent. Phillips (1982) cautions, "once a generalization has been translated into numbers, it proceeds to operate according to the rules of numbers, not according to the things from which the numbers were derived. What this means is that statistics are accurate to the extent that the things they represent behave enough like numbers to justify the use of the numbers."

Although not a subject appropriate for this text, our ability to analyze statistical information is fundamental to our overall competency. The information age brings us more and more data we do not experience personally. We increasingly rely on the way others compile information, what their interpretations are, and the perceived impact. Without a basic ability to understand the generalization of numbers, we place ourselves in the position of accepting interpretations of others, a position that limits our ability to influence decisions and solve problems. Phillips (1982) suggests that statistical proofs can take several forms:

1. *DEMOGRAPHIC statistics describe proportions of occurrences in whole populations. Income ranges, housing types, jobs performed by people in a community, number of marriages in a community, and size of family are all examples of demographic statistics.*
2. *ACTUARIAL statistics are predictions and trends. They operate on an "all other things being equal" basis; that is, things will remain the same if events remain the same. If there are intervening events, new calculations must be made.*
3. *INFERENTIAL statistics are really statements of the odds that events and/or conditions are not connected by accident. Medical research for example is based on a process of gathering information under carefully controlled conditions so that accurate statements can be made about the causes or treatments of particular diseases.*

We may want to compare our percentage of absenteeism in manufacturing to other parts of the company. We may want to explore absenteeism in other industries. We may want to examine the use of sick leave by employees in manufacturing as compared to other functions. All are questions requiring an understanding of the interpretation of numbers. When problem-solving group members are confronted with numerical generalizations they do not understand, their most appropriate course of action is to find resources to help make accurate analyses.

Observation

Personal observation is an important, although often unrecognized, fact-finding technique. We continually engage in observing and interpreting events around us. We use these interpretations both consciously and unconsciously as proofs essential to the development of our understanding and opinions. It is important, therefore, that we develop good observational techniques in order to use our personal experiences most productively. When we observe a peer sitting at his or her desk and staring into space, what interpretation do we make of this observation? Do we consider our peer to be lazy, engaged in reflective thinking, daydreaming, or aloof? Have we considered all of the possible explanations for our peer's behavior? How can we verify our understanding?

Observation is important when considering human communication competencies. We observe communication behavior all around us. We base assumptions about the competencies of others on our observations. The accuracy of these observations is an important part of our assessment process.

As supervisors working on the absenteeism problem, we will bring our personal observations to the problem. In fact, the causes of the problem may well be within the range of observations group members can make. Do we observe and verify from records that more absenteeism occurs on Fridays and Mondays than other days? What might be a reason? Do we observe that certain individuals are repeat offenders? Have we documented this observation? What do our observations tell us about the boredom level of the jobs, the adequacy of the reward systems, and how workers interpret enforcement of company policy? Our observations can form a basis from which to evaluate the relevancy, sufficiency, and plausibility of other information sources. It is important, therefore, to attempt to be precise in observation and to explore through questions, research, or further observation perceptions that are unclear or appear contradictory.

Fact-finding and evaluation skills are fundamental to effective problem solving. Interestingly enough, we do not often emphasize that one of the most important experiences in our formal education process is the training of individuals to be good fact-finders with abilities for critical evaluation.

SUMMARY

Decision making is the process of choosing from among several alternatives, and problem solving is a multistage process for moving an issue, situation, or state from an undesirable to a more desirable condition.

Groups make decisions and solve problems through a variety of methods, including leader mandate, majority rule, powerful minority influence, and consensus. Organizational culture, the problem itself, technical competencies, and communication competencies all influence decision-making and problem-solving processes. Barriers to problem solving can be identified in task, procedural, and interpersonal areas. Problem-solving processes include the Standard Agenda, brainstorming, Delphi technique, Single Question approach, Ideal Solution approach, and nominal group process. Each represents a different process for solving problems and different interpretations of how groups come to decisions. Decision-making and problem-solving effectiveness can be increased by developing fact-finding and evaluation skills, which include informational interviews, data analysis, and observation. In addition, effectiveness can be improved with positive interaction processes.

WORKSHOP

1. You have been studying a variety of approaches to decision making and problem solving. You will now be asked to assume the position of training manager for Food Service Industries. As training manager you are responsible for making a series of routine business decisions. You are returning from your annual vacation and find a number of decision items in your in-basket. For each item, describe what you would do and what criteria you are using for each decision. Small groups or the class as a whole will compare and discuss responses. (See pages 329–331.)

2. Solving a Campus or Community Problem is designed to build skills important for problem analysis, data gathering, problem solving, and solution presentation. Because the activity requires the gathering of information from those involved with the problem, you and your group will require two to three weeks to complete your assignment. Specific stages in this activity are described. (See pages 331–332.)

3. Our next in-basket activity asks you to become Dave Fedderson, the acting director of the Clark Home for Boys. In addition to building your decision skills, this in-basket requires you to select appropriate channels and structure messages to communicate your decisions. (Dave Fedderson's in-basket can be completed individually or done as a small-group project.) (See pages 332–335.)

4. To illustrate similarities and differences in decision-making and problem-solving approaches among class members, select a current problem familiar to class members. (Cases and in-basket items are also appropriate for this activity.) Divide the entire class into groups of six members each. Each group will appoint one member to be a fa-

cilitator. All groups need flip-chart paper and Magic Markers. Each group will have fifteen minutes to find possible solutions for the problem. (All solutions are taken even if other group members disagree.) At the end of fifteen minutes each group will spend five minutes choosing their top three solutions (through consensus or majority vote). The top three solutions will be recorded on flip-chart paper and posted for the entire class to review. Each group facilitator reads the top three to the entire class. The class then goes "shopping" for ten minutes. "Shopping" is simply walking around the room and recording any solution that individual group members believe is especially productive. Groups again convene for twenty minutes. Group members begin by adding from "shopping" any solutions they want discussed. Within the allotted twenty minutes each group will rank their top two solutions one and two. Facilitators again record these decisions on flip-chart paper, post the findings, and report to the entire class. Discussion follows about the process and the similarities and differences in solutions.

The Training Manager of Food Service Industries
In-Basket Exercise

Instructions: You have been away on your annual vacation. Upon your return, the following items have been marked with a priority stamp by your secretary. For each item, describe what you would do next. Can you make an immediate decision? What additional information do you need? Are you going to involve other people? Describe your criteria for each decision.

Item 1

```
To: YOUR NAME, Training Manager for Food Service
Industries
From: Mike Barnes, Vice President of Major
Accounts

 I have just received two complaints about one of
our newest salespersons. Topco Foods and Bestway
both said Jim Johnson was rude and did not
effectively represent our product line. I thought
he had just been in one of your training sessions.
How would you evaluate his performance? Please
advise immediately?
```

Item 2

To: YOUR NAME, Training Manager for Food Service
Industries
From: Jane Connors, Chair, Community Service
Speakers Bureau, the _____ Chamber of
Commerce

We know your company is an active and vital
member of this community. As chair of the Speakers
Bureau for our Community Outreach Program, I would
like to invite you to give a motivational talk on
leadership at our September banquet. Mike Barnes
of your company recommended you and felt you were
just the person to do the job. Our program goes to
press next week, so we need your response as soon
as possible.

Item 3

To: All Department Heads
From: Finance

Because of a downturn in our profit projections
for the next quarter, each department is being
asked to reduce its fourth quarter budget by 2
percent. Because each department's spending
authority is established through finance, we need
a list of those items or events you want to
eliminate. Thank you very much for your
cooperation in this matter. The list should be in
our office no later than Friday.

Item 4

To: YOUR NAME
From: Jerry Masters, Head of Manufacturing
Services

I have a problem and know you can help. We have
hired six new people for our new manufacturing
process group. We had not budgeted any training
courses for the six, as we did not anticipate

starting the group before the first of next year.
Company policy requires me to schedule them for
new employee orientation, but I don't have the
training funds available to reimburse your
department. Please advise how I should handle this
situation.

Item 5

Dear YOUR NAME

I was in your June 4th class on managing poor
performance. I tried everything you said and now
am really in a mess. In fact, the subordinate in
question has gone to my manager and made a formal
complaint. I just want you to know I told my
manager it was all your fault and they should
really look at what people are taught in those
supervision classes.

Sincerely,

John Price

Solving a Campus or Community Problem

The class should be divided into groups with six members each. An un-
solved problem of current interest on the campus should be identified. The
problem should be complex and of a nature that allows information gathering by the class. Groups will be asked to use the Standard Agenda for
problem solving.

STEPS IN THE ASSIGNMENT

1. Each group should meet and determine how they will approach the
   problem. During this meeting, fact-finding responsibility should be
   established.
2. Fact-finding is done by group members.
3. Following fact-finding, group members will use the standard agenda
   for problem solving. Once solution agreement has been reached,
   group members will determine how to present findings to the remainder of the class.

4. Class presentations of findings are made.

5. Discussion follows about similarities and differences in recommendations between and among groups. Also, discussion includes experiences with the Standard Agenda process.

(A variation on this activity includes using more than one campus or community problem. It is important, however, that all group members have some awareness of selected problems. It is recommended that at least two groups work on similar problems. The comparisons of their findings are informative for analyzing group problem-solving efforts.)

David Fedderson's In-Basket Exercise

Instructions. Your name is David Fedderson. You are the acting director of the Clark Home for Boys. You have just returned from a five-day vacation and find your in-basket full of a variety of items in need of immediate response. Respond to each item separately, choosing the appropriate channel for response and structuring the best message.

In-Basket Background Information

The Clark Home provides residential, educational, recreational, and counseling care for boys between the ages of thirteen and seventeen who have been assigned to the home by court order. At the present time, 120 boys are in residence. A seven-person board of directors is responsible for filling administrative positions and defining policy.

You were appointed acting director six months ago when Jim Chelton, executive director for ten years, resigned over a disagreement with the board of directors regarding appropriate disciplinary measures at Clark. You had served as director of educational services for five years under Chelton. You now are a formal candidate for permanent executive director. The board of directors has seven applicants for the job and will begin the final selection process shortly.

The staff at Clark consists of six residential counselors, two social workers, an accountant, two recreation directors, four teachers, a director of residence halls, a staff psychologist, your administrative assistant, and two part-time secretaries. You remain as director of educational services while serving as acting executive director.

Background on Several Staff Members

Jane Andrews, Administrative Assistant to Executive Director. Jane has been at Clark since Jim Chelton first became director. She is loyal to Chelton and has been upset by his resignation. She is very competent and has been valuable to you in the last six months. You do wonder at times if she questions your loyalty to Chelton.

Mike Simms, Director of Residence Halls. Mike has been at Clark for eighteen months. He is a retired military officer. He is sincerely concerned for the boys' welfare but he and Chelton disagreed on disciplinary measures. Mike felt that Chelton was much too lenient. Mike also disagrees with the staff psychologist, Amy Fielding, on several issues. Mike frequently socializes with several members of the board of directors.

Dr. Amy Fielding, Staff Psychologist. Amy became staff psychologist at Clark three years ago. She has good rapport with most of the boys and participates with them in numerous recreational activities. She gets along well with the staff except for Mike Simms, whom she considers autocratic. Her concern about Chelton's resignation and the uncertainty of a new director have contributed to her consideration of another job. She has not yet reached a decision about leaving Clark.

In-Basket Item 1

```
   Dave—While you were gone Simms disciplined
Dolphie Evans far too harshly. Dolphie came to me
and indicated he is afraid of Simms. I have just
about had it with this type of staff action. I am
scheduled to work with Dolphie on Tuesday. I need
to tell this kid something. Please advise.

Amy
```

In-Basket Item 2

```
Federal International
Clark County Chapters

May 17

Mr. David Fedderson
Clark Home for Boys

Dear Mr. Fedderson:

  As you know, the Federal Clubs of Clark County
were responsible to a small extent for the
beginning of Clark Home for Boys. We are proud of
our participation in this effort. For the past
several years, Jim Chelton has spoken to our
annual budget committee meeting and detailed how
Federal Clubs might continue to participate in the
work of Clark.
```

The meeting this year is scheduled for May 25 at 12:00 noon at the Federal Clubs' Hall. I am hopeful that you will be able to meet with us and help us determine the work we can do together. I must advise you that you can expect questions concerning what effect the change in directors is anticipated to have on the general program at Clark. I certainly hope you can be with us. I will be looking forward to hearing from you.

Sincerely,

Mac Conneville
Chairman, Budget Committee
Federal Clubs of Clark County

In-Basket Item 3

May 18

Mr. David Fedderson
Clark Home for Boys

Dear Mr. Fedderson:

In beginning the final selection process for the position of Executive Director of the Clark Home for Boys, I have been asked to contact the top three applicants and request they submit an additional statement of philosophy with regard to the position. The selection committee narrowed the candidate field from the detailed résumés you and the other applicants submitted in your original applications.

The type of additional information we are seeking deals with a statement of your philosophy concerning the operation of an educational and rehabilitation facility for boys who have become wards of the court. Any statement you care to make will be confidential to the selection committee. You will be asked to comment relative to your statement and answer other questions that selection committee members might have on May 30 at 8:30 a.m. in the Board Room at the Clark Home for Boys. If this time is not convenient for you, please advise me as soon as possible.

Sincerely,

Jerry Danforth
Selection Committee Chairman
Board of Directors, Clark Home for Boys

In-Basket Item 4

```
Notes from Jane

To: Dave
From: Jane
Date: Friday

  The counselor in South Hall, Rick Newhouse,
called and wants to speak with you personally. He
says there is a matter in South that bothers him.
He seemed upset to me.

  J.
```

In-Basket Item 5

```
Clark Home for Boys
M E M O

Date: May 16
To: Dave Fedderson
From: Mike Simms
Subject: Revision of conduct standards and
         operating procedures for Residence Halls

  Recommendations for the following operating
procedure and conduct standard changes will be
made to my Advisory Board next week at our regular
monthly meeting. I have talked informally with my
Advisory Board members and believe these changes
are in keeping with their thinking on running the
residence halls. I need your approval as soon as
possible to finalize the written report to the
Board.

  1. Eliminate first-name basis when students
     address counselors.
  2. Establish hall regulations eliminating
     differential curfew by age and institute
     lights-out policy at 9:00 p.m.
  3. Institute regular residence inspections rather
     than leaving this responsibility to individual
     residence counselors.
  4. Institute a formal demerit system. Withdraw
     privileges systematically when demerit limit
     is exceeded.
  5. Establish a work program that will replace
     five hours of recreational activities per
     week.
```

SUMMARY OF COMPETENCY COMPONENTS
KNOWLEDGE, SENSITIVITY, SKILLS, VALUES

KNOWLEDGE

Decision making is defined as a choice among alternatives.

Problem solving is defined as attempting to change an undesirable state.

Problem-solving processes are identified and described as Standard Agenda, brainstorming, Delphi technique, Single Question, Ideal Solution, and nominal group process.

Fact-finding and evaluation are based on information-gathering techniques such as interviews, data analysis, and observation.

Components for effective presentations are identified.

SENSITIVITY

Organizational culture, the problem, technical, and communication competencies are described as influencing the quality of decisions and problem solving.

Individual behavior is identified as important for group effectiveness.

Positive individual behaviors support effective group processes.

SKILLS

Fact-finding, interaction process, and presentation skills are identified.

Fact-finding, interaction process, and presentation skills are applied and practiced through case studies, in-basket exercises, and group experiences.

Analysis skills are applied to group interactions, case studies, and in-basket exercises.

VALUES

Decision making and problem solving are described as important processes for organizational excellence.

Effective decision making and problem solving require critical thinking and evaluation of the best available information.

Decision making and problem solving grow more complex in an information society.

REFERENCES AND SUGGESTED READINGS

Baird, J. E., Jr. 1982. *Positive personnel practices, quality circles leader's manual.* Prospect Heights, IL: Waveland Press.

Brilhart, J. K. 1986. *Effective group discussion.* 5th ed. Dubuque, IA: Brown.

Cummings, H. W., L. W. Long, and M. L. Lewis. 1983. *Managing communication in organizations: An introduction.* Dubuque, IA: Gorsuch Scarisbrick.

Dewey, J. 1910. *How we think.* Boston: Heath.

Fisher, B. A. 1980. *Small group decision making.* 2d ed. New York: McGraw-Hill.

Gouran, D. S. 1979. *Making decisions in groups: Choices and consequences.* Glenview, IL: Scott, Foresman.

Harris, T. L., and W. E. Schwahn. 1961. *Selected readings on the learning process.* New York: Oxford University Press.

Hirokawa, R. 1988. Group communication and decision-making performance: A continued test of the functional perspective. *Human Communication Research* 14(4): 487–515.

Jones, S. E., D. C. Barnlund, and F. S. Haiman. 1980. *The dynamics of discussion communication in small groups.* New York: Harper & Row.

Kahn, R., and C. Cannell. 1964. *The dynamics of interviewing.* New York: Wiley.

Kepner, C. H., and B. B. Tregoe. 1985. *The rational manager.* New York: McGraw-Hill.

Larson, C. E. 1969. Forms of analysis and small group problem-solving. *Speech Monographs* 36: 452–55.

Phillips, G. M. 1982. *Communicating in organizations.* New York: Macmillan.

Scheidel, T., and L. Crowell. 1964. Idea development in small discussion groups. *Quarterly Journal of Speech* 50: 140–45.

Simon, H. A. 1960. *The new science of management decision.* New York: Harper & Row.

Tompkins, P., and G. Cheney. 1983. Account analysis of organizations: Decision making and identification. In *Communication and organizations: An interpretive approach,* eds. L. Putnam and M. Pacanowsky, 123–46. Beverly Hills, CA: Sage.

Wilson, G. L., H. L. Goodall, Jr., and C. L. Waagen. 1986. *Organizational communication.* New York: Harper & Row.

Wood, J. T., G. M. Phillips, and D. J. Pedersen. 1986. *Group discussion: A practical guide to participation and leadership.* 2d ed. New York: Harper & Row.

CHAPTER

~ T E N ~

Presentations in Organizations: Developing Important Oral Competencies

Developing competencies through . . .

KNOWLEDGE

Describing types of organizational presentations
Identifying basic formats for presentations
Relating presentations to problem solving and decision making

SENSITIVITY

Considering ethical and credibility issues for presentations
Describing audience concerns
Understanding coping with anxiety

SKILLS

Assessing individual presentation needs
Practicing analysis capabilities for presentations

VALUES

Understanding the importance of ethical and credible individual behaviors for organizational effectiveness
Relating effective presentations to overall organizational effectiveness

The Spending More to Save More Presentation Case

Nancy Winslow was concerned about next week's manufacturing staff meeting. She had wanted to be scheduled to talk to management about her training budget but not necessarily in such a potentially difficult setting. Nancy had just been notified that she was to make a formal presentation justifying her request for $100,000 to train assembly workers on new equipment requiring improved reading comprehension and mathematics skills. Nancy knew the need for skills training was great among assembly workers, but she was also aware that several influential managers opposed spending training time and money in favor of replacing the most deficient employees. Nancy had hoped to convince the manufacturing manager of her plan before meeting with his staff. Now it was obvious that she would not have that opportunity and could expect serious challenges to her proposal. Nancy began to think about the needs assessment she had recently conducted among assembly workers. The data supported her training proposal, yet her findings were not designed to demonstrate whether training was a better investment than hiring new employees. Nancy wondered if she should consider collecting information to support her point of view or leave that decision for the manufacturing management staff. The memo indicated she was to have approximately twenty minutes to present her plan, with an additional hour for questions and answers. Nancy did not mind presenting her information but wondered exactly what her presentation goals should be. She felt uncomfortable about attempting to persuade management to train versus replace workers although she strongly believed that training was a better solution. She also was nervous about the "grilling" questions she could expect from at least two members of the staff. Nancy was apprehensive as she began to prepare her material. What information should she present? Was something missing? How could she plan to respond to tough questions and challenges?

INTRODUCTION

Nancy is facing a typical organizational situation requiring presentation skills. She must convince management of her training plan and, in so doing, will influence what happens to the employment future of several assembly workers. She wants to do a good job not only for the assembly workers but also for her reputation with the manufacturing staff. Nancy is experiencing what most of us can expect in our work lives. We will be asked to make presentations about our work and we will be challenged by those who may disagree with the position we represent. The decision at hand and our professional reputation will be affected by the competencies we bring to these situations.

Think about some of your experiences with presentations? What went through your mind as you began to prepare? Do you believe your current skills are adequately developed for most organizational situations? The chances are that most of us have concerns about our organizational presentation capabilities. We realize that unlike the somewhat structured evaluation of our abilities during school, at work we will continually have to demonstrate our abilities by explaining and supporting our positions during both formal and informal presentations.

Presenting information, supporting positions, or asking for resources are frequent subjects of organizational presentations. In Chapter 9 we talked about important skills for problem solving and decision making. Presentation skills are an extension of these capabilities. We solve a problem and make a decision. The decision must be announced to others. Management must be convinced of our solution. We may need to persuade others to support us with money and people. In fact, it is fair to say that presentations are a natural consequence of problem solving and decision making.

This chapter will describe important characteristics of organizational presentations and relate presentations to problem solving and decision making. Types of organizational presentations will be discussed, as will ethical and credibility issues. We will build presentational competencies through an understanding of personal credibility, audience and context analysis, preparation of material, coping with anxiety, presenting as an individual or as part of a team, and handling audience participation. Specifically, knowledge competencies will be developed through examining a variety of types of organizational presentations and considering basic formats for presentations. Sensitivity will be encouraged by considering ethical and credibility issues, describing audience concerns, and understanding coping with anxiety. Skills are practiced through case analysis and activities. Value development is encouraged through an understanding of the importance of ethical and credible individual behaviors during presentations and by relating effective presentations to overall organizational effectiveness.

PRESENTATIONS IN ORGANIZATIONS

Most jobs today, and more in the future, will require employees to give presentations. We are asked to describe to management the status of a project. We train other organizational members on the use of equipment or a process. We report conclusions from our quality circle meeting. Organizations in our information society depend more than ever before on individuals transferring information through **presentational speaking.**

Blue-collar workers and executives alike make presentations as part of their regular job responsibilities. Presentations are used in organizations to train, inform, critique plans of action, and persuade others to support

Presentational speaking— speaking in organizations designed to educate, inform, or persuade.

decisions. Our ability to present material effectively will contribute to our organizational credibility and influence the progress of our career.

Surveys of top management in major organizations consistently suggest that employees have deficiencies in presentation skills. Companies annually spend thousands of dollars developing oral competencies. Fully competent organizational members face the reality that they will be asked to give speeches and others will evaluate their overall effectiveness and the quality of their efforts.

Many people dread presentations. Highly apprehensive individuals will avoid job responsibilities requiring talking before groups, and when that happens both the individual and the organization lose. Excellent organizations need contributions from all members. When fear blocks an individual from contributing, the individual loses an ability to influence decisions and the organization loses a valuable resource.

Once we become aware of the likelihood and importance of making presentations in organizations, we start thinking about how to develop our own competencies. We ask questions about what to expect in professional settings and how to evaluate our current skills. We will begin to answer some of these questions by discussing general characteristics of business presentations.

Frank Dance (1987) has suggested that presentational speaking in organizations can be described in general categories: how the topic is selected, orientation of topic, time constraints, audience composition, expectation of audience participation, focus of responsibility for activity, expected degree of speaker expertise and preparation, decentering, degree of perceived spontaneity, use of audiovisual aids, and question and answer period. Generally speaking business presentations occur on the business site with a topic chosen to fit a particular problem or issue. Topics are specific and speakers are expected to adhere to announced agendas. Presenters are expected to respect time constraints while effectively covering important and often complex details. Unlike many public speaking settings, the audience is usually known to the speaker and may comprise peers, subordinates, and managers. In other words, the speaker will probably be involved in a continuing working relationship with members of the audience. Furthermore, most audience members will attend presentations as part of their job requirements.

Organizational presentations are characterized by a high degree of audience involvement. The presenter is frequently interrupted with questions and at times challenged on positions or technical information. Both the audience and the presenter accept responsibility for information exchange. Most effective organizational presenters are skilled at both clear and concise presentation of information and the handling of audience interactions.

The audience holds the presenter responsible for preparation and topic expertise. In fact, the overall organizational credibility of an individual can be adversely affected if he or she does not adequately prepare or presents information not credible to the audience. Dance (1987) relates audience expectations to the concept of "decentering," or "the degree to which the speaker/presenter is expected to make a serious effort to take the conceptual point of view of the audience members. In public speaking, the speaker's efforts at decentering are often subtle and understated, while in presentational speaking, the audience members expect the presenter to demonstrate an effort to address their specific points of view and needs overtly."

Organizational presentations are usually less spontaneous than presentations designed for public settings. More detail intensive, organizational presentations frequently use audiovisual supporting materials and audience handouts. Those skilled in business presentations become familiar and comfortable with a variety of technologies important for enhancing understanding and retention of information. Overhead projectors, video playback machines, tape equipment, computers, teleconferencing equipment, and other devices are all used for business presentations.

Finally, most organizational presenters must respond to questions and answers during and following presentations. The ability to respond to questions influences the credibility of the information transmitted and may contribute as much as the formal presentation to overall effectiveness. As Nancy Winslow begins to prepare for her presentation to the manufacturing staff she will consider what information they currently have about the skill level of assembly workers. She will prepare visuals to detail her budget. She is considering gathering data to compare training costs to the costs of hiring new, more skillful employees. Additionally, she is thinking about how she can answer managers who do not believe that training skill-deficient employees will meet the organization's needs.

Nancy currently works with most of the managers to whom she will make the presentation. She knows that her credibility will be on the line because she is advocating a position that at least two powerful members of the group oppose. How would you advise Nancy to prepare? Should she attempt to persuade the group to her position or simply make them aware of all of their options? What responsibility does she have to the assembly workers? What responsibility does she have to herself? The next several sections of our chapter will describe the types of presentation options Nancy has, discuss ethical and credibility issues she should consider, and make specific recommendations for increasing her effectiveness.

TYPES OF ORGANIZATIONAL PRESENTATIONS

Organizational presentations can be divided into three broad types: educational, informational, and persuasive. Educational presentations literally teach others information relevant to the organization. Informational presentations transmit knowledge from one organizational member or unit to another, and persuasive presentations are aimed at helping the organization solve problems or make decisions. Many presentations will be combinations of all three, requiring competent organizational presenters to develop skills in educating, informing, and persuading.

Educational Presentations

Educational presentations literally teach organizational members their jobs. Groups of people are trained in new processes, interpersonal relations, communication skills, or new technologies. Presentations are designed to help others utilize the information the presenter has learned and is responsible for transmitting to others. Giving instructions is perhaps the most common form of an educational presentation. In either a group or individual setting, the presenter is responsible for organizing information clearly and concisely to enable others to meet the expectations of an assignment or task. Giving instructions may be the most frequent of all educational presentations. When given effectively, instructions can contribute to the overall productivity of the organization. Instructions that fail to convey effective information cost organizations money in mistakes, poor-quality decisions, frustration of employees, and a variety of other, less obvious ways.

Responsibility for giving instructions is usually assigned to supervisors or those considered technically competent in an issue or task area. Unfortunately, the expertise an individual has is often the reason the "expert" does a poor job of educating others. Many people who are technically competent give accurate but ineffective instructions because they know their material thoroughly but not their audience. They speed through the information at a rate few can comprehend. They end their presentations by asking if they were understood, are pleased when everyone nods yes, and are surprised when people cannot complete the assignment or mistakes occur. A better understanding of the group to whom they were giving instructions would help explain their failures. Most people in organizations, and elsewhere, who receive instructions want to appear competent to their "teacher." When material is presented in a fashion that makes understanding difficult, a frequent tendency is to fake understanding with the intention of figuring out the situation later with peers or in other ways. The trainees respond that they understand when they don't and make mistakes they do not intend as a result of multiple misunderstandings. Effective organizational presenters learn that although accuracy is necessary for giving instructions, it is insufficient for effective communication of information. Giving instructions takes a thorough understanding of receivers, their needs and levels of comprehension.

Educational presentations also include technical training, basic skills training, interpersonal development and management training, and introductions of new concepts or technologies. These presentations are typically several hours in length and include diverse types of audience participation. Educational presentations that train or introduce new concepts require competency in holding people's attention over a period of time while providing material in enough detail to generate understanding. Educational presentations are specific career responsibilities in a variety of jobs (see Chapter 11 for a more complete description) and temporary responsibilities of those with expertise in a particular area. As your educational experiences in your school will almost certainly confirm, some presenters are better than others in generating understanding. Think about a time when you were part of an effective training program. What did your instructor do well? How might you use your observations to build your skills? Now think of a time when you were not pleased with the results of your training. What made the difference? Can your observations help you understand what to avoid?

Informational Presentations

Information is the life blood of organizations. Problems surface through information exchanges and problem solving occurs as individuals and organizations seek to discover information alternatives on which to base decisions. In Chapter 9 we spent considerable time discussing the importance of relevant, sufficient, and plausible information for problem solving and decision making. Now we will describe the role that informational presentations play in generating that information.

Informational presentations occur in a variety of organizational settings. Managers brief their subordinates on organizational policy. Individual contributors brief management on the status of a work project. A project team may review for management staff the technical problems associated with product design. Although similar to educational presentations, informational presentations are focused on providing the most current information available as opposed to teaching the audience new information. Unlike educational presentations, which frequently assume the audience has minimal familiarity with the topic, most informational presentations assume a reasonable degree of subject familiarity by the audience. In fact, many organizational presentations that are primarily of an informational nature will begin from the point of the last information exchange as opposed to the beginning of the project or issue. A common example of this type of informational presentation is the checkpoint meeting, in which an individual or team will report on the status of a project based on progress from the last checkpoint. Although introductions in these presentations frequently summarize the project, little attention is paid to details previously communicated.

Management teams request informational presentations to solve problems and make decisions. Nancy Winslow is asked to bring information to the manufacturing management staff of her organization. They need to make important decisions about assembly-line workers. She is considering expanding their request to attempt to persuade them to her point of view,

Informational presentations—presentations focused on providing the most current information available. Common examples are management briefings, checkpoint meetings, and technical reports.

yet her basic assignment is to inform them with relevant, sufficient, and plausible information.

Persuasive Presentations

If Nancy Winslow decides to attempt to influence the decision of the manufacturing staff, she will be engaged in persuasive communication. She will seek to influence the attitudes and beliefs of others by the arguments she makes. She will attempt to get manufacturing managers to interpret her data as she does and support her recommended training plan. Organizational members frequently are requested to make recommendations. In a very basic sense, recommending a course of action is a persuasive process.

Persuasive presentations are made to request resources, gain approval of an idea, sell a product or process, convince others to make changes, gain support for a course of action, and critique the efforts of others. Persuasive presentations are focused on getting an audience to adopt the point of view of the presenter based on relevant, plausible, and sufficient arguments. These presentations guide the audience to the conclusions the presenter favors. They ask for support, ask for business, ask for change, and make a variety of other requests.

Persuasive presentations in organizations are usually task related and contain more factual support than is common in other settings. Essentially, persuasive presentations are asking for a decision from the audience that supports the intentions of the presenter. Effective presenters realize that for a persuasive presentation to be successful they must not only understand what information their audience is likely to have on the topic but also consider relevant attitudes and issues. Nancy Winslow, for example, is aware that two powerful managers generally oppose training and prefer to replace deficient workers. This awareness will drive her strategies if she decides to try to persuade the manufacturing staff. If that opposition were not present, her presentation might be organized very differently. Given her knowledge of the manufacturing managers, what advice would you give Nancy? Can she afford to ignore these two men? Should she state her opinion but make no real effort to change their minds? What would you do if you were Nancy?

There are ethical implications in Nancy's concerns. She is concerned about the assembly workers. She can choose information for her presentation that primarily supports her training request or she could let the managers develop their own data on replacement costs. She has a number of other options based on her evaluation of what is right and wrong in this context. Regardless of what she chooses, Nancy is engaged in making decisions that will affect her credibility with the manufacturing management staff. The next section of our text will discuss how ethics and credibility relate to presentational speaking in organizations.

Persuasive presentations—presentations that attempt to influence the problem solving or decision making of the organization. Common examples are sales presentations, action recommendations, and resource requests.

ETHICS AND CREDIBILITY

Whether we are teaching, informing, persuading, or any combination of the three, we are making choices about ethical behaviors that affect our overall credibility. The past several years have seen an increased awareness of the importance of ethical behaviors for organizational effectiveness. And nowhere is the need for ethical behaviors more apparent than in the information organizations use for problem solving and decision making. As we have previously discussed, it is impossible to make the best decision when information has been withheld or distorted.

The question of what is right or wrong in a given context is a difficult one. Nancy Winslow is struggling with whether she should attempt to influence the decision of the manufacturing staff. She holds a strong opinion, but her decision also includes concerns about who has the right to make the decision and what her role should be.

William Howell and Ernest Bormann (1988) have suggested six general guidelines for ethical behavior during presentations:

1. *The presentation should be factually accurate and representative of conditions. It should contain no significant omissions or distortions as to facts. In commonsense language it should be truthful.*
2. *The intent of the presenter should be revealed to the audience.*
3. *Pseudo-logic, the use of logical forms and language to camouflage unsound material, is to be avoided.*
4. *The presenters should not rely on arousing intense emotions to facilitate persuasion.*
5. *Presenters should accept full responsibility for the changes they are attempting to bring about.*
6. *Presenters should be open; that is, all relevant points of view should be welcomed and discussed fairly in an atmosphere of free inquiry.*

Put simply, ethical communication for presentational speaking includes being truthful, informed, concerned with the audience, prepared, and understandable. Chapter 12 will be devoted exclusively to the important topic of organizational ethics and values.

Closely related to ethical behaviors is the concept of **credibility,** or the assessment of the overall reputation and competence of an individual. When applied to presentational speaking, credibility is the quality of persuasiveness that is based on the audience's perception of the character and competence of the speaker. Put another way, the credibility of the speaker is based on the audience's subjective and objective assessments of his or her integrity and capabilities. Indeed, Aristotle some 2300 years ago said that confidence in the character of the speaker was related to whether the speaker exhibited good sense, good moral character, and good will. Think for a moment about speakers you believe to be high in credibility. How do they behave? Now identify speakers you believe lack credibility. Compare them to your highly credible list. What makes the difference?

Credibility—quality of persuasiveness that is based on the audience's perception of the character and competence of the speaker.

Most of us want to be credible to others. Certainly if we expect professional success we will need to have others evaluate us as competent and worthy of trust and influence. But how is credibility formed? What can we do to enhance our personal reputation? Simply put, credibility is formed from our past interactions and how those interactions are described to others and then is confirmed or refuted by our presentation.

Initial credibility—credibility based on reputation, position, department or organization, and other general perceptions of competencies.

We begin any presentation we make with what is described as **initial credibility.** Our initial credibility is based on our past reputation, our job, the department or organization we represent, and any other general perceptions of our competencies. When we are new to an organization we have little initial credibility. We have to establish ourselves. If we have performed effectively, our past accomplishments contribute to the receptivity of our audience. If we have performed poorly, we may have to overcome negative attitudes based on past circumstances. Part of our preparation for presentation will include an assessment of how our intended audience will receive us.

Derived credibility—credibility based on the actual presentation; related to preparation, verbal, and nonverbal behaviors.

Our **derived credibility** comes from the actual presentation we make. The presentation reveals our level of thinking and preparation, and our delivery and nonverbal behaviors affect our credibility to a particular audience. Generally speaking audiences assess credibility on vocal qualities such as loudness, pitch, articulation, quality, rate and rhythm, dialect, and style. Audiences also evaluate eye contact and gestures.

Terminal credibility—credibility based on the evaluation of the presentation when the merits of the ideas are tested over time.

The credibility process continues beyond the actual presentation. Our **terminal credibility** is established as people evaluate the merits of our ideas over time. In other words, terminal credibility is an evaluation of our competencies after people have an opportunity to test the relevancy, sufficiency, and plausibility of our instructions, information, or recommendations. Terminal credibility is especially important in organizations. As we said earlier, most presentations in organizations are given to people with whom we have an ongoing relationship. If our terminal credibility is high, if our ideas stand the test of time, the chances are our initial credibility will increase for our next presentation. We will have more influence because we have established a track record of success.

How do we establish that successful record? The next section of the chapter helps develop our competencies by describing ways we can increase our credibility by understanding audience and context analysis. Additionally, we will discuss preparation of material, coping with anxiety, presenting as an individual or as part of a team, and handling audience participation. At the completion of the chapter, including the Workshop, you should be able to determine what you need to do next to establish your own presentational competencies.

INCREASING PRESENTATION EFFECTIVENESS

Thus far we have discussed the importance of presentational speaking in organizations and described a variety of types of common organizational presentations. We have considered important ethical and credibility issues.

Now we will attempt to identify ways in which individual competencies can be developed for presentational speaking.

Increasing Credibility

Although credibility evaluations rest with audiences, we can enhance the likelihood of a positive rating if we consciously think about how to describe ourselves, our intentions, and our concerns. We can begin by considering what our initial credibility is likely to be with a particular group. What do they know about our background? How much have we interacted before? What were the results of previous exchanges? If our task competence or subject expertise is unknown to our audience, we may want to begin by briefly describing our training or experience. If our expertise is known but our position controversial, we may want to cite research and stress the competence of our sources. Additionally, we can avoid needlessly calling attention to our inadequacies.

In many organizational settings, questions and challenges to presenters are common and appropriate for decision making. We can usually increase our credibility by stressing our fairness, demonstrating that we have examined various alternatives, not just the ones we are recommending. We can stress our concern for enduring values such as quality, creativity, or team play. We can stress our similarity with our audience in terms of beliefs, attitudes, values, and goals. We can point to our long-term consistency and demonstrate our concern for others through nondefensive behaviors during questioning and challenges. In general, we can increase our credibility by demonstrating that we support the welfare of the group or organization, not just our own concerns. Finally, we are more likely to be perceived as credible if we present a positive orientation to the situation, are assertive, and are generally enthusiastic.

Audience and Context Analysis

When thinking about establishing our personal credibility, we began to think specifically about our audience and the context or circumstances of our presentation. Earlier we described effective communication as resulting from meanings being understood among people as accurately as possible. This base of interpersonal communication obviously remains true for the presentation. How can we ensure that the results of our problem solving or work accomplishments are best represented to those who have a need to know? Who are our potential audiences and what do we want them to do? Effective presentations reflect good decisions about our potential receivers.

At times, our audience will be a management team who will grant final authority or resources to implement the proposed solution. They must be convinced by our presentation of what we expect to achieve by our solution or a particular course of action. At other times, we will be announcing decisions to people who are affected by them. In this case, the decision implementation and how it affects the receiver may be more important than any explanation of our decision process.

John Baird (1982) has suggested four important questions for **audience analysis.**

Audience analysis—assessment of what receivers are interested in, what they know, what their attitudes and values are, what they are wanted to know, what the speaker's probable credibility is, and what format will be most effective.

1. *What are they interested in?*
2. *What do they already know?*
3. *What are their attitudes?*
4. *What are their values?*

Additionally, it is necessary to consider these questions:

5. *What do we want them to do?*
6. *How much credibility do we have from their viewpoint?*
7. *What presentation format is likely to be most effective?*

Preparation of Material

After questions about the potential audience have been satisfactorily answered, we can proceed to the selection of material for presentation. Selection of material depends on audience analysis and the assignment at hand.

We select material with relevancy, sufficiency, and plausibility criteria. These criteria must be met for us individually before we can make projections about how they can be met for our expected audiences. Once material has been selected we begin the organizing process.

Material can be organized in a variety of formats. A few of the common formats are as follows: chronological, question/answer, topical, problem/ solution, solution/problem, and recency/primacy. Table 10.1 defines and gives examples of these patterns.

Once decisions are made about the material to be included and the organizational sequence, introductions and conclusions should be developed. Introductions attract audience attention, establish credibility for the presenter or presenters, and clarify the purpose of the presentation. As with all other presentational decisions, introductions are most effective when careful consideration is given to the needs and interests of the audience. It is very difficult to capture attention if the introduction to a presentation is poorly planned.

Baird (1982) suggests a number of devices that are effective for introductions:

A famous, thought-provoking quotation. . . . An interesting story or illustration, perhaps giving an example of the problem to be discussed. . . . A description of important events which have occurred recently. . . . A series of rhetorical questions which arouse listeners' curiosity, such as: 'What's the most dangerous situation to be found right now? What's the greatest source of dissatisfaction among all employees? We're going to answer those and other important questions during this speech.'. . . . A startling statement—one

TABLE 10.1
Formats for Organizing Presentations

Patterns	Definition	Example
Chronological	Arranges events, group process, implementation plans in a sequence one after another, a first-to-last time sequence	"First, the group defined the problem as _____, next we evaluated each solution, and finally we are recommending this decision."
Question/answer	Proposes questions considered by the group or potentially in the minds of the audience and then provides answers	"As a group we first considered how to understand the problem of absenteeism. We wanted to know what caused this problem in other companies. We found out that . . ."
Topical	Arranges topics by logical groupings or subgroupings	"We studied the problem of absenteeism in each of three areas: what other companies are experiencing, how the manufacturing function compares to the rest of our company, and what are typical causes of work force absenteeism. We will now report our findings in each of these areas."
Problem/solution	Defines and describes the problem, followed by solution proposal	"We have come to believe that the problem of absenteeism can be understood as _____ . From this description of our problem we can provide the following possible solutions."
Solution/problem	Describes a solution strategy and then details the problems the strategy will solve	"We are happy to announce that we believe the new training program will be in place by this fall. We expect this approach will favorably affect the problems we encountered."
Recency/primacy	Describes most recent events and details how those events were influenced by previous events, a reversal of historical chronological order	"This month our absenteeism rate is only 9 percent. We believe the decrease is a result of certain decisions all supervisors made even while still participating in the management task force. If we go back six months we can see. . . . ."

which shocks the audience through its dramatic force. . . . Humor, although it must be both appropriate and well done. . . . A simple statement of the topic, provided you know that it is of high interest to the audience.

Conclusions, particularly crucial to the success of presentations, summarize the key elements in the presentation and restate and call for needed action on the part of audience members. Effective conclusions leave the audience with a short and concrete summary of what the presenter has decided is most important to know. Conclusions are last impressions and influential in setting the tone for what happens next. Sometimes conclusions return to introductions to emphasize how the presentation has met the goals established then. At other times, the conclusion focuses on the needed action from the audience and solicits questions to gain more direct involvement.

Coping with Anxiety

Many people are apprehensive about presentational speaking. Giving a speech is the last thing they want to do. In fact, some students reading this text are dismayed to realize how many presentational speeches are required for most careers. We worry about being evaluated by others and wonder if we will ever get over the stress associated with speaking before people.

The fear of presentational speaking is real; literally thousands of individuals report that speaking before groups is among their greatest fears. However, as we have discussed, anything that blocks us from communicating limits both individual and organizational effectiveness. The following suggestions will not eliminate fear but are offered as coping strategies to deal with the concern for talking in front of groups of people.

1. *Fear is normal.* When we worry about our effectiveness we are exhibiting a healthy concern for our self-esteem. The issue is to manage the fear, concern, or apprehension and not treat it as abnormal behavior. You can't wait until it goes away to give your first presentational speech.

2. *Preparation is key for management of fear.* When we prepare for speaking we eliminate many of the ambiguities of the situation. We know our topic, we have analyzed our audience, we have selected material appropriate to both, and we have considered which formats for presentation are best. We may still worry about the actual delivery of the speech, but we gain confidence from our preparation.

3. *Practice is an essential fear management strategy.* Practice helps us "hear ourselves before others do." We can control our concerns by going over our presentations with the help of friends or peers. Their participation can help us prepare for tough questions and provide feedback important for improvement. We can see if our notes or materials work in the setting in which we will deliver the speech. Can our visual materials be seen? Do we know how to operate the equipment we will be using? Practice reduces uncertainty and usually increases effectiveness. Practice is so important, in fact, that one major electronics firm requires all managers to rehearse operating status reviews with their peers before making presentations to corporate evaluation teams. A major aerospace company has a practice room dedicated for any employee to reserve in preparation for a technical briefing or other type of presentation.

4. *A sense of humor helps.* Many of us overestimate the impact on our lives and careers of one presentation. We exaggerate our concerns by state-

ments such as "I'll be fired if this isn't good" or "I can never face my boss again if we don't get this order." In reality, although our presentations are important, they are only one of many measures of our organizational competencies. We need to be able to laugh at ourselves and put in perspective the real requirements of the situation. Chances are we are not expected to be eloquent, dynamic speakers. We are expected to be clear, concise, and knowledgeable.

5. *Physical exercise releases tension.* A moderate amount of physical exercise before a presentation can relax tense muscles and control physical symptoms of stage fright. Walking and climbing stairs are recommended as long as the amount of exercise is reasonable and does not fatigue to the point of reducing energy for the presentation.

6. *Training and experience help anxiety.* In most cases the more training we have in presentational speaking, the more relaxed and effective we will be. For some highly apprehensive individuals training can heighten anxiety, and for those people additional personalized assistance is desirable. For most of us, however, giving presentations and studying effective ones give us an experience base important in developing our competencies. If you are among those highly apprehensive individuals who find this strategy less than helpful, talk with your instructor about other options to help manage communication apprehension. The long-term positive impact on your career from learning to manage anxiety is well worth the investment of time and energy.

Preparation for Presenting

We have been talking about preparing material for presentations and coping with anxiety. In either case the word *preparation* is the key. Preparation generally increases effectiveness and helps us manage most presentational situations.

Personal preparation for presenting includes rehearsing the speech, working with visual aids, preparing notes, and timing the presentation. Additionally, it is a good idea to check specific details in the room scheduled for your presentation and to arrive early to confirm arrangements. Personal preparation also includes selecting clothing that is appropriate for the occasion and comfortable for the presenter. A rule commonly recommended is that you never wear new clothing or new shoes for a presentation. Anything that introduces newness or uncertainty should be reserved for less stressful situations.

Many organizational presentations are prepared and presented by teams or groups of individuals. Many of you may have worked on a group project for which certain team members did not adhere to their allotted presentation time, making life miserable for other presenters. Groups need to rehearse and time presentations just as much as individuals do. Additionally, team presentations are most effective when all team members have tightly coordinated information so that segments of the presentation are not unnecessarily repeated.

Handling Participation

We have previously discussed the frequency and importance of audience participation during most organizational presentations. We have talked about the necessity to respond to differing ideas and challenges. We have not yet described some basic ways to handle audience participation.

Effective presenters anticipate lines of questions they might get from their audience. They not only prepare the formal presentation but also practice answers to expected questions or challenges. Effective presenters learn to analyze questions and ask for necessary clarification before responding. If a group is relatively large, repeating a question so all can hear increases the perception that the speaker is interested in the audience and in answering the questions.

Effective presenters respond to all audience members and control domination attempts from one or two individuals. Effective presenters also ask the audience for ideas or critiques. At times skilled presenters have questions for their audience to increase ownership of a decision or position. Perhaps most important, effective presenters maintain supportive, non-defensive behaviors that encourage a sense of "we," or belonging with the audience. This sense of "we" is especially important in ongoing organizational relationships.

SUMMARY

Most jobs today, and more in the future, will require employees to give presentations. Blue-collar workers and executives alike make presentations designed to educate, inform, or persuade. Surveys of top management consistently suggest that employees are deficient in presentation skills, and fully competent organization members realize that speaking before groups is part of most job responsibilities. Organizational presentations usually occur on the business site, with topics focused on specific problems or issues. Most presentations are made to groups with whom the presenter has an ongoing working relationship, and both the presenter and the audience are responsible for information exchange. Organizational presentations are characterized by a high degree of interactivity between the presenter and an audience who generally has considerable familiarity with the subject. Organizational presentations can be divided into three broad types: educational, informational, and persuasive. Educational presentations literally teach others information relevant to the organization. Informational presentations transmit knowledge from one organizational member or unit to another, and persuasive presentations are aimed at helping the organization solve problems or make decisions. Ethical communication for presentational speaking includes being truthful, informed, concerned with the audience, prepared, and understandable. Closely associated with ethical behaviors is the concept of speaker credibility, or the audience's perception of the character and competence of the speaker. Initial credibility is based on our past reputation, our job, the department or organization we represent, and any other general perceptions of our competencies. Derived credibility comes from the actual presentation, which reveals our level of preparation and critical thinking as well as our delivery and nonverbal behaviors. Terminal credibility is established as people evaluate the merits of a speaker's ideas over time. Credibility can be enhanced by consideration of how best to describe ourselves and our positions to an audience. Audience and context analysis helps us make decisions about establishing credibility as well as the selection of material and actual organization of the presentation. Preparation of material includes the selection of content and organizational sequences based on the goals of the presentation. Anxiety and apprehension can be managed by remembering that fear is normal, by preparation and practice, by development of a sense of humor, through physical exercise, and with training and experience. Personal preparation for presenting includes rehearsing the speech, working with visual aids, preparing notes, and timing the presentation. Group presentations have the same requirements, with additional emphasis on group content and timing coordination. Effective presenters encourage audience participation with supportive, nondefensive behaviors. Questions are answered honestly and directly, with emphasis on establishing a sense of belonging with the audience.

WORKSHOP

1. Identifying your presentational strengths and weaknesses is a good way to improve your presentational abilities. List five presentational strengths you currently practice. List five presentational weaknesses. In small groups discuss what you can do to improve the weaknesses. Describe how your strengths were developed and how they might be utilized to work on weaknesses.

2. Divide the class into groups of five members each. Ask each group to develop a list of three national figures, all of whom the group can support as sincere and believable. Each group should be prepared to describe why they selected these individuals. Compare lists and discuss reasons for selection.

3. Individually or in small groups, identify individuals who might be credible for each of the following subjects: health, fashion, entertain-

ment, politics, music, football, social change, and business. Discuss why they are credible to you.

4. Identify an upcoming presentation in your community designed to educate, inform, or persuade. Attend the presentation and utilize the evaluation form that follows. Report your observations to your class.

Presentational Speech Evaluation Form

CONTENT

		DELIVERY
Introduction	_____ Attention	Vocal Behaviors
	_____ Audience rapport	_____ Pitch
	_____ Clarity	_____ Speech speed
	_____ Length	_____ Pronunciation
Body	_____ Organization	Nonverbal Behaviors
	_____ Logic	_____ Appearance
	_____ Language use	_____ Posture
	jargon	_____ Gestures
	technical terms	_____ Eye contact
	_____ Attention	Use of Materials/Visuals
	_____ Audience rapport	_____ Notes
	_____ Clarity	_____ Handouts
	_____ Length	_____ Audio/visual aids
Conclusion	_____ Summary	
	_____ Clarity	
	_____ Sense of completion	
	_____ Length	
Audience participation	_____ Questions	
	_____ Clarity	
	_____ Tone	
	_____ Satisfaction	
	_____ Content	

For each of the areas for evaluation use the following scale: 1 = very poor; 2, 3, 4 = needs improvement; 5 = average; 6, 7, 8 = generally effective; 9, 10 = excellent.

SUMMARY OF COMPETENCY COMPONENTS
KNOWLEDGE, SENSITIVITY, SKILLS, VALUES

KNOWLEDGE

Presentation skills are described as an extension of problem solving and decision making.

Organizational presentation types are educational, informational, and persuasive.

Most jobs require presentational competencies.

Types of credibility include initial, derived, and terminal.

SENSITIVITY

Ethics and credibility are important for presentational effectiveness.

Fear is a normal human emotion related to presentational situations.

Effective presenters are concerned with audience reactions.

SKILLS

Analysis skills are developed through exercises and self-analysis activities.

Skills are practiced through exercises.

VALUES

Presentational speaking is important for organizational effectiveness.

Credibility is necessary for presenter effectiveness.

Ethical presentation behaviors are necessary for organizational effectiveness.

REFERENCES AND SUGGESTED READINGS

Baird, J. E., Jr. 1977. *The dynamics of organizational communication*. New York: Harper & Row.

Baird, J. E., Jr. 1981. *Speaking for results: Communication by objectives*. New York: Harper & Row.

Baird, J. E., Jr. 1982. *Positive personnel practices: Quality circles leader's manual*. Prospect Heights, IL: Waveland Press.

Dance, F. E. X. 1987. What do you mean presentational speaking? *Management Communication Quarterly* 1(2): 260–71.

DeVito, J. A. 1984. *The elements of public speaking*. 2d ed. New York: Harper & Row.

Howell, W. S., and E. G. Bormann. 1988. *The process of presentational speaking*. 2d ed. New York: Harper & Row.

Kelly, L., L. Lederman, and G. Phillips. 1989. *Communicating in the workplace: A guide to business and professional speaking*. New York: Harper & Row.

CHAPTER

Applications of Organizational Communication

Developing competencies through . . .

KNOWLEDGE

Describing influences for career decisions

Identifying career option areas and educational preparation for organizational communication

Discussing responsibilities of communication professionals

SENSITIVITY

Developing awareness of personal influences for career decisions

Understanding the occupational exchange

SKILLS

Assessing individual career development needs

Practicing analysis capabilities in the role of a communication professional

VALUES

Relating personal and organizational values to the occupational exchange

Understanding change as an important organizational process

Describing organizational change as an important responsibility of the communication professional

The "Where Do We Go From Here?" Case

As John walked toward the student union to join his friends, Jill and George, he thought about his round of upcoming interviews. Jill, George, and John were all scheduled for several of the same companies and he knew they were concerned as well. Being almost ready to graduate had some advantages, but this job search thing was tough. Not only was John trying to determine what were good companies and how to sell himself to them, but also he was thinking about what parts of the country he would like and how it was going to feel to leave his friends. He hadn't realized it was going to be that difficult. Well, at least he wasn't alone; Jill and George were having some of the same problems, too.

As Jill waited for John and George, she began to rehearse mentally questions and answers for her upcoming interviews. Six companies scheduled in the next two days—that will put her skills to the test. Jill is wondering if John and George are right about taking the offer with the best salary. What else should she be considering and what about cost of living in various parts of the country? The companies she will talk with in the next two days are in four different states several hundred miles apart. What other considerations should she make?

John and George enter the union at the same time and spot Jill.

GEORGE: Sorry I'm late, I went by the library to check the annual report of Randel Corporation. John was right that their expansion has been slowing for the last two years. I will probably not consider them as seriously as I thought.

JILL: George, are you sure that is an appropriate approach? You have really liked the type of job that Randel is describing; growth certainly isn't everything. What do you think, John?

JOHN: I have been thinking that we should all take the best salary offer, but I am beginning to have second thoughts. How much consideration should we give to where we want to live and the type of products and services the company produces? I have interviews scheduled with a defense contractor, computer manufacturer, retail chain, and that government job. They all need training specialists and I think I qualify for what they want, but they do very different things.

JILL: I was just sitting here thinking about what factors are most important to me. I expected to be so excited when this time came. I can hardly believe I am fearful of making the right choice.

INTRODUCTION

John, Jill, and George are experiencing the concerns of many of us when we begin to make important decisions about the beginning of our careers. What company would be best? What factors deserve the most weight in our decision? Which choice will work best in the long term? We almost need a crystal ball to help us find answers.

But our concerns really begin much earlier than during the job search process. John, Jill, and George chose organizational communication as their major. As you would expect, they are thinking about job choices that will use the skills they have developed during their four years in the communication program. In a real sense, their career choices began when they selected their majors and the abilities they wanted to develop with their education. The jobs they now take will reflect that overall direction and those decisions.

This chapter is designed to increase awareness of communication-related career choices. We will discuss how to begin planning a career, what general career choices are available to those studying organizational communication, what skills are important, and what types of education are required. We will also present a self-analysis process for career planning. Finally, the chapter addresses the role of the communication professional in organizational change. The change-agent role is described as a professional responsibility of most of the career options we will be discussing.

This chapter is designed to increase *knowledge* through the presentation of career options for organizational communication, through the identification of individual and organizational factors influencing careers, by describing basic requirements for an organizational change agent, and by identifying a change process and models for client and change-agent interaction. *Sensitivity* is developed through self-analysis of personal experiences influential in career choices, through identification of primary responsibilities for major career options, and by understanding the assumptions underlying selection of one change model over another. Analysis *skills* are practiced with the self-analysis process through the selection of intervention models, and by gathering data with informational interviews. *Values* are presented as important in career planning, integral to the individual and organizational relationship, and central to all professional organizational change activities. Finally, *knowlededge, sensitivity, skills,* and *values* are applied to our interpretation of organizational problems requiring the expertise of communication professionals.

CHOOSING A COMMUNICATION CAREER

In one sense, all careers are communication careers. The majority of our organizational time is spent communicating, whether we select communication or a seemingly unrelated field as our primary area of emphasis.

As we have proposed throughout this book, organizational communication competencies are important for all of us, regardless of career choices. Although this chapter focuses specifically on communication careers, the factors important for selecting a communication career also are applicable to other choices and are basic for understanding both individual and organizational needs.

Careers are the sum total of our job experiences over time. Careers involve decisions about personal interests, aptitudes, educational preparation, and the match of our individual competencies to the needs of particular organizations. Career planning should begin while pursuing our education but continues throughout our work life and even into retirement. We usually think of career planning as it relates to paid employment, but in reality career planning is the process by which we plan to use our competencies as they relate to all types of work environments. As such, careers are best understood as an integral part of our total lives.

How, then, should we begin to plan our careers? Figure 11.1 presents key factors in what we will call the **occupational exchange** between individuals and organizations.

Occupational exchange— when individual competencies match organizational competencies and the individual becomes a working member of the organization.

As you can see from Figure 11.1, we have used our competency framework—knowledge, sensitivity, skills, and values—to describe individual competencies as they interact with organizational competencies in an oc-

---

FIGURE 11.1
Factors In Occupational Exchange

Individual Competencies	*Organizational Competencies*
Knowledge	Knowledge
Occupational information	Functional requirements
General knowledge	General knowledge
Sensitivity	Sensitivity
Expectations of organizations	Expectations of individuals
Orientations to work life	Orientations to work and
(family, role models,	workers
experiences)	Market/environmental
Self-awareness	awareness
Skills	Skills
Technical qualifications	Technical requirements
General communication abilities	General communication abilities
(ability to translate skills to	(ability to define needed
organization)	requirements for workers)
Values	Values
Occupational interests	Product/service interests
Socioeconomic goals	Socioeconomic goals
Achievement aspirations	Achievement aspirations

cupational exchange. Put simply, an occupational exchange occurs when individual competencies match organizational competencies and the individual becomes a working member of the organization. Figure 11.1 describes what individuals bring to the employment process and what organizations seek when offering employment. The occupational exchange is important for understanding how individuals select jobs and how organizations select individuals for employment. Awareness of these factors is necessary for effective career planning.

Knowledge for the Occupational Exchange

Individuals base job and career choices on occupational information. They base jobs and career options on what they know is available and usually with incomplete understanding of all that is possible. We gather occupational information from past experiences, the people around us, exposure during our education, media, and in a variety of less systematic ways. Sometimes we are aware of skill and educational requirements associated with particular occupations, while at other times we have only a vague understanding of what competencies are required in a given profession. Individuals also have general knowledge that applies to almost all occupations. The depth and breadth of this general knowledge contributes to occupational flexibility, or the ability to fit oneself for a variety of job positions. General knowledge includes communication competencies, organizing abilities, time-management skills, critical-thinking abilities, and decision-making capabilities.

Organizations develop knowledge about the functional requirements they need in specific occupational categories. A human resource development position may carry similar responsibilities from organization to organization; however, a specific human resource development position will have job-specific requirements. A human resource position in one organization might require extensive training experience, whereas a similar position in another company would not include the training responsibility. In addition, organizations require the general knowledge base that we previously described for individuals. Indeed, one of the difficulties for most organizations during inteviews is assessing the somewhat subjective, yet critically important, areas of general knowledge exhibited by job applicants. Research on who is promoted into top management in U.S. corporations suggests that general knowledge in communication and decision making may be more important for long-term advancement than most technical skills.

Sensitivity for the Occupational Exchange

Individuals bring a variety of expectations to the job search process. Salary, position responsibilities, and advancement opportunities are only a few of the expectations individuals seek to clarify in interviews. Individuals also have expectations about how employees should be treated and the type of work environment that is personally desirable. We have been oriented to work by our family experiences, by those who have acted as role models for us, and by our previous work experiences. Research indicates that we are likely to be influenced in occupational choices by direct contact with individuals in specific occupations and advice from individuals personally close to us. It is not unusual, therefore, to find similar occupational choices—such as law, medicine, and education—made by several members of one family. However, these orientations can be limiting. A woman, for example, who is surrounded by those who believe her best occupational choice is teaching may or may not consider other possible alternatives suitable for her abilities. That is not to say the teaching profession would be inappropriate, but to the extent it is a stereotypical expectation (a choice appropriate for women), her potential may be limited. The same is true for men. Occupational expectations of parents and influential role models can both encourage and restrict the range of possibilities considered when making educational and career choices.

Self-awareness also is an important sensitivity for career choices. What types of competencies do we bring to an employment situation? What competencies remain in need of development? What are our preferences regarding work? How do our communication, conflict, and leadership preferences influence career choices and the jobs in which we will be comfortable and productive? How well do we know ourselves and our needs?

Organizations are sensitive to finding employees who meet their expectations. Organizations develop work norms and behavior expectations they believe contribute to productivity in their particular environments. Some organizations, for example, expect workers to put in numerous hours of overtime. In an interview, the answers a prospective employee gives to questions about work and time commitments may be pivotal to the organization's assessment of the prospect's future. Organizations also develop sensitivities to changing markets and environmental needs that require new skills and abilities from their work force. In today's labor market most organizations expect computer competencies from prospective employees; little more than a decade ago there was only marginal concern for computer skills.

Skills for the Occupational Exchange

Individuals bring a variety of technical qualifications to their job search. The technical qualifications an individual develops should support occupational choices because technical qualifications or the lack thereof limit choice. We know that without certain skills we cannot consider certain occupations. Only the rare individual will attempt to land a computer programming job without having technical preparation on computers. Unfortunately, far more individuals attempt to occupy essentially communication jobs without the training or background appropriate for these responsibilities. Because we have all been "communicating" for as long as we can remember, many take for granted the technical preparation necessary for excellence in communication jobs. Yet our technical preparation is fundamental to success in the job search and in the job itself.

Our ability to translate our knowledge, sensitivity, skills, and values to a prospective employer will in large measure determine the types of jobs we are offered. Few job interviews begin with an objective test of the skills and abilities of applicants. Most organizations rely on communication exchanges—interviews, résumés, letters of application—for initial if not final screening of potential employees.

Individuals bring their technical qualifications to the job search in hopes of matching those qualifications with the organization's technical requirements. Rarely, however, is there a perfect match. Organizations generally seek the best available match between an individual's technical background and the technical requirements of a particular job. Organizations also weigh the applicant's general knowledge in communication, decision making, critical thinking, time management, and leadership. They make judgments about the current skill level of the applicant and the amount of training time necessary for the applicant to become a productive employee. Just as the individual must be able to communicate adequately his or her abilities, organizations attempt to define for the applicant the needed requirements of the job and any additional relevant information. This match between abilities and requirements is fundamental for the occupational exchange to work successfully.

Values in the Occupational Exchange

As in all other aspects of our life, values are a central factor in career decisions. What is important to us and what we find desirable, interesting, and stimulating all relate to the values we hold. Our career interests are reflections of our value system. The socioeconomic goals we hope our employment will support are a product of a complex set of values that have developed throughout our life experiences. Even our achievement aspirations can be described as an extension of our personal value system. Understanding what is important to us should guide overall career choices as well as decisions about whether or not specific jobs meet our needs. One of the most common employment mistakes is the acceptance of a job because it represents a good financial offer, regardless of whether the job is of interest and supports other needs. A "good offer" in the fullest sense is an offer than helps us support our value system.

Organizations also have value systems. Earlier in the text we referred to the importance of organizational culture and values. Cultures help to define what is expected and valued within particular organizations. Products, services, resource allocations, and development interests all reflect the values of organizations. As do individuals, organizations have socioeconomic goals and overall achievement aspirations. For a successful occupational exchange, the individual's values and the organization's values need to be in harmony—if not in all respects, at least in those areas central to job performance.

An individual should begin career planning with the concept that jobs and ultimately careers are continual exchanges of individual knowledge, sensitivity, skills, and values with organizational knowledge, sensitivity, skills, and values. The success of these exchanges for both individuals and organizations begins with the ability to define and articulate competencies, a process fundamental for effective organizational communication.

Self-Analysis for Career Planning

For the remainder of the chapter to be more meaningful and practical, the following self-analysis activities for career planning should be completed. This self-analysis will give you personal information with which to evaluate the rest of the chapter.

The purpose of a self-analysis is to help you understand personal influences on career choices. to identify achievements that have been valuable to you, to define skills used in important achievements, and to make projections of the type of career and lifestyle you desire for the future. Your self-analysis is designed to guide decisions about competency development and to identify any limitations in occupational choices you may have inadvertently created for yourself. Figure 11.2 summarizes the self-analysis activity. A worksheet and examples of each of the activities are found on pages 386–392.

Influences on Career Choices

Identify by name those individuals who have been most influential in helping you form expectations about work, occupations, and achievements. What have these individuals told you about what is possible? How satisfied are they with their work? How would they profile the successful person? What types of occupations have they suggested you should pursue? What have they told you is a waste of time?

After you have identified important "work" messages from those around you, write a one-paragraph description of your ideal occupation. Include the responsibilities the occupation entails, the skills the occupation uses, and how individuals in this occupation will know if they are successful.

Next, compare your "perfect" occupation paragraph with your answers to questions about how key people have influenced your occupational choices. Can you see their influence in your "perfect" occupation? If so, how? If not, what other influences have contributed to your selection?

Identification of Achievement Skills and Values

The next portion of your self-analysis requires careful reflection. Identify four major achievements in your life. These achievements must have one important quality: They must be very personally important. Others may

---

FIGURE 11.2
Summary of Self-Analysis Activities for Career Planning

1. Identify specific individuals who have been influential in shaping your concept of work and occupational choice.
   What have they told you about possibilities?
   How satisfied are they with their work?
   How would they profile a successful person?
   What occupations have they suggested to you?
   What occupations do they not suggest for you?
2. Describe your ideal occupation in terms of responsibilities, skills, and measures of success.
3. Compare your "perfect occupation" to messages from those who have influenced you.
4. Define four important achievements with skills used for each achievement and values satisfied.
   Identify common skills used and values satisfied among the achievements.
   List ten skills and ten values that seem to be predictive for you of achievement and satisfaction.
5. Write a narrative describing your desired lifestyle for a five-year span following your formal education. How should this narrative influence your career choices?
6. Make ten statements about your current career planning.
   Identify ten questions you need answered for career planning.

---

have considered the achievements you identify as significant, but that is not the most important qualification. The achievements you choose should be of high personal value, regardless of external evaluation. In fact, it is common for an achievement in this category to be something of which few others are aware. These four achievements also must be achievements in which your personal efforts were primary contributions. Many people might say, for example, that they consider their family life to be an achievement, and of course it may be. However, for purposes of this activity, writing a poem, building a piece of furniture, conquering your fear of public speaking, or learning to use a computer are better examples of achievements for which you have had primary responsibility. Once the achievements have been identified, list the skills and abilities you used in these achievements and the values each achievement satisfied. (A partial skill and value list is provided in Figure 11.3.)

When you have listed important achievements, skills, and values, identify those skills and values that have contributed to more than one of your achievements. We are beginning to identify through this activity those skills and values that have been most important to you over time. Which additional skills should be on your "most important" list? Which additional values? Next, list ten skills and values you believe are most likely to con-

---

FIGURE 11.3
Partial Skills and Values List

Partial Skills List

mathematical	administrative	documentation
analytical	planning	speaking
creative	organizational	financial
managerial	writing	graphic
communication	artistic	team building
persuasive	athletic	motivational
listening	research	teaching
decision making	problem solving	delegation

Partial Values List

security	family happiness	power
geographical location	wisdom	expertness
justice	autonomy	love
humanitarianism	leadership	aesthetics
recognition	honesty	service
enjoyment	self-actualization	health
achievement	material wealth	knowledge
prestige	emotional well-being	religion
fame	social	creative

---

tribute to a sense of personal achievement. This list, if thoughtfully constructed, should be influential in career planning and occupational choice.

Describing a Desired Lifestyle

Next, write a one-page narrative describing all aspects of your most desired lifestyle for the five years immediately following completion of your education. Describe where you think you want to live, what leisure activities you envision, what family and social relationships you prefer, and how work relates to these choices.

Include in your narrative a desired level of income and any other important choices you want to consider. (We are not attempting to suggest that it is possible to define perfectly all of these issues; however, general themes usually can be discovered.) What do these preferences say about your choice of work? Should they be considerations in your career planning? What other influences are important?

Identifying Current Status of Career Planning

After completing all of the analysis activities, list ten statements you can make about the status of your current career planning. These statements should relate to choices you have already made, skills you want to use in your future occupation, and values you want to satisfy through work. (Don't forget to refer to the examples on page 389 if you need help.) Finally, develop ten questions you want answered as a result of your self-examination. What do you need to know about occupational choices? How can you find out? Who would be good information sources? Much of what we have discussed in the decision-making and problem-solving chapter should be used to help you examine your personal career planning needs.

CAREER CHOICES IN ORGANIZATIONAL COMMUNICATION

Figure 11.4 identifies eight major career option areas and job titles within each area for those planning careers in organizational communication. As we describe each of the eight areas in terms of job responsibilities and required skills, think about your self-analysis and what you will need to know to select a communication career.

Internal Communication

The **internal communication careers** that follow were collected by a committee for the International Communication Association (ICA) Organizational Communication Division (Petrie et al., 1975). The synthesis of these collections suggested that those working in internal communication have the following responsibilities:

> *Provides consultation, assistance, and guidance to management on matters relating to employee and management communication; coordinates employee communication programs and activities; coordinates publishing of regular employee media; advises, coordinates, and conducts attitudinal and other polls among employees; provides editorial and publishing services; produces, edits, and distributes special publications.*
>
> *Develops and maintains informational unit to serve the needs of senior management and the communication department.*
>
> *Develops, coordinates, and implements small group, face-to-face communication programs to facilitate team building, problem identification, and problem solving.*

Internal communication careers—work within an organization to assist management in employee and management communication, coordinate a variety of training activities, coordinate internal communication media, facilitate team building, and develop numerous other communication activities.

Internal communication specialists must have extensive backgrounds in interpersonal and organizational communication with an emphasis on human relations. These specialists are familiar with principles of instructional design, can evaluate the designs of others, can plan and implement their own programs, and have well-developed presentational skills. In addition to speaking skills, internal communication jobs require good listening skills and an ability to write clearly. They also may be required to understand technical print production for internal publication responsibilities. They must be able to analyze data and must be skilled in a variety of data-gathering techniques. Most internal communication specialists are

FIGURE 11.4
Career Options In Organizational Communication

Option Area	*Job Titles*
Internal communication	Human resource specialist
	Training and development specialist
	Personnel liaison
	Internal publications coordinator
	Internal communication specialist
	Organizational development specialist
	Internal consultant
External communications	Advertising specialist
	Public relations coordinator
	Industrial media producer/director
	Technical writer
	Telecommunications coordinator
	Editor
	Community affairs coordinator
Sales	Account representative
	Retail salesperson
	Marketing specialist
	Media salesperson
	Advertising salesperson
	Real estate, insurance, products, etc. salesperson
Human services	Fund-raiser
	Counselor
	Career development specialist
	Program specialist
Education	Teacher/professor
	Administrator
Research	Associate
	Business analyst
	Marketing research analyst
	Social science specialist
Management	Trainee
	Section/branch manager
	Store manager
	Regional manager
	Corporate staff
	Sales manager
	Personnel director
	Media manager
	Advertising manager
	Human resource development manager
	Corporate communications manager

Consultant (external to employing organization)	Organizational development specialist Human resource development specialist Trainer Analyst

required to have a basic understanding of statistics and the use of computers.

External Communications

The ICA report found the following responsibilities common among those with **external communications careers:**

Is responsible for a full range of external public relations activities: corporate advertising; community, shareholder, financial, and government relations; produces corporate literature, sales promotions, and special productions.

Directs and coordinates all activity in the development, implementation, and administration of a corporate identification system covering all aspects of visual communication, material, and media.

Has administrative responsibility for public relations and development departments.

External communications specialists also may be responsible for community relations, telecommunications systems, and the public relations contacts for specific individuals within or related to the corporation.

External communications specialists may be required to have a broad range of journalism and media production skills. These specialists design and produce media in addition to supervising others (such as advertising agencies) in the design of corporate identifications ranging from logos to television commercials. They understand the fundamentals of public relations and have skills in written communication and audience analysis. Some external communications jobs require financial background in order to direct public relations efforts in financial markets.

Sales

Those with **sales careers** represent products and services to potential customers. Sales responsibilities include preparing sales presentations, analyzing the market or audience, soliciting accounts, making sales presentations, taking and handling orders, and servicing accounts. Those in sales positions are primary representatives of the organization to its external public.

Salespeople need abilities in interpersonal and organizational communication, market analysis, and the preparation and presentation of both

External communications careers—responsibility for external public relations activities; corporate advertising; community, shareholder, financial, and government relations; corporate literature, sales promotions, and special productions.

Sales careers—representing products and services to potential customers.

oral and written materials. Sales positions also frequently require technical ability appropriate to specific products or services and a basic understanding of budgeting, costing, and accounting procedures.

Human Services

Human service careers—responsibility for fund-raising, grant writing, and other formal budget justification processes. Human service professionals engage in counseling, design, administration, and evaluation of programs; they also engage in responsibilities similar to internal communication careers.

Human service careers generally involve nonprofit or government organizations. Job responsibilities include fund raising through public solicitation of funds, grant writing, and other formal budget justification processes. Human service specialists may engage in individual counseling on subjects ranging from managing personal finances to job search skills. They design, administer, and evaluate a full range of programs that provide human services.

In addition to those job titles listed in Figure 11.4 for human service specialists, many of the job titles listed for the internal communication option also apply. In fact, the skills required for internal communication positions also are needed in the human service area. In addition to those skills common for both internal communication and human service positions, human service jobs may require knowledge of direct mail, persuasive appeals in fund-raising, cost accounting, budgeting, and program evaluation.

Education

Careers in education—teaching in high schools, junior colleges, and universities.

Careers in education require professional certification and advanced degrees. Those with communication backgrounds teach primarily at high school, junior college, and college and university levels. Job responsibilities include instructional design and development, presentation of educational materials, evaluation of student performance, and individual counseling and guidance.

In addition to professional certification required for high school teachers and elementary and high school administrators, teachers need interpersonal, small-group, and organizational communication abilities. Listening is a necessary skill, as is the ability to speak and write well. Graduate degrees are required for almost everyone entering the field of education. Masters degrees are necessary for elementary and secondary education positions, and doctorates are required for most postsecondary and administrative positions. Educators are responsible for developing expertise in particular subjects, for conducting research, and for presenting material appropriate to these subjects. Educational administrators also need skills in finance, personnel management, and public relations.

Research

Research careers—responsibility for the design and development of research programs to support the ongoing activities of the organization or to chart a course of change.

Those with **research careers** are responsible for the design and development of research programs to support the ongoing activities of the organization or to chart a course of change. Research specialists conduct interviews and surveys, evaluate data, commission data collection, and co-ordinate research forums. These specialists are involved in business trend analysis, marketing and demographic research, and a broad range of social science applications to organizational life. They evaluate organizational performance with both qualitative and quantitative measures.

Depending on the focus of the position, research specialists are required to exhibit capabilities in social scientific research methods, marketing research, and financial analysis. Research specialists must understand data collection and evaluation procedures. They must be familiar with needs analysis techniques and a variety of types of data interpretation. Research specialists also are responsible for interpreting their findings to the organization, which requires good skills for oral and written presentations. By far the majority of research positions require extensive knowledge of statistics and computers.

Management

People with **management careers** are responsible for planning, coordinating, supervising, and controlling many of the activities described in the other career options. Managers guide and direct subordinates to achieve organizational goals. Thus, managers involve themselves in a variety of personnel activities such as interviewing, hiring, performance evaluation, and employee goal setting. Managers also help to direct the activities of the organization through the use of both human and material resources. They perform communication activities to guide and direct subordinates, solicit subordinate feedback, and exchange information with other management levels and the organization's public. Managers fulfill the formal organizational role of coordinating information and activities.

Managers are generally required to have at least basic technical skills in the areas in which they manage. Advertising managers, for example, usually bring to their positions technical knowledge about media production. Managers need interpersonal, small-group, and organizational communication competencies. They should be able to listen, think critically, lead group decision making and problem solving, and generally speak and write well. Managers also may be required to exhibit competence in business management, finance, economics, and law.

Management careers—responsibility for planning, coordinating, supervising, and controlling many of the activities of the organization.

Consulting

Those with **consulting careers** are hired by organizations to provide expertise either not in existence in the organization or more objectively supplied by someone not directly employed by the organization. Consultants help organizations identify problems, evaluate performance, find problem solutions, and implement a wide variety of change activities. Consultants design data-collection activities, collect and evaluate data, and make rec-

Consulting careers—work as an external adviser to organizations to identify problems, evaluate performance, find solutions, and implement a wide variety of change activities.

ommendations for organizational improvements. Consultants design, conduct, and evaluate training programs. Typical topics for such programs include interpersonal communication, small-group processes, leadership, conflict management, and problem-solving processes. Consultants also prepare a variety of written reports summarizing assignment findings.

Consultants combine many of the skills required for internal communication and research positions. They must be able to assess quickly the quality of information they are receiving and establish working relationships appropriate for their assigned responsibilities. Consultants need awareness of interpersonal, group, and organizational communication processes as well as the ability to effectively seek information both orally and in writing. Graduate degrees and extensive work experience are desirable for consulting positions.

Additional Options for Organizational Communication

Organizational communication backgrounds frequently are used as pre-professional preparation for training in law, social work, and business. Many of the competencies developed in an organizational communication program are favorably evaluated for entrance into a wide range of graduate programs, including, of course, graduate programs in communication. Numerous students throughout the country have creatively combined organizational communication competencies with other interests such as engineering, medicine, art, or science.

EDUCATIONAL PREPARATION FOR ORGANIZATIONAL COMMUNICATION CAREERS

Educational preparation for organizational communication careers is most often based on a broad liberal arts background with particular emphasis on a combination of theory and practical courses. Developing competencies for the career options we have described begins with an overview of the human communication process, an introduction to basic concepts and theories in organizational communication, and an understanding of how theories of organizations relate to human communication. The first part of this text was designed to introduce you to these concepts.

Preparation for a communication career also requires development of oral skills for interpersonal, small-group, and public settings. Basic research methods and statistics are essential for evaluating and collecting data, a responsibility of many communication positions.

For those selecting internal communication, human service, and research options, particular emphasis should be placed on social science courses that contribute to understanding human behavior and research techniques appropriate for behavioral science data collection and interpretation. Preparation for external communications positions is found in journalism, technical writing, public relations, and media production courses.

Courses in instructional design are important for those in education, training, and consulting. Understanding how to develop effective learning situations requires a mix of theory and practice courses and opportunities.

Those entering sales and management positions can benefit from courses in interpersonal communication, persuasion, interviewing, small-group processes, and conflict management. These option areas are also supported by courses in business management, finance, and economics.

As stated earlier, most of the option areas also require a basic understanding of statistics and computers. In fact, leading organizational recruiters suggest that communication professionals can best prepare themselves for good entry-level positions if they have competencies in organizational communication accompanied by special skills in video production, computers, statistics, or program design and evaluation.

For most students today, educational preparation will not stop with an undergraduate degree. Many students will continue through graduate programs and most will participate in continuing education, whether or not in the pursuit of a formal degree. Our fast-paced information age requires flexibility and change not only from organizations but also from all of us. Part of the ability to make necessary changes comes from identifying how educational preparation strengthens our competencies and enables us to be productive members of the organizations for which we work.

PROFESSIONAL APPLICATIONS OF ORGANIZATIONAL COMMUNICATION: HELPING ORGANIZATIONS DEVELOP AND CHANGE

Inherent in most of the career options we have been discussing is the responsibility of communication professionals to help organizations identify needed change and to develop strategies and tactics appropriate for productive change. Because of the rapid changes associated with an information society, increasing importance is being attached to organizational positions responsible for guiding and directing change and development. Most of the communication positions we have been discussing are directly or indirectly associated with identifying, conceptualizing, introducing, teaching, and evaluating change. Thus, helping organizations develop and change is a primary professional application of organizational communication competencies.

But what exactly is this professional responsibility we are alluding to and how does a communication professional prepare himself or herself for a role in change and development processes? Warren Bennis (1969) suggests that **organizational development** (OD) is needed for dealing with

Organizational development—educational strategies intended to change the beliefs, attitudes, values, and structure of organizations.

continuing change and can be described as "a complex educational strategy intended to change the beliefs, attitudes, values and structure of organizations so that they can better adapt to new technologies, markets, and challenges, and the dizzying rate of change itself."

Fundamental to the Bennis notion of organizational development is the ability to identify needed change, to develop educational strategies (internal communication, training, publications, advertising, public relations) that help bring about change, and to evaluate the results of these efforts. If you will refer back to the responsibilities and skills required for most of the communication career options, you will see that problem identification, design of educational strategies, and evaluation techniques are primary responsibilities for communication professionals.

Closely aligned with Bennis's description of organizational development is Wayne Pace's definition of human resource development. Pace (1983) suggests that **human resource development** (HRD) "refers to a set of activities that prepare employees to perform their current jobs more effectively, to assume different positions in the organization, or to move into jobs, positions, and careers that are yet unidentified and undefined." Pace contends that the importance of human resource development rests on seven basic assumptions:

> (1) That human beings are important in their own right as resources to achieve organizational goals; (2) that human beings have the right to be satisfied with ways in which they contribute to the organization; (3) that changing conditions, environment, markets, and resource demands necessitate the continual preparation of human beings to assume different positions; (4) that human beings do not come to the organization with all of the knowledge and skills they need to fulfill any and every demand placed upon them; (5) that a pool of developing workers, supervisors, and managers constitute a body of individuals who can help meet future human resource needs; (6) that development constitutes more than technical training, but involves an understanding of human behavior, how people respond and relate to one another, how human beings contribute to organizational productivity as well as to their own well-being; and (7) that the quality of work life is a legitimate and valuable concern of human beings in all areas of development.

Both internal and external communication specialists have professional responsibilities for organizational and human resource development. Whether as an employee of the organization or as an external consultant, communication specialists collect and evaluate data, interpret data to those responsible for decision making, develop processes and plans for solutions, and evaluate the results of change and development efforts.

The manner in which communication specialists provide these professional services can be described by three general models: purchase, doctor-patient, and process. Each model reflects different assumptions about the role of the communication specialist; the abilities of individuals, depart-

Human resource development—sets of activities that prepare employees to perform their current jobs more effectively; to assume different positions in the organization; or to move into jobs, positions, and careers that are yet not defined.

ments, or entire organizations to define their own problems; and who has responsibility for problem solving.

The Purchase Model

In the **purchase model**, the organization relates to communication specialists, whether they are organizational employees or external consultants, by requesting particular services to meet a need the specialist has not been involved with identifying. The communication professional may be requested to conduct a training class, write a news release, or design a publication announcing a new policy. The parties requesting the specialist's services assume they understand their own needs and have identified the specialist as capable of meeting those needs. In other words, they are purchasing the desired services. This model can be an efficient use of resources if the assignment is well defined and the specialist capable of implementing the desired request. This model is ineffective, however, when the client does not thoroughly understand the problem or requests of the specialist services beyond the specialist's scope of responsibility or capability.

Purchase model—consulting model in which the organization relates to the specialist by requesting particular services to meet a need the specialist has not been involved with identifying.

The Doctor-Patient Model

The **doctor-patient model** is based on assumptions very different from the purchase model. In the doctor-patient model, the communication professional acts in much the same manner as a medical doctor, who examines patients, identifies their symptoms, and prescribes treatment. In the organizational setting, the doctor-patient model requires the communication specialist to examine symptoms of organizational problems and prescribe appropriate solutions to meet the identified problems. As in the purchase model, the results are effective if the specialist has abilities appropriate to the task and if the organization readily accepts the diagnosis and treatment. One of the primary problems with the doctor-patient model is in the lack of organizational acceptance of proposed solutions when organizational members have little or no input into the process.

Doctor-patient model—consulting model in which the organization expects the specialist to diagnose problems and prescribe solutions.

The Process Model

The **process model** for organizational development finds members of the organization working hand in hand with the communication professional to identify problems, propose solutions, implement action, and evaluate results. In the process model, the communication specialist is responsible for guiding organizational members through inquiry and problem solving. Basic assumptions underlying the model are that organizational members are more likely to be committed to solutions they have helped generate and that the talents of the specialist are best used when working directly with those affected by the problem.

Process model—consulting model in which the organization and specialist work jointly to diagnose problems and generate solutions.

Planned Development and Change

Regardless of the model or models from which the communication professional works, four basic activities occur in the process of planned development and change: data collection; data evaluation; planning and implementation of development, solutions, and change; and evaluation of results. The effectiveness of each of these activities contributes to the overall effectiveness of development and change. Although the activities are closely related one to another, they each require unique skills for effective performance.

Data Collection

Primary techniques for data collection include questionnaires, audits, interviews, performance data, cost analysis, and trained observation. Each technique can yield useful information, and often the techniques are combined to provide a more comprehensive understanding of potential problems and issues.

Questionnaires contain open-ended or closed questions. Entire populations may be asked to respond, or sampling techniques may be used to survey part of a population from which to generalize the results. For questionnaire data to be useful in planned change, questions must be relevant, well framed, and valid, with respondents representing a population who can be expected to understand the problem.

Organizational communication *auditing* is a particular type of questionnaire currently gaining in credibility and use. Such auditing is the periodic examination of important communication activities such as message-sending and -receiving activities as they relate to important organizational outcomes. As Gerald Goldhaber (1986), one of the leaders in communication auditing, suggests,

> *Organizations which conduct a communication audit will derive valid information about their communication systems. With this information, they will become aware of current behaviors and practices and also the likelihood of future successes and failures. They can take the initiative in planning for their future rather than defensively react to communication crises. Valid information gives an organization the freedom to choose from alternatives which path it wants to follow as it grows and develops.*

Numerous audit instruments exist and numerous others are tailored for particular organizations. Audits are used to design communication strategies, assess needs, and evaluate practices. Regardless of the procedure used, organizational communication specialists are expected to understand auditing's basic principles and to be able to use the approach as part of planned change activities.

Interviews can contribute a rich amount of data important for change and development. Whether informal or tightly scheduled, interview data can expand understanding of complex problems and identify resistance to organizational change. Interviewing requires problem knowledge, the ability to be understood by others, the ability to understand others, and skills for meaningful interpretation of interview results.

Questionnaires and interviews are techniques that gather data the organization does not already have. Other data, called *performance data*, exist as a result of the daily operation of the organization. These performance data come from sales reports, turnover rates, employee absenteeism, quarterly profit statements, and a host of other routine organizational measures. These data all too often are not thoughtfully used along with questionnaire and survey data to better understand needs. Communication specialists often find such performance data useful to substantiate or expand understanding of problems identified with questionnaire and interview techniques.

Gathering data about the cost of a problem also contributes to directing action toward solutions. *Cost analysis* may range from determining a ratio of return on an advertising campaign to assessing the dollar value of employee time spent in meetings as compared to the value derived from decisions made in meetings. Cost analysis is based on the assumption that communication behavior has both human and financial consequences. From this perspective, a seemingly inexpensive training program that fails to explain an important concept is costly. Gerald Wilson, H. Lloyd Goodall, and Christopher Waagen (1986) propose a six-step process for analyzing communication costs in task behaviors:

1. *Describe the task to be costed in terms of behaviors.*
2. *Identify behaviors involving communication.*
3. *Describe communication network coordinating communication behaviors.*
4. *Determine the time spent by each person involved with the task in various communication functions.*
5. *Value time spent by each person.*
6. *Compute total cost of communication for the task.*

Although cost analysis can be used to determine the cost efficiency of particular types of communication (television commercials or newspaper advertising), the primary purpose of collecting cost data is to understand the financial consequences of the event, task, or behavior within the broader context of what the organization needs. Thus, communication cost analysis frequently becomes the responsibility of the communication specialist.

Finally, *trained observation* is a valid technique for data collection. The communication specialist, either as a participant-observer or as an observer alone, may collect data about group processes such as decision making and problem solving. Specialists assess the effectiveness of training approaches by observing participant interactions and abilities to perform behaviors proposed during training. Skilled observation can also uncover information not previously known to the organization and therefore difficult to collect in formal questionnaires or interviews. One communication specialist's observation, for example, discovered unexpected resistance to a new policy eliminating an eating area near a production line. Although the organization provided an attractive alternative area, employees were disgruntled. Observation of the displeasure led the specialist to investigate further, finding that the production manager had increased the number of breaks per shift for each employee but had reduced the amount of time for each break. The quality assurance manager, concerned with removing food from the product assembly area, had moved the new break area further from the production line, requiring more walking time per break. The two changes, each well founded, were not compatible.

Data Evaluation

Once data are collected, evaluation and interpretation begin. In the case of questionnaires and audits, answers are tabulated and statistical analysis is used to develop a numerical description of the issues or problems under consideration. The use of appropriate statistical tests, an understanding of the limits of particular tests, and an ability to translate the numerical data into the essence of the problem are important in data evaluation. Interviews are coded to discover recurring themes or identify unique problems and creative solutions. When interview and survey data are collected for the same general problem area, data are examined for convergence—that is, whether the two forms of data yield essentially the same understanding of the problem. When they do, the specialist has added confidence in the accuracy of the findings. When findings are dissimilar, additional data may be needed to understand discrepancies.

Cost analysis data are used to evaluate communication efficiency and effectiveness and to understand the financial impact of issues and problems. These data may be used to make decisions about the amounts of organizational resources needed for change and development. Cost data also contribute to a better understanding of questionnaire and interview results. Finally, observation data are used to confirm understanding from other data, stimulate the identification of additional data needs, and bring subtle yet often crucial interpretation to data collected with more formal techniques.

Once data have been analyzed, the communication professional is responsible for interpreting data to those involved in developing solutions and making decisions about change. Data interpretation, therefore, must fit the needs of the proposed audience while thoughtfully and honestly reflecting the findings. This feedback stage can be especially difficult if the specialist has data that may not meet with the approval of key decision makers.

A dilemma faced by a communication consultant in a large East Coast manufacturing plant illustrates this problem. The consultant was hired to help management understand why several key supervisors had requested transfers to other divisions within the organization. Also, turnover rates for the plant exceeded the company average and absenteeism was at an all-time high. Management was perplexed because of the long-time excellent reputation of their division and the recent installation of new state-of-the-art manufacturing equipment designed to improve both quality and quantity of output. Data collected by the consultant revealed that supervisors were asking to leave because they did not trust the motives of management with regard to the new equipment. Many supervisors, and a significant number of workers as well, believed management was planning to use technology to eliminate jobs, or at best to reduce advancement opportunities by requiring fewer and fewer lead positions on the manufacturing line. Many of the top supervisors were young and wanted to continue their career advancement, which they believed to be jeopardized by management planning. The consultant knew that management would not be pleased with these findings, although the findings accurately reflected the data. The consultant was faced with the problem of presenting findings for maximum problem understanding while directing management toward generating a solution.

A communication professional is concerned with how to facilitate understanding without placing blame and with how to generate commitment for a problem solution. This component of the change process can be especially difficult for the internal communication consultant who may gain his or her primary visibility with management during the discussion of difficult problems. The ability to be effective in this type of circumstance requires careful planning and broad-based communication competency.

Data are reported in written and oral form. Raw data and interpretations of data are identified and carefully separated. Interpretations are labeled for source and basis. Limitations of data also are specified. Frequently, reports will contain only portions of a data set. Decisions about what data to include are based on relevancy to the problem, the audience for the report, and the audience's ability to use data for problem solving. Reports identify the existence of additional data should the people involved need more detailed information.

Planning and Implementing Solutions

The planning and implementing of needed change come about in diverse ways. At times the communication professional is charged with the responsibility to develop and propose plans for change that are subject to management approval. At other times the specialist may be charged with developing and implementing plans as part of regular job responsibilities. For example, communication professionals frequently are responsible for determining organizational training needs and providing training services appropriate to those needs. In other types of problem situations, the communication professional may act as a group facilitator, with others responsible for decision making and problem solving.

The communication professional is most likely to be involved with the following types of change activities: policy changes, process changes, training and development activities, and advising and counseling. Although the responsibility and level of involvement for each activity will vary from organization to organization, these primary change activities are fundamental for organizations to improve their adapting, coping, and problem-solving capabilities.

Policy refers to formally established decisions about organizational operating procedures. Organizations have personnel policies, financial policies, and customer service policies, to name just a few. For policies to be effective, they must reflect not only what the organization does but also what the organization should be doing. Effective organizations have dynamic policies that reflect changes in changing environments. Communication professionals are involved in developing personnel policies, customer relations policies, policies that govern relationships with suppliers to the organization, advertising and public relations policies, and policies that prescribe what information will be available to all organization members.

Communication professionals also involve themselves in needed *process changes*. Performance appraisal, meetings, decision making, and problem solving are only a few examples of organizational processes in which communication professionals develop plans for training organizational members in their effective use or make recommendations for process improvements.

Training and development activities are formal education strategies to help organizations perform more effectively. As we have already discussed, training is a primary responsibility for communication professionals. Effective training can help individuals and entire organizations develop better self-awareness, incorporate the use of new skills and processes, and adapt to the changing needs of dynamic environments. Training also is used to transmit organizational beliefs, attitudes, and values. As such, training reflects organizational culture and becomes part of the shared realities of organizational members.

Policy, processes, and training and development activities are generally somewhat formally structured and part of the planned operation of the organization. *Advising and counseling activities* are both formal and informal responsibilities of the communication professional. Personnel liaisons, for example, meet regularly with departments and department managers to provide advice and counsel. Counseling may examine specific behaviors, include improved ways of doing things, or focus on career development. Communication professionals, however, frequently are sought for informal advice about human relations problems and personal dilemmas organizational members face. The ability to understand and represent both the interests of the individual and the organization requires sensitivity and strong interpersonal communication skills. Effective advice and counseling help individuals reach good decisions and improve behaviors—both vital processes to organizational adaptation and change. This advising and counseling role is essentially important in organizations undergoing rapid change. When individuals are asked to acquire new skills and face somewhat uncertain futures, they may need assistance in planning their personal response to the circumstances around them. The communication professional can assist the entire organization in developing flexibility for an information society by individually helping members maximize their personal coping mechanisms.

Evaluating Results

Changes in policies, processes, training and developmental activities, and advising and counseling are part of the ongoing process of organizational life. However, almost everyone recognizes that change for the sake of change may or may not be organizationally effective. The final component of the change and development process, therefore, is the evaluation of the results.

Change can be evaluated in a number of ways and with a number of different criteria. Organizations frequently use performance measures such as profiit and loss, sales quotas, manufacturing output, quality defects, and employee turnover to measure change. When a sales and profit problem has been caused by quality defects on the manufacturing line, the effectiveness of improvement efforts is measured against previous sales, profit, and defects figures.

Many organizational change efforts, however, are not directly linked to quantifiable measures of performance. Attempts to generate increased teamwork, for example, although ultimately related to profit and loss figures, cannot be immediately measured in terms of dollars and cents. Evaluation of this somewhat subjective problem can be established by looking for changes in the data that identified the problem. Data gathered by one consultant identifying a teamwork problem indicated that instead of peers and supervisors working together to solve problems, supervisors routinely went to managers for decisions they should have been making themselves. The consultant evaluated whether her team-building efforts had generated improvement by determining whether managers were still being asked as frequently for solutions. Effectiveness of teamwork efforts also was evaluated by asking the supervisors themselves how they felt about change efforts. Thus, trained observation can also be important in evaluation of change efforts not suitable for direct performance measures.

Finally, additional data collection serves a useful role in the evaluation of change. Questionnaires, auditing, interviews, and the other techniques discussed in the data-collection phase of change can be used to determine the effects of educational strategies for organizational development and change. In one very real sense, evaluation is not the end of the change process but instead is the way the process begins again. The evaluation of change gives us a new organizational point of reference from which additional change efforts can occur. Figure 11.5 illustrates how the four components of the change process can be visualized as a cyclical process, with evaluation efforts influencing subsequent data collection and problem identification.

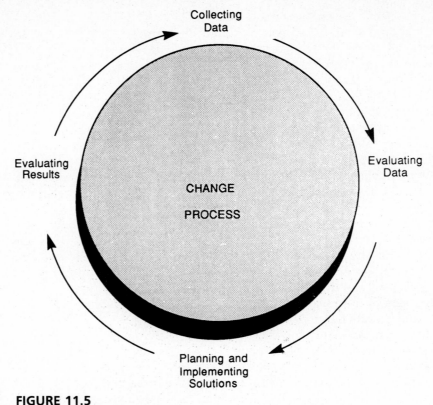

FIGURE 11.5
Illustrates the cyclical nature of the change process.

Most researchers and business practitioners agree that the rate of change in organizational life will continue to escalate as we come fully into the information age. If these predictions continue to prove true, organizational communication competencies will be increasingly desirable for those responsible for organizational decision making and problem solving. Professional positions for managing change will continue to be important; however, managing change will increasingly become everyone's responsibility. Indeed, the challenges of change in an information society suggest the growing importance of communication professionals for effective organizations of the future.

SUMMARY

Careers are the sum of our job experiences over time. Careers involve decisions about personal interests, aptitudes, educational preparation, and the match of our individual competencies to the needs of particular organizations. This match is referred to as an occupational exchange based on the knowledge, sensitivity, skills, and values of both the individual and the employing organization. Self-analysis helps generate awareness of influences for our occupational choices and can be used to develop important criteria for career planning. Self-awareness, in turn, can help us evaluate the major career options in organizational communication: internal communication, external communications, sales, human services, education, research, management, and consulting. Each of these areas requires educational preparation and a diverse set of communication skills. Described by various job titles, communication professionals frequently are responsible for helping organizations develop and change. This general responsibility, usually referred to as organizational development and human resource development, refers to the identification of needed change followed by the development, implementation, and evaluation of educational strategies that help bring about change. Communication professionals work with organizations in purchase, doctor-patient, and process models. In all three models, the process of change is based on data collection, data evaluation, planning and implementing of solutions, and evaluation of results. Change activities are predicted to become increasingly important for organizations in an information age.

WORKSHOP

1. A work sheet and examples for self-analysis activities for career planning follow. (See pages 386–392.)

2. Locate five advertisements requiring communication competencies in each of three newspapers: (1) your local paper, (2) a national paper such as the *Wall Street Journal* or the *Washington Post* national edition, and (3) a paper from a major city other than the one in which you live.

   Compare the fifteen advertisements. Identify the skills and experiences wanted by potential employers. What are the salary ranges? How can you prepare yourself for these opportunities?

3. Select the communication career option area (or areas) that interests you most. Identify a local professional who is employed in this career area. Develop a list of questions you would like answered. Make an appointment and interview this person. Report your findings to the class. (This activity can be accomplished in pairs or teams. The exercise is more meaningful if all eight option areas are reported to the class.)

4. Dr. Don Morley reflects on communication careers in his essay "So What Are You Doing After Graduation? Some Reflections of a Former Xerox Salesperson." Have you considered sales as a communication career? Should you? (See pages 392–395.)

5. In the Communication Professional at Work Activity, organizational situations are presented that require the services of a communication professional. You are the professional consultant chosen to work with these organizations. (See pages 395–397.)

6. Susan Bowick, in an essay entitled "Communication as a Management Tool," describes a deliberate communication strategy to deal with change. Read her "change strategy" and discuss it with your class. (See pages 397–399.)

Work Sheet and Example of Self-Analysis Activities for Career Planning

NAME_____

Achievements are observable results of individual skills in action. Achievements that have lasting importance normally satisfy key values in an individual's life. This exercise is designed to help you identify both skills and values that have contributed to your personal achievements. Identification of important skills and values is a fundamental step in successful career and life planning.

Instructions. Read the instruction for each activity, reflect on it, and then write your response. Be as brief or extensive as you like.

1. Identify specific individuals who have been influential in shaping your concept of work and occupational choice.
   What have they told you about possibilities?
   How satisfied are they with their work?
   How would they profile a successful person?
   What occupations have they suggested for you?
   What occupations do they not suggest for you?

2. Describe your ideal occupation in terms of responsibilities, skills, and measurement of success.

3. Compare your perfect occupation to messages from those who have influenced you (Exercises 1 and 2).

4. Identify and list four important achievements, skills used for each achievement, and values satisfied.

    Identify common skills used and values satisfied among the achievements. List ten skills and ten values that seem to be predictive for you of achievement.

ACHIEVEMENTS	SKILLS USED	VALUES SATISFIED

COMMON SKILLS USED   COMMON VALUES SATISFIED

TEN SKILLS PREDICTIVE OF ACHIEVEMENT/TEN VALUES PREDICTIVE OF ACHIEVEMENT

5. Write a narrative describing your desired lifestyle for a five-year span after your education is complete. How should this narrative influence your occupational/career choices?

6. Identify ten statements you can make today about your current career planning. Identify ten questions you need answered for career planning.

TEN STATEMENTS	TEN QUESTIONS
1.	1.
2.	2.
3.	3.
4.	4.
5.	5.
6.	6.
7.	7.
8.	8.
9.	9.
10.	10.

Self-Analysis Activities: Example.

NAME: MARTIN EMMONS*

1. Identify specific individuals . . .

   The individuals who have been most influential in shaping my concepts of work and occupational choices have been Ted Roel, Robert Emmons, and Gayle Emmons. These people showed me a wide range of different possibilities of work that I could go into. However, they suggested that in all of those possibilities there were certain areas in which I would excel. They tried to show me the different virtues and vices that each job would have and indicate what skills were needed.

   The occupations they most highly recommended for me were management, engineering, selling, and personnel management. Those occupations that I was not encouraged to pursue were social service, medicine, and politics. These are not all of the areas that I explored but these were the ones that come to mind.

   I respect the opinions of these people because the work that they produce brings them great personal satisfaction, a comfortable life, happiness, and a sense of accomplishment. All in all, they respect themselves and others also respect them. I feel these values are important. These people would consider a successful person by how much respect, personal satisfaction, and motivation that a person has. The idea of money and wealth does not make a person successful. However, it can make a person comfortable.

* Martin Emmons completed these activities while a student at the University of Colorado at Colorado Springs.

2. Describe your ideal occupation . . .

My ideal occupation would be owning my own successful small business. The responsibilities are tremendous. However, the bottom line of the success of the business is one's own. The ideal part of being your own businessman is that you are the boss. You will make or break your business.

There are many skills needed in running a business. I feel that the most important are leadership, motivation, and innovation. With these skills I would hopefully run a successful business or find the people that could help. I would consider myself successful if I were providing the best service to my customers while having self-respect and a sense of accomplishment in my life. And, of course, a small profit to be able to live a comfortable lifestyle.

3. Compare your perfect occupation . . .

In comparing my perfect occupation to the occupations of those who have influenced me, I see some of the same types of occupations. In many respects a salesman is his own boss and the same with an upper-level manager. However, these people do not have the same freedom of choices as a small-business owner does. In any of the jobs that were suggested to me, I could produce and be happy. However, the lure of being self-employed is hard to ignore.

4. Define four important achievements . . .

ACHIEVEMENTS	SKILLS USED	VALUES SATISFIED
1. Starting a mail order business	Personal communication Written communication Motivation Time management Resource management Salesmanship Organization management Verbal communication	Sense of accomplishment Self-respect Responsibility Independence Happiness Monetary
2. Teaching myself to do blacksmithing	Use of tools Motivation Innovation Ability to research information	Sense of accomplishment Pleasure Wisdom Self-respect Capable
3. Teaching myself how to do research	Time management Motivation Written communication Discipline Organization	Sense of accomplishment Responsibility Equality Wisdom Logic

4. Learning a martial art

Time management
Body control
Mind discipline
Motivation

Sense of accomplishment
Inner harmony
Self-respect
Self-control
Pleasure

COMMON SKILLS USED

Motivation

Time management

Written communication

Organization

COMMON VALUES USED

Sense of accomplishment

Self-respect

Pleasure

Responsibility

TEN SKILLS
  PREDICTIVE OF ACHIEVEMENT

1. Motivation
2. Time management
3. Resource management
4. Organization
5. Written communication
6. Body control
7. Mind discpline
8. Innovation
9. Verbal communication
10. Ability to research information

TEN VALUES
  PREDICTIVE OF ACHIEVEMENT

1. Self-respect
2. Happiness
3. Sense of accomplishment
4. Responsibility
5. Equality
6. Wisdom
7. Inner harmony
8. Independence
9. Pleasure
10. Self-control

5. Within the next five years after my education is complete, my goal is to be living in Colorado. I would like a ranch in the mountains with a small amount of land surrounding it. With this living situation I can be away from the fast-paced world that we live in. I enjoy the competition of life but would like to be able to rest in the leisure of my own home.

I envision that my leisure activities would become more people-oriented. I would quit ignoring my friends in favor of studying. Also, all of the projects that I have put aside for years can be completed.

I am not ready to be married, but I would like to renew some of the old friendships and relationships that I have put on hold while going to school. At some point I would like a family but not necessarily within the five-year time frame of this narrative.

With the choices that I have in mind with my social relationships and lifestyle, I feel that a job with a large corporation as a salesperson would be ideal. I envision working for a company like AT&T or Hewlett-Packard. During this time I would like to save enough money to obtain my ultimate goal of owning my own small business.

I feel that being a salesperson will give me enough freedom, responsibility, and self-respect. This position will also let me work and produce as much as I am capable of.

6. Statement about Occupational Choice

TEN STATEMENTS

1. I want to have self-respect in the occupation that I work in.
2. I want to work where I have a sense of accomplishment.
3. I want to be able to take responsibility.
4. I want room for advancements, both monetary and responsibility.
5. I want enough income to lead a comfortable life.
6. I would like to lead rather than be led.
7. I want to have enough freedom to be innovative.
8. I would like a job that I can take pleasure in doing well.
9. I want a job where there is equality in the working environment.
10. I would like a job where I can be independent in the working environment.

TEN QUESTIONS

1. Do I need more education or knowledge to handle all of the responsibilities?
2. Where can I find this information?
3. How much freedom am I going to have in producing my work?
4. Am I going to be happy in this occupation?
5. Can I handle all of the responsibilities?
6. Am I going to use the skills that I have been taught?
7. Do I have enough information about occupations to make a good choice?
8. Where can I find out about occupational choices?
9. Is this the company I want to work for?
10. How can I find out more about a company?

So What Are You Doing After Graduation? Some Reflections of a Former Xerox Salesperson

Donald D. Morley, Ph.D.*

In the spring of my senior year the not-so-sudden realization set in that I was about to graduate and had to find a job. Armed with a soon-to-be-granted bachelor's degree in communication and a desire not to be chained

* After receiving his bachelor's degree in communication, Donald Morley was a sales representative for Xerox Corporation. After leaving Xerox he received his master's and Ph.D. in communication and currently is an associate professor of communication at the University of Colorado at Colorado Springs. His major teaching and research interests are in persuasion, organizational communication, and research methods.

to a nine-to-five desk job, I decided that something in the area of sales might be a logical choice. In retrospect, it was a good choice for a substantial number of communication graduates. The problem is that very few communication majors know much about (1) the different types of sales positions that exist, (2) how to find a good entry-level sales position, and (3) how to minimize the pitfalls that await the new sales representative. This essay offers some reflective advice on these issues.

All too often the mention of "sales representative" conjures up a stereotypic image of a pushy, arm-twisting, aggressive person. At the mention of sales as a possible career, one student replied that she did not even like salespeople—much less want to become one. Although the stereotype is at least partially accurate, few people recognize that sales jobs vary a great deal in the amount of assertiveness or push required of the sales representative.

The major determinant of required assertiveness is the type of sales. Outside retail sales, where the salesperson seeks out a customer who is the ultimate consumer of the product or service, requires the type of salesperson that can (1) be creative in locating and identifying the prospective customers within the territory; (2) convince high-level people within the organization who don't really want to talk to them to do so; (3) get around receptionists whose job is to greet others but to keep you away from their bosses; and (4) be dynamic, trustworthy, competent, confident, and persuasive enough within minutes to close the order successfully or at least close for some intermediate step leading to an order. In short, we are talking about a comparatively aggressive salesperson with a rare combination of abilities. Because outside retail sales is a difficult high-pressure business, salespeople generally command substantial commissions.

Wholesale and industrial sales representatives stand in sharp contrast to outside retail representatives. Unlike the retail salesperson, whose products are more often than not perceived by customers to be increased overhead, the wholesale representative supplies customers with products or materials the customer will eventually resell for profit. This being the case, prospective customers are more likely to hear out the salesperson in anticipation that the transaction will be mutually profitable. Furthermore, since the product is resold, these sales representatives have repeated contact with their customers and selling per se becomes more a process of servicing accounts than trying to talk someone into buying something.

Like the retail sales representative, the wholesale representative must be creative in identifying prospective customers within his or her territory and must be good at developing small "foot-in-the-door" accounts into substantial profitable accounts. Even more than the retail sales representative, these representatives need to be highly organized, excellent recordkeepers, excellent time managers, and in short must give their customers the impression that they are on top of everything because they *are* on top of everything.

Assuming that you are interested in sales, just how do you find a *good* sales job? Every newspaper in every city is full of advertisements for sales representatives. Many promise fun, excitement, hundred-thousand-dollar-plus incomes, and products that sell themselves. Unless you just fell off the turnip truck, however, you know nobody is going to pay you a hundred thousand dollars to sell something that sells itself. In fact, only a small percentage of the sales positions advertised in newspapers are worth looking into. The reason is that there seems to be an unwritten rule among sales professionals that the true salesperson is an actively creative person who finds a sales position in the same way he or she finds potential customers. So how do you find and recognize a good sales position?

First, get involved in the community and network. When a company treats its salespeople right, only a few openings will arise and when they do the word tends to spread informally. Second, recognize that the first product you will sell is yourself—and that's also probably the most expensive product you'll ever sell. Xerox, for example, estimated that it cost more than forty thousand dollars to hire and train a new sales representative. If you look around your home, work, and environment in general you will realize that the potential list of companies that will "buy you" is enormous. Every product and service that you look at has been sold by somebody a multitude of times. While you're looking around, write out a list of companies for which you might want to work and research them. I find it perplexing that students will spend over forty hours in the library doing research for a term paper, but not even forty minutes researching a potential job. In addition to library research, talk to people who already sell for the company. For example, I recently ran into a factory representative for a well-known manufacturer of camping equipment. Within a short time I learned that he had been with the company over twenty-five years, was very happy with his job, made a great deal more money than a university professor, and that the president of the company personally interviewed and hired all the factory representatives. And yet I doubt that the thought of selling for this particular company, and hundreds of others like it, ever occurs to many people on the job market. In contrast, the big-name companies like Xerox are flooded with applications, hire only a few, and have a persistent tone of "You're replaceable."

Once you know a fair amount about some companies—go after them. If they say they are not interested—go after them again. After all, sales requires a degree of tasteful persistence and an initially uninterested sales manager might start seeing that you have what it takes.

There are a number of sales jobs, however, that you should avoid. I call them "sink-or-swim" positions. Essentially, these are companies that put little time, effort, and money into training their salespeople. If they need five good sales representatives, they hire a hundred, knowing full well they will fire ninety-five of them within a year. I was once offered a headhunter fee by a life insurance broker for every college graduate that I sent him. He made it clear that he was out to hire as many as he could, because he knew that only a few of them would work out and all of them could at least sell life insurance to their family and friends before he had to let them go. I never sent him anybody. In short, take a good hard look at what the company is going to invest in you before you invest in them.

Even after you've landed a good sales position, a number of pitfalls await you, the major one being that you don't sell enough to make a good living, or worse yet, keep your job. It is hoped your selection of the right company, good training, and hard creative work will go a long way in avoiding this pitfall. However, the organizational structure of most sales divisions tends to foster a self-fulfilling prophecy for success or failure. It works something like this: Your immediate sales manager's income and performance depend on how you and the rest of the sales team perform. In turn, the district manager's performance evaluations depend on how well the sales managers do, and so on up the organizational hierarchy. Although this is generally a good system, what happens is that this mutual dependency causes organizational superiors to assign their best sales territories to what they *perceive* to be their best salespeople and the lesser territories to what they perceive to be their weaker salespeople. As a result, the prophecy is fulfilled when the good sales representative outsells the weak ones. The lesson is simple: Be perceived as a strong sales representative. Dress and act professionally, make sure your accomplishments are known, do not dwell on your failures, and most important, be positive. Managers will not entrust a major accounts package to people who fail to display the confidence and optimism that they not only can do the job but also can do it better.

Professional salespeople are not peddlers and charlatans. Rather, they perform a valuable service to the people and organizations to whom they sell, while earning themselves a good income. Before anyone looks down at sales as a career, they would be well advised to remember that Lee Iacocca started his career in sales and that much of what he learned in those early days was pivotal in preventing the demise of Chrysler Corporation.

QUESTIONS FOR DISCUSSION

1. The author points to the problem of how the organizational structure of most marketing divisions results in a self-fulfilling prophecy. What are some alternatives that might avoid this problem? What are their advantages and disadvantages?

2. Even if you do not choose to go into sales, you will someday have to market yourself. What ideas do you have about finding a prospective employer and convincing that company to hire you?

The Communication Professional at Work Activity

Each of the following organizational situations will result in a request for the services of a communication professional. As you read each case, try to determine which of the consulting models you would recommend and what types of data must be collected to initiate the change cycle.

Jane Edwards's Problem Employee

Jane Edwards was proud of the people who worked for her in the data-processing department. They were capable and had shown a great deal of commitment and creativity during the last few difficult months of program expansion. With such a positive performance by the entire department, Jane could hardly believe the reports she was getting about George Jones. He was one of her most capable programmers. Could he really have been responsible for major errors in the new program? Did he really walk away last Friday, threatening never to come back? Should she go to him directly? Jane decides to contact her personnel liaison, Jim Hillis. She wants to know how Jim can help her understand what, if anything, is happening to George.

QUESTIONS FOR DISCUSSION

1. What model is Jane putting in place to work with Jim?

2. What data does Jane have?

3. If you were Jim, what data would you need to help with Jane's problem?

The Case of the Poorly Written Manual

John Howard was shaking his head as he left the meeting with his boss, Joe French. Joe was right, the new technical manual was simply not up to the company's standards. Yes, he had told Joe that there were three new people in the test group, but that was no excuse. The three apparently were simply not capable writers; maybe capable product engineers, but their writing was terrible. John called the training department and asked for Susan Harris. Could Susan schedule his three new employees in her next technical writing course?

QUESTIONS FOR DISCUSSION

1. What model is John putting into place to work with Susan?

2. What are his assumptions in making this decision?

3. Is this an appropriate approach for solving his problem?

The Transition of Stanley Manufacturing

Stanley Manufacturing has enjoyed a fine reputation in the small home-appliance industry. Since its beginning some sixty years ago, Stanley has prided itself for maintaining a family atmosphere for its employees, who are expected to stay with Stanley for their entire working careers. But times have changed. Stanley's management team sees profits being eroded and more and more competitors using innovative manufacturing processes, enabling them to produce a quality product at a price lower than the Stanley line. Stanley's management team understands that Stanley Manufacturing must undergo major changes to regain a prominent position in the market.

They decide to hire a consultant external to the Stanley organization to help them begin a change process.

QUESTIONS FOR DISCUSSION

1. Which model is the Stanley management team putting in place?
2. If you were the consultant, what type of data would you collect?
3. How would you involve people in the Stanley organization?
4. Can an external person be useful in this situation?

Communication as a Management Tool

Susan Bowick*

The notion that part of a manager's job is talking to people in his or her organization is certainly not revolutionary. Walk into any book store in America today, and you will see shelves of books that focus on performing the managerial job more effectively. Much of the information in current management literature deals with the importance of translating a manager's vision into a clear agenda, with priorities that employees can readily understand.

Robert Waterman, Jr., coauthor of *In Search of Excellence*, the bestseller on well-managed companies, notes, "In all our basic research, C.E.O.s were constantly telling us that you can't reiterate your corporate vision and goals enough. It's just amazing how fast people lost direction and wandered from the basics." Effective corporate leaders also understand the power of infectious enthusiasm. "If a company's in deep yogurt," says Waterman, "a good policeman can turn it around. But to make it a great company requires a cheerleader."

The importance of having a strong communications philosophy has been brought home to me many times as a manager at Hewlett-Packard Company. Being part of the high-tech business sector means constant change. The Lake Stevens Instrument Division of HP is no exception, as the management team quickly evolved business strategy from one traditional instrument product line (which employees knew well and loved!) to four different product lines. The future of our business was with new products and new customers that were not understood by employees. This change created lots of apprehension about why the new strategic direction was necessary, who was responsible for the decisions that propelled us into the new business, and most important, the uncertainty individual employees experienced as they tried to figure out what their role might be in the new scheme of things.

* Susan Bowick is personnel manager at the Lake Stevens Instrument Division of Hewlett-Packard Company. She joined Hewlett-Packard twelve years ago as a secretary after spending several years in the public sector as a business teacher.

In the midst of the changing business strategy, I noticed some interesting phenomena taking place. Much of the panic and uncertainty being felt by employees was based on a lack of information. In the absence of accurate, current information, employees were creating information by speculating and sharing what information was available. Employees were acting on this information without verifying the accuracy of it. The grapevine was humming—but with the wrong tune.

After looking at the communication occurring within the organization, the reasons behind much of the uncertainty became clear. Most managers were communicating within their departments but, sure enough, managers were talking about lots of different things. Managers were choosing various times and ways to communicate. What was being said reflected individual views and priorities, so a cohesive business picture was just about impossible to sort out. It became apparent that if we wanted employees to support the organization through the change in business strategy, the management team needed to take the lead in communicating more information to employees.

Our business needed a way to answer employees' questions. We needed our employees to be able to count on hearing information on a regular basis. All employees in the organization needed to hear a consistent message—not just a few people close enough to the decisions to be "in the know." Individual managers needed to do a better job explaining overall business strategy, then translating that into specific plans for each department. And we needed to figure out what information employees wanted to hear. The managerial role in communicating had just become more complex than any of us had realized!

The communication challenge was treated as any other business problem to be solved. We developed an objective and designed a communication program that specified the who, when, and what of sharing our business strategy with employees. Ways to measure the effectiveness of the communication were also defined. The matrix that follows became the Lake Stevens Instrument Divisions' communications strategy.

The expected result is being achieved. Employees are hearing consistent, frequent information. We have asked for feedback from employees about the communication and found out that there are no William Jennings Bryans among us, so the entire senior management team is taking a class to become more effective presenters. The role of manager as communicator is taken seriously.

Audiences	Message Content	When	How	Who	Measurement of Effectiveness
All LSID employees	Division objectives, current year (Emphasize LSID tactical plans, why, when, link to long-term strategies) Communicate current results, new LSID issues	Quarterly	Quarterly communication sessions	Division Manager	Employee interviews Number of questions received about business direction
Mgrs/Supv "Leaders of Change"	LSID strategic direction, key organizational issues, visibility into planning process and resource allocation Emphasize why and relationship to other functional areas	At least two times/year or as needed	LSID Management meeting	Division Manager and functional managers	Questionnaire at end of meetings Number of questions from employees
Each functional area	Impact of above on functional area Plans to manage within functional area Department results, issues	Monthly, or as needed	Coffee talks, cracker barrels Department meetings	Functional managers	MLMS results for goals, orderly work planning, upward communication Does dept. have tactical plans linked to strategy? Have those plans been presented to all employees?

Matrix from *Soper Hill Views*—LSID Publication. Reprinted with permission.

SUMMARY OF COMPETENCY COMPONENTS:
KNOWLEDGE, SENSITIVITY, SKILLS, VALUES

KNOWLEDGE

Careers are described as the sum of our job experiences over time.

Career options in organizational communication include internal communication, external communications, sales, human services, education, research, management, and consulting.

Responsibilities of communication professionals include helping organizations develop and change.

Organizational development is described as strategic educational activities designed to help organizations improve their adaptability, coping processes, and problem solving.

Consultants work with organizations in three models: purchase, doctor-patient, and process.

Professional responsibilities in change include data collection, data evaluation, planning and implementing change, and evaluating results.

SENSITIVITY

Orientations to work, expectations from work, and self-awareness all contribute to occupational choice.

Self-awareness is developed through evaluation of influences, identification of achievements, reflection on desired work life, and projection of desired lifestyle.

Communication careers require sensitivity to interpersonal, small-group, and organizational communication.

SKILLS

Analysis skills are practiced through self-awareness exercises.

Skills are practiced through case analysis and exercises.

VALUES

Occupational exchanges are influenced by personal and organizational values.

Self-awareness is fundamental to good career planning.

Change is described as important for organizations in the information age.

Managing change is a valued responsibility of communication professionals.

REFERENCES AND SUGGESTED READINGS

Bennis, W. 1969. *Organization development: Its nature, origins, and prospects.* Reading, MA: Addison-Wesley.

Bennis, W., K. Benne, R. Chin, and K. Corey. 1976. *The planning of change.* 3d ed. New York: Holt, Rinehart & Winston.

French, W. L., and C. H. Bell. 1973. *Organization development: Behavioral science interventions for organization improvement.* Englewood Cliffs, NJ: Prentice-Hall.

Goldhaber, G. M. 1986. *Organizational communication.* 4th ed. Dubuque, IA: Brown.

Pace, R. W. 1983. *Organizational communication: Foundations for human resource development.* Englewood Cliffs, NJ: Prentice-Hall.

Petrie, C., E. Thompson, D. Rogers, and G. Goldhaber. 1975. Report of the ad hoc committee on manpower resources. Report prepared for the Division IV meeting of the International Communication Association, April, Chicago.

Schein, E. H. 1969. *Process consultation: Its role in organization development.* Reading, MA: Addison-Wesley.

Wilson, G. L., H. L. Goodall, Jr., and C. L. Waagen. 1986. *Organizational communication.* New York: Harper & Row.

PART ~IV~

Organizational Communication: Values/Ethics/Dilemmas

Part Four illustrates the importance of individual and organizational values and ethics for organizational communication. Whereas the previous chapters have addressed values and ethics, no one chapter has focused specifically on the relationship of values and ethics to effective organizational communication. Part Four is designed to help us understand organizational value systems and how the roles, relationships, and responsibilities we assume in our organizational lives reflect our values and decisions about ethical behavior. Although the material in Part Four contributes to *knowledge, sensitivity*, and *skills*, the discussion of values, ethics, and dilemmas is specifically designed to develop the fourth component in our competency framework, *values*. As we have discussed throughout this text, the fully competent communicator brings knowledge, sensitivity, skills, and values to all communication interactions. The ability to understand our individual values and to assess the value systems within organizations is an important ingredient for our personal and professional decisions about ethical communication behaviors. This discussion of values and ethics is based on an important foundation of our text, namely, that the fully competent and effective communicator both exhibits and encourages ethical communication behaviors.

CHAPTER

Headlines in photograph courtesy Colorado Springs *Gazette Telegraph*.

Organizational Communication: Values and Ethical Communication Behaviors

Developing competencies through . . .

KNOWLEDGE

Describing individual and organizational values

Defining ethical communication

Identifying criteria for the evaluation of ethical communication behaviors

SENSITIVITY

Awareness of our personal value systems

Understanding the complexity of ethical dilemmas

Distinguishing between what we *would* do and *should* do

SKILLS

Assessing personal value systems and behaviors

Applying skills to case and dilemma analysis

VALUES

Relating values to individual behavior and organizational effectiveness

Understanding ethical behavior as contributing to choice, growth, and development

The Presidential Fact-Finding (Witch-Hunt?) Case

Alyne Carter was surprised to receive a call requesting her to come to the office of the president of Melton Corporation. Alyne had never had an appointment with the president and she was concerned about what he wanted to discuss. The president was relatively new to Melton and rumor had it that the board of directors had hired him as a "hatchet" man to terminate some long-term Melton managers who were associated with the failure of one of Melton's major land-development projects. Alyne's boss, Jim Johnson, had received criticism from some board members, although he was not directly involved with the development project.

Melton had a long history of being a good place to work, with open communication and support for taking risks, even though risks sometimes resulted in failures. Management at Melton had traditionally believed that their speculative land-development business would be most successful if they developed properties other companies had chosen to ignore. The strategy had generally worked, with the Briarwood project a major and important exception. The failure of Briarwood and the loss of several million dollars had upset important board members and contributed to the resignation of Melton's president.

Alyne Carter did not work on the development side of Melton's business. She reported directly to the vice president in charge of personnel and human resource development, Jim Johnson. Alyne and Jim had a good working relationship based on mutual trust and admiration. Alyne was concerned when she heard criticism of Jim as well as the general rumors that people were going to be fired. The upcoming meeting with the new president increased her fears.

When Alyne left the meeting, she knew her concerns were real. The discussion with the new president had confused her and left her wondering what to do. Although he had been perfectly pleasant, she knew he was looking for information to use against her boss. The president had begun the meeting by asking her to describe her work at Melton. He then said he needed to ask her some hypothetical questions about her department's management, recruitment, and promotional practices. Following several general questions, the president said that the rest of their conversation must stay within his office. He then proceeded to ask her if pressure had come from certain managers to hire several key individuals thought to be responsible for bad decisions in the Briarwood project. The president specifically asked if Jim Johnson had approved her hiring recommendations and whether any of her recommendations had been reversed in the last six months. Alyne attempted to answer the questions directly, although she felt as if she were walking into some unknown trap. She wished she had called Jim and told him she had been asked to see the president. He might have been able to give her some insight about what was going on. The president closed the meeting by again suggesting that their conversation was not to leave the room. He also made a somewhat vague reference to his responsibility to make unpopular changes in the best interest of Melton. He hoped she would understand and realize he had to do his job in the best way he saw fit.

Alyne could not believe this type of meeting had taken place at Melton. The rumors about a "hatchet" man certainly seemed correct. She knew she had been told not to talk about her discussion with the president, but she felt Jim should know. Was it unethical to break her promise to the president? Where did she owe her loyalty? Was the president engaged in fact-finding or in a witch hunt?

INTRODUCTION

Alyne Carter is faced with a question of values and ethics. She has inadvertently become involved in a communication situation that makes her uncomfortable and violates what she believes to be basic Melton company values. Alyne has been told by the president of Melton that their conversation should be kept in confidence, yet she believes that her boss, Jim Johnson, should know about the president's "fact-finding" and veiled threats of future action. Alyne is caught between respecting directions from the president and valuing her loyalty to her boss. She has to decide about her values in this situation and what constitutes ethical behavior. Part of her decision will be based on a determination of whether Melton's president has engaged her in unethical communication.

Although an uncomfortable situation, Alyne's dilemma unfortunately is repeated hundreds of times day in all sizes and types of organizations. Individual and organizational values clash, making determinations of ethical behavior difficult. Organizational values appear to change, leaving employees perplexed about what communication behaviors are valued and what behaviors should no longer be exhibited. Individual organizational members try to determine whether personal ethics and business ethics can or should mix.

This chapter is designed to help you think about how values and ethics influence human communication within organizations. The chapter also introduces you to value and ethical dilemmas commonly encountered by communication professionals. The chapter attempts to contribute to the development of your *knowledge* by defining values and ethics, identifying individual and organizational values, and establishing frameworks for evaluating ethical communication behaviors. *Sensitivity* is developed for relationships among organizational cultures, values, ethics, and decision making. Analysis *skills* are practiced through personal assessment of values, by identifying value themes in organizational philosophy statements, and by evaluating ethical behaviors in typical organizational communication situations. *Values* development is encouraged through an understanding of the importance to organizations of personal and organizational value systems and through discussions of the role of ethical communication behaviors for communication competency and effectiveness. All four competencies—knowledge, sensitivity, skills, and values—are applied to a case study, practical examples of value and ethical dilemmas, a decision-making simulation, and the development of a personal values and ethics statement for organizational communication.

VALUES IN ORGANIZATIONAL COMMUNICATION

Although most of us frequently use the word *value*, we often do not stop and thoughtfully consider what the concept really means to us. If asked, could you readily identify your value system for others? How did it develop? Who or what has influenced your choices? How does your value system influence your communication behaviors?

Generally speaking, the word *value* refers to the relative worth of a quality or object. Value is what makes something desirable or undesirable. **Values** are subjective assessments, and as Joseph DeVito (1986) suggests.

Values—concept that refers to the relative worth of a quality or object.

> *a value is an organized system of attitudes. If, for example, we have a cluster of favorable attitudes pertaining to various issues relating to freedom of speech, then we might say that one of our values is that of free speech. In another sense, a value is an organizing system for attitudes. If we have a particular value, say financial success, then this will give us guidelines for developing and forming attitudes. Thus, we will have favorable attitudes toward high-paying jobs, marrying into a wealthy family, and inheriting money because of the value we place on financial success. Values also provide us with guidelines for behavior; in effect, they direct our behavior so that it is consistent with the achievement of the values of goals we have.*

Richard Johannesen, in his important book *Ethics in Human Communication* (1983), states that "values can be viewed as conceptions of The Good or The Desirable that motivate human behavior and that function as criteria in our making of choices and judgments." Family belonging, achievement, financial security, prestige, and hard work are all values that have some degree of importance for most of us. Johannesen and others suggest that the importance of our personal values influences a wide variety of our decision-making activities and behavior choices. In other words, we are more likely to make choices that support our value system than choices that will not. Let's say that financial security is a strong value for an individual. When faced with a choice of jobs, chances are the individual will carefully examine each organization for potential financial and job security.

The job applicant who values financial security may well take a lower salary offer with a well-established company over a higher-paying offer from a new, high-risk venture. Another job seeker with diferent values, possibly adventure and excitement, might choose the newer company simply for the potential risk and uncertain future.

Values, therefore, become part of complex attitude sets that influence our behavior and the behavior of all those with whom we interact. What we value guides not only our personal choices but also our perceptions of the worth of others. We are more likely, for example, to evaluate highly someone who holds the same hard work value we do than someone who finds work distasteful, with personal gratification a more important value. We may even call this person lazy and worthless, a negative value label.

Before reading further in this chapter, stop for a few minutes and attempt to describe your personal value system. What are your priorities? Have you ever stopped to think about their influence on your activities and your evaluations of others? Think about how your personal values may influence your communication behavior.

Organizational Value Systems

Part of the unique sense of a place we call organizational culture develops from the values held in common by organizational members. Leonard Goodstein (1983) goes so far as to suggest that "many persons who are seriously interested in organizational behavior now believe that organizations are best regarded as cultures, with all that the term 'cultures,' in an anthropological sense, implies. In my opinion, the most important implication of this position is that organizations, like persons, have values and that these values are integrated into some coherent value system."

Milton Rokeach (1973) has defined a value system as "an enduring organization of beliefs concerning preferable modes of conduct or end-states of existence along a continuum of relative importance." Based on the Rokeach definition, Goodstein (1983) contends that "in any organization, the members generally have a set of beliefs about what is appropriate and inappropriate organizational behavior. Furthermore, these beliefs can be ordered in importance in a reliable fashion by the members of the organization." In other words, organizational value systems help organizational members to understand what the organization holds as important and how the unique sense of the place should influence their personal decision making and behavior.

Terrence Deal and Allen Kennedy (1982) describe organizational values as "the bedrock of any corporate culture" and link value systems to overall organizational effectiveness. They state, "As the essence of a company's philosophy for achieving success, values provide a sense of common direction for all employees and guidelines for their day-to-day behavior. These formulas for success determine (and occasionally arise from) the types of corporate heroes, and the myths, rituals, and ceremonies of the culture. In fact, we think that often companies succeed because their employees can identify, embrace, and act on the values of the organization."

Values are part of the shared realities generated through organizational communication. These shared values are reflected in organizational myths, stories, decision making, and thematic and tactical communication rules. Indeed, it is fair to say that organizational values are transmitted, maintained, and changed through organizational communication processes.

As described in Chapter 3, thematic communication rules are general prescriptions of behavior reflecting the values and beliefs of the organization. Tactical rules prescribe specific behaviors as related to the more general value themes. In fact, several tactical rules may evolve from one general thematic rule. We gave an example of a Midwest computer manufacturer with a strong value theme of "Communicate your commitment to the company." Based on that value theme, employees reported tactical rules, including "Come in on Saturday to finish up—but make sure you tell someone," "Complain about how tough the challenge really is," and "Use the term *family* to refer to the company." These tactical rules supported an important value theme in that particular company. Employees exhibiting compliance with thematic and tactical rules were generally considered to have been well socialized into the organization and supportive of its values.

In addition to thematic and tactical communication rules, stories, and myths, organizational values are seen in the decisions members make. Deal and Kennedy (1982) suggest that "if employees know what their company stands for, if they know what standards they are to uphold, then they are much more likely to make decisions that will support those standards." Research conducted by David Palmer, John Veiga, and Jay Vora (1981) supports the important link between values and decision making. They found that "value profiles were relatively successful in predicting managers' decision preferences and in providing further evidence of the linkage between personal values and decision making." In other words, an individual's value system, when coupled with the more general value system of the organization, influences the decisions individual organizational members will make. Deal and Kennedy contend that "shaping and enhancing values can become the most important job a manager can do." They further suggest that successful companies stand for something (clearly communicated values), that managers put effort into shaping and fine-tuning values, and that values are shared realities at all organization levels.

Organizational values not only influence the behaviors of current members but also contribute to the type of person who gets hired and the types of career experiences employees are likely to have. Some organizations value very specific types of educational backgrounds, whereas others are more likely to look for particular work experiences. Some organizations value promotion from within, whereas their counterparts never fill important vacancies from among existing employees. During times of economic difficulty, organizations valuing long-term commitment to their employees may reduce work hours or salaries for everyone rather than lay off a portion of their work force. Other organizations with less employee-centered values may decide that layoffs are the most efficient and effective way to deal with a business downturn. Arguments can be made for either position. The values of the organizations, however, are likely to guide the alternatives even considered by their respective management teams.

Think about the values of your school. Can you describe these values in any order of priority? How do they influence the policies and procedures that you as a student are asked to follow? What kinds of formal and informal messages transmit these values to students? What values do students transmit to the administration and faculty?

Figure 12.1 provides three examples of organizational value statements. Each statement is taken from the new employee handbook of the three

---

FIGURE 12.1
Organizational Value Statements

Company A

As a company, we want to share timely and accurate information on policies, programs, and activities. We want the information to be consistent and available to all employees. This is a goal that all managers should help to achieve. The company believes communication about our business creates a motivated and creative workforce.

Company B

The mission of Company B is as follows:
Command, control, and support the work force.
Modernize the work place.
Prepare to support other divisions of the company.
Train, motivate, and maintain individual capabilities.
Provide a motivated environment that will attract and retain motivated and challenged workers.

Company C

Our philosophy in managing is to plan aggressively and anticipate events rather than letting them drive us. Our program for our personnel must include fair compensation, appropriate benefits and working conditions, and an opportunity for advancement based on skills and ability. Our company will endeavor to participate in and offer educational programs necessary to assure the qualified training of personnel, with a primary emphasis on improving customer service. All of these efforts are adopted to support our goal of excellence.

organizations. Without knowing anything else about these organizations, think about the value systems you believe the messages represent.

Which of the three most closely fits your personal value system? Which least fits your values? Would value statements such as these make a difference in the organizations for which you would want to work? If so, why? If not, why not?

Individual Values

Although we have been discussing organizational value systems, we should remember that organizations are really groups of individuals working together in goal-directed activities. This means that organizational value systems are a collective interpretation of the values individual organizational members share in common. As Leonard Goodstein (1983) suggests, "in the final analysis, we are talking about the values and beliefs of individuals. Organizational values are the modal or general values that are espoused by most of the organization's members and the ones that are put forward as representing 'organizational truths.' New members are recruited into the organization by their willingness to accept these 'truths,' and much of the focus of organizational socialization is to shape these values and beliefs."

Numerous other organizational researchers have come to believe, as does Goodstein, that the more similar organizational and individual values are, the more likely the individual is to identify positively with the organization. In other words, a closeness between "this is the way I believe things are" and "this is the way I believe things *should be*" generally means the individual is satisfied with the organization and can personally commit to organizational values and beliefs. One of the difficulties, of course, is thoughtfully understanding the real values of an organization before one becomes a member. The process of matching individual and organizational values also is complicated by the lack of individual understanding of how value systems relate to work life. (As you will recall, the self-analysis exercises for career planning located in Chapter 11 were designed to help you think about your values as they might relate to career and job selection.)

Value Orientations

Personal values have been discussed in a variety of ways. Gordon Allport, Philip Vernon, and Gardner Lindzey (1960) suggest that personal values can be described in terms of six orientations: theoretical, economic, aesthetic, social, political, and religious. *Theoretical* values focus on the discovery of truth, knowledge, and order, whereas *economic* values focus on the useful and practical and on material acquisition. *Aesthetic* values are expressed in our concerns for artistic experiences and in our desire for form and harmony. *Social* values are expressed in our relationships with others and our love and service commitments. *Political* values relate to needs for power, influence, leadership, and domination, and *religious* values are expressed in needs for unity and meaningful relationships to the world.

Terminal and Instrumental Values

Rokeach's (1973) value survey identifies terminal and instrumental values. **Terminal values** can be viewed as concern for "end states of existence," or desirable goals, and **instrumental values** are desirable behaviors or modes of conduct that are related to and influence terminal values. The terminal values that Rokeach identifies are a comfortable life; an exciting life; a sense of accomplishment; a world at peace; a world of beauty, equality, family security, freedom, happiness, inner harmony, and mature love; national security; pleasure; salvation; self-respect; social recognition; true friendship; and wisdom. Instrumental values are the qualities of being ambitious, broad-minded, capable, cheerful, clean, courageous, forgiving, helpful, honest, imaginative, independent, intellectual, logical, loving, obedient, polite, responsible, and self-controlled.

A possible relationship between terminal and instrumental values can be illustrated through the example of someone with a high priority on the terminal value of accomplishment and instrumental values of being ambitious, capable, imaginative, intellectual, logical, and self-controlled. We are not suggesting, of course, that these are the only instrumental values that go hand in hand with a sense of accomplishment. Obviously, there could be others. We are suggesting, however, that terminal values are generally accompanied by combinations of instrumental values that individuals perceive to be harmonious.

> **Terminal values**—concerns for end states of existence or desirable goals.

> **Instrumental values**—desirable behaviors or modes of conduct that are related to and influence terminal values.

Work Values

The personal values we have been discussing apply to all aspects of our lives, not just the time we spend in organizations. Until recently few attempts have been made to explore personal values as they specifically apply to work environments. Roger Howe, Maynard Howe, and Mark Mindell (1982) identify five value dimensions that they believe affect our organizational lives: locus of control, self-esteem, tolerance of ambiguity, social judgment, and risk taking.

Locus of control refers to the value we place as organizational members on connections between our efforts and the success or failure of the organization. In other words, do we value personal control over success or failure, or do we value an organizational environment in which circumstances beyond our control contribute to success or failure? Do we, for example, want to be personally responsible for meeting sales quotas or do we prefer to provide support to others who have the final quota responsibility? Our locus of control value also relates to whether we value organizational advancement as a result of our own efforts (personal control) or as the result of luck, politics, or random selection (external control).

> **Locus of control**—value we place as organizational members on connections between our efforts and the success or failure of the organization.

The **self-esteem** dimension relates to the value we place on recognition for work, positive feedback, and the use of our contributions. This value

> **Self-esteem**—value we place on recognition for work, positive feedback, and the use of our contributions.

represents our concern for being trusted and perceived as making worthwhile contributions to the organization.

Tolerance of ambiguity as a value refers to the importance we place on structured or unstructured work environments. Our preference for "one right answer" on our comfort with a variety of possible approaches for decision making relates to the level of ambiguity we personally value. Those with a low tolerance for ambiguity may value "one right answer" and structured environments, whereas those higher in tolerance for ambiguity may prefer less structure and more opportunity for creative and diverse approaches.

The value we place on the feelings of others and our general assumptions about why people work can be described as our **social judgment**. Our concerns for sensitivity, empathy, and social insight are related to the importance we place on working relationships with others.

Risk taking concerns the importance we place on quick rather than deliberative action and whether we prefer our own sense of job fulfillment as opposed to job security. Our risk-taking value influences the degree of security we require in work situations, our tolerance for ambiguity in decision making, and whether we are willing to attempt tasks we have not previously encountered or have few qualifications for accomplishing.

Figure 12.2 summarizes the three value approaches we have been describing. After reviewing these lists, consider which additional values you would add. Which of the three approaches best represents your personal value system? Could the three be combined?

Tolerance of ambiguity— value or importance we place on structured or unstructured work environments.

Social judgment—value we place on the feelings of others and our general assumptions about why people work.

Risk taking—value that explores the importance we place on quick rather than deliberative action and whether we prefer our own sense of job fulfillment as opposed to job security.

APPRAISING YOUR INDIVIDUAL VALUE SYSTEM

Understanding what is important to us and what our values are contributes to our ability to identify the careers and organizations in which we can be the most productive and satisfied. Personal value assessment also helps us identify the ways values influence behaviors and evaluations of whether communication is ethical or not. Before we begin to explore ethics in organizational communication, a self-analysis of personal values is provided to give you insight into your value system. This assessment exercise is based on the assumption that our consistent behaviors reflect our value systems. Our approach in Figure 12.3 is by no means the only valid measure of a value system. We present this scale as a useful way to begin to think about the relationship of values and behaviors. As you complete the appraisal, consider additional questions that might be asked and additional values not represented in the appraisal. The scoring form for your appraisal is located on page 430.

FIGURE 12.2
Three Approaches to Describing Personal Values

Value Orientations

Theoretical
  Truth
  Rationale
  Order
  Knowledge
Economic
  Material acquisition
  Usefulness
  Pragmatism
Aesthetic
  Artistry
  Harmony
  Form
Social
  Love
  Concern for others
  Service
Political
  Power
  Influence
  Domination
  Leadership

Work Value Dimensions

Locus of Control
  Internal
  External
Self-Esteem
  Recognition
  Trust
  Worth
Tolerance of Ambiguity
  Structured work
  Unstructured work
Social Judgment
  Assumptions about others
  Interpersonal sensitivity
Risk Taking
  Action oriented
  Uncertainty as challenging

Rokeach Terminal and Instrumental Values

Terminal Values

A comfortable life
An exciting life
A sense of accomplishment
A world at peace
A world of beauty
Equality
Family security
Freedom
Happiness
Inner harmony
Mature love
National security
Pleasure
Salvation
Self-respect
Social recognition
True friendship
Wisdom

Instrumental Values

Ambitious
Broad-minded
Capable
Cheerful
Clean
Courageous
Forgiving
Helpful
Honest
Imaginative
Independent
Intellectual
Logical
Loving
Obedient
Polite
Responsible
Self-controlled

FIGURE 12.3
Values Appraisal Exercise

Instructions: Read the following twenty-four statements, which indicate six defined values. Circle the number for each question that is most descriptive of you. Use this scale:

4 = definitely true
3 = mostly true
2 = undecided whether statement is true or false
1 = mostly false
0 = definitely false

1. I intend to retire by age fifty with enough money to live the good life.   4 3 2 1 0

2. I take pleasure in decision making, particularly when other individuals are involved.   4 3 2 1 0

3. I enjoy now, or have enjoyed in the past, a close relationship with one or both of my parents.   4 3 2 1 0

4. I especially enjoy and appreciate beauty and beautiful objects, events, or things.   4 3 2 1 0

5. I enjoy creating projects of my own.   4 3 2 1 0

6. I feel a rich life has many friends and much friendship in it.   4 3 2 1 0

7. I am most valuable to clubs and groups when I am an officer rather than just a member of the group.   4 3 2 1 0

8. I enjoy both giving and going to parties.   4 3 2 1 0

9. I would choose a class in art, drawing, or sculpture over a class in math.   4 3 2 1 0

10. I think holidays should be spent with family and close relatives.   4 3 2 1 0

11. I like fine things and have expensive tastes.   4 3 2 1 0

12. I think decorating one's apartment or house is a fun thing to do.   4 3 2 1 0

13. I expect to earn more money than the common person on the street.   4 3 2 1 0

14. I take pleasure in buying special gifts for members of my family.   4 3 2 1 0

15. I am often considered a take-charge type of person in small groups and organizations.   4 3 2 1 0

16. Had I the talent, I would write, draw, or create art of some kind.   4 3 2 1 0

17. I have a close friend with whom I talk about almost everything.   4 3 2 1 0

18. I enjoy owning good music, literature, and artwork.   4 3 2 1 0

19. I think it is good and fun to make something out of nothing.   4 3 2 1 0

20. I agree with the phrase that money can't buy happiness but it sure makes life much more comfortable.   4 3 2 1 0

21. I think that spending time with one's family is an activity that is both necessary and enjoyable.   4 3 2 1 0

22. I often have to aid those close to me in making choices regarding both important and unimportant things in life.   4 3 2 1 0
23. I would give up sleep in order to spend time with some good friends.   4 3 2 1 0
24. When I see a new building or house, I first think about how it looks and then how it will be used.   4 3 2 1 0

This scale was prepared and tested by Sherwyn P. Morreale.

ETHICS IN ORGANIZATIONAL COMMUNICATION

Defining Ethics

We have described *values* as that which makes something desirable, a subjective assessment of worth that motivates human behavior and serves as a yardstick against which we measure choices. **Ethics**, although related to values, are the standards by which behaviors are evaluated for their morality—their rightness or wrongness. When applied to human communication, ethics are the moral principles that guide our judgments about the good and bad, right and wrong, of communication, not just communication effectiveness or efficiency.

Ethics—right or wrong of a given behavior or situation.

Johannesen (1983) helps us make the distinction between values and ethics.

> Concepts such as material success, individualism, efficiency, thrift, freedom, courage, hard work, prudence, competition, patriotism, compromise, and punctuality all are value standards that have varying degrees of potency in contemporary American culture. But we probably would not view them primarily as ethical standards of right and wrong. Ethical judgments focus more precisely on degrees of rightness and wrongness in human behavior. In condemning someone for being inefficient, conformist, extravagant, lazy, or late, we probably would not also be claiming they are unethical. However, standards such as honesty, truthfulness, fairness, and humaneness usually are used in making ethical judgments of rightness and wrongness in human behavior.

From this perspective it is fair to say that our values influence what we will determine is ethical; however, values are our measures of importance, whereas ethics represent our judgments about right and wrong. This close relationship between importance and right and wrong is thought to be a powerful influence on our behavior and how we evaluate the behavior of others.

Defining Ethical Communication

Is it ever ethical to tell a lie? Am I being ethical if I deliberately withhold information I know you need but have not asked for directly? Should I compliment a person to be pleasant, even though the compliment may be insincere? Is it ethical to withhold from my boss information about a mistake I have made? How honest should someone be in giving criticism to another? Chances are you have had to answer several of these questions in your personal determination of ethical communication behaviors. Daily we come into contact with situations requiring us to make judgments or choices about what is right, ethical, or moral. In the case of a compliment, we may spend little time debating what is ethical, whereas a decision to withhold information from our boss requires serious consideration and considerable worry.

We all face the question of trying to decide what is ethical communication behavior. Our answers to ethical questions are based on our communication competencies—knowledge, sensitivity, skills, and values—and are related to our overall communication effectiveness. As we have previously discussed, ethical communication is an important prerequisite for effectiveness both for individuals and entire organizations.

Choice making—selection of options based on knowledge of alternatives.

Ronald Arnett (1985), in synthesizing the status of ethics scholarship in communication, points to communication behaviors that support **choice making** as a "central component in the ethics of communication." Joseph DeVito (1986), in contrasting ethical and unethical communications, suggests that ethical communication "facilitates the individual's freedom of choice by presenting the other person with accurate bases for choice." In contrast, unethical communications "interfere with the individual's freedom of choice by preventing the other person from securing information relevant to the choices to be made; for example, lying, extreme fear and emotional appeal, and prevention of interaction."

Thomas Nilsen (1966) describes communication he believes to be morally right as that which "contributes most to the listener's opportunity for significant choice, which provides the information and the reasoning from it that makes possible the most rational decision among the alternatives, and which motivates the listener to such choice." As Arnett's (1985) status of ethics scholarship suggests, although there is disagreement about what is ethical, "there is clear agreement on the centrality of choice making in a communication ethic."

Paul Keller and Charles Brown (1968) suggest that ethical communication fosters conditions for growth and development. Keller (1981) further contends that it is possible to be committed to a position while at the same time remaining open to new information. This openness to new information is viewed as fundamental for growth and development. Ethical communication can also be described as based on values that support the innate worth of individuals. Communication is ethical when it values the essential dignity of human beings and supports the ability of individuals to realize their full potential. Whether ethical communication is described as supporting informed choice making, contributing to growth and development or valuing the innate worth of human beings, it depends on individuals taking responsibility for personal behaviors. This personal responsibility underscores the importance of developing criteria or guidelines for ethical communication behaviors.

Influences for Ethical Organizational Communication

Individual value systems, organizational value systems and cultures, and the standards of given professions all influence the ethics of organizational communication. Employees have individual value systems and make individual judgments about the rightness or wrongness of communication behavior. Even in organizations in which openness is encouraged, an individual employee may choose not to notify a supervisor of a serious mistake. The individual judges this behavior as ethical because of his or her intent to correct the problem. The employee's supervisor, on the other hand, may consider it unethical to withhold information that could affect the productivity of the group. An absolute judgment about the rightness or wrongness of the employee's behavior is difficult. It is possible to understand, however, that individual and organizational values can differ, contributing to differing interpretations of ethical behavior.

Organizational communication also is influenced by ethical standards of particular professions. In fact, developing ethical standards is central to any concept of professionalism, and according to Gordon Lippitt and Ronald Lippitt (1978), every profession has found it necessary to establish a code of ethics. Codes of ethics help individuals define behavior within a profession, articulate relationships between professionals and those with whom they come in contact, provide protection to users of the professionals' services against abuses of professionalism, and guide advancement in the state of knowledge in a discipline. The importance of ethical standards for the communication professional is underscored by W. Charles Redding (1979), who describes the impact of consultants on the careers or earning capacities of large numbers of individuals. Specifically, Redding contends that irreparable damage can be done in these high-risk consultant-client situations. Jo Sprague and Lucy Freedman (1984) underscore this concern with the argument that professional consultants should be bound by a code of ethics as rigorous as all other members of the helping professions.

Formal codes of ethics such as those that guide the medical and legal professions are not as common in the communications professions. Codes of ethics for journalists do exist; however, codes are yet to be developed for the more general organizational communication professions.

Particular emphasis has been placed on developing ethical standards for the communication consultant. Behaviors related to client contact, skill representation, establishment of fees for services, handling of client information, and termination of the client-consultant relationships are all subject to standards of ethics. With specific emphasis on the training responsibility for communication professionals, Redding (1979) has proposed the following guidelines for all training activities:

1. *Respect for the integrity of the individual trainee*
2. *Providing opportunity for self-actualization*
3. *Encouraging the exercise of critical faculties*
4. *Devoting explicit attention to ethical problems and issues*
5. *Concern for long-term development of trainees*

These guidelines suggest that not only the content of the training but also the presentational approaches and overall responses to trainees should foster an environment in which trainees will explore, think critically, and examine alternatives.

Evaluating Ethical Behavior

Most of us do not continually think about evaluating our own behavior and the behaviors of others along ethical lines. We do, however, tend to make conscious ethical evaluations when in doubt about what we should do or when the behaviors of others cause us concern about the rightness or wrongness of their actions. An important part of our communication competency, therefore, is determining how we should approach evaluating ethical communication behaviors.

Karl Wallace (1955), has developed a set of guidelines for the evaluation of behavior which he first applied to our political system and which Rebecca Rubin and Jess Yoder (1985) have extended to the assessment of communication skills in an educational setting. These guidelines are appropriate for consideration in most organizational communication situations.

Habit of search—ethical communication that explores willingly the complexity of any issue or problem.

Habit of justice—ethical communication that presents information as openly and fairly as possible with concern for message distortion.

Habit of public versus private motivations—ethical communication based on sharing sources of information, special opinions, motivations, or biases that may influence positions.

Habit of respect for dissent—ethical communication that encourages opposing viewpoints and arguments.

1. The **habit of search**. Ethical communication explores willingly the complexity of any issue or problem. This exploration requires generating valid information and evaluating new and often controversial findings.
2. The **habit of justice**. Ethical communication presents information as openly and fairly as possible and with concern for message distortion. Not only is information accurate, but also information is presented for maximum understanding. When we receive and evaluate information, the habit of justice requires that we examine our own evaluation criteria and potential biases that contribute to distortion in meaning.
3. The **habit of public versus private motivations**. Ethical communication is based on sharing sources of information, special opinions, motivations, or biases that may influence our position. Hidden agendas are discouraged for both message senders and receivers.
4. The **habit of respect for dissent**. Ethical communication not only allows but also encourages opposing viewpoints and arguments. This habit of respect for dissent in an open environment supports generation of the best ideas through thoughtful examination, disagreement, and new idea presentation.

When applied to the organizational setting, these guidelines suggest that individuals and groups are engaging in ethical communication behaviors when they thoughtfully analyze problems and issues, are open to diverse types and sources of information, conduct their deliberations openly without hidden agendas, and not only respect differing viewpoints but also encourage disagreement and dissent to produce superior ideas and solutions. From this perspective, unethical organizational communication behavior suppresses the examination of issues, withholds relevant information to pursue personal interests or motivations, and uses dissent to press for personal rather than organizational advantage.

ETHICAL DILEMMAS IN ORGANIZATIONAL COMMUNICATION

Although ethical issues can arise over virtually any type of communication, several recurring organizational communication situations have ethical implications. These situations (representing skills and abilities, communication behaviors related to money, communication behaviors related to information collection and dissemination, personal communication behaviors, and planned organizational communication) are frequently encountered by the communication professional.

Representing Skills and Abilities

All of us present our skills and abilities to potential employers when seeking a job. The way in which we communicate what we know reflects an ethical decision about fair representation of our abilities. Most of us have known someone who has told an interviewer about a skill we knew the individual did not possess. Although we would say that this is not strictly ethical behavior, we know our friend is highly motivated and will attempt to do a good job if hired. But does this motivation make the behavior acceptable? What is the ethical standard we should apply?

Once hired, we may attempt to seek good assignments designed to help us advance. How do we represent our abilities as compared to others in our work group? Do we keep information about mistakes from our supervisor to appear more competent than our peers? Do we blame others for problems even though we legitimately bear part of the responsibility? How can we behave ethically and still risk what others might think about our competencies if they know we have made a major mistake?

When in a supervisory or managerial position, we are responsible for giving feedback to others about their performance. Are we hesitant to give negative information to a problem employee, thereby creating a false sense of security? Are we making an important ethical decision or are we making a realistic appraisal that the person in question can't handle bad news and would be demoralized if we were more direct?

The representation of skills and abilities also influences problem identification. Consultants and human resource development specialists frequently are asked to help define organizational problems and propose training and related development activities for problem solution. These professionals are continually faced with the dilemma of defining a problem they may or may not have the skills to solve. When the consultant is external to the organization, defining a problem as needing skills other than those the consultant possesses costs the consultant potential earnings. The organization must hire someone else to meet its needs. On the other hand, defining the problem or need in terms of services the consultant can provide is subject to serious questions of integrity. The concerns are much the same for the internal communication professional.

An example from the development of the training plan of a major East Coast retailer can help to illustrate this dilemma. The company's personnel director, at the request of the president, designed and administered a company-wide training needs assessment survey to develop a training program for all employees. The company's previous training efforts had been sporadic and generally were in response to requests from particular departments. As a result, sales employees had received more training than any other single group. The personnel director, who specialized in sales training, was sensitive to the president's request and interpreted it as an implied criticism of his past efforts. The training survey contained twenty-four items assessing needs relating to interpersonal relationships and ten items relating to specific areas such as performance appraisal, affirmative action, and administration of company benefits. Critics of the personnel director's efforts pointed out that the organization would continue to emphasize sales training based on the content items in the survey. They noted that most of the twenty-four items relating to working relationships were items covered in courses already offered through personnel. Although a training plan and budget were established from the survey, the personnel director's credibility with some of the president's staff was eroded because of their questions about his ethics in assessing the real needs of the organization rather than the needs he was capable of meeting. In reality, the personnel director may have been correct that the items represented in the survey were the most crucial for overall needs assessment. Our example does not define for us whether or not the personnel director engaged in ethical behavior. The example illustrates the dilemma the director faced and how his behavior was subject to the ethical evaluations of others.

Communication Behaviors Related to Money

Communication surrounding fees for services, salaries, and personal versus corporate money is subject to ethical evaluation. The communication consultant, in pricing a training program to a potential client, must base the worth of services on personal credentials, program complexity, general market value of the program, and fees the consulting organization is expecting to pay. Should a consultant, for example, charge different organizations different fees for essentially the same services? How should fees and services be described? How can the consultant establish charges for diagnosing a problem that is not fully understood? The answers to these and other questions represent decisions about ethical communication.

An ethical question is whether general salary information should be available to all employees or whether salaries should remain confidential to individual employees. The communication of performance review and wage administration information is also a management communication decision with ethical consequences. Individuals communicate their ethical standards regarding organizational money when they use expense accounts, buy services or products for the organization, and establish department budgets. One way to examine our communication behaviors relating to organizational money is to determine whether we would approve of our behavior if we were the sole owner of the company.

Many communication professionals face ethical dilemmas as a result of payment for services. It is not uncommon, for example, for a communication consultant to work simultaneously for competing organizations. Do both clients need to know that the consultant is employed by the other? Internal communication specialists encounter information concerning personal problems of employees such as alcoholism or drug abuse. Are these specialists ever entitled to withhold information from the organization that pays their salary? How should these decisions be examined? All of these questions and more have ethical implications for the behaviors of individuals and for overall organizational policy.

Communication Behaviors Related to Information Collection and Dissemination

Most communication professionals are involved in collecting organizational information. They interview, conduct surveys, facilitate meetings, advise and counsel individuals, review documents, and in a variety of other ways generate data important to the conduct of their jobs. During data-collection activities, ethical decisions are made concerning what should remain confidential, who has a need to know, how accurate the information is, and what the criteria for interpretation are. These same ethical issues are related to information dissemination. Should sensitive information be kept private, going only to affected individuals? Does a guarantee of confidentiality prohibit the use of the information, even though the organization could be improved if the information surfaced? Who has a need to know? How accurate is the information and is it subject to varying interpretations? Most experienced professionals know their ability to handle these sensitive questions ethically contributes to their personal credibility. Even if ethical considerations were not important in and of themselves, practicing communication professionals find that the exercise of ethical standards is essential to their overall organizational effectiveness. Research on effective leaders supports this perspective. As you will recall from Chapter 8, Bennis and Nanus (1985) found that a characteristic of effective leaders was their ability to generate trust and behave consistently. Outstanding leaders practiced their individual standards (ethics and values) in a manner that helped others accept the challenge of their organizational vision.

Personal Communication Behaviors

Thus far we have been talking about the ethics of organizational communication as related to specific types of organizational responsibilities. Although these areas include personal behaviors, there is yet another area of personal behavior important for our consideration. This area, broadly described as our personal communication style, refers to the ethics of our individual behaviors, regardless of our job responsibilities. Do we, for example, behave autocratically, attempting to win at any costs? Is this autocratic preference ethical when it stifles the good ideas of others? Do we, as a result of high communication apprehension or a preference for conflict avoidance, refuse to participate in decision making even though we have information appropriate to the decision? When employed by the organization, is it ethical to withhold the best of our thinking? Does our style help others to examine issues critically or do we use the power of our position or force of our personality to get our own way? How can we examine the ethics of our approaches? These questions and others can be answered through self-assessment and understanding of our personal ethical standards.

Planned Organizational Communication

Planned organizational communication such as advertising, public relations, and government and stockholder interactions is more likely to be governed by formal codes of ethics or legal standards and requirements than other aspects of organizational communication. Advertising is subject to government regulations that include ethical standards about what constitutes "truth in advertising." Full disclosure of financial information is required for stockholder and government relationships, and public relations efforts are subject to ethical standards established by the journalism profession. Despite these standards, we can all think of times when we have questioned the ethics of advertising and can remember when organizations attempted to manipulate the public with less than full disclosure about products or services.

DEVELOPING ETHICAL STANDARDS
IN ORGANIZATIONAL COMMUNICATION

We have been discussing how we can determine whether communication is ethical and have identified some common ethical dilemmas faced by communication professionals. We have not, however, attempted to apply ethical standards to the behavior choices we can expect to encounter in organizational settings. The following shortened versions of ten organizational dilemmas were encountered during my consulting experiences. For each dilemma, attempt to determine what you would actually do if faced by this situation and what you should do. If what you would do and should do are different, state why. Finally, after analyzing all ten situations, attempt to determine what criteria you were using in applying ethical standards.

Ethical Dilemmas in Organizational Communication

1. You are the newly appointed personnel director for a large beverage distributor. Your new job responsibilities include screening all applicants for promotions to management positions. Your company's usual procedure is for the personnel director to screen applicants and select the top three for further interviews with management. You also know that the president of the company does not want a woman on his personal staff. Your current decision is difficult because your most recent vacancy is on the president's personal staff and your top three applicants are female. You can send the three applicants to the president and wait to see what happens. You can rethink your selection criteria and try to have a male applicant in the top three. You can reopen the position, hoping to attract additional qualified applicants. You can confront the president about his discriminatory posture. You also have other options. *What would you do? What should you do?*

2. You are part of a team of people who is involved in administrating and interpreting an in-depth set of surveys designed to help managers in your company better understand how their managers and subordinates view their effectiveness. The results of the surveys are intended to be developmental, and individual members of your team will meet with each manager to interpret the results and develop action plans for improvements. You are puzzled when you see the first computer printouts of the survey results. Managers who you know are well respected and effective are receiving low scores as compared to a national sample of managers from similar industries. You contact the company that compiled the results and ask questions about their sample. Your contact does not provide satisfactory information. Your peers believe you should go ahead and interpret the results to the managers. You believe the results are suspect and question whether they should be presented. Your boss believes the results should be presented. After all, corporate headquarters uses the survey with no problems. You can do as your peers want you to do. You can ask for a meeting with your peers and your boss in hopes of convincing them of your concerns. You can present the results to your group of managers and tell them you don't have much confidence in the findings. You can refuse to participate further in the program. You have other options. *What would you do? What should you do?*

3. A crew member from the night shift's manufacturing group has come to you as her personnel liaison with a concern about drug use on the

production line. She won't give you any specific details for fear of those involved finding out who has turned them in. She suggests you should investigate immediately but warns against involving her in any way. She asks you not to tell the other personnel liaisons because the grapevine has it that one of them may be involved. You can go to your boss and work with her in deciding what to do next. You can try to investigate on your own. You can bring up the drug problems the plant is experiencing at a staff meeting and watch closely to see if there are any unusual reactions from your peers. You can tell your source to give you more specific information before you will do anything. You can ignore the problem because of lack of evidence. You have other options. *What would you do? What should you do?*

4. You are in the training department of a large West Coast hospital. Your department is responsible for all training for nonmedical staff and management training for medical department supervisors and nursing staff. Your boss has been in his position for twenty-two years. When asked to develop a five-year report of your department's activities, your analysis of the records shows that one consultant has been paid over $50,000 for approximately six training sessions per year. This fee schedule is more than twice what other consultants working in similar subject areas have charged the hospital. You decide to pull the consultant's file and investigate. Much to your surprise, there is no formal contract or course evaluations. You ask your boss about the consultant in question, only to be told he is none of your concern. The secretary in your department warns you that the consultant is a special friend of your boss and that you had better let the matter drop. You can forget the whole thing and finish the report. You can press your boss for more information. You can ask the secretary to help you locate the missing information. You can go to the finance department and ask for its copy of the contract. You can put this deficiency in your final report. You have other options. *What would you do? What should you do?*

5. You have overheard a conversation between your manager and the manager of a department where your best friend is employed. From their conversation, it is apparent that your friend is not pleasing her manager and she will definitely be passed over for the promotion she badly wants. You don't want to see her hurt, and you happen to know she has a job offer from another group within your organization. Should you tell her about the conversation and urge her to take the new offer? Should you remain silent because of the manner in which you heard the information? Should you go to your boss and tell him you accidentally overheard the conversation and are concerned because your friend might turn down a good job offer? Should you urge your friend to confront her boss? You have other options. *What would you do? What should you do?*

6. You are the lead copywriter in an advertising agency handling a major chemical products account. Your copy is frequently criticized by the chemical manufacturer's marketing director. He wants a stronger sell, even

if that means omitting much of the disclaimer information associated with the safe use of the products. He contends that people buying chemicals should take individual responsibility for safety and that the company should not be required to devote scarce ad and package label space to full disclosure of the potential hazards. You realize he may even be willing to test whether government regulating agencies will restrain his actions if he refuses to comply with industry product labeling requirements. The issue comes to a head when you receive copy proofs changed by the marketing director to omit disclosure information you believe should remain in the new ad series. Your immediate boss is out of town on vacation and cannot be reached. You either have to let the changes go or confront the man. You know he will not appreciate your interference. You can let the copy go as is. (You have documented evidence that the marketing director, not your agency, made the changes.) You can refuse to make the changes, thereby jeopardizing the account. You can ask to be removed from the account. You can go to the marketing manager's boss in the chemical company. You have other options. *What would you do? What should you do?*

7. You are a consultant specializing in management communication training programs. You have been hired by a prestigious building products manufacturer to conduct a series of programs for its top management staff. The programs go well and you are excited about future business with other branches of the organization. The president of the company invites you to lunch and congratulates you on your work. He has recommended extending your contract and indicates that this will be the beginning of a long and mutually satisfactory relationship. He then tells you of an unwritten condition in your contract: He wants a quarterly report made directly to him on promising individuals in the branch offices. He believes your contact in the training classes will give you the opportunity to spot talent that he may have little opportunity to recognize. He insists the report should be confidential, as his personnel department would object. You can do as the president requests. You can advise him of your concerns about evaluating people during training sessions not designed for that purpose. You can object to the need for secrecy in your appraisals. You can say nothing and think about what to do next. You have other options. *What would you do? What should you do?*

8. You have received a job offer from one of your current employer's principal competitors. The offer was unsolicited and has come as a surprise. Although this type of offer is not uncommon in the advertising business, you are unsure how to respond. The vice president who is urging you to come to work for her also mentioned that one of your current employer's largest accounts is talking with her group about changing agencies. You have reason to believe the account is pleased with your work and wonder if her offer is not aimed at increasing the chances of taking business away from your employer. So far the vice president has not asked you any questions about the account. You are scheduled to meet her for lunch next week. Should you tell your employer you are considering another position?

Should you refuse to discuss the account in question if the vice president mentions it? How can you learn whether the offer has a hidden business agenda? Do you have a responsibility to your current employer to tell him a major account is being solicited by another firm? *What would you do? What should you do?*

9. You are the newest member of your company's field sales staff. Before being assigned to your own group of accounts, you spent three months making sales calls with experienced sales personnel. During that time, you became aware of customer complaints about quality defects in two of the six product lines your represent. The salespeople you worked with assured you that the company was aware of the problem and was working hard to lower the defective shipments. In your first solo presentation, your potential customer asks you about rumors that some of your product lines are having defect problems. He wants to know very specifically what he can expect if he places a large order. You want to make the sale. You have not investigated the extent of the defects problem or when the company expects to have it solved. You know your manager expects you to secure an order from this customer. How should you answer the customer? Can you make the sale if you admit the defects problem? What will happen if you don't? What would your manager have you do? What are your other options? *What would you do? What should you do?*

10. You are the member of a task force asked to recommend to the city council how the city's Park and Recreation Department can better serve low-income members of your community. Two members of your group believe city government should reduce its budget and view your assignment as an ideal way to make that statement. You disagree. The task force is charged with making programming recommendations. The Park and Recreation Department is charged with incorporating those recommendations into their budget, which must be approved by the council. You think that increased programs for low-income areas of your community are positive and hope some of your recommendations will be part of the final report. Several of the group's members agree with you, two strongly disagree, and several are undecided. At the next-to-last task force meeting before the report is due to council, a reporter asks to interview a member of the task force in order to get a progress update. The two members with whom you have had the most disagreements are late to the meeting. Others in the group suggest you talk with the reporter. You agree, hoping this will be an opportunity to express your support for low-income programming. As the interview begins, you wonder whether your remarks should reflect the various perspectives present in the group or whether it is appropriate to represent your personal view. Should you tell the reporter that members both support and disapprove of increased park and recreation programming? Should you tell the reporter that the final report to council is very likely to contain a dissenting opinion and you are not sure which side of the issue will receive majority support? Will this type of dissent weaken the effectiveness of the report? Should you represent your

position since the other two members are late and would have had an opportunity to speak to the press had they arrived on time? *What would you do? What should you do?*

After analyzing these examples, would you say that the behaviors you *would* do and *should* do were always the same? If they were different, what caused the difference? What contributed to similarities? Was it difficult to determine what was ethical in a given situation? Can you identify the standards you used as your criteria? As a result of these examples, can you see the relationship between competency and ethics?

SUMMARY

Values are the subjective assessments we make about the relative worth of a quality or object. These assessments are thought to guide our behavior in making choices and judgments. Both individuals and organizations have value systems that are expressed through communication behaviors. In an organizational sense, values are part of the shared realities generated through organizational communication. These shared values are reflected in organizational myths, stories, decision making, and thematic and tactical communication rules. Individual values have been described as theoretical, economic, aesthetic, social, and political. Work place values include concern for locus of control, self-esteem, tolerance of ambiguity, social judgment, and risk taking. Rokeach has identified both terminal and instrumental values. Appraising an individual value system is important for job and career decisions. Ethics are the standards by which behaviors are evaluated for morality, for rightness or wrongness. When applied to human communication, ethics are the moral principles that guide our judgments about the good and bad, the right and wrong of communication, not just communication effectiveness or efficiency. Ethical communication is an important prerequisite for communication effectiveness and has as a central focus behaviors that encourage choice making, foster conditions for growth and development, and value the innate worth of human beings. Individual and organizational value systems and the standards of a given profession all influence the ethics of organizational communication. Ethical communication can be evaluated by using Wallace's criteria of the habit of search, the habit of justice, the habit of public versus private motivations, and the habit of respect for dissent. Finally, ethical communication results from thoughtful analysis of potential dilemmas in organizational communication.

WORKSHOP

1. Divide into groups of four or six members each and discuss the ten examples of ethical dilemmas presented earlier in this chapter. Com-

pare your individual responses to those of other group members. As a group, what would you do; what should you do?

2. Either individually or in small groups write a statement describing the values of your ideal organization. Describe your organization's ethical communication behaviors.

3. Organizations A and B have differing value systems. Divide the class in groups and assign each group an Organization A or Organization B value system. Both organizations face the same problem. Using the stated values as a basis, each group should determine how its organization would solve the problem. Report your solutions to the class as a whole. (See pages 431–432.)

4. Judge Bernard Baker, in an essay entitled "Ethics and a Look at the Law as a Communications Forum," raises important questions about "honest" communication. His essay can be used for individual reflection or class discussion. (See pages 432–434.)

5. The Coronado Youth Employment and Recreational Services Case illustrates value and ethical differences between a board of directors and an executive director. These clashes result in serious authority and responsibility problems. Describe this case in terms of values and ethics. Prepare to advise Margaret Rims and the board of directors. (See pages 434–436.)

Scoring the Values Appraisal Exercise

Instructions (Part 1). These are the six defined values that are indicated by the twenty-four statements. Enter the number you circled for each statement next to the number for that statement. Then total your score for each value.

VALUES:	MONEY	POWER	FAMILY	AESTHETIC	CREATIVE	SOCIAL
	1 _____	2 _____	3 _____	4 _____	5 _____	6 _____
	11 _____	7 _____	10 _____	9 _____	12 _____	8 _____
	13 _____	15 _____	14 _____	18 _____	16 _____	17 _____
	20 _____	22 _____	21 _____	24 _____	19 _____	23 _____
TOTALS:	_____	_____	_____	_____	_____	_____

Instructions (Part 2). Now plot your own personal values profile. Use the preceding totals for each of the six values and plot them on the chart on page 431.

	MONEY	POWER	FAMILY	AESTHETIC	CREATIVE	SOCIAL
16						
15						
14						
13						
12						
11						
10						
9						
8						
7						
6						
5						
4						
3						
2						
1						
0						

Organizational Values and Decision-Making Exercise

Organization A Value System

Locus of control. Little emphasis on connection between individual efforts and the success or failure of the organization.

Self-esteem. Little emphasis on recognition for work or positive feedback.

Tolerance of ambiguity. Low tolerance for ambiguity and high support for "one-right-answer" approach.

Social judgment. Little specific concern about working relationships with others.

Risk taking. High need for security and deliberative action.

Organization B Value System

Locus of control. High emphasis on connection between individual efforts and the success or failure of the organization.

Self-esteem. High emphasis on recognition for work; positive feedback.

Tolerance of ambiguity. High tolerance for ambiguity and low support for "one-right-answer" approach.

Risk taking. Low need for security and high support for risk taking.

The Problem

Reducing the work force through layoffs.

The Situation

The company for which you work is faced with a decreased demand for several of its products. As a result, the company president plans to announce and implement a 3 percent reduction in the staff of your division. The actual reduction will consist of about 50 employees from a division work force of 1,350. The layoffs could start as early as the first week of January. It is now the middle of October.

The Assignment

Given the values of your organization, decide how you should implement this reduction in force. Your plan for implementation will be conveyed to the company president.

Ethics and a Look at the Law as a Communications Forum

Bernard R. Baker, District Judge*

Aristotle was the first recorded thinker to bridge the disciplines of ethics and communication (e.g., rhetoric). He defined "ethos" as the distinguishing character, "moral nature," or guiding beliefs of a person, group, or institution. Further, he defined "ethics" as the discipline dealing with what is good and bad (i.e., with moral duty and obligation). Ethics are, therefore, the principles of conduct governing an individual or a group—that is a theory or system of moral values.

The Preamble to the Code of Professional Responsibilities for lawyers states,

> *The continued existence of a free and democratic society depends upon a recognition of the concept that justice is based upon the rule of law grounded in respect for the dignity of the individual and his capacity through reason for enlightened self-government. Law so grounded makes justice possible, for only through such law does the dignity of the individual attain respect and protection. Without it, individual rights become subject to unrestrained power, respect for law is destroyed, and rational self-government is impossible.*
>
> *Lawyers, as guardians of the law, play a vital role in the preservation of society. The fulfillment of this role requires an understanding by lawyers of their relationship with and function in our legal system. A consequent obligation of lawyers is to maintain the highest standards of ethical conduct.*

The thrust of this essay is to analyze the law as an ethical system in conjunction with being a prime forum of communication. It is, therefore, a micro-macro of value-oriented or ethical communication. How are ethics (values) practiced day to day in the courtroom by trained communicators, i.e., lawyers and judges?

* Judge Bernard R. Baker presides as a district court judge in the 4th Judicial District in Colorado Springs, Colorado, where he administers over the full spectrum of justice in the criminal, civil, domestic, and probate law areas. Judge Baker received his doctorate in the philosophy of law from Indiana University. He also holds a degree in economics and business administration from Northwestern University.

First, lawyers are advocates. Judges are arbiters, i.e., decision makers. The whole theory of the adversary system of law is like that of a college debate team. Each side will do its utmost to win, provided its conduct falls within a given standard of *ethics* or *values*. Of primacy, therefore, is that each side must speak the truth. Objective facts must be distinguished from inferences, conjecture, or at worst mere hyperbole. I must state, as a judge, that many lawyers forsake truth in argumentation in favor of the proverbial "play on words." Attempts are made to make black look white and vice versa, in the strange alchemy of verbal message. Some lawyers rationalize that their play on words will be equalized or critically minimized by the judge and/or jury. They "shotgun," and leave it up to the judge and/or jury, sitting in the middle, to discern the truth. This is *not* ethical communication. One must never assume that someone else is going to discover untruth or various gradations, thereof. This flies in the fact of the Kantian moral imperative that one basically ought to do that which would be right in the eyes of the doer. This is, of course, only a sophisticated rendition of the Golden Rule.

I consider it a fundamental tenet of "natural law" (absolute, universal, immutable moral truth) that all of us want to be told the truth. It therefore follows that we utter *only* the truth in ethical communication. We now convert the micro of the law into the macro of ethical communication. We know, as a society, that organizations and institutions are inherently not conducive to fact-finding and truth. The reasons are myriad. I will dwell on only one: competition—the will to win, or more basally put, the will to survive. This is where some trial lawyers go wrong ethically. It's win at any cost, with the familiar "We're getting paid to win, aren't we?" The profit-oriented corporation is in business to make a profit, isn't it, regardless of the cost to truth? The whole realm of business organization, from external advertising to internal reports, all suffers from this same advocacy perspective—a perceived need to put things in the best light possible at the expense of truth. This is the ultimate ethical problem for the law, for the government, for business organizations, and for our society.

How do we face this naked truth about human behavior since it factors down to survival instincts? I submit that we as individuals, and collectively as a society, learn to "bite the bullet"; that truth, the ultimate principle of ethical communication, prevail over the need to look good. The communication goal, therefore, is to state the truth and bear the consequences.

As we commenced with Aristotle, we will close:

> *Or is it quite wrong to make our judgment depend on fortune? Yes, it is wrong, for fortune does not determine whether we fare well or ill, but is, as we said, merely an accessory to human life; activities in conformity with virtue constitute happiness, and the opposite activities constitute its opposite. . . .*
>
> *For no function of man possesses as much stability as do activities in conformity with virtue: these seem to be even more durable than scientific knowledge. . . .*

The happy man will have the attribute of permanence which we are discussing, and he will remain happy throughout his life. For he will always or to the highest degree do and contemplate what is in conformity with virtue; he will bear the vicissitudes of fortune most nobly and with perfect decorum under all circumstances, inasmuch as he is truly good and "four-square beyond reproach."

QUESTIONS FOR DISCUSSION

1. If ethical communication is "honest" communication, is it possible to be honest in a contemporary organization and at the same time survive and serve your own needs and goals?

2. If your own best foot is somewhat dirty, do you still put it forward?

3. Can an organization tolerate "honest" communication if the particular truth is critical of the organization and could affect its very survival?

4. When, if ever, is it right for an individual, an organization, or even a nation, to lie to its own people and/or to others?

The Coronado Youth Employment and Recreational Services Case

The Youth Employment and Recreational Services (YERS) program has a long and distinguished history in Coronado, California, a growing city of 1,200,000. However, in recent years minority community members have pressed for increased services and facilities in parts of town with substantial minority populations. These requests have created dissension and growing controversy among YERS staff and members of the board of directors.

Margaret Rims was promoted to executive director of the Coronado YERS in 1983 after having been with the organization for twenty-five years. Margaret began her career in recreational development while attending Coronado University and has seen the YERS program grow from a one-person staff with limited programs in a single location to a staff of fifteen offering services at seven Coronado sites.

Over the years, Margaret Rims has been given credit for the growth of the recreation program. She has also been asked by the National Council of Youth Employment and Recreational Services to lead several regional and national workshops on recreation program development.

When Margaret Rims applied in 1983 for the position of executive director, several staff and board members were surprised because most assumed Margaret was happy in her recreational development role. Several members of the board voiced concern regarding Margaret's overall administrative qualifications, but the prevailing sentiment supported her promotion.

Margaret Rims became executive director of the Coronado YERS in the climate of mounting pressure to increase services and facilities in the heavily populated minority areas of northeast Coronado. Several local groups also questioned minority representation on the YERS staff and board. Margaret felt these pressures were best ignored. She disagreed with several members of the board and staff who urged her to develop plans to increase minority involvement.

Margaret's strongest staff support came from her friend and personnel director, Jack Smith. Jack has been YERS personnel director for eighteen years. He has not been pleased with increasing personnel requirements established by the national executive council of YERS. Specifically, he has disagreed with detailing job descriptions and the institution of grievance procedures for employees. Jack believes employers should have more latitude than these policies and procedures afford. Some minority job applicants have charged that Jack was responsible for keeping them from being employed at YERS.

In early 1984, several influential minority community members met with Margaret Rims to discuss YERS program expansion. Margaret told the group she could not recommend the expansion they desired. At the meeting, Bill Hillis, a black lawyer in Coronado, confronted Margaret with questions about Jack Smith's hiring practices. Margaret stoutly defended Jack.

The citizens group was not content with Margaret's responses. Bill Hillis contacted the YERS president, Dr. Atkins, and requested a formal meeting with the board of directors. The group, with Hillis as spokesperson, also expressed concern to national YERS officials. National YERS funds, along with membership dues, are the primary source of funding for YERS programs.

The national director of YERS contacted Dr. Atkins to express his concern. He further stated his apprehension that any publicity of the issue might adversely affect the YERS fund drive scheduled to begin within the month.

Unknown to Margaret Rims, the board of directors met with Bill Hillis and the group who originally confronted Margaret. Dr. Atkins and the board pledged support of program development in northeast Coronado and promised to look into the hiring practices directed by Jack Smith.

At the next formal meeting, the board informed Margaret of the need to include this promised expansion in 1985 planning. No specific actions were taken regarding either Jack Smith or current hiring practices. At the same meeting, the firm of Jones and Belew, certified public accountants for YERS, reported revenues from membership were down 10 percent from the previous year and facilities maintenance costs were increasing an unexpected 8 percent. Those board members who had originally questioned Margaret's capabilities became vocal in their criticism.

In the next few months, the division between the board and Margaret Rims became open and hostile. Dr. Atkins received reports that Margaret stated in a staff meeting that she had been at YERS before any of the board and would be there when all of them were gone.

The rift flared into the open when Margaret submitted the YERS program proposal for 1985 to the board of directors. No inclusion of the promised programming in northeast Coronado was made. Margaret walked out of the meeting in anger. She refused to return telephone calls from Dr. Atkins.

Dr. Atkins called an emergency meeting of the board of directors. Sentiment ran high, and the board voted to terminate Margaret Rims. Two members objected, claiming the action was in direct violation of national YERS policy, which called for warning and probation before termination of any employee. One member further expressed concern about community reaction to terminating a twenty-five-year employee.

Community leaders openly criticized both Margaret Rims and the board. Margaret retained a lawyer and named Dr. Atkins and several members of the board in a defamation of character suit. She also claimed specific damages for loss of retirement benefits because of termination. During the initial months of 1985, membership revenues dropped by 12 percent and staff morale and productivity were extremely low. Jack Smith was believed by Dr. Atkins to be a focal point of internal disruption and a source of continuing information for Margaret Rims. Amid these problems the search for a new executive director began.

QUESTIONS FOR DISCUSSION

1. What are the ethical and value issues in this case?
2. Describe how the flow of information throughout YERS affected the problem.
3. How would you describe this communication climate?
4. What should Margaret Rims do? What should the board do?

SUMMARY OF COMPETENCY COMPONENTS:
KNOWLEGE, SENSITIVITY, SKILLS, VALUES

KNOWLEDGE

Values are described as individual assessments of what is desirable that motivate behavior and guide choice and judgment.

Ethics are identified as the rightness or wrongness of behavior.

SENSITIVITY

Values are shared realities generated through organizational communication.

Values influence decision making and problem solving.

Values and ethics are important for communication competency and organizational effectiveness.

Understanding personal values is important for career choice.

SKILLS

Analysis skills are practiced through value assessment.

Analysis skills are developed and practiced through case and dilemma analysis.

VALUES

Individual, organizational, and professional values guide behavior and effectiveness.

Ethical communication behavior contributes to choice making, contributes to growth and development, and values the innate worth of individuals.

REFERENCES AND SUGGESTED READINGS

Allport, G., P. Vernon, and G. Lindzey. 1960. *Study of values.* Boston: Houghton Mifflin.

Arnett, R. C. 1985. The status of ethics scholarship in speech communication journals from 1915 to 1985. Paper presented at the Speech Communication Association Convention, November, Denver.

Bennis, W., and B. Nanus. 1985. *Leaders: The strategies for taking charge.* New York: Harper & Row.

Deal, T. E., and A. A. Kennedy. 1982. *Corporate cultures: The rites and rituals of corporate life.* Reading, MA: Addison-Wesley.

DeVito, J. A. 1978. *Communicology: An introduction to the study of communication.* New York: Harper & Row.

DeVito, J. A. 1986. *The interpersonal communication book.* 4th ed. New York: Harper & Row.

Goodstein, L. D. 1983. Managers, values, and organization development. *Group and Organization Studies* 8(2): 203–20.

Howe, R., M. Howe, and M. Mindell: 1982. *Management values inventory.* San Diego: University Associates.

Johannesen, R. L. 1983. *Ethics in human communication.* 2d ed. Prospect Heights, IL: Waveland Press.

Keller, P. W. 1981. Interpersonal dissent and the ethics of dialogue. *Communication* 6: 287–303.

Keller, P. W., and C. T. Brown. 1968. An interpersonal ethic for communication. *Journal of Communication* 18(1): 73–81.

Lippitt, G., and R. Lippitt. 1978. *The consulting process in action.* LaJolla, CA: University Associates.

Nilsen, T. R. 1966. *Ethics of speech communication.* Indianapolis: Bobbs-Merrill.

Palmer, D. D., J. F. Veiga, and J. A. Vora. 1981. Personal values in managerial decision making: Value-cluster approach in two cultures. *Group and Organization Studies* 6(2): 224–34.

Posner, B., J. Kouzes, and W. Schmidt. 1985. Shared values make a difference: An empirical test of corporate culture. *Human Resource Management* 24(3): 293–309.

Redding, W. C. 1979. Graduate education and the communication consultant: Playing God for a fee. *Communication Education* 28(4): 346–52.

Redding, W. C. 1984. Professionalism in training—Guidelines for a code of ethics. Paper presented at the Speech Communication Association Convention, November, Chicago.

Rokeach, M. 1973. *The nature of human values.* New York: Free Press.

Rubin, R., and J. Yoder. 1985. Ethical issues in the evaluation of communication behavior. *Communication Education* 34: 13–17.

Shockley-Zalabak, P., and D. Morley. 1989. Adhering to organizational culture: What does it mean? Why does it matter? *Group and Organization Studies* 14(4): 483–500.

Sprague, J., and L. Freedman. 1984. The ethics of organization intervention. Paper presented at the Speech Communication Association Convention, November, Chicago.

Wallace, K. R. 1955. An ethical basis of communication. *Speech Teacher* 4(1): 1–9.

~ A P P E N D I X ~

Putting It
All Together

The next several pages of the text contain a self-assessment instrument, cases, and guest essays designed to develop communication competency by applying the theory you have been studying and to practice analysis opportunities. The self-assessment instrument has been designed to help guide your choices about additional educational preparation and to identify areas for continuing competency development.

The seven cases in the Appendix are taken from real experiences of individuals with organizational communication responsibilities. Four guest essays are provided to help us think about important issues raised in the cases. Essays have been written by people with degrees in organizational communication and by those employed in professional communication jobs. Their perspectives are useful as you consider your knowledge, sensitivity, skills, and values for organizational communication.

These final pages have been designed to help you pull together the various competencies this text has been seeking to develop. We suggest you again complete the self-assessment of competency needs that was presented in Chapter 1 (Table 1.1). Compare your answers from the beginning of the course until now. What have you accomplished? What remains to be done?

After you have completed your self-evaluation, compile a list of competencies you rate as highly developed. Next compile lists for those competency items rated moderately developed, somewhat limited, and needing development. What is your plan for continued growth?

TABLE A.1
Self-Assessment of Personal Development Needs

The following organizational communication competencies are presented for your self-evaluation. For each area you are asked to determine whether your present competencies are highly developed, moderately developed, somewhat limited, or needing development.

As I complete this course I would describe my KNOWLEDGE in . . .	Highly Developed	Moderately Developed	Somewhat Limited	Needing Development
1. defining and understanding organizational communication as . . .				
2. understanding major theories of how organizations work as . . .				
3. determining how an individual experiences organizational life as . . .				
4. describing what organizational conflict is and how it relates to productive organizations as . . .				
5. identifying characteristics of leadership and management communication as . . .				
6. understanding decision making and problem solving as . . .				
7. locating career opportunities in organizational communication as . . .				
8. distinguishing between values and ethics in organizational communication as . . .				
As I complete this course I would describe my SENSITIVITY to . . .				
9. my personal responsibilities for organizational communication as . . .				

As I complete this course I would describe my SENSITIVITY to . . .	Highly Developed	Moderately Developed	Somewhat Limited	Needing Development
10. how "shared realities" are generated through organizational communication as . . .				
11. why and how people work together as . . .				
12. what motivates me and what is likely to motivate others as . . .				
13. the importance of interpersonal relationships with supervisors, peers, and subordinates as . . .				
14. personal preferences for a variety of approaches to conflict as . . .				
15. personal preferences for leadership and management communication as . . .				
16. organizational influences for decision making and problem solving as . . .				
17. past achievements, values, and skills that can guide career choices as . . .				
18. how values and ethics contribute to organizational effectiveness as . . .				
As I complete this course I would describe my SKILLS in . . .				
19. analyzing a variety of organizational problems as . . .				
20. developing effective organizational messages as . . .				
21. engaging in active listening as . . .				
22. contributing to supportive organizational environments as . . .				
23. participating in productive conflict management as . . .				
24. leadership communication as . . .				
25. leading and participating in effective group meetings as . . .				

(continued)

TABLE A.1 (*continued*)

As I complete this course I would describe my SKILLS in . . .	Highly Developed	Moderately Developed	Somewhat Limited	Needing Development
26. fact finding and evaluation as . . .				
27. gathering information for decision making and problem solving as . . .				
28. analyzing data for decision making and problem solving as . . .				
29. developing and making public presentations as . . .				
As I complete this course I would describe my VALUES for . . .				
30. accepting personal responsibility for communication as . . .				
31. relating individual communication behavior to organizational effectiveness as . . .				
32. using conflict for productive outcomes as . . .				
33. determining how leaders and managers should behave as . . .				
34. influencing my career choices as . . .				
35. understanding organizational values, ethics, and dilemmas as . . .				

CASES

The following cases are taken from real experiences of individuals with organizational communication responsibilities. "A Conflict of Interest" and "Can Newspeople Challenge My Company?" stimulate our thinking about important issues of ethics and values while "Who Gets Cut?" raises both communication and decision-making concerns. Guest essays have been written by people with degrees in organizational communication and by those employed in professional communication jobs.

A Conflict of Interest

Gerald Burnes, M.D., is administrator of St. Vincent's Hospital Laboratory.* The twenty-four-hour-a-day, seven-day-a-week operation employs 165 people. Bob Warft is the lab's medical technologist. Bob holds a master's degree in business administration and oversees production, budgeting, and quality control. He reports directly to Dr. Burnes. Bob also is in regular contact with seventeen supervisors who monitor their own sections.

George Rogers is the supervisor of a small section with three employees with very specific subspecialty training. Testing and the evaluation of this group's results are shared only by members of this section and the pathologist, Dr. Burnes. George has worked for Dr. Burnes for fifteen years. Janice Pearson has been in this section, reporting to George, for six months. She is conscientious, eager, and a recent graduate of medical technology school. Janice is determined to do well, as there are few available jobs in this subspecialty.

Over the years, George and Dr. Burnes have developed a personal relationship similar to that of father and son. Their lack of objectivity with each other has created past problems when determining a diagnosis. Instead of offering two clear perspectives, they will agree to avoid a conflict. George's technical skills are good when he is attentive to details. After fifteen years at the same job, however, he has become less quality conscious. George works fewer total hours than the other supervisors and does not keep regular hours. Also, George is the only supervisor who reports directly to Dr. Burnes. He uses their relationship to register lab complaints and personal problems.

Bob Warft does not attempt to deal with George as long as George is under Dr. Burnes's supervision and protection. Bob can only register complaints from other supervisors about George's attitude and special privileges.

Although interpersonal relationships have been strained, George's position did not seem to affect patient care. Recently, however, Janice uncovered some serious errors George had made. Janice took the cases to Dr. Burnes, who quietly corrected the diagnoses. The time lapse between the initial and the corrected diagnoses was several months. These mistakes could have serious consequences for the patients. Dr. Burnes did not formally reprimand George Rogers or take other action.

QUESTIONS FOR DISCUSSION

1. What are the organizational communication problems in this case?

2. What should Janice do?

* This case was prepared by Summer Kircher (CT, A.S.C.P.), cytologist, Albany School of Medicine. Summer is a graduate student at the University of Colorado and a research assistant in the communication department.

3. How would you advise Dr. Burnes?

4. How can this problem be prevented in the future?

Can Newspeople Challenge My Company?

John Tyler is public relations director for a midwestern power company in the process of constructing a nuclear power plant to expand customer service.* Local residents in the areas to be served by the new nuclear plant are mixed in their reactions to the facility going up in their backyards. As a result of continuing national media coverage of nuclear power issues, local media have begun frequent coverage of the plant's progress. In particular, media attention has focused on the power company's requests to the local commerce commssion for rate increases and the cost overruns and delays encountered in plant construction.

John Tyler has been advised by his board of directors that he should escalate company public relations efforts in order to ensure a more favorable climate for the utility as it prepares to again ask the commerce commission for a rate increase. Amid preparation of an aggresssive campaign on the benefits of nuclear power, John receives a call from a network news team desiring to interview management involved with plant construction. The news team assures John of fair and balanced coverage and agrees that power company officials can tape everything the network shoots for its story.

John is worried because he knows that construction cost overruns have contributed to the utility seeking its latest rate increase. He is concerned that network reporters could use this fact to generate negative publicity, just what his management is attempting to avoid. John also knows that refusing to speak with the press can be interpreted as hiding important information to which the public has legitimate access. He also is troubled by potential conflict between his management and high journalistic standards.

QUESTIONS FOR DISCUSSION

1. Should John agree to the interviews?

2. What might happen if he refuses?

3. How can he advise his management to deal with this situation?

4. What are the ethical and value issues involved?

5. How would you advise John to proceed?

---

* This case was prepared by Dr. Kim Walker following his research on interactions between Illinois Power and the crew of the television program "60 Minutes." Although the case is fictional, it addresses critical issues about the public's right to know, journalistic responsibility, and the role of the communications professional in controversial organizational situations.

Dr. Walker (B.A., Millikin University; M.S., Ph.D., Southern Illinois University) is on the faculty at the University of Colorado, Colorado Springs, and is director of the Media Center and telecommunications facilities for the campus.

What Gets Cut?

The staff of the local Boy Scout council is in conflict regarding some editorial decisions on a recently completed promotional film for the Boy Scout program.* The five-person executive staff handled the production of the half-hour film, which is intended to be used to promote membership and to raise funds in the local community. Part of the film was shot at the local Boy Scout camp. Several young scouts, who happened by chance to be black, were shown riding horseback without the use of protective riding helmets.

The executive staff is meeting to decide how to handle the part of the film shot at the local Boy Scout camp. The finished film has been viewed. Seven of the thirty minutes are questionable and perhaps should be edited. The portion in question is aesthetically effective but does show several scouts without riding helmets. If the seven minutes are cut out, the film will be less effective and will be too short for the media purposes for which it was intended. But if that portion is not edited out, the lack of safety gear may raise some controversy in the local community. It is almost winter, so new footage that will blend seasonally with the existing film is not possible.

Present at the staff meeting are the following five persons:

Barbara, the executive director of the staff, who was hired by an all-white board of directors, is held in low esteem by her staff. The staff resent having a female director of a boys' organization. Barbara's position is that any decision that satisfies all the staff members is satisfactory with her.

Gary, the camp director, has extensive camping background. He is accustomed to making all decisions for the camp himself. It is his position that the film must be edited and the questionable seven minutes cut out.

Craig, the public relations director, has extensive background in the Boy Scout program. He grew up as a Boy Scout and has worked professionally for this council for several years. He is sensitive to the program's public image but also values the moral standards that Boy Scouting represents. Craig is ambivalent regarding the course of action for the questionable footage.

Sam, the fund development director, also has background in the Boy Scout program, but only recently began to work for the local council. He was hired by Barbara because of his ability to raise funds for the program. He is of the opinion that cutting the film will negatively impact on the fund-raising efforts already planned for the upcoming year. He believes the motivation for editing the film relates to the appearance of more black than white scouts in the footage and not to safety standards or the lack of safety helmets.

* This case was prepared by Sherwyn P. Morreale.

William, the membership director, is the only black staff member. He was passed over by the board of directors when Barbara was hired as executive director. He has worked for the local council for many years and was considered well qualified for the position of director. He believes that some discriminatory attitudes may be impacting on the editing decision, but believes the best decision for the upcoming membership drive should be made. He is not sure what that decision is.

QUESTIONS FOR DISCUSSION

1. If you were the executive director of the Boy Scouts council, how would you proceed?

2. What are the communication issues in the case?

3. What type of decision-making process would you use?

CASES AND COMMENTS

Our final set of cases is accompanied by commentaries from professionals addressing the issues raised in each situation. After studying each case and reading its companion essay, identify the knowledge, sensitivity, skill, and value competencies important for problem resolution.

Karen Mason's Management Briefing Disaster

Karen was humiliated. How could they? Why did John and Shirley have it in for her? Everyone at the meeting knew she was embarrassed, and no telling what most of the managers thought of her.

Karen Mason was upset as a result of a practical joke her two co-workers, John and Shirley, had played on her during her first presentation at Quality Products' quarterly management meeting. They knew she was nervous and wanted to make a good impression. John and Shirley thought putting cartoon slides in place of her opening graphs would be funny and appreciated as a good joke by both Karen and the management team. After all, they had her original slides ready to hand to her as soon as the laughter subsided. They had no way of knowing that the joke would totally unnerve her. Although everyone had laughed initially, Karen knew most felt sorry for her as she ended up reading her remarks.

John and Shirley thought Karen was being ridiculous. Their department was known for practical jokes and Karen should be expected to join in if she really wanted to be accepted. Neither John nor Shirley had intended to disrupt the presentation. Karen should have better control of herself.

Does Karen have a right to be angry? Is it possible that she doesn't have a sense of humor? Or are John and Shirley to blame? Can it be that both are correct? What would you do if you were Karen, John, or Shirley?

Michael Hackman offers suggestions for understanding the problems Karen, John, and Shirley are experiencing in his commentary that follows.

Some Ideas on the Use of Humor in Organizations

Michael Z. Hackman, Ph.D.*

The ability to create and appreciate humor seems to be unique to human beings. Indeed, humor plays an integral and vital role in the human communication process. Hardly a day goes by without exposure to humor in some form. From the internal laughter that may be generated by our own perceived futility to the amusement and pleasure received from listening to a good joke to the hilarity of witnessing someone slip on a banana peel, we are virtually surrounded by events we perceive as humorous. Humans, even in the most dire of circumstances, seem to engage in humorous interaction. Famed psychotherapist Viktor Frankl, for example, reports that even among prisoners in Nazi concentration camps, a degree of humor persisted. This is not completely surprising in light of the important role humor plays in the communication process.

Explanations for the significance of humor in human communication are plentiful. Literally hundreds of theories or variations of humor theories exist. Integrating these many perspectives on humor is not an easy or enviable task. In the simplest terms, humor seems to serve a number of internal and external functions in the human communication process. Internally, humor allows individuals to deal with socially unacceptable or threatening materials in a healthy, socially acceptable fashion. Humor allows us to look at the negative or anxiety-provoking aspects of our lives in a way that makes these events less threatening. By laughing in the face of adversity, we use humor to reduce tension and threat.

Humor aimed at ourselves, known as self-disparaging humor, also serves an internal anxiety-defusing function. By using ourselves as the brunt or object of a joke, we defend against attacks from others by attacking ourselves first. Most often individuals rely on self-disparaging humor in situations in which they feel uncomfortable or awkward. The ability to laugh at our own shortcomings may help to reduce the threat associated with our perceived weakness. If we can find the courage to laugh about it, how bad can it really be?

Humor also serves external, interpersonal functions. Humor is a social bonding mechanism. In the words of Victor Borge, "laughter is the shortest distance between two people." Beginning with the laughter and smiles we share with infants, appropriate humor serves to cement our interpersonal relationships. Appropriate and effective humor enhances interpersonal attractiveness and brings people closer together.

Humor is as important in organizational communication as in other settings. Humor helps establish bonds among those who work together, bonds that flourish when communicators use humor appropriately and

* Michael Z. Hackman is assistant professor in the Department of Communication at the University of Colorado at Colorado Springs. He received his Ph.D. in speech communication from the University of Denver. His research interests include human communication theory and humor and communication.

effectively. Some basic principles to follow in organizational settings include

> Never use humor that could potentially offend anyone who might hear it. If you offend even one person, your humor has failed.

The humor you use in the organization must be appropriate for every possible receiver of your message. In one particularly unfortunate situation, a superior and a subordinate who routinely exchanged "humorous" memos were both fired when an upper-level manager intercepted one of the memos. The idea of exchanging humorous memos seems innocuous enough, but the individuals in this example failed to recognize the potential their humor had for offending others within the organization.

> In meetings and presentations, use only humor that is relevant to the subject of discussion. Excursions from the subject may be perceived as foolish.

Humor can be very effective in meetings and presentations, particularly when used to defuse anxiety or tension. Humor that is not relevant to the discussion may serve as a distraction, and worse yet may serve to lead to a perception that the speaker is foolish or unprepared. Use humor to your advantage. Only use humor that helps you achieve the specific purpose of your communication. Never begin a meeting or presentation with unrelated jokes. Use only humor that is germane to the subject of discourse to put an audience at ease and capture attention.

> Use moderation. Too much humor, like anything else, can result in reduced effectiveness.

Don't act like a frustrated comedian. Too much humor can damage your image and detract from your message. Remember, there is a time to be serious. Be aware of your audience and the degree to which they are "in fun." Individuals fluctuate in and out of fun. Be sensitive to how your humor is being received.

> Realize that the use of humor, for all of its benefits, does involve risks. Under certain circumstances, the use of humor has resulted in lowered ratings of source credibility and interest.

Most of the negative impact of humor has been associated with the inappropriate use of humor that is either irrelevant, distasteful, or excessive. All in all, however, research indicates that the moderate use of appropriate, relevant humor most often results in a more favorable reaction to an individual.

QUESTIONS FOR DISCUSSION

1. Based on Hackman's guidelines, did John and Shirley use humor appropriately and effectively? How should they use humor in the future? Did Karen overreact?

2. How might a manager meeting with a group of subordinates facilitate a feeling of "fun"? Would a subordinate meeting with a group of superiors need to use different techniques?

3. Do any particular types of humor seem inappropriate for the organizational setting? Why?

The "I Thought I Gave Them Everything" Case

Henry Gonzales has been the manager of Quality Foods's 7th Street store for four years. Henry is considered among Quality's top managers for making the once-unprofitable store the sales leader of the company. Gonzales works hard and expects the same of all store employees. He emphasizes financial rewards for hard work and has initiated a pay incentive plan for supervisors who are able to cut costs or increase sales in their respective departments.

Henry was angry and upset when the personnel director for Quality informed him that two of his leading supervisors had requested transfers to other Quality stores. Didn't they realize they were in the best of Quality's stores and making more money than their counterparts in less profitable operations? Did they really need more of his time, as the personnel director intimated? Why should grown people need hand-holding? Didn't they recognize he was busy and always worked for the best interests of the store and his supervisors?

Henry wondered what he should do next. He felt inclined just to let them leave and see how they would like to work under another manager. On the other hand, they were good workers. Should he talk with them? What would he say?

Henry Gonzales is like many busy managers who lose touch with the wants and needs of those who work for them. In the following commentary. Richard Little describes how managers like Henry Gonzales often confuse material rewards with motivation. As you study Henry's problem and read the commentary, think about what you would advise Henry to do. What does he need to know about communication competency?

Communicating the Motivation Process

Richard Little, Ph.D.*
Managers have endured endless hours learning the proper managerial techniques, nuances, and theories concerning how to properly motivate

* Richard Little currently serves as director for the Center for Business and Management, Division of Professional Development, University of Oklahoma. He is responsible for all non-credit program activity in the business management, finance, and executive programs. Dr. Little works extensively, to develop programs for business, industry, and the public sector. Organizations with which he has worked include Exxon, RCA, Digital Equipment, Hewlett-Packard, Burlington Industries, Magnavox, Pemex Oil of Mexico, Borg-Warner, Morton Salt, International Harvester, and Goodyear Aerospace.

subordinates and individuals. Much of this time was devoted to theories postulated by Douglas McGregor, Abraham Maslow, Frederick Herzberg, and others. However, the end product always seems to revolve around the same issue: How do we motivate people? All this knowledge of principle and theory are only so much rhetoric if the manager doesn't understand and practice the art of communicating the motivation process. The higher the level of management, the more likely the problem is communication. Therefore, if managers truly want employees doing what they (managers) want done because they (employees) want to do it, it is imperative that motivation be communicated effectively. It is fair for a manager to say, "How do I motivate my people?" The answer is provided through the communication of the concepts of ACT—Awareness, Commitment, Time.

Awareness—Understanding the Process

The basic theory of motivation is getting results through people because they want to do the work. The process has been debated by psychologists, but the underlying premise is fundamental—understanding and meeting the needs of employees. Unfortunately, these needs are not uniform in nature or specific to all. Employees are complex individuals who present myriad problems. One often wonders why anyone would want to become a manager, thus becoming accountable for all the characteristics necessary not only to understand people but also to properly manage them for results. Thus, Maslow's "hierarchy" and Herzberg's "hygiene-motivators" are theories that should be understood before beginning the practice of communicating the process. Interestingly, it is usually through the communication of the theory that the process breaks down. The theory is textbook, the application is real-world. As Frederick Herzberg said, "Do we want motivation or do we want movement?" Most managers want both but get only the latter. Understanding the theory—awareness—is the first step in communicating the process. Communicating effectively is the product of developing an awareness of motivation.

Commitment—Applying Motivation

Commitment to the motivation process is integral to results and performance. Many managers profess a profound commitment, yet there must be a reciprocal interactive relationship between manager and subordinate for motivation to be realized. This is not formally stated between manager and employee in the form of a contract or agreement. Rather, commitment to motivation is communicated by both parties through verbal and nonverbal channels. It becomes imperative that managers understand these channels, for, right or wrong, employees subjectively assess and evaluate their managers' commitment through their communication. It is not surprising to discover that what managers say they want is motivation and what actually is expected is often contradictory. For example, managers may communicate a message that implies delegation of responsibility for a task assignment. However, the accompanying authority is retained by the manager, forcing the employee to rely on the manager's input for the final decision. The process is initially perceived as motivational by the manager, but in reality is merely task assignment. The manager reacts to the situation with the perception that all criteria were evident for motivation to occur, failing to recognize that the fundamental variable for true motivation—authority—was not communicated. Understanding the communication process is therefore fundamental for managers to create effectively a climate conducive to motivation.

Time—The Motivational Product

Invariably, managers and individuals profess an awareness of the process of motivation and a commitment to the process, but the end result is consistently influenced by the variable of time. Time can be used as an excuse to thwart the actual commitment to motivate, thereby blocking implementation. Time must be dedicated to implement the motivation process effectively. This is perhaps the single most difficult aspect of communicating real motivation. Managers who understand the process and are aware of the implications of true motivation may project a solid commitment but find that the organization does not provide the true time for motivation.

Time is one of those important organizational variables that is compared to bottom-line results and the proverbial return on investment (ROI). Organizations often argue that the time lost in providing for motivation actually retards production and ROI. This is not the case when organizations want true motivation. Research emphasizes that traditional organizations perceive three primary factors—salary, job security, and promotion—as motivators. These are actually maintenance factors that by definition, are short term, providing satisfaction and not necessarily motivation. An organization subscribing to such a philosophy may use the argument of cost and time to argue substantially against the value of motivation. Such organizations, in fact, may satisfy the initial needs of wages, security, and promotion, while not providing any genuine commitment to motivation. Too often this is a conscious decision rather than accidental, resulting in a climate of maintenance rather than motivation.

Managers who communicate awareness and commitment can reasonably cope with the variable of time. Employees who are reasonably satisfied within their organizations require more than salary or security for motivation. Recognition is an example of a universal need that applies to most individuals. Interestingly, recognition does not require additional money from the organization. It is one of the least understood motivators by managers and only requires time. Managers who communicate recognition are involved in creating a positive climate for motivation. However, as managers become vertically mobile in organizations, they tend to communicate less and thus contribute to suppressing motivation.

In a cost-benefit analysis, organizations focus on the three needs that actually cost the organization money. Focusing on these areas may provide satisfaction, but not motivation. Recognition, achievement, and challenge are less costly for the organization and more beneficial. The cost to the organization is not primarily financial, but rather an investment of time. Time devoted to recognition pays dividends to managers and organizations.

Conclusion

Communication is essential to successful motivation. Creating a climate where employees function in a positive, innovative, and creative fashion does not magically occur. Organizations and managers must first deal with the question "Do we really want motivation?" If the answer is yes, then the process includes (1) *awareness*—"What is motivation?"; (2) *commitment*—"How to communicate the process"; and (3) *time*—"Implementation with accountability" for proper effectiveness. The ACT concept is fundamentally dependent on communication and an awareness of a complete understanding of how to communicate the motivation process. ACT is conceptually motivational, but only theoretical in nature without effective communication. Just as a manager experiences the real-world application and benefits of motivation, an awareness of how the communication process contributes to success is basic to such achievement. Motivation is thus not merely awareness, commitment, and time; it is also communication.

QUESTIONS FOR DISCUSSION

1. Can you apply the ACT process to Henry Gonzales' problem?

2. Discuss the relationship of communication and motivation.

3. Defend the statement "Motivation should be used by all managers in all organizations."

Ann Cartwright, Vice President of Drummond Industries

Ann Cartwright was perplexed and disturbed by the conversation taking place in hushed tones outside her office door. Apparently Tom Jackson and Jim Jurgers, both Drummond vice presidents, didn't realize Ann's door was open and that she could hear their remarks. They were saying that Ann had been promoted to vice president of marketing because she was a woman and that the president, George Miller, was unwilling to criticize her because he didn't know how to deal with a woman on his staff.

Ann had been promoted six months ago when her longtime boss, the vice president of marketing, had retired. Ann had been successful as the manager of marketing and was widely credited with developing excellent marketing plans for several new product lines and for expanding the services of the marketing department to assist the product development group in its identification of potential new lines. Her subordinates, both male and female, liked to work for her and believed Ann to be fair and direct. In fact, almost everyone seemed genuinely excited and pleased when her promotion was announced.

Ann wondered what the conversation meant and what she should do. She knew she needed both men's cooperation and certainly the trust of Drummond's president. Should she confront Tom and Jim? Should she go to the president? Should she ignore the remarks and act as if nothing has happened? What, if anything, does this mean for her future?

Ann Cartwright's experience is similar to those reported by female professionals in all types of organizational positions. Although the number of women managers increases daily, acceptance into previously all-male management teams is mixed, often affecting the quality of working relationships. Sherwyn Morreale provides, in the following essay, a commentary useful for understanding Ann's problem. Think about what Ann should do as you read. What communication competencies does Ann need in order to work with Tom and Jim?

Male and Female Managers: Is There a Difference?

Sherwyn P. Morreale, Ph.D.

As society and our contemporary organizations move headlong into the twenty-first century, an interesting phenomenon is occurring. The nature of the contemporary work place, in terms of the sex composition of middle management, is changing. Males and females now are working side by side in the highly competitive ranks of middle management. As more females are entering the work place and successfully scaling the managerial ladders to organizational success, numerically there are nearly as many women managers as men. But despite the fact that males and females now are holding similar managerial and administrative positions, gender-related stereotypes of men and women, as managers and as communicators, persist. And frequently, the characteristics associated with the stereotypical male manager are deemed more desirable than the characteristics associated with the stereotypical female manager.

An array of questions arises related to these changing roles of male and female middle managers in contemporary organizations:

First, what is the nature of the gender-stereotypical picture that may still be held of the typical male manager and the typical female manager? Is it an accurate and fair picture? That is, is it really descriptive of what male and female managers are like in contemporary organizations? And second, do the actual management and communication behaviors of male and female managers conform to what might be expected, based on any gender-stereotypical picture held of them? Or are male and female middle managers actually more alike than unlike?

> First question: Are gender-based stereotypes still operating in today's organizations? If so, what is their nature? For our discussion gender stereotypes are considered simply overgeneralizations about male or female managers based on their sex.

A review of research in this area suggests that some gender-stereotypical perceptions of male and female managers still persist. Despite a discordant and often contradictory collection of research findings regarding gender-related perceptions of managers, the position of "manager" appears to continue to be identified and described in primarily masculine terms. Traditionally, the "successful manager" has been considered to possess traits or characteristics more commonly viewed as descriptive of men than women. More specifically, "some research regarding attitudes toward women in management reveals a perception that men, because they possess masculine characteristics, are more capable, more acceptable, and more preferred for management positions" (Wheeless and Berryman-Fink, 1985, p. 137). For example, one research study indicated that the possession of masculine or instrumental behavioral skills was prerequisite to demonstrating the managerial aptitudes of leadership (Evangelist, 1981). Another repeated set of studies found that a "good manager" was described in masculine terms and not seen as androgynous, that is, possessing both masculine and feminine characteristics (Powell and Butterfield, 1979, 1986). And surprisingly, in a study in which the subjects were both male and female managers, all subjects regardless of their own sex indicated a preference for male stereotypic management behaviors over feminine or even androgynous behaviors (Brenner and Bromer, 1981). Finally, and as recently as 1987, a study of perceptions of mangement/behavioral styles concluded that sex-differentiated management models of male and female managers may still exist (Statham, 1987).

If indeed gender-stereotypical perceptions of managers are operating in contemporary organizations, what are the stereotypical behaviors, characteristics, or traits deemed to be descriptive of the male manager and of his female counterpart (see table)?

Male Stereotype of Masculinity: *Instrumental/Leader Behaviors*	*Female Stereotype of Feminity:* *Socioexpressive Behaviors*
Acts as a leader	Gentle
Has leadership abilities	Tender
Dominant	Understanding
Aggressive	Warm
Willing to take a stand	Sensitive to needs of others
Forceful	Compassionate
Assertive	Sincere
Strong personality	Helpful
Competitive	Eager to soothe hurt feelings
Independent	Friendly

Note: These descriptors are derived from Wheeless and Dierks-Stewart, 1981.

Typically, the male stereotype or masculine model incorporates a set of characteristics suggestive of instrumentality, or a task-oriented nature or personality. The female stereotype or feminine model incorporates a set of characteristics suggestive of emotionality, or a socioexpressive orientation or personality. The male stereotype suggests a concern for the job or task at hand; the female stereotype, a concern for people or relationships.

Next Question: Considering the dichotomous nature of the gender-stereotypical picture of male and female managers, the next logical question relates to the accuracy of these gender stereotypes. Do the actual management, leadership, and communication behaviors of male and female managers reflect a goodness of fit and conform to the behaviors described in the gender stereotypes?

A review of recent research studies suggests that in actuality, there may not be such significant differences in managerial and leadership skills between male and female managers. In contrast to the descriptive dichotomy and behavioral differences suggested by the research on gender stereotypes, another body of research indicates that male and female managers and leaders actually are exhibiting similar behaviors. Some exemplary studies of middle managers from "real world" organizations indicate that contrary to the stereotypes, male and female managers behave alike. For example, in a study of male and female leaders in a hospital setting, regarding perceived leadership behaviors and subordinate satisfaction, no significant differences by sex were discovered (Bartol and Wortman, 1975). In a study of working managers/leaders selected from a military and a civilian organization, there was no significant difference between males and females in terms of leadership style or in terms of interpersonal versus task orientation (Chapman, 1975). Another study of male and female managers, from both industry and the federal government, examined differences in managerial thinking styles and attitudes (Feuer, 1988). Only one of twelve lifestyle scales indicated a difference by sex, the "conventional" scale; women were less concerned than men with appearing normal and meeting the expectations of those in power (p. 27). In a study of male and female manager/entrepreneurs, no differences by sex were found in risk-taking propensity and behaviors (Masters and Meier, 1988). And in an examination of sex stereotypes in two large mental health systems, manager/leaders' sex did not appear to have a consistent influence on either leader behavior or subordinate satisfaction (Osborn and Vicars, 1976). Finally, in a gender study of organizational influence strategies and leadership behaviors of managers from a financial institution, a municipal service agency, and a state library, no significant differences by sex were discovered (Rizzo and Mendez, 1988).

In response to the original questions regarding the changing nature of middle management and the changing roles of male and female managers, two conclusions can be drawn. Gender-related stereotypes of managers do appear to be operating in contemporary organizations. But contrary to the gender stereotypes, male and female managers may, in fact, be more alike than not.

REFERENCES

Bartol, K. M., and M. S. Wortman, Jr. 1975. Male versus female leaders: Effects on perceived leader behavior and satisfaction in a hospital. *Personal Psychology* 28: 533–47.

Brenner, O. C., and J. A. Bromer. 1981. Sex stereotypes and leaders' behavior, as measured by the agreement scale for leadership behavior. *Psychological Reports* 48: 960–62.

Chapman, J. B. 1975. Comparison of male and female leadership styles. *Academy of Management Review* 18(3): 645–50.

Evangelist, M. A. 1981. Managerial aptitude as a function of sex-role orientation. *Dissertation Abstracts International* 41(12): Order No. 8109064.

Feuer, D. 1988. How women manage. *Training* 25(8): 23–31.

Masters, R., and R. Meier. 1988. Sex differences and risk-taking propensity of entrepreneurs. *Journal of Small Business Management* 26(1): 31–5.

Osborn, R. N., and W. M. Vicars. 1976. Sex stereotypes: An artifact in leader behavior and subordinate satisfaction analysis? *Academy of Management Journal* 19(3): 439–49.

Powell, G. N., and D. A. Butterfield. 1979. The "good manager": Masculine or androgynous? *Academy of Management Journal* 22(2): 395–403.

Powell, G. N., and D. A. Butterfield. 1986. The "good manager": Does androgyny fare better in the 1980's? A paper presented at the Annual Meeting of the Academy of Management, Chicago.

Rizzo, A., and C. Mendez. 1988. Making things happen in organizations: Does gender make a difference? *Public Personnel Management* 17(1): 9–20.

Statham, A. (1987). The gender model revisited: Differences in the management styles of men and women. *Sex Roles* 16(7/8): 409–29.

Wheeless, V. E., and C. Berryman-Fink. 1985. Perceptions of women managers and their communication competencies. *Communication Quarterly* 33(2): 137–48.

Wheeless, V. E., and K. Dierks-Stewart. 1981. The psychometric properties of the Bem Sex Role Inventory: Questions concerning reliability and validity. *Communication Quarterly* 29(3): 173–86.

QUESTIONS FOR DISCUSSION

1. In your view, what barriers does Ann face? What barriers exist for women in organizations?

2. If you were a corporate president or C.E.O., what specific measures might you take to ensure equality between the sexes in your organization?

3. What can women themselves do to accelerate more favorable attitudes toward managerial women?

The Rule Here Is to Do What Management Wants

Jim Robinson liked people on his staff to get along with each other and support group decisions. As president of Firetone Insurance, he had a history of promoting mostly white males who agreed with him. He was known for avoiding men or women who engaged in confrontation and disagreement. Jerry Douglas ought to know that. He had been the sales manager for Firestone for five years and only lately was exhibiting a level of disagreement that made Robinson uncomfortable. Also, Sally Marshall, the head of finance and Firestone's only woman manager, seemed to be siding with Douglas.

Jerry was contending that Firestone had to hire a more diverse sales staff as additional competitors entered several of their good sales territories targeting Firestone customers with international affiliates. Unlike these competitors, Firestone's field sales staff were mostly white males with no international experience. Jim and others on his staff felt Jerry was being pessimistic and negative. Sally seemed to agree with Jerry, although she wasn't as outspoken.

Jerry was disgusted with all of his peers except Sally. The others knew he was right but were afraid to confront Jim. They told Jerry to be patient and Jim would eventually see his point of view. Jerry believed that being patient would cost Firestone considerable money and might cause them to lose key accounts currently being pursued by their competition.

Both Jim and Jerry were concerned. Neither liked what was happening. What would you advise Jim to do? Jerry?

Adelina Gomez, in her commentary that follows, discusses the implications of valuing diversity in an environment increasingly characterized by business across national boundaries and cultures. As you read her commentary, think about how Jim is influencing the diversity in his organization. Consider what Jerry should do.

Valuing Diversity

Adelina Gomez, Ph.D.

The study of organizational communication should be considered incomplete if it fails to recognize the significance of cultural differences in the work place and the impact they have on interpersonal and working relationships. The influx of a culturally diverse work force and the increase of multinational corporations in the last two decades have outdistanced studies of and training in cross-cultural relations. That is why it is imperative that we strive to develop a culturally literate work force in the same way that we strive to develop a skilled work force.

In the 1980s, business between the United States and other countries continues to flourish. For example, studies show that United States companies formed more than 800 joint ventures in one year with the People's

Republic of China as compared with only about 900 in a previous five-year time frame. What this means for both the domestic and world market is more and more cross-cultural interaction for a less and less trained work force. If we are to compete effectively, cross-cultural training and understanding must go hand-in-hand with business and technology training. A long-standing lament has been that Americans are experts in transfering business and technology across cultures but dismal in cultural understanding.

All this demonstrates the lackluster performance and seeming apathy that has prevailed since the civil rights movement of the 1960s. Progress toward cultural diversity, although slow, has been consistent; educational enlightenment about cultural differences has not kept pace. It is not enough to count the numbers of minorities and foreign nationals that are employed at any given time in any given organization. It is time that schools of business, schools of engineering, schools of education, and certainly departments of communication become more committed to the development of these skills in their students.

How do we go about developing these skills? Before we can understand and appreciate another culture, it is first necessary to understand our own. While there are countless cultural variables and it is impossible to know and understand each one, there are specific ones we can identify that are useful in understanding ourselves and in helping us develop the skills to understand others. We should be conscious of our culture's impact on our world view; on our pattern of thought; and on our assumptions, attitudes, values, and beliefs. Without this understanding we will persist in our ethnocentric views and fail to be objective about those who are different from us. For example, we may perceive another cultural group as less intelligent simply because they speak our own language with a pronounced accent. We often perceive others as less motivated simply because their behaviors are different. Speaking more than one language is laudable and motivation may be different from culture to culture—not more or less, only different. The Japanese, for example, have a saying that they believe strongly: The nail that sticks out is soon hammered down. The statement reflects a culture that is more group- than individual-oriented. To become objective in our perceptions is to recognize and respect these differences. Recognition and respect mark the beginning of our understanding of others. Of course, understanding and respect are merely the beginning of the development of intercultural skills. Intercultural skill development requires consistent effort because it involves changes that are not always easy.

Change begins when we develop an understanding of our culture and recognize that those whom we perceive as different are very likely to remain that way. Recognition of cultural differences reduces ethnocentric behaviors as we move toward understanding other cultures and the positive diversity that exists. The objective, then, is to relate the basic elements of one's own culture to those of another. For example, human needs are universal, but the means of satisfying them differ among cultures. The importance of this notion is that universal goals and/or needs are often obscured in different cultural settings and in the ways needs are expressed. That is why looking for equivalence in the other culture is useful. A good example is language, which is used differently in different cultures. Especially among Eastern societies what is left unsaid is as important as what is said. In Western cultures we emphasize forcefulness, explicitness, and verbal completeness.

Learning to communicate successfully with people from other cultures means making a commitment and working hard. Lest the reader assume that the recommendations above are all-inclusive, please remember what someone once emphasized: Productive cross-cultural communication requires each individual to have the flexibility to adapt, adjust, and react appropriately to the daily challenges of hundreds of communication differences encountered.

QUESTIONS FOR DISCUSSION

1. Describe the culture of Firestone Insurance. How does Jim's world view influence what is happening between Jim and Jerry?

2. What can Jerry do to influence Jim's thinking?

AUTHOR INDEX

SUBJECT INDEX